DESIGNS ON EMPIRE

Designs on Empire

AMERICA'S RISE TO POWER IN THE AGE OF EUROPEAN IMPERIALISM

Andrew Priest

Columbia University Press
New York

Columbia University Press
Publishers Since 1893
New York   Chichester, West Sussex
cup.columbia.edu
Copyright © 2021 Columbia University Press
All rights reserved

Library of Congress Cataloging-in-Publication Data

Names: Priest, Andrew, author.
Title: Designs on empire : America's rise to power in the age
of European imperialism / Andrew Priest.
Other titles: America's rise to power in the age of European imperialism
Description: New York : Columbia University Press, [2021] | Includes
bibliographical references and index.
Identifiers: LCCN 2020056827 (print) | LCCN 2020056828 (ebook) | ISBN 9780231197441
(hardback) | ISBN 9780231197458 (trade paperback) | ISBN 9780231552172 (ebook)
Subjects: LCSH: United States—Foreign relations. | Europe—Foreign relations—
Public opinion, American. | Europe—Foreign relations—United States. | United States—
Foreign relations—Europe. | Imperialism. | Elite (Social sciences)—United States—
Attitudes. | Public opinion—United States.
Classification: LCC E183.7 .P75 2021 (print) | LCC E183.7 (ebook) | DDC 327.73—dc23
LC record available at https://lccn.loc.gov/2020056827
LC ebook record available at https://lccn.loc.gov/2020056828

Columbia University Press books are printed on permanent and durable acid-free paper.
Printed in the United States of America

Cover image: © Getty Images/Ideabug

For Megan

Contents

Acknowledgments

I began thinking about writing this book more than a decade ago. At the time, I was working in the Department of International Politics at Aberystwyth University. My colleagues and friends there encouraged me and gave me the confidence to pursue the project, and I thank all of them.

The generous research leave provision at Aberystwyth allowed me to spend a year in Washington, DC, at the outset. There, David Painter hosted me as a visiting fellow in the Department of History at Georgetown University and allowed me to present my initial ideas to his graduate students. I am very grateful to David and hope he will be pleased that the book is finally here. At Georgetown, the late Larry Kaplan also enthusiastically discussed the project with me in its earliest stages. Many other people welcomed me to DC and exchanged ideas with me. Particular thanks go to my friends Tammy Barnett and Steve Galpern.

Funding for the project has come from Aberystwyth University, the University of Essex, and the Eccles Centre at the British Library in London, which awarded me a visiting fellowship.

I have been fortunate to receive valuable feedback from many people on different parts of this book. I especially want to thank Robert Julio Decker, Joseph A. Fry, Barbara Reeves-Ellington, Frank Schumacher, Jay Sexton, Steve Tuffnell, and Kevin Waite. Since coming to the University of Essex, I have been lucky to work with wonderful colleagues who have supported me along the way. I am especially grateful to members of the Political Cultures and Citizenship research cluster in the Department of History who read and commented on various chapters: Alix Green, Matthew Grant, Nadine Rossol, and Felix Schnell. I want to thank Sean Kelley, Tracey Loughran, and Alison Rowlands for their good advice, especially on the publishing process. I have also had excellent comments and constructive criticism from several anonymous readers. Needless to say, all errors and omissions are mine alone.

Stephen Wesley at Columbia expressed his enthusiasm for this project from our first correspondence and he has maintained it throughout the publishing process. He has also offered excellent advice and been very patient. Thanks, Stephen.

My good friends Andrew Johnstone and Carl Watts deserve a special mention. We get to see each other too rarely these days, but we always have a great time when we do and enjoy keeping up with each other's work. I also want to thank people I now see even more rarely: my mentors from various stages of my career: Nick Cull at the University of Southern California, Scott Lucas at the University of Birmingham, and Martin Alexander, emeritus professor at Aberystwyth. Each has encouraged me and shaped my work in different ways.

My extended family remains a happy reminder that there is more to life than the American Empire. As I write these words, I, like so many others, am separated from them. I would like to be able to give copies of this book to them in person, but, even if I can't, I hope that this is a reminder of how much they all mean to me. In Canada, Barb Rosser and Chuck Daigle have welcomed me into their home and their lives. In the UK, the Priest-Poulton clan goes from strength to strength. They may not realize the extent to which they have helped me in doing my work, but they have. Much love to my parents, Mike and Shirley, and to Suzy, Jon, Gary, Isabela, Milly, Freya, and Amalia.

Finally, my partner, Megan, has endured the slow progress of this book during our time together with great fortitude. She has also read and commented on various parts of it, and been a constant source of strength, support, and encouragement. This book is for her with all my love and thanks for everything she has done.

Parts of chapter 3 and brief sections of chapter 1 of this book appeared in "Thinking About Empire: The Administration of Ulysses S. Grant, Spanish Colonialism, and the Ten Years' War in Cuba," *Journal of American*

Studies 48, no. 2 (2014): 541–58 © 2013 Cambridge University Press. They are reprinted with permission. I also draw on some ideas developed in an earlier article, "Imperial Exchange: American Views of the British Empire During the Civil War and Reconstruction," *Journal of Colonialism and Colonial History* 16, no. 1 (2015).

DESIGNS ON EMPIRE

Introduction

The Challenge of the American Empire

Unlike the old empires, we don't make . . . sacrifices for territory or for resources. We do it because it's right.

—BARACK OBAMA

I n March 1899, less than a year after the United States had won its war with Spain, James Bryce responded to a request from *Century* magazine's editor, Richard Watson Gilder. In the space of a few short months beforehand, the United States had acquired effective control of Cuba, Puerto Rico, Guam, and the Philippines from Spain, and annexed Hawaii.

Gilder asked Bryce, the British Liberal Party politician, academic, and soon-to-be ambassador to the United States, to write an article for Americans about the lessons they could learn from the experiences of the imperial powers of Europe now that they were faced with administering their own colonial acquisitions in the Caribbean and Pacific. Bryce was delighted to accept. He wrote of the various challenges that the British and others had encountered in their imperial endeavors—the climate, social structures, and religions of the societies they had come to rule—and how Americans might consider the British responses to these challenges to help them administer their new territories. "The United States is entering upon a novel course," he concluded, "a difficult, though splendid, experiment watched with interest by the whole world."[1]

Bryce astutely observed that American interest in other empires had increased hugely in the months since the United States acquired its overseas territories, but he was wrong in suggesting that this was a new phenomenon. Many leading Americans—journalists, politicians, government and military officials—had in fact spent a great deal of time considering contemporary European empires in the years and decades before 1898. They were curious about Europe, Europeans, and the global reach of their governments. Many of these elites were careful observers of the international scene, and, from the Civil War onward, the United States' own growing regional and international interests had brought the activities of colonizers and colonized peoples around the world into mind.

This book is about this American thinking on empire. It examines the views of these European colonizers, their governments, peoples, and their systems of establishing and maintaining global power, and how they all shaped thoughts on empire in the United States. American attitudes to European imperial and colonial policies were important themes in the development of an expansionist thought in the United States at a crucial period in the history of its foreign policy and in the formation of the American worldview. The book contends that the decades between the Civil War and the conflict with Spain saw a particularly vibrant debate about European imperialism based on the challenges and opportunities that these imperial policies and practices presented. Americans who participated in these debates were sometimes interested in such questions for their own sake, but in doing so often articulated their views about the world and the roles that great powers played. Many also wondered aloud what these issues meant for the future of the United States, and whether the American empire would become like those of the Europeans, for better or worse, if it had not already.

These Americans were the elites of the foreign policy establishment who saw the parameters of the state in a more and more dynamic international setting. Such people were often influential figures in developing and promoting the diplomatic and ideological norms of the day. They included secretaries of state like William Henry Seward and Hamilton Fish, and congressmen like Charles Sumner and Carl Schurz. They also included lesser-knowns who were nonetheless influential. We will also consider the views of some of these people, especially those involved in the U.S. diplomatic and consular service around the world—such as William L. Dayton, John Bigelow, Caleb Cushing, Simon Wolf, N. D. Comanos, and John Kasson—as well as others in the military and the press. As the historian Frank Ninkovich has shown, many journalists and editors also engaged in debates about profound overseas issues, shaping views among the interested public and in turn influenced by the domestic milieu in which they operated.

Ninkovich argues that many of these people had a keen interest in the global progress of what they termed "civilization," which featured prominently in American magazines such as the *North American Review, The Nation*, and *Century*.[2] Rather than focusing on literary culture and the writers who sought to shape middle-class opinion, however, our primary focus here is political discourse.

This book's interest in the hierarchical world of foreign policymaking means a privileging of white, elite males that is all but unavoidable in a study of this period, before the advent of survey data to gauge public opinion on particular issues of the day and with upper-class men dominating all aspects of politics and society. At this time, the machinery of politics and foreign policy was operated by a small group of men living and working in or near the White House in Washington, DC. The city of Washington itself was still underdeveloped, with unmade roads and animals wandering the streets, and many prominent foreign representatives considered it to be a diplomatic backwater. The Department of State had a minuscule staff. It became much more important over the course of the nineteenth century, but the sometimes haphazard approach to United States foreign policymaking was reflected in its diplomatic and consular services, which were often staffed by people with more political connections than diplomatic talent. This led to numerous incidents, which occasionally had serious diplomatic consequences, emphasizing the elitist nature of the approach to foreign affairs and internationalist thought reflected in this book.[3] Other voices were present in foreign policymaking and are present here—including some women and African Americans—but they also tend to be elites in their own way, having left the clearest imprint in the documentary record: suffragists like Elizabeth Cady Stanton and Julia Ward Howe, and campaigner and diplomat Frederick Douglass. It would be fascinating to discover how a wider swath of Americans understood European empires, but we find only occasional glimpses in letters published in newspapers or private missives to politicians—and we cannot know whether even these represent wider sentiments.

The privilege of those most engaged in foreign policy matters is important here, as it positioned them as participants in *worldmaking*—the international beliefs and policies that historian David Milne has explored in later generations.[4] Those in positions of power and others close to them tended to guide the electorate in political matters, especially concerning foreign policy, which often appeared complex, arcane, and distant from people's everyday lives. Because we have few other choices and because privileged voices tended to be the loudest, we can regard much of what they say as characteristic of broader attitudes toward particular international issues, such as the dominance of the imperial powers.

Debating Empire

The United States is a postcolonial nation. Because of this, we might expect it also to be an anti-imperial one. In some ways it is. Many of the people featured in this book expressed opposition to European empires. This could be because of the United States' own path to independence from colonial status, or because of these empires' actual or imagined threat to the well-being of the United States. This was a period of crystallization of Europe's global influence as various rivals sought to carve out new colonial territories, the period that historians have called "high" or "new" imperialism, and this had a direct, material impact on the United States.

Many Americans objected to European empires on ideological grounds, observing their iniquitous systems of rule—systems that Americans themselves had campaigned against during the Revolution. Most of these Americans believed that the United States eschewed such actions from its position as an exemplary nation with a written constitution and supposedly benign foundations. Its overseas expansion was, to their minds, strictly commercial, not territorial, and certainly not deliberately exploitative of faraway peoples and lands outside of any meaningful legal or moral framework. Thus, many Americans resisted—and continue today to resist—the idea that the United States was an empire. They posit instead that it was an opponent of the practices of other empires, and suggest—somewhat like Barack Obama, whose statement opens this introduction—that the United States was essentially *unimperial*.[5]

This American anti-imperialism was not monolithic, however. Rather, it was brimming with tensions, ambiguities, ironies, and contradictions. It was also somewhat elastic and could accommodate many imperialist assumptions.[6] There certainly was anti-imperialist sentiment from the beginning of the republic that came from opposition to the British Empire, but some citizens often expressed this by opposing what they saw as the United States government's desire to expand and control territories across North America for the purposes of practicing slavery. The prominence of a public, anti-imperialist rhetoric did not preclude the existence of a thriving, concomitant, albeit usually more covert imperialist rhetoric. Notable Americans in the late nineteenth century frequently argued in favor of expansion abroad beyond the purposes of commerce and trade. While outright calls for conquest and governance of overseas territory were rare, elite Americans often wanted to incorporate new contiguous territories into the Union: to secure coaling stations for the merchant fleet, to gain regional economic hegemony, and to influence the political affairs of other nations. The diplomatic historian William Appleman Williams characterized this as "imperial anticolonialism" or "noncolonial imperial expansion . . . under which America's preponderant economic power would extend the American system throughout the world without the embarrassment and inefficiency of colonialism."[7]

Scholars usually categorize Williams as a member of the Wisconsin school, which used the terms *empire* and *imperialism* to describe the American trajectory from continental to extracontinental nation.[8] This cut against the grain of earlier work that had seen the territorial growth of the United States as broadly benevolent, incorporating purportedly sparsely occupied lands to the west whose small populations the nation could easily assimilate. This work also argued that the United States government's decision to embrace colonialism from 1898 was merely a blip in the transition from regional to world power.[9]

Wisconsin scholars counteracted the idea that the United States was an exceptional nation that had arisen largely because of the unusual circumstances in which the founders conceived it and the pathbreaking nature of its political settlement. Because its government's mandate has always derived from the people (however exclusionary this mandate was in practice) rather than from an autocrat or monarch as in Europe, America positioned itself to be fundamentally different. Proponents of this exceptionalism applied their logic particularly to empire. The United States acquired territory to incorporate it into the Union under one form of rule, they argued, making it different from, say, the British Empire, which controlled its vast territories very differently than how it governed at home. As the Wisconsin school pointed out, however, despite the rapid growth of its democracy, the United States was an empire in how it imposed its will on territories and peoples—including with violence—regardless of whether they were part of the American continent or lived beyond its shores.[10]

In spite of developments in writing on the United States over the past few decades, several gaps remain in the historiography of the American empire. This book examines two of them. First, because many scholars continue to overemphasize the significance of the fin de siècle crisis of the 1890s and the war with Spain in 1898 as particular moments in the imperial history of the United States, this book focuses on the years before 1890. The pre-1890 period was replete with examples of American leaders searching for influence and even territory abroad as the United States vied with the main European imperial powers within its hemisphere and beyond. During the post–Civil War Reconstruction period alone, the United States faced real and perceived threats from European empires, as well as debating the possibilities for its own expansion into places like Alaska, Mexico, Canada, Cuba, Hawaii, and Santo Domingo. Second, rather than economics or culture, this book considers as a central theme the ideology of empire, and how leaders in the United States observed, discussed, supported, and opposed other contemporary empires.

Ideas and ideologies are too often downplayed or taken as given in studies of foreign policy. As Michael Hunt suggests in his classic study, ideology should not be reduced to a static concept connecting domestic economic exigencies with overseas expansion. Instead, Hunt encourages us to consider the domestic social dimensions of ideology—such as race, religion, and region—to understand drivers in foreign policy. While perhaps less secure and ultimately less satisfying than a more parsimonious explanation of the mechanics of foreign affairs focusing on national security or economics, understanding ideology in these terms can expand rather than reduce the range of explanatory possibilities. In this sense, the lack of clarity is what gives it strength.[11]

Opening up discussions about empire in this way reveals what was, and, equally, what was not possible at a particular time. The post–Civil War period was important in its own right, but it can also be seen in the ways it framed the 1898 period, often seen to be so crucial in announcing the arrival of the United States on the global scene. The United States was an increasingly active and activist nation during this period, and it made deliberate choices about how it viewed and operated in the world. Of course, these were often circumscribed by the material realities that leaders confronted, but these leaders were developing a worldview that the nation's growing hemispheric power increasingly allowed it to realize. This has important implications for our understanding of the United States as an empire. It helps us to comprehend the ways in which the United States was born of empires, surrounded by, and bound up in them. It also demonstrates a continuum of American power that puts less emphasis on 1898 as a significant break in the evolution of that power. Furthermore, while the United States became increasingly entangled in imperial environments over the course of the nineteenth century, it shows that it was not predestined to become a colonial power in the way that it did. Politicians and others made the decision that this would happen, and others supported them.

Certainly, many Americans *were* often suspicious of aspects of European imperialism at this time, when they defined themselves and their nation in opposition to Europe.[12] American leaders routinely attacked European politics, monarchy, and forms of overseas expansionism in speeches and writing, while newspapers were often even more vocal. They tended to focus particularly on economic issues to argue that the European imperial systems effectively kept the United States in a form of economic bondage, either because these empires maintained closed economic systems, or, paradoxically (especially in the case of Great Britain), for exactly the opposite reason: that they practiced free trade, undercutting nascent American industries. Domestic debates about economic growth showed the complexities in the broader ideology of empire and American encounters with colonies and the powers that controlled them, even if they do not tell us everything we need to know about the way the United States made policy toward these empires.

Equally essential was the issue of race. Race was a defining feature of American society, made all the more relevant by the battles—figurative and actual—over chattel slavery and its aftermath. These struggles were compounded by a widely accepted view among ruling elites in Europe and North America that race determined the capabilities and limitations of different groups of people, which allowed them to propose that there was a racial hierarchy. Black people were at the bottom of this hierarchy, considered at best to be intellectually inferior to their white counterparts and at worst to be a violent and marauding threat to them. Such views had disastrous consequences for generations of African Americans, whose subjugation was both justified and prolonged by these prejudices. In contrast, the highest tiers were occupied by whites, whose success and dominance in domestic and international affairs was evidence enough of their own intellectual and moral superiority. In-between were other races that Americans encountered. Most obviously, these were the large number of Native

American tribes, which were generally seen as an impediment to white settlers in North America who spread out across the continent in search of territory. Settler attitudes and government policies toward natives were complex, often contradictory, and changed over time. Broadly, they ran from a rejection of the notion that the tribes had any redeeming features at all and so should be destroyed, through to a paternalistic belief that they could be "civilized" to become more like the whites who wanted to take their lands, and ultimately assimilated into white society. This racial hierarchy was also applied to peoples in various empires, colonies, regions, and nations in the Americas, Europe, Africa, and Asia.[13]

In approaching the topic of race in this way, we can see how elite attitudes were central to framing American approaches to the world, to foreign nations, and to empires. In the wake of the Civil War, the racial lenses through which elites in the United States viewed domestic politics and society led them to view the United States' imperial rivals and those they ruled in markedly different ways. This phenomenon was particularly pronounced among liberal Republicans, a group that dominated intellectual life in the United States. These men—and again they were all men—were ensconced at the highest levels of American society, in government, the press, and at universities. They generally regarded excessive government interference in public life as dangerous to human progress, and particularly decried the political spoils system, which they believed corrupted American politics, and sometimes what they saw as government overreach in foreign policy. They were also often deeply suspicious of people who were different from themselves: immigrants, the poor, and people of color.[14] This was especially significant at a time when huge numbers of new immigrants came to the United States to live and work in its thriving industries. This brought more Americans into contact with the world outside than ever before, generating nativist and xenophobic responses among established white groups, and in turn influencing elite approaches to different nations and colonies.[15]

Many of these liberals, as well as some other Republicans and even some Democrats, took an increasingly internationalist view of the Monroe Doctrine, President James Monroe's 1823 statement proclaiming that the United States would resist further European colonization in the Americas. While the doctrine was primarily an anti-colonial tract, its growing salience in American political discourse as the century progressed also saw it morphing into a justification for United States dominance in the Western

Hemisphere.[16] American commentators often adopted pseudoscientific notions suggesting that those of European stock, and especially the much-lauded "Anglo-Saxons" of Britain and their descendants abroad, evinced a natural superiority and proclivity for successful government. Because of this, they possessed more "civilization" than other groups. Those who adopted such theories contended that others required tutelage. This meant that few Americans wanted to incorporate peoples from other races, whom they considered inferior, into their nation, and usually urged caution when confronting plans for expansion in the Caribbean and elsewhere.

While scholars have posited these racial attitudes in the final decades of the nineteenth century as major impediments to territorial acquisitions by the United States, such views also further reinforced American inclination toward European colonizers.[17] Most people in the United States, and especially the liberal, internationalist Republicans who dominated the apparatus of foreign policymaking, felt more affinity for the imperial powers of Europe—Britain especially, but also sometimes France, increasingly Germany, and to a lesser extent Spain—than they did for millions of colonized peoples in the Americas, Africa, and Asia. Although they often expressed distaste toward European imperial encroachments and transgressions of humanitarian norms, leading Americans usually felt a closer connection with European powers—which were at various stages of political reform at home and thus supposedly becoming even more "civilized"—than with their neighbors in the Americas.

In delineating the attitudes toward empire that existed at the time, this book explores the range of different ideas about empires during the period in which European powers dominated the global scene. It does so by combining imperial and anti-imperialist thought at the highest level—in the realm of policymaking—to trace new contours in the landscape of the American empire. Beginning from a number of episodes in which the American official mind registered European imperial and colonial practices, it makes the case that understanding contemporary European empires was an important element of elite American international thought and policy. Two of these cases were close to home—Mexico and Cuba—and two of them were farther afield—Egypt and what people knew as the "Congo" in West Africa. Each brought about an encounter between contemporary American thinking on empire and concrete European empires' moves on the world stage. These empires were the French, Spanish, British, and German, as well as some others, including the Ottoman and Belgian.

Of course these views were not static. They varied among different groups and regions and over time. There were dominant themes and ideas that united all elite Americans, but there were also sharp divides, and even those who agreed on certain principles and approaches might do so for different reasons. Broadly in the period from the time of the Civil War to the 1890s, there appears to have been a distinct trend toward an acceptance of British models of empire, and especially ones emphasizing commercial dominance. But there was also a growing sense among some key figures that imperial intervention to control regions could be a necessary evil in the contemporary world. This view was not fixed, consistent, or universal, but it suggested a range of possibilities that leaders increasingly entertained.

This book begins by exploring American attitudes toward European empires in the context of its early history. There are three main ways policymakers believed the United States was fundamentally different from its European counterparts. First, the notion that the powers of Europe were involved in aggressive empire building and colonial rivalry from which the United States had absented itself, only becoming involved when it was necessary and then often only because the European powers themselves directly threatened U.S. interests. They ultimately wanted these powers to leave the Western Hemisphere, often believing that this was an inevitable development over time because colonialism was an outdated feature of the international system and so they were only hastening this process. The second theme was the belief that U.S. forms of continental territorial expansion were, in the main, different from European patterns of empire. Most obviously, this was because most people saw geographical expansion to the south and west of the United States as part of a "natural" process of contiguous growth, even though it involved a fundamental dismissal of Indian cultures. The third was the increasing salience of the Monroe Doctrine, designed to separate the American and European spheres and thus immunize the United States from further imperial intrigues. This encouraged American policymakers and others to think of their nation as adopting a doctrine of nonintervention, deriving from George Washington, which guided policy into the era of the Civil War and beyond.

Immediately after the Civil War, France intervened in Mexico. This episode was part of a broader imperial project by French emperor Napoleon III to install a European nobleman, Maximilian, on the Mexican throne.

While the United States could do little to influence the diplomatic outcome of this maneuver, there was no shortage of ideological responses to
this imperialist threat in a border republic. Particularly important were
American conceptions of nonintervention and the Monroe Doctrine—
never promulgated by the government in Washington during this crisis
but also never far from the surface. While the American press was sometimes loud and vituperative on the matter, official language tended to stress
the common interests the United States had with the former republican
government in Mexico. But this stance on Washington's disagreement with
Paris did indicate a growing sense of leadership on the part of the United
States over other nations within the Americas, which was also increasingly
at these other nations' expense. Political leaders therefore defined nonintervention narrowly to serve the interests of the United States at a time of
national calamity. The episode also confirmed elite American preconceptions about the untrustworthiness of the French government, while
Napoleon's ultimate failure to establish a new monarchy reaffirmed the
limitations of French imperial policies and colonial projects.

At the same time, during Reconstruction in the United States, Spain
was building up its colony in nearby Cuba. While often challenged by the
British, this island had long been a part of the Spanish empire, and the eruption of a brutal war for independence there in 1868 tested the government
of the United States as well as Spain. Not unlike in Mexico, many American commentators urged their government to rally to participate in what
was later known as the Ten Years' War, encouraged by the prospect of
Cubans escaping the bonds of colonialism. Yet, Washington rarely did so,
due, in part, to a number of contingent factors like the continued paralysis
in government brought about by the failures of domestic Reconstruction
and the inherent conservatism of the administration of Ulysses S. Grant.
More than this, however, the conflict revealed some of the limits of American anti-colonial sentiment as the government and its supporters elected
to prioritize diplomatic relations with Spain over support for those seeking to break free from the Spanish Empire. It also illustrated the racial
dimensions of American imperial thought: because of long-held attitudes
about the political capacity of Cubans, the U.S. government in Washington could rationalize a policy that it claimed was evenhanded while it tacitly prioritized continued Spanish control. This applied especially to their
perceptions of the brutality of the fighting, which they deemed "uncivilized." In their minds, this violence signified Cubans' unfitness for self-rule,

even though the Spanish forces were also engaged in it. All this was complicated by the continuation of forms of slavery on Cuba at a time when the United States was still dealing with the repercussions of its own emancipation policies.

Around 1882, a few years after the official end of Reconstruction, Egypt rebelled against its colonial overseers. The rebels were brutally suppressed. While American commercial and political interests in North Africa were slight at this time, Egypt's strategic importance and exoticism made it alluring to some Americans. Simultaneously, reports of the mighty British Empire—at the height of its powers—interfering politically in Egypt, culminating in the savage military subjugation of the population, riled many. Influenced by racial prejudices and notions of civilization and progress, leading Americans proffered a range of responses to Britain's actions, providing a window onto aspects of American thought about British imperialism at this time. Many expressed shock that the British could engage in such slaughter, although others believed that violent actions were sometimes necessary if underdeveloped areas like Egypt were to be brought into the modern age.

Divergent views also appeared around the so-called Scramble for Africa, which saw European nations compete for territory and influence across the continent. The administration of Chester A. Arthur made a decision: to participate in the Berlin West Africa Conference in late 1884 and early 1885. At this time, many leading Americans continued to regard their nation as different from the other powers and thus exempt from the ongoing imperial intrigues they observed. But while diplomatic participation in the conference was the closest Americans came to engaging in the Scramble for Africa, U.S. discourse on sub-Saharan Africa, with its emphasis on commerce and "civilization," was, at times, distinctly European. American participants in the conference, and others who supported them, may have felt that the United States could be a moderating influence on those who would bring violence and injustice to the colonized Africans. Yet, the United States also sought economic exploitation of the region, and one of the primary reasons it did not become more fully involved was because of its growing cynicism about the rewards of doing so. As in the other cases, such views were predicated on particular racial views, in this case of native black Africans whom Americans often considered to be incapable of working but also highly belligerent and more susceptible than whites to the temptations and effects of alcohol. To that end, American participation at Berlin was significant in itself, even though the diplomatic expectations for the United States were ultimately unfulfilled.

In examining these cases, the book argues that we should understand the United States as an imperial power in an imperial world. To be sure, many American elites opposed European empires for what they represented, as well as what they did, and balked at the notion that the United States should emulate them. Still, many of these elites had at least a grudging admiration for the way the European powers and the British in particular were amassing economic power. They were often jealous of how Britain sought to gain the benefits of imperial dominance, often without the constraints of formal political control, and they increasingly sought to mimic that approach. This meant that, although they could loudly denounce Britain and the British, as Edward Crapol puts it, "at the subconscious level, Britain epitomized America's image of the successful world power."[18] More than this, they could even support colonialism, the taking and administratively organizing territories overseas, going beyond imperial policies of economic domination, if they believed it was beneficial—perhaps even necessary—to bring native populations in line with European-American sociopolitical values and practices. Far from being anti-imperialist, these attitudes were consonant with the broader concerns of British liberal imperialists.

American leaders thus operated within an imperial context during the nineteenth century. This was, after all, the age of high imperialism in which the dominant European nations sought to expand their economic influence and territory as never before. Such actions had profound impacts on the United States, impelling those in authority to grapple with their manifold implications. While we inevitably view the period before 1898 from the vantage point of knowing what happened next, there is also no doubt that many politically engaged Americans were concerned with empires, with their place in global politics, and with their positive and negative ramifications for United States foreign policy long before U.S. ships of war sailed into the harbors of Havana and Manila.

America Among Empires

Over the past couple of decades, especially following the 9/11 attacks and the wars in Iraq and Afghanistan, reassessments of the American historical empire have dovetailed with renewed interest in the contemporary global role of the United States. These events have spurred historians to explore links between present-day America and other empires of the past, particularly the British one, its closest associate and rival.[19] This, in turn, has encouraged people to treat the United States like other empires to explore its development in terms of *transimperialism*, including the effects of its imperial encounters on the metropolitan center.[20] Placing empire at the heart of the American experience in this way expands the horizons of the study of the United States, "the single greatest achievement of a historiography no longer content with writing solely about U.S. foreign relations," as one group of scholars has put it.[21] Yet the fact that Barack Obama—a liberal, Nobel Peace Prize–winning president who placed great emphasis on downgrading the American military presence in the Middle East—could still reject the idea that the United States has ever been an empire shows that the subject deserves reexamination. Obama may have been repeating a popular mantra that fit with the expectations of his audience (in this instance, it was significant that he was speaking to members of the military, but he made a similar statement in another context and no doubt knew it played to wider perceptions).[22] The notion that the United States was different from other empires, or that its empire did not really begin until 1898, if at all, is surprisingly widespread in the academic community.[23]

Ultimately, understanding United States history necessitates an explicitly imperial historiography. Participating in such a project compels us to interpret the development of the nation not in terms of its isolationism or difference but rather how it was enmeshed in imperial networks, which in turn influenced American elites' beliefs and practices. The period between the Civil War and the 1890s was more than merely prelude to the advent of American imperialism after 1898. In studying the United States over time, we must take seriously the idea that it was an empire that simultaneously incorporated, imitated, and also *rejected* many of the traits of its contemporaries.

The historian Dane Kennedy has recently argued that it is incumbent upon historians to examine their reasons for undertaking projects about empire, and acknowledge the contemporary motivations and concerns that drive them to ask certain questions.[24] In choosing to write this book, there is no doubt that I have, in part at least, been motivated by witnessing (mostly from Great Britain) the way the world's sole superpower has used its vast resources around the world, and especially during the wars in Afghanistan and Iraq. However, I hope that I have not undertaken this study with what one scholar, writing about the battles between the left and right over the history of empires, characterized as "an almost deliberate disregard for the complexity of an opponent's position."[25] I do not suggest that there were no voices expressing other ideas about the world, or that empire was the sole preoccupation of American elites at home and abroad. As David Hendrickson has shown, and again not unlike in the world today, myriad movements and beliefs jostled for prominence in domestic debates about the international system, and discussions of the advantages and disadvantages of empires and imperialism for the United States unfolded amid competing and complementary ideas.[26] There certainly were other strands to debates about internationalism. There were many opponents of empire in the United States. And many of the debates that took place at this time had important implications and echoes in the period after 1898 and well beyond, right up to the present day.

CHAPTER I

The United States and European Empires

T he Civil War marked a pivotal moment in the history of the United States and a transitional period in its foreign policy. It also precipitated a tumultuous and transformational moment of reconstruction, both literal and ideological, in its wake. The devastating conflict signaled the beginning of the end of the United States' continental expansionism and the acceleration of imperial growth beyond its borders, but it also saw a consolidation of its relations with the other powers of the day as its own political future became more assured. Elite views of these powers were crucial in shaping views of its own growth.

The era saw the climax of a struggle between at least two competing visions of the United States, both of which were fundamentally imperialist in nature. The first was primarily a Northern vision that privileged industrial growth. With time, proponents of this vision came to oppose slavery, seeing it as an outdated legacy of Britain's imperial past. The other vision rejected this basic premise, predicating its version of the American system on the continuation and even expansion of the slave system. It also saw the federal government's efforts to curtail slavery as inimical to the founding principles of the United States and representative of a tyrannical form of government, akin to that same British imperialism. In their different ways, therefore, American policymakers and others around them generally regarded their nation as anti-imperial even as they advanced their own forms of empire and their own visions of an American future.

In large part, this rejection of empire was based on views of the empires of the day. From its inception, the United States was—and continues to be—defined by its political leaders in relation to other nations. It was born as part of a political experiment in representative government, and early American leaders struggled to balance their desire for isolation for their fragile nation with the reality of nearby dangers and the necessity of being part of an Atlantic system. As the country became stronger—economically, militarily, and diplomatically—it looked more and more to its allies and rivals, both past and present, to understand its changing place in the world.

Opposition to, and accommodation of, the empires that surrounded the United States and shaped the world in which it operated were central to this process. First among these was the British Empire,[1] but also the empires of France, Spain, Russia, and Germany. Having lost much of its North American territory to the rising Britain, France made renewed and often successful attempts from the mid-nineteenth century onward to carve out influence in the Americas, Africa, and East Asia. Despite its precipitous decline as an empire between 1810 and the early 1820s, Spain was also central to American thinking, because it still held on to a few territories in the Caribbean—most notably Cuba—that were within the United States' growing orbit. Later in the century, Americans became more concerned with Russia and a united Germany as these nations' power grew and they vied for influence in various regions, while many people in the United States also took sporadic and often superficial interest in other empires outside of their immediate spheres of interest, including those of the Hapsburgs and Ottomans. Commentators often expressed opposition to these nations projecting their power overseas and exerting economic control in order to gain advantages over rivals. They particularly decried colonialism—the seizing, holding, and politically controlling of overseas territories with a view to exploit their lands and native populations—especially colonialism in the Americas. Such an acquisitive and domineering mode of interaction with the world, many leading Americans argued, was inimical to a United States that its founders had conceived as an anti-colonial nation. They often claimed to want no part in these intrigues, portraying imperial influence, and particularly colonialism, as anathema to the American people, their traditions, and their republican system of government.

Professed ideological opposition to empires was thus deeply ingrained. Americans had, after all, declared independence from their colonial master, Great Britain, in 1776 in protest against what they perceived to be the undue imperial burdens that Britain had placed on them through taxation. They then consolidated their national power in the first decades of the nineteenth century, seeking no overseas colonies for themselves. Some Americans were also reflexively suspicious of European politics and diplomacy, which had seen the continent in almost perpetual conflict for the previous two centuries. Finally, Americans' self-declared rejection of imperialism was also the result of the impact of these imperial powers on the United States itself, particularly through European trade that either excluded the United States or impinged upon it, but also through European wars that detrimentally affected American shipping and commerce as well as sometimes leading to the impressment of American citizens.

Its resistance to involvement in European balance-of-power politics and imperial intrigues, however, obscures aspects of the United States' own imperialistic agenda both at home and abroad. Some of the central traits of imperialism, such as aggressive economic and territorial expansionism, were elemental to the formation and enlargement of the American nation. Indeed, a logic of expansionism predated the foundation of the United States itself. The American Revolution came about in large part because the American subjects of the British Empire were considerably *more* expansionist—especially in acquiring land at the expense of indigenous tribes and confederations—than were politicians in London. The American founders therefore initially celebrated the growth of the British Empire, only to become disillusioned with it, frustrated by its limitations and impositions.[2]

Nonetheless, Americans could not avoid imperial entanglements in the pursuit of their independence and in its aftermath, and so the assistance of the European empires was sometimes necessary to ensure the survival of the fragile Union. Coming in the wake of the British victory over the French in the Seven Years' War, a conflict for imperial dominance that encompassed North America, as well as Britain's subsequent attempt to consolidate its North American empire by military and fiscal means, the American Revolution was inevitably an international and imperial conflict.[3] The imperial dimension was even evident in the particular commodity—tea from the British East India Company—whose taxation by the government in London led to the most infamous event in the developing American rebellion, the so-called Boston Tea Party of 1773. These developments among the European empires forced the American revolutionaries to rely on another empire, France, to provide them with economic and material support. Even after independence, the United States faced the need to forge diplomatic relationships with imperial powers and to operate in the international trading system dominated by them, however limited U.S. engagement in trade was in the early years of its existence.

Perhaps because of these kinds of interactions, American anti-imperial and even anti-colonial attitudes were, in fact, far less absolute than they might otherwise have appeared. Many in the United States looked on approvingly at aspects of imperial control—including some of those practiced by Europeans—and wanted to learn from them. While they did not necessarily like the limits that they believed imperialism and colonialism placed on American economic growth, they believed that imperial practices could impose order and stability on entire regions and engage these regions in processes of modernity that would ultimately benefit them and their peoples, whom they often saw as "backward" or "uncivilized." Some Americans were prepared to accept, and even aspired to replicate, strands of the British imperializing process, which they often believed dovetailed with the white settlement and "civilization" of the American West and which they increasingly practiced at the expense of indigenous populations. Americans thus inherited beliefs in social and racial hierarchies from the European imperial powers, however much they wanted to escape from Europe's diplomatic practices. This meant that inhabitants of the United States could oppose Great Britain as an oppressive, tyrannical power that had made undue demands on Americans, and would do so again if it could, while simultaneously celebrating and promoting a form of American empire that subjugated those they considered inferior and who were on the margins, or outside, of the state, based on the British model. These Americans thus, at least implicitly, began to regard themselves as the natural successors to the British Empire, even if they would not have put it in these terms.[4]

Many of these views were predicated on racialized assumptions and theories that often imagined certain peoples as being unprepared for independence and self-rule, or at least that they required help and tutelage from the "civilized" powers to get there. It could apply to people in the United States such as African Americans and Native Americans, near neighbors like Haitians, Mexicans, or Cubans, or those who lived in faraway places such as Egypt or West Africa. Reasons for taking such a position varied according to the case, but, with notable exceptions—such as Greece in the 1820s and Hungary from the late 1840s—it usually made American leaders reticent to support nascent or fully fledged independence movements abroad, and especially violent revolutions that threatened to upset the existing political order without pursuing a reasonable set of political goals.[5] In turn, American elites—especially those in or close to the centers of power—felt more comfortable in supporting imperial and even colonial orders that they claimed to oppose.

During these formative years, such paradoxes contributed to the ways that American leaders developed their understandings of the United States' relationship with European forms and practices of imperialism as a way to explain and justify the growth of American economic influence and territory. These Americans had to balance the need to develop diplomatic relations and trade with the stronger European powers while simultaneously resisting European interference in their own affairs. In doing so, political leaders articulated a vision of republicanism and self-determination in opposition to what they saw as the most malign practices of imperialism, even as they sought to grow and consolidate their own territorial holdings and regional hegemony.

This chapter establishes three interrelated themes to explore the ways in which the United States interacted with these other empires. All three demonstrate how the United States saw its own "empire" as different in fundamental ways from other European forms. The first theme concerns Americans' ideological attitudes toward these European empires: how they had to operate within an imperial Atlantic system after independence, and how they measured the European imperial powers against their own standards of rule. The second, following on from this, deals with American approaches to their own territorial growth over continental North America and how they generally rationalized this as a natural process, as opposed to what they saw as the aggressive expansionism of European empires. The final theme is the one that increasingly dominated elite American thinking as the nineteenth century progressed, and which to these Americans was perhaps the primary factor that made them exceptional: the notion that they were noninterventionist, refusing opportunities to interfere and dominate other nations and regions. This idea was based around the increasing salience of the 1823 Monroe Doctrine, the proclamation made by the administration of James Monroe resisting further European colonization of the Americas, which positioned the United States as ideologically separate from the Europe nations that frequently engaged in wars for imperial gain.

Early American Views of the European Empires
in the Americas

European empires dominated the early decades of the United States' existence. They controlled the Atlantic world, and political independence in fact gave the United States little autonomy. In practice, this meant that the United States conducted its economic and diplomatic business within a complex web of imperial interactions led by the growing British Empire, which had consolidated its power in the Americas after the loss of the colonies, and the empires of France and Spain. Thus, as American leaders struggled to define their new polity as an independent state, they also faced the challenge of separating themselves from the imperial intrigues of the great powers—powers that in effect had to allow Americans to forge their own nation if it was to survive.[6]

Left to their own devices, American leaders might have preferred to raise the political and diplomatic drawbridge, but they knew that this was impossible: Europe was too important a part of American life. By necessity, American elites were often astute readers of European government and society, and sometimes minor but significant players in its power politics. The most prominent foreign policy protagonist of the revolutionary era, Thomas Jefferson, was one such leader, who could, as one scholar has put it, "never escape Europe."[7] Jefferson acknowledged what he saw as the many shortcomings of the European system. He grounded his ideas about the creation and growth of the United States on his view of Europe, and particularly on his association of the European powers with inherited monarchy, which he thought corrupt, despotic, and outdated, and which he believed stood in striking contrast to the growing republican virtue of post-independence America. He also objected to the British monopolies that forced the United States to trade on British terms and threatened the long-term future of the Union. Once an enthusiastic subject of the British Empire, Jefferson had effectively admitted the failure of American attempts to enact reforms from within it in his *Summary View of the Rights of British America* (1774), and then in the Declaration of Independence itself two years later.[8] Thus, despite his long-term admiration for Britain's rival, France, Jefferson claimed in 1797 that it had been his "constant object through public life" to remain "perfectly neutral and independant [sic] with all nations" and "with respect to the English and French in particular."[9] Yet, although he sought a new kind of diplomacy that rejected war as a means to achieve America's ends, when in office he sometimes willingly participated in European diplomacy. As we shall see, in coveting lands to the west of the United States in the great Louisiana territory owned by France when he was president, Jefferson became entangled in European diplomacy. He even entertained an alliance with the British (or at least gave the impression that he did) to force the French to consider his terms.[10]

Jefferson's contemporaries also struggled to escape from imperial intrigues. His archrival Alexander Hamilton also advocated neutrality, believing that the United States was politically distinct from the major European nations and therefore should remain separate from them. Despite their differences, Hamilton expressed somewhat similar views to Jefferson about the malign influence of European empires and urged that the United States not follow their example. In *The Federalist Papers*, for example, Hamilton observed that the world was divided into four different areas—Europe, America, Africa, and Asia—each of which had its own distinct sets of interests:

> Unfortunately for the other three, Europe, by her force of arms and by her negotiations, by force and by fraud, has in different degrees extended her dominion over them all. Africa, Asia, and America have successively felt her domination. The superiority she has long maintained has tempted her to plume herself as the mistress of the world, and to consider the rest of mankind as created for her benefit. . . . Let Americans disdain to be the instruments of European greatness![11]

However, Hamilton's apparent neutrality saw the young United States tilt distinctly toward Britain. Born in the British West Indies, Hamilton had come to resent British colonialism but he also appreciated the advantages that British power could bring to the United States over the Spanish and French possessions in the Americas.[12] In 1790, he even advised George Washington to acquiesce in a quarrel between Britain and Spain when British forces threatened to march through the Mississippi Valley to engage the Spanish in Louisiana.[13] Crucially, he also saw Britain as a relatively benign regional force that would not attack the United States without very good reason. If they were given such a reason, however, he recognized Britain's potential to threaten the feeble new nation, not just because of its military might but also because the United States imported so many British goods and benefitted from British dominance of the seas.

Britain's continued challenge to the United States economically through its "informal" or "free trade" empire caused much resentment, because American leaders increasingly tended to see it as limiting their own possibilities for trade. Although they did not invent the terms, John Gallagher and Ronald Robinson discussed and popularized the concepts of a historical British Free Trade Empire in the 1950s. Gallagher and Robinson argued that historians had tended to focus too heavily on the areas of the world in which the British had actually taken political control, and assumed that there was a lack of political will to shape the areas in which they had not. They suggested that a number of factors—including the political and economic structures of a particular region, and the relative power of other interested empires in the area—explained why Britain chose to control some places as formal colonies and others by extending its influence through economic means. Thus, the British practiced what Robinson and Gallagher characterized as "a policy of commercial hegemony in the interests of high politics" and "the use of informal political supremacy in the interest of commercial enterprise."[14] This was especially relevant in the Americas, where the British held some colonies in the Caribbean but chose not to extend their formal dominion to many places in South America even as the Spanish Empire disintegrated in the early nineteenth century. This led some in the United States to believe that the British continued to count the newly independent United States as being a part of their commercial domain. Many people in the Southern states in particular regarded British formal colonialism and informal empire as part of an effort to undermine the American slave economy by building up industries in India and the West Indies while monopolizing the production and controlling the prices of various staples, including cotton.[15] This was exacerbated considerably after Britain's abolition of slavery in its empire in the 1830s, and many politicians in the South suspected a British conspiracy to undermine American cotton interests.[16] Americans thus actively sought to develop countermeasures to it, including by promoting tariffs and policies of reciprocity to gain commercial advantages, especially in opening up British colonial holdings and dependencies.[17]

In part based on this suspicion and outright disdain for the powerful British, American elites often expressed antipathy toward European colonialism and trade practices. This meant that they also provided rhetorical support for peoples struggling for independence, as they increasingly believed that the days of European empires in the Americas were coming to an end. In the early nineteenth century this applied especially to Spain, which had lost ground to Britain and France and whose tenuous grip on its American possessions grew weaker by the year. However, more generally, many commentators could not see how European nations could hold on to territories so far away from their own centers of power when revolutionary ferment was in the air. "Colonies universally, ardently breathe for independence," observed the second president, John Adams, toward the end of his life. "No man, who has a soul, will ever live in a colony under the present establishments one moment longer than necessity compels him."[18]

Although many agreed with Adams's opposition to colonialism, attitudes toward empire increasingly revealed the growing regional divisions in the United States. Certainly, Adams's suspicions reflected a broader trend in American society at the time that was not just confined to the non-slaveholding and industrializing north. In the rural South and West, jingoistic attitudes toward Britain and Spain were rife. People saw the monarchical powers of Europe subverting republican ideals, and, as revolutions against Spanish imperial rule in South America took hold, many viewed the United States as the vanguard of an emerging and dynamic pan-republicanism in the Americas. Yet opposition to empire—and particularly the British forms of empire—away from the metropolitan centers was often based as much on economic as on ideological motives. This was because Southerners and Westerners felt financially squeezed by the dominant regions of the Northeast, and they saw the opening of other markets as a way out of their economic constraints. One of the most prominent opponents of the British Empire was Kentucky representative Henry Clay. In his most famous speech, made when he became a senator in 1832, Clay focused on the free trade of the British Empire that he argued limited the growth of the United States and, by implication, the colonies and nations that the British controlled.[19] Clay also argued in favor of providing assistance for the emerging South American republics and dismissed the possible consequences of doing so. Other Southerners supported Clay, including those who saw the rapidly burgeoning British Empire as a direct threat to American—and specifically Southern—interests. "At this moment she presents to the civilized world the spectacle of the greatest military and commercial power in combination ever known," South Carolina representative Francis W. Pickens observed of Britain in 1841. Pickens had watched Britain's recent imperial progress in the Mediterranean, and the Near and Far East, as well as in the Western Hemisphere with alarm. Its "peculiar commercial system" made Britain "the reservoir of the wealth of nations," and this, married with its willingness to press its diplomatic and military power, made it a direct threat to the United States, he said, especially those slaveholding states: "She has moved steadily upon her objects with an ambition that knows no bounds. And wherever she has had a conflict of interest she has rarely yielded to any power."[20]

There were compelling practical reasons for close political ties with Great Britain, however, despite misgivings about its intentions and outlook. John Adams's son, John Quincy Adams, for example, who served as ambassador to London for two years from 1815 was no lover of the British Empire and as secretary of state supported President James Monroe's rhetorical attack on British imperial and colonial policies.[21] Adams particularly detested colonialism—the taking and ruling of overseas territories—considering it outdated and even conspiratorial, because colonial powers operated together to ensure their continued international dominance. In an exchange with the British minister to Washington, Stratford Canning, in 1821, Adams castigated Britain for its territorial claims and influence around the world, listing the places where Britain asserted its influence, prompting the supercilious Canning to enquire whether Adams thought Britain also claimed "a piece of the moon." Adams responded: "I have not heard that you claim exclusively any part of the moon; but there is not a spot on *this* habitable globe that I could affirm you do not claim."[22] Adams thus sought to undermine both the formal holding of colonies as well as the informal economic forms of (British) empire that he believed restricted American trade, an increasing concern in both the north and south of the country.[23]

Because of the great power of the European nations, however, leaders often tacked toward them rather than their own neighbors in the Americas. In the early years of the republic, this was especially notable during the revolts in Spain's colonies in the 1810s and 1820s. American writers may have engaged in what Adams called "warfare of the mind," in which they railed against monarchism and colonialism, but the United States remained economically vulnerable after the War of 1812 with Great Britain, now that the British were preeminent on the global stage.[24] Adams recognized this.

Moreover, growing personal affinities between leading figures in Washington and London encouraged reconciliation shortly after the war. Such feelings were evident in the signing of the Rush–Bagot Pact in April 1817, which, among other things, demilitarized the Great Lakes.

Moreover, while people like Adams may have longed to see European imperial influence curtailed in the Americas, they often balked at the prospect of actually supporting the fight against colonialism there and rejected connections between the independence struggle in the United States and the developing anticolonial movements elsewhere in the Western Hemisphere. Elites were generally of the opinion that, unlike in the United States, some peoples were simply not ready to free themselves from the tyrannies of European colonialism to become nations. Such racialized views indicated that American leaders often had a greater affinity with the European powers themselves than with independence-seeking colonies that resisted them. In one illustrative example, at the end of the eighteenth century the United States actively opposed the independence of the French Caribbean island colony of Santo Domingo when it rebelled against French rule, fearing the prospect of a black-ruled nation, under the leadership of the charismatic former slave Toussaint Louverture, so close to the United States. The British and American governments worked together to oppose a return to French dominion, but also to exploit the considerable economic possibilities that the lucrative sugar trade held for both sides. U.S. policies thus reflected an economic pragmatism, but one predicated on eschewing unity with the islanders who hoped to achieve their freedom, amid fears about slave uprisings in the Southern United States.[25] The United States did not recognize Haitian independence until 1862, a highly significant moment of its own Civil War.

Policymakers in the United States thus often supported colonial subjects who began to strive for independence only in the broadest rhetorical terms, with practical assistance usually lacking and outright opposition sometimes in evidence. They generally based this stance on the ethnic makeup and supposed lack of aptitude of such people for self-rule. In 1817, John Quincy Adams recoiled from the prominent role that blacks played in the emancipation of the Spanish colonies, publicly expressing his disdain for the revolutionaries and claiming that the "ferment of the Spanish colonies" was not "founded on principles," but had "merely grown out of circumstances." As a result, he erroneously suggested at one point, the colonial rebellions against Spain had "been put down in great measure by the dissensions of the colonists and the misconduct of their leaders."[26] By 1821, and despite the success of many of the colonies in resisting Spain, Adams concluded that Spanish rule had left them without "the first elements of good or free government. Arbitrary power, military and ecclesiastical, was stamped upon their education, upon their habits, upon all their institutions."[27] As we shall see, Adams's successors took up this view of rebellious colonists who were unworthy of independence.

Even his father John Adams's comments about the iniquities of colonialism should not disguise his low opinion of the people of the American colonies to the south of the United States. John Adams believed that they lacked the maturity to be independent republics and so would become subject to the very monarchical intrigues and alliances from which they wanted to escape. Here, Adams suggested that the Spanish colonial system had enfeebled the population, including the Creoles. Spanish Americans were steeped in "general ignorance" and superstition when compared to even the Italians or French, he said, and certainly not "England, English America, and all other Protestant nations" because these Spanish Americans believed that only they and the Spaniards of Europe were chosen by God to be saved.[28] In this sense, then, the enervating effects of colonialism that had acted on these societies for generations apparently precluded meaningful independence for their inhabitants.

This applied especially to Spain's colonies. Spain's supposedly particularly aggressive and violent form of colonial acquisition and control had long-term effects on the colonized peoples. Adams's views were manifestations of the "Black Legend," which gave an especially negative account of the Spanish empire and its effects. Historian Charles Gibson has defined the Black Legend (*Leyenda Negra*) as an "accumulated tradition of propaganda and Hispanophobia according to which Spanish imperialism is regarded as cruel, bigoted, exploitative, and self-righteous in excess of the reality."[29] Despite the assistance Spain provided to the United States during its struggle for independence, such derisive views of Spanish imperialism contributed to the development of what María DeGuzmán has identified as a distinct national identity in the United States based on tension with, and sometimes in opposition to, Spanish figures in cultural contexts. DeGuzmán notes that this phenomenon only intensified as the nineteenth century progressed, despite Spain's weakening position in the Americas, and it contributed to a perception that, even after independence from Spain, Latin America was still distinctly Spanish. DeGuzmán therefore concludes that Americans saw Spain as something of a "bridge" between "colonizer and colonized" rather than simply a white, Catholic colonizer. This, combined with Americans' desire for land that Spain occupied, inevitably brought mutual suspicion and mistrust that was, in James Cortada's words, "virtually institutionalized" by both governments in the first years of the U.S. republic, continuing for decades afterward.[30]

Early Views of Other Empires

Throughout the United States' formative years, Americans struggled to understand European empires that held territory far from the United States, often because they had limited knowledge both of the empires themselves and the territories they occupied. Sometimes they viewed these empires positively, especially if they posed no obvious threats and upheld what they perceived to be broadly defined norms. So while Thomas Jefferson objected to many of the features of European monarchical systems, he was also an admirer of Tsar Alexander I of Russia, believing that the tsar represented a more enlightened form of autocracy than other monarchs. Jefferson thought that the dynastic inheritance of European empires had led to degeneracy among their ruling families, but that this had not yet occurred in Alexander, the grandson of Catherine the Great. Jefferson explicitly contrasted Alexander's inherited rule with the self-appointed French emperor Napoleon, whom Alexander had helped to defeat, and he even had busts of the two leaders set opposite each other in his house at Monticello to represent this dichotomy.

Jefferson based his admiration on Russia's continental growth. For much of the previous century, Russia had been steadily expanding into northern, central, and southern Europe, often at the expense of other continental empires. While Alexander continued this expansion, he also flirted with social and political reform early in his reign. Encouraged by such moves, in 1806 President Jefferson told the Russian emperor, "It will be among the latest and most soothing comforts of my life, to see advanced to the government of so extensive a portion of the earth, and at so early a period of his life, a sovereign whose ruling passion is the advancement of the happiness and prosperity of his people." Over the next two decades, however, American observers would come to perceive Alexander as an increasingly autocratic figure, described by *Niles Weekly Register* at the time of his death in 1825 as "the most dangerous man of modern times." In his final years, even Jefferson became suspicious of him.[31]

Like Jefferson, other Americans also came to view the politics and foreign policy of the French Empire with caution, seeing France's continental dominance during the Napoleonic Wars as increasingly dangerous and tyrannical. Alexander Hamilton, for example, believed that France was "marching with hasty and colossal strides to universal empire." This, he said, was because "after binding in chains their own countrymen, after prostrating surrounding nations, and vanquishing all external resistance to the revolutionary despotism at home," they persisted in a policy of war to perpetuate their power.[32] Thus, although many Americans celebrated the fall of the Bastille, subsequent events that led to the outbreak of general war in Europe troubled all but the most ardent Francophiles, and reinforced ideas that France was a lesser nation—and therefore a lesser empire—than Britain.

The domestic instability during the decades that followed Napoleon's defeat did little to counter such perceptions of France's inferiority. Extremism that became evident in the 1848 European revolutions dashed American hopes for a durable French republic. Many Americans saw the coup d'état by Louis Napoleon, Bonaparte's nephew, as especially egregious, countering the evolution of liberal institutions in France, a fact that, as one scholar has argued, "made it extremely difficult for many Americans to pay France the respect the French people so ardently desired."[33] Louis Napoleon, who became Napoleon III when he declared himself emperor of the French in 1851, came to embody all that was wrong with European politics and empires. As Richard Koebner writes, in the English speaking world (and particularly in Britain) during this period, use of the largely negative term "imperialism"—embodying such features as the rapid acquisition of power and money, despotism, and an extravagant royal court, as well as extraterritorial campaigns—was increasingly associated with Napoleon III's rule.[34] The first known use of the term "imperialism" in the United States was by an anonymous author in 1852, who claimed:

If there be a system of a doctrine utterly hideous and detestable to an American, it is imperialism.

Deriving its power from the ambition of an army, and the fear and admiration of an ignorant multitude, it ignores the liberty and sovereignty of the individual and of the state.

The right of self-government is taken away, as is the right of opinion by the Papacy. The right of cities and of states to regulate their internal affairs is annihilated by its centralization—a polity necessary to imperialism as the hand to the brain, the body to the soul.[35]

In this instance, the author's focus was on "imperialism" as a domestic phenomenon dominated by an overweening Catholic centralism, but during the course of the next decade, Americans discussed its foreign implications more freely.

Spain's demise, Britain's rise, and France's ambitions meant that these three nations dominated American elite thinking about contemporary empires, but other imperial entities also occupied American attention. The Ottoman and Hapsburg empires were more challenging to imagine because they were of peripheral interest to most Americans, including political elites. As one scholar has recently noted, the U.S. populace "likely had only a hazy knowledge" of the Ottoman Empire and the places it ruled at this time, and they tended to see the metropolitan center, often simply called "Turkey," as only "half civilized." By the time of the American Revolution, most of the Americans who knew anything about it already regarded the empire as corrupt and in decay. In *The Federalist Papers*, for example, Hamilton drew a negative comparison between the United States and the Ottoman Empire, which he noted had no powers of taxation over its dominions and allowed local governors to take from the people for themselves or for the purposes of the state, without accountability.[36] In this instance, the *lack* of power and authority of the metropolitan center generated negative views.

Much of this discussion was also cultural, specifically religious. Most Americans assumed that Protestantism was superior to other denominations and religions. In practical terms, this meant that the early American missionaries operating in different contexts around the world were united in a belief that Christianity's power was in part derived from its association with, and contribution to, more advanced forms of civilization. This often led them to support the growth of the British Empire in order to help spread the Christian faith.[37] They and many others placed Islam on a particularly low rung of their religious hierarchy.[38] As Karine Walther has recently shown, this influenced not only those American Christian missionaries working in the Ottoman Empire and beyond, but also politicians and other leaders in the United States. Such people may have placed

Muslims higher on the racial ladder than others, notably African "heathens," but because religion was the defining factor in American assessments of the Islamic sphere, it trumped other qualities and became its own racial category. This had important political ramifications for both the United States government and for how many saw the outside world. Encounters with the Barbary States in North Africa—three of which were nominally under the control of the Ottoman Empire—reinforced early American beliefs that Islam itself made its adherents violent and uncivilized. American support for the Greeks during their independence war in the early 1820s, which garnered much interest and even encouraged a movement advocating for intervention, and again during the Cretan insurrection at the end of the 1860s, undoubtedly rested in part on religious grounds. Americans involved in such campaigns largely saw the Ottoman Empire as being against the natural order of global politics and international law, because it placed Muslims above both Christians and Jews in the religious and racial hierarchy. This could also lead them to support Christian empires claiming territories in Muslim lands, as in the case of the French extending their influence into Morocco during the early nineteenth century.[39] As Walther puts it, these attitudes "depended on the assumption that Muslims required outside intervention and the abandonment of their faith to make any civilizational advances."[40]

American views of the Ottoman Empire began to improve over the course of the nineteenth century, and especially in the years before the Civil War. The short-lived Young America movement within the Democratic Party in the 1840s and 1850s advocated American expansionism to the south, as well as support for reformist, anti-monarchical institutions in Europe. In keeping with this, it opposed Russia, which it regarded as expansionist and oppressive, and supported the Ottomans because of their apparently reformist agenda. Young America's leader Edwin De Leon was a Southerner who would become President Franklin Pierce's consul to Egypt from the mid-1850s, but his group's activities in the United States caused some concern that it would assist and encourage illegal support for anti-imperial movements in Europe. Some feared it might persuade the government to become more heavily involved in European politics by acquiring a naval base in the Mediterranean, an idea raised by De Leon himself.[41] More broadly, the years before the outbreak of the American Civil War saw a tentative but expanding dialogue between American leaders and their counterparts in the Ottoman Empire, not just at the diplomatic and military levels but also in trade and technology. This was perhaps best captured by representatives of Samuel Morse's telegraph company gaining the attention of Sultan Abdulmejid I, leading to the introduction of this new means of communication in the empire during the Crimean War of the 1850s.[42]

Engaged Americans were similarly uncomfortable and often ill-informed about the Hapsburg Empire, with its convoluted geography, multilingualism, and complex ethnic makeup. Most knew little about its rulers or inhabitants, and struggled to draw comprehensible parallels between Hapsburg rule and the experience of Americans under the British Empire. The Hapsburg Empire's association with conservatism, Catholicism, and nobility did not help to dispel this ignorance. And any negative perceptions that people had were further reinforced by the events that unfolded over the course of the nineteenth century, when possibilities for reform and independence for many of its inhabitants were frustrated. Such movements culminated in the revolts of 1848—which may ideologically have borrowed heavily from the American Revolution—in such places as Italy and Hungary, and encouraged a transatlantic exchange of ideas, but became violent and lapsed into what for most American policymakers looked like extremism. There were party and regional variations in responses to the prospects of these revolutions. Conservative Whigs' studied suspicion of revolutionary fervor contrasted with the intuitive response of nascent Free Soilers, who saw obvious alliances with the Europeans struggling to throw off the chains of monarchy. Southerners were usually cautious about any prospect of radical change—especially following France's abolition of slavery in its colonies at this time—while the many in the Midwest, home to the anti-imperial Young America movement as well as a higher concentration of immigrants than much of the rest of the nation, more broadly embraced the cause.[43] While these European uprisings piqued American interest and some considerable enthusiasm especially in their early stages—including some significant diplomatic tensions over the possibility that the United States government might attempt to mediate in some way—the ultimate failure of revolutionary movements across Europe and the emergence of absolutist figures such as Napoleon III and Emperor Franz Josef of Austria confirmed to most interested Americans that Europe was simply not well suited to republicanism. Many of the émigrés from the Hapsburg Empire who settled in the United States, some of whom became prominent figures in American society—like Karl Heinzen, Friedrich Kapp, Carl Schurz, and August Willich—reinforced such ideas.[44]

Finally, Americans—even those most engaged in thinking about the rest of the world—also often ignored vast areas of the world that were subject to European imperial competition. While a commentator in the *North American Review* provided an account detailing the devastating losses the Afghans had recently inflicted upon British colonial troops at the end of the First Anglo-Afghan War in 1842, for example, he had to provide much context and explanation for his readers. The author said he wrote the article because he believed it would "not be without interest," but conceded it was likely that there were "not many of our countrymen who have watched the course of events in that war."[45]

Territorial Expansion

Despite their habitual skepticism about aggressive empire building in continental Europe, great power acquisition of overseas colonies, and European control of international trade, leading Americans were also often enthusiastic empire builders themselves. Indeed, ideas about territorial growth were ingrained in the fabric of American politics and society. The founders formed the United States as an expansionist state and were optimistic that augmentation of both population and territory would soon allow it to challenge the dominant European empires.[46] Benjamin Franklin's *Observations Concerning the Increase of Mankind* (1755) was explicit about such ambitions, contrasting America as a land that offered the space to grow with the limited opportunities to do so in Europe. To Franklin and others, theirs was an empty continent whose security was threatened by the presence of the empires of Spain, France, and then Britain, as well as Native American tribes. If they could remove these powers, they reasoned, the land would open up for them to take.[47] The incorporation and rule of various territories thus meant that the nation was involved in an expansive project from its very beginnings as it took in new territories to become what one historian has recently called the "Greater United States."[48]

As several authors have noted, the first generations of American leaders held a particular notion of an American "empire" that justified territorial expansionism. Richard Immerman contends that "*empire*, as a noun, was value-free at the time the United States gained its independence," while Michael Vlahos suggests that the term was "entirely descriptive of the free space they sought."[49] Richard Van Alstyne concurs, noting that these leaders did not object to the idea that the United States was an expanding empire; indeed, they often embraced the term. There are many examples of this: George Washington's view of the United States as a "rising American empire," Jefferson's "empire of liberty," and Hamilton's declaration that the new American nation was "the embryo of a great empire" of republicanism.[50] For these protagonists, building an empire primarily meant gaining contiguous territory with few, if any, perceived connotations of domination, because the government would incorporate the land into the Union. Crucially, few associated an American empire with overseas conquests and attendant exploitation of the kind they believed characterized European growth.

For early American leaders, the need for territorial expansionism was axiomatic, because external threats exacerbated the fragility of the political union. The prospect of expelling the European powers from the continent was therefore intimately intertwined with the perceived need for additional territory, including Spanish holdings to the south—Florida during the first decades of the republic, but also land west of the Mississippi. Furthermore, it included British Canada to the north, which Americans had been trying to annex since even before the war of independence, establishing a pattern that continued until the beginning of the twentieth century and went beyond the need to maintain basic security. In making such claims, some Americans displayed an inherent certainty that the United States would soon inherit the land occupied by the European powers: "If we want it, I warrant it will soon be ours," as the geographer of the United States, Thomas Hutchins, put it in the 1780s.[51]

Such confidence was evident in Thomas Jefferson's 1803 purchase of the massive Louisiana territory. Prior to this, Jefferson faced a reassertion of French power in North America following Napoleon Bonaparte's secret agreement with Spain for the retrocession of Louisiana to France in late 1800. Yet, although the French first consul saw the land as a bulwark against the expansion of the United States, Jefferson was able to exploit Napoleon's weaknesses in the region, and especially in the Caribbean, to convince him that he could not afford a rift with the United States and so should sell the territory. The traditional view has been that in acquiring the 828,000 square miles of Louisiana for a mere 60 million francs (about $15 million, or four cents per acre) through a combination of skillful bargaining and luck, Jefferson effectively removed the French threat from the continent.[52]

To Jefferson, this growth was not just beneficial but necessary for the success of the republican project, associating the healthy future of the nation with the augmentation of its territory and population. His "empire of liberty" was designed to integrate new lands into the Union, but also to keep these lands from others, and to demonstrate the strength of republicanism when it was under threat in Europe. In the words of one particularly admiring historian, his empire's "domain and compulsion would be in the realm of the mind and the spirit of man, freely and inexorably transcending political boundaries, incapable of being restrained, and holding imperial sway not by arms or political power but by the sheer majesty of ideas and ideals."[53] Jefferson's vision was of a homogenous people whose strength in numbers would allow them to oppose external threats: "But who can limit the extent to which the federative principle may operate effectively?" he asked in his second inaugural address. "The larger our association the less it will be shaken by local passions; and in any view is it not better that the opposite bank of the Mississippi should be settled by our own brethren and children than by strangers of another family?"[54] In this sense, Jefferson saw U.S. expansionism as the antithesis of European colonialism.

Jefferson's purchase of Louisiana brought him much closer to a policy of empire in the European mold than he recognized, however. His ideas of an integrated, ethnically homogenous people implied exclusion, conquest, and domination of those who did not conform or who resisted. Moreover, as Robert Lee has recently contended, the $15 million price tag is dwarfed by successful claims made by numerous tribes since the late nineteenth century against the U.S. government arising out of the purchase. Jefferson's policies also exposed a series of issues that went to the heart of republican government and its place in the imperial world. In addition to the question of whether the president possessed the constitutional authority to make such a deal, perhaps the most important element was reconciling this massive territorial expansion with his philosophy of government based on decentralized power and the primacy of small agrarian farmers. Critics wondered how this republic could expand to such an extent without the exploitation and domination inherent in European expansion, at their most extreme seeing Jefferson as a New World Bonaparte. His expansionist vision encouraged American leaders to strive for greater acquisitions as they sought to gain regional dominance, expanding the reach of

American slavery westward while looking toward commercial expansion in the Pacific and beyond. Indeed, many saw further growth as both natural and relatively simple in light of the ease with which Jefferson had effected the Louisiana concession from the French.[55]

To the north, this expansionist fervor focused on Canada, which many believed would inevitably become part of the United States. Although recent accounts have downplayed the American desire for Canadian territory as a cause for the declaration of war against Great Britain in 1812, many Americans supported the invasion of British North America, because they believed it would give them an effective monopoly in the lucrative fur trade and potentially increase commercial opportunities in other parts of the British Empire, especially the West Indies. Yet, while in declaring war President James Madison rejected the charge that territorial aggrandizement was his primary motivating factor, he acknowledged in private that relinquishing territory captured in an invasion would be difficult, and that denying the British an empire in North America would reduce its power significantly and force it to reckon with the United States.[56] As Jefferson (now in retirement) put it at the start of the war, gaining Canadian territory at least as far as Quebec would "be a mere matter of marching" and it would lead to "the final expulsion of England from the American continent."[57]

Americans also strove for greater territorial acquisitions to the south, most immediately obtaining Florida from the Spanish. Beyond the desire for more territory, white settlers on the southern and western frontiers resented continued Spanish control of land and river routes. They were also suspicious of the Spanish settlers' relations with the Native tribes—claiming that they encouraged aggression toward Americans—and of Spain's relationship with Britain. Alexander Hamilton had outlined the problem in *The Federalist Papers*:

On the one side of us . . . are growing settlements subject to British dominion. On the other side, and extending to meet the British settlements, are colonies and establishments subject to the dominion of Spain. This situation and the vicinity of the West India Islands, belonging to these two powers, create between them, in respect to their American possessions and in relation to us, a common interest. . . .

[The] savage tribes on our Western frontier ought to be regarded as our natural enemies, their natural allies, because they have the most to fear from us, and most to hope for from them.

Taken together with the possessions of Britain and Spain, Hamilton suggested, the land occupied by the Native tribes "encircle[d] the Union from Maine to Georgia."[58] Not only would the Spanish be able to use Florida as a base in any putative conflict with the United States, but also the alliance between Spain and Britain against France held out the possibility that the two would act in concert against the United States. These fears grew as relations with the British deteriorated, leading to a joint congressional resolution in 1811 warning President Madison that the United States should not allow Spain to pass "any part" of the territory "into the hands of any [other] foreign power."[59] Although plans for gaining all of Florida foundered in the years before and during the 1812 war, American desire for it remained, as did their determination to prevent the British from acquiring it.

As with other lands, rather than satisfying American appetite for territory, the eventual acquisition of Florida in 1819 under the stewardship of James Monroe's secretary of state John Quincy Adams merely exacerbated it. Like with many of his predecessors and contemporaries, Adams's dislike of European empires did not preclude a belief in the United States' destiny to be a great continental power, and he had supported (with some caveats) Jefferson's purchase of Louisiana. Historians disagree, however, on the broader significance of Adams's expansionist vision. According to William Earl Weeks, Adams "conceived of the North American continent as the proper laboratory for the great experiment in human freedom, and early on he determined to devote his energies to the expansion of the nation's limits." In contrast, Greg Russell suggests that Adams carefully considered his ideas about territorial growth. Russell disagrees with those who claim that Adams's foreign policy ethics were little more than a cover for his empire building by pointing out his stiff opposition to the acquisition of the independent republic of Texas (1845) and the war with Mexico (1846–1848) toward the end of his life.[60]

In some ways, Adams's objections to these acquisitions of territory during the 1840s were understandable, because the United States became increasingly aggressive in pursuing them. While the 1840s saw Washington negotiate with a stronger power, Great Britain, over the Oregon territory, it threatened war before doing so. By the time it gained Oregon in 1846, it had also annexed Texas, and it then took military action against its weaker neighbor Mexico to gain the vast swathes of land—including California and New Mexico—that extended the reach of the United States to the Pacific Ocean. But American leaders saw this as materially different from European attempts to gain overseas colonies, because their form of expansion promised statehood and citizenship for most of the territory's people. In his infamous finding on the fate of slave Dred Scott in 1857, for example, Justice Roger Brooke Taney asserted that while the Constitution provided the power for Congress to expand into contiguous land with a view to bringing it into the United States, it had "no power . . . to establish or maintain colonies bordering on the United States or at a distance, to be ruled and governed at its own pleasure." In this instance, Taney suggested, certain rules applied as soon as the United States laid claim to the land, including rights of property that, ironically, helped to deny Scott his freedom.[61]

The phrase "Manifest Destiny" (coined by journalist John O'Sullivan in 1845, writing about his desire to annex Texas and what he saw as an impending war with Britain over Oregon) may be popular shorthand for this American continental expansionism, yet the term tells us relatively little about what motivated the expansionists or indeed about the results of their actions. For example, Thomas Hietala has emphasized the specific conditions at this particular moment in the 1840s arising from deep divisions over domestic issues such as industrialization and race, which generated demands for growth. The notion of Manifest Destiny also ignores the inheritance of European colonial ideas about the Anglo-Saxons' right to rule over "lesser" races and it implies a unity of purpose among Americans that never existed. Many members of Congress objected to the incorporation of Texas as a state, and the measure ultimately only barely passed. The war with Mexico from 1846 to 1848 caused even greater uproar as both Whigs and Democrats rebelled against President James K. Polk's policies and the problems of incorporating the land taken from Mexico. While many of these fears rested on chauvinistic views of the Mexicans and a disinclination to include them as Americans, some also saw threats to republican values in this new militarism. A prominent opponent was the veteran Democrat senator from South Carolina, John C. Calhoun, who supported the acquisition of Texas and desperately wanted to prevent the government from placing any limits on the extension of slavery, but who vigorously opposed the war with Mexico, because he saw the United States becoming like imperial Britain or Spain.[62]

While Southern proponents of slavery could reject expansionist methods based on what they saw as their tendencies to extend executive imperial authority along the lines of the European powers, Northerners could support territorial growth if it fit with their vision of the United States as a benign expansionist force. John Quincy Adams may have sided with the dissenters on Mexico in his final years, even if he vehemently disagreed with figures like Calhoun about the extension of slavery, yet it is clear that his long-term aim was to see the United States as the dominant power in North America. This would be at the expense of the European powers, but also its native inhabitants as well as other nations in the region. In deciding to pursue the acquisition of Florida a quarter century before, Adams had followed his predecessors in recognizing that as long as the European empires occupied contiguous territory, then the United States was subject to their interests and rivalries. While he welcomed Spain's decline in the Americas, he also feared that powerful Britain would take its place, and sought assurances from London that it was not seeking to acquire Florida or Cuba from its ally. He then took advantage of Spain's growing weakness while keeping the Spanish guessing about American intentions, and even deigned to recognize the belligerents in Spain's American colonies. The 1819 Transcontinental Treaty in which the Spanish ceded Florida to the United States ultimately relied on a combination of General Andrew Jackson's military aggression against Spain and the Seminoles in Florida (as well as a good deal of semantic maneuvering about Jackson's actions on the part of the secretary of state himself) and Adams's ability to manipulate Spain's regional weaknesses to complete what Samuel Flagg Bemis calls "the greatest diplomatic victory won by any single individual in the history of the United States."[63]

There were opponents of this expansionism on moral grounds. Writing in 1850 in the wake of the war with Mexico, for example, female suffrage campaigner Elizabeth Cady Stanton decried American expansion in the south and west, because it was "stained with the guilt of aggressive warfare upon such weak defenceless nations as the Seminoles and Mexicans." Her argument was predicated on the notion that if women participated fully in politics then they could prevent such imperial aggression.[64] Likewise, abolitionist Martin R. Delany noted that the American negotiator in Mexico, Nicholas Trist, was a supporter of slavery and had been implicated in the slave trade during his period as a U.S. consul in Havana. Now Trist, as the "representative of a nation making high pretensions to justice," was tasked with ending a war with Mexico, a nation that had ended slavery. Intriguingly, in singling out the United States, Spain, and France as arbiters of what he called "slaveholding power," Delany contrasted them with England, which he said was "the master spirit of the world" whose "every example is to promote the cause of Freedom."[65]

In contrast, Adams and the expansionists of the 1840s shared a belief that it was the inherent right of the United States—and no other power—to expand across the continent. What they disagreed about was exactly which areas and whether they should use them for the purposes of slavery. As Adams said of Great Britain to the American minister in London, Richard Rush, in 1818: "If the United States leave her in undisturbed enjoyment of all her holds upon Europe, Asia, and Africa, with all her actual possessions in this hemisphere, we may very fairly expect that she will not think it consistent either with a wise or a friendly policy to watch with eyes of jealousy and alarm every possibility of extension to *our natural dominion of North America*, which she can have no solid interest to prevent, until all possibility of her preventing it shall have vanished."[66] Therefore, Adams may have objected to subsequent American expansion, which he perceived as aggressive and undemocratic, but it followed the precedents that he had set over Florida, in turn building on the Louisiana Purchase. Even the intermittent discussions and occasional negotiations about bringing Cuba into the Union broadly adhered to Adams's logic that some territories were naturally part of it.

This perceived right was the essence of Manifest Destiny as justification for American expansion, and its supporters—whether from the North or South—generally continued to see the territorial growth of the United States as being very different from the empire building of the European powers. In October 1845, for example, the *New York Morning News* argued that many in Europe were misguided about the nature of the Texas acquisition:

It is looked upon as aggression, and all the bad and odious features which the habits of thought of Europeans associate with aggressive deeds, are attributed to it . . . But what has Belgium, Silesia, Poland or Bengal in common with Texas? It is surely not necessary to insist that acquisitions of territory in America, even if accomplished by force of arms, are not to be viewed in the same light as the invasions and conquests of the States of the old world . . . We are contiguous to a vast portion of the globe, untrodden save by the savage and the beast, and we are conscious of our power to render it tributary to man.[67]

They also had to oppose these empires in order to allow their expansion to take place. A reason for taking Texas, for example, was to keep it from the British and stop them from interfering in American affairs.[68] One of the most famous interventions in this debate came from retired president Andrew Jackson, whose private letter to Representative Aaron V. Brown was published in 1844, without Jackson's permission, to enlist support for the annexation. Jackson told Brown that "the welfare and happiness of our Union" relied on gaining Texas and expressed regret that he had not been able to see it through during his presidential term. Rather than risking disunion by acquiring additional territory, as many believed would happen, he thought that incorporating Texas would prevent it from forming an alliance with Britain and thus prevent what he called "a servile war" in the South and West begun by the British, inciting slave insurrections. According to Jackson, the United States could only avert this apocalyptic outcome by extending the western boundary to the Rio Grande to make the nation "invincible." As he put it, if the United States had this reach, "the whole European world could not, in combination against us, make an impression on our Union." Jackson may have been interested in spreading American institutions, democracy, and peace, but his priority was the extension of the borders of the United States to avoid what he called "the probabilities of future collision with foreign powers."[69]

Moreover, the idea that the land was "untrodden" (to quote the *Morning News*) further exposes the paradox of an American mindset assuming a separation from European imperialism but incorporating many of its prejudices and practices. As Carroll Smith-Rosenberg has suggested, this complex sense of identity meant that Americans tended to consider themselves to be anti-imperialist when they looked east toward Europe, but were imperialist when they looked south and west. Somewhat similarly, Kariann Akemi Yokota has explored the process by which, in becoming American citizens, Americans had to "unbecome" British and navigate a complex path to escape from Britain's empire while also oppressing those indigenous populations within their expanding borders. In this way, Yokota suggests, the United States can be seen as a postcolonial nation, albeit one in which "the boundary between colonizer and colonized is ambiguous."[70]

Such notions of domination presupposed American institutional as well as racial superiority, traits that were intimately interconnected. Anders

Stephanson has suggested that American ideas about their divine mission and, later in the nineteenth century, the spread of "civilization" across the continent set them apart from Europeans, because Americans conceived of the United States as a utopian, globally transformative project with a unique ideological and spatial reach. Long before the founding of the United States, however, the logic of European diplomacy had already enveloped many Native American tribes and confederations, drawing them into commerce, treaty making, and alliances with the white settler. As the United States became more powerful, the possibilities of assimilation of indigenous peoples generally gave way to the adoption of increasingly coercive and violent methods that Europeans had employed against "savages" in Europe, Asia, and North America. While this should not obscure the agency of the many Native American tribes that struggled to retain their lands and identities, it does suggest a homogenizing view among white Americans of a Native "problem" that had to be solved. Paradoxically, these Americans believed that almost no matter what action they took toward indigenous people—amity, assimilation, or war—it was for the natives' benefit, or at the very least for the greater good. In this respect, the teleology of what Richard White has called American "imperial dominance" was little different from that of the European colonizing mission.[71] Thus, adding territory did not mean simply occupying empty lands and spreading American ideals; it meant taking territory from, and struggling for control over, others.[72]

Finally, it was no coincidence that many advocates of continental growth in the pre–Civil War decades thought about an American future beyond the American continent. Most prominently this meant in Asia. Adventurers and merchants had often traveled and traded there and wanted to compete with their European counterparts. China in particular was a source of mystery and fascination to many of them—and many others—conjuring up what Gordon Chang has called an "imagined future" in which the United States would become an influential force in Asian affairs.[73] The outbreak of the First Opium War (1839–1842) thus concerned many American elites, as the British engaged in gunboat diplomacy to open up Chinese ports. Curiously, one of the few prominent people to speak out in favor of Great Britain was John Quincy Adams, who claimed that the Chinese were effectively resisting British attempts to practice free trade and thus contravening natural laws and civilized norms. While Adams's views were highly controversial among his contemporaries, they were important in influencing more outward-looking Americans to consider the role their country should play in encouraging Chinese engagement with the rest of the world.[74]

Such people were already associating agricultural overproduction with the need to search for new markets far from American shores: in Hawaii and Japan, as well as China and elsewhere. The numerous initiatives and treaties signed during this period—including the two major naval expeditions to explore the Pacific undertaken from the late 1830s, the 1844 treaty with China brokered by Caleb Cushing in the wake of the First Opium War, and Commodore Matthew C. Perry's mission to open Japan in the early 1850s—attest to this spirit. Therefore, as Americans were increasingly able to unify their rapidly expanding nation through technological innovations—primarily railroads and the telegraph—they were also imagining the nation's future abroad, even as the question of slavery was tearing their country apart.[75]

Nonintervention

United States interest in Spanish America during the nineteenth century grew in proportion to the demise of Spain as a colonial power. However, just as American policymakers had often approached the former Spanish colonies with some caution and even apprehension, because they were unconvinced they were worthy of nationhood, so did they increasingly eye the successor nations as potential rivals. Many people in the United States applauded the colonies for striving to escape from the confines of imperial control to become sovereign nations. This, after all, mirrored the experience of the United States and fit with the founders' ideology—albeit an often abstract one—about the wider regional applicability of the republican model. It also reinforced a sense of common purpose among American nations deriving from their shared experiences of European empires but a separation from Europe. Yet these new countries were also threats to the preeminence of the United States, which had been the only independent republic in the Americas up to this point. If the Americas did become a multipolar continent, some Americans reasoned, it might also lead to growing regional rivalries and ultimately end up replicating the worst aspects of the European balance-of-power system.[76]

In reacting to these independence movements, American leaders continued to adhere, rhetorically at least, to the established principle of noninterference first promulgated by George Washington in his farewell address. Most famously, John Quincy Adams suggested in 1821 that the United States had always "respected the independence of other nations, while asserting and maintaining her own" and "abstained from interference in the concerns of others, even when the conflict has been for principles to which she clings, as to the last vital drop that visits the heart." He set out a vision of the United States that went "not abroad in search of monsters to destroy." Instead, he said,

> she is the well-wisher to the freedom and independence of all. She is the champion and vindicator only of her own. She will recommend the general cause, by the countenance of her voice, and the benignant sympathy of her example. She well knows that by once enlisting under other banners than her own, were they even the banners of foreign independence, she would involve herself, beyond the power of extrication, in all the wars of interest and intrigue, of individual avarice, envy, and ambition, which assume the colors and usurp the standard of freedom. The fundamental maxims of her policy would insensibly change from liberty to force. The frontlet upon her brows would no longer beam with the ineffable splendor of freedom and independence; but in its stead would soon be substituted an imperial diadem, flashing in false and tarnished lustre the murky radiance of dominion and power. She might become the dictatress of the world: she would be no longer the ruler of her own spirit.[77]

Adams therefore argued that the United States did not, and indeed should not, become involved in imperial intrigues or in other nations' affairs, even to encourage independence or the adoption of republican government, because to do so would negate its founding principles and pose a danger to the body politic. He thus reinforced the notion that the United States occupied an ideological position that was fundamentally at odds with that of the European powers, a point reinforced by his calling at the end of the speech for Britain to follow the American example.

The subtext of this anti-imperialist rhetoric was Adams's concern about European machinations in the Americas. He was especially worried about the possibility of intervention by the newly formed Quadruple Alliance (Austria, Prussia, Russia, and Britain, which became the Quintuple Alliance with the subsequent inclusion of France), and eager to prevent an increase in Russian power in the American Northwest. His response to these monarchist challenges signaled a distinct shift in American international thought. Written largely by Adams and given as part of President Monroe's message to Congress in December 1823, the so-called Monroe Doctrine expounded a worldview based on two interrelated issues: the separation of the old and new worlds, and the "non-colonization" principle. In his declaration, Monroe claimed that the "American continents" were "free and independent," and so the United States would not accept colonization of any part of the Americas by any European power, although it would not interfere with existing European colonies. Simultaneously, he promised that the United States would refrain from interfering in Europe's affairs.[78]

While the doctrine initially made little impact, it had profound long-term significance. Jay Sexton notes the ambiguity of the original statement that was intended as much for public consumption as it was for foreign powers. It was somewhat ironic then that its early reverberations were limited and largely negative even in the United States, as Congress resisted being drawn into hemispheric matters. The doctrine also had no standing in international law and so the European powers did not initially regard it as important. The British tacitly accepted it and allowed it to be maintained through the strength of the Royal Navy, but they had originally suggested a joint Anglo-American declaration against Russian or French intervention, so it broadly represented their interests as well. But its flexibility, alongside growing U.S. power, allowed politicians to adapt and manipulate it for numerous different purposes in the decades that followed.[79]

The doctrine blended republican and anti-colonial principles while effectively placing the United States at the head of the emerging nations in the hemisphere. It also acknowledged the dissatisfaction of many Americans with monarchical systems of government, but did not commit the United States government to do anything about them. At the time, many prominent public figures, including Henry Clay, Daniel Webster, and Edward Everett, looked to intervene to aid the Greek rebels in their war against the Ottoman Empire. Adams and Monroe placed limits on such assistance, suggesting that, for the time being at least, the United States would be an ideological rather than a geographical empire. This was, however, a strikingly bold move by a power that was weak in the face of those it challenged and notably did not preclude future ventures or acquisitions. While Adams rejected British overtures for a joint declaration against the possible extension of Russian or French control in the Americas, because he was concerned that the American public thought of him as an Anglophile, it is notable that he also rebuffed London's call for a clause renouncing British and American claims to Texas and Cuba. As one British newspaper put it, "The plain *Yankee* of the matter, is that the United States wish to monopolize to themselves the privilege of colonizing . . . every . . . part of the American continent."[80]

Moreover, not all in the United States were satisfied with the prospect of continued nonintervention. The clamor for assistance to Greece rumbled on into the mid-1820s, and by the 1830s, some were openly calling for the United States to conduct its own widespread policies of annexation and protectionism, particularly in the Caribbean and Latin America, to compete with those of Great Britain.[81] The quartermaster general of the United States Army, Thomas S. Jesup, was one such figure who looked forward to the day when the United States would challenge Great Britain on land and sea. He worried that Britain continued to pose a threat to the United States on the continent and would augment its power if it gained other territories, complaining that the United States had "adopted the maxim, whether wisely or not time must determine, of non-interference under any circumstances, with the affairs of other nations." If it could promise protection to other nations in the region, he believed that they would "gladly receive" it, although at that time only Britain could do so. "Her colonies, therefore, and their consequent influence are a guarantee to her against our commercial, maritime, and political ascendency, so long as she holds them."[82]

Despite the lofty rhetoric of Adams and Monroe, many in the new South and Central American republics realized that Washington's assistance would only extend so far, and as Dexter Perkins has noted, in the years that followed, it "was readier to be bold in speech than it was to be decisive in action."[83] Furthermore, as we have seen, the United States government's attachment to the principle of nonintervention did not preclude aggression to gain more territory in the 1840s. Nor did it prevent private individuals from interfering illegally in other countries. American newspapers began to call this process "filibustering" in response to Narcisco López's attempt to end Spanish rule in Cuba in 1850–1851, and such activities continued even after the American Civil War.[84] Simultaneously, American companies began to reach into nearby nations and regions, transforming the territories, extending their influence, and fomenting nascent anti-Americanism.[85] The United States' neighbors thus bore the brunt of its growing power and increasing competition with the other imperial nations in Latin America.[86]

The impact of this growing strength was felt especially in Mexico and Cuba, both of which continued to be buffeted between the European empires and the United States. While Cuba remained a Spanish colony, its proximity to Florida and its symbolic power meant that many prominent Americans looked to bring it into the Union, especially as a way to expand the institution of slavery and the power of the slaveholding South. Such ideas went back at least as far as Thomas Jefferson and culminated during the antebellum period in the 1854 Ostend Manifesto, an annexationist tract that further tainted U.S.–Cuban relations and raised the ire of many Northerners in the United States. American attitudes toward Cuba were complex and often contradictory. During the 1840s and 1850s, Northerners as well as Southerners often supported annexation even if, as over so many other issues, they disagreed on how and why they would try to achieve it. Somewhat similarly with Mexico, growing U.S. power, continuing European interest in the country, and chronic domestic instability ensured a generally poor state of relations with Washington. As Karl Schmitt characterizes them, American governmental and private interests toward Mexico during this period broadly focused on "revolutionizing it, or colonizing it, or conquering its border provinces."[87]

Conclusion

By the time of the American Civil War, the patterns of responses to empire were well established. As the power of European global influence crested, there was a reflexive suspicion of their attempts to gain and maintain overseas colonial territories and unfairly control global trade, especially when these actions impinged directly on the United States. Simultaneously, the growing domestic significance of the Monroe Doctrine reinforced the need to oppose—rhetorically at least—Europe's regional influence.

The Civil War period consolidated debates about how the United States government would deal with the burgeoning European imperial might. Ideologically, the war itself, as well as its aftermath, pivoted around questions of territorial expansion and the power of centralized political authority. In diplomatic terms, it forced the United States to engage much more with European allies and antagonists, increasing American fears about the role of Europe in the Western Hemisphere and even raising the possibility of some of its nations' interference in the politics and territory of the United States. It also foreshadowed a growing confidence on the part of American policymakers who looked beyond American shores for inspiration and education, even as "high" or "new" imperialism, in which the main European powers looked to extend their influence and consolidate their power, took hold.

The weakness of the United States at this time provoked one of these powers, France, precipitating a crisis over Mexico. French intervention in Mexico in the 1860s and reactions to it highlighted many of the important features of the United States' relationship with the European powers during the age of high imperialism. It was a direct challenge by a major European nation to an independent former colony in the Americas bordering the United States, amid the greatest existential domestic crisis in the United States since independence. It was also part of a broader tapestry of international interventions and threatened interventions in the Americas at this time, including other European imperial maneuvers and the direct threat of British interference in the Civil War. More than any of these factors, however, it was a test of U.S. moral leadership in the Americas.

Jay Sexton has posited the idea that between 1861 and 1865, both the Union and Confederacy believed that they were fighting against imperial forces, utilizing the language of anti-imperialism—especially by deploying ideas about the Declaration of Independence—to proclaim their respective causes. For leaders in the North, this entailed a struggle against the expansion of slavery, an explicitly imperialist endeavor that had brought the Union to the brink of collapse by the early 1860s. As Sexton points out, however, in order to deal with this threat and reestablish the Union, Lincoln built and augmented a strong, centralized federal authority, which, while appealing to popular ideals of decentralization, reinforced a pervasive belief in the Southern states that the North was itself an imperialist force bent on subjugation.[88] Thus, the Civil War era needs to be understood as one in which the United States dealt with questions of empire, both internal and external, and navigated the myriad and liminal complexities these questions presented. How it dealt with them would help define such issues as U.S. identity, ideas of nationhood, and its sense of place in the world during the years that followed.

CHAPTER II

France and the Mexican Intervention

On Sunday, June 12, 1864, Archduke Ferdinand Maximilian of Austria and his wife Carlota entered Mexico City for the first time on what would seem to have been the most auspicious of occasions. The Mexican people had apparently received the young couple enthusiastically since their arrival in the country two weeks earlier, and now, in what would become the capital of Maximilian's New World Empire, large, cheering crowds from all sectors of Mexican society greeted them. Arches, flags, and red carpets festooned the city, and church bells rang. Dressed in full regalia, the emperor and empress, recently elected by a popular plebiscite, passed through the throng in their state coach. People threw flowers and firecrackers, joining in a frenzied celebration of the monarchs whom they believed would save their country from an ongoing civil war. Then, following ceremonies at the cathedral to inaugurate their reign, Maximilian and Carlota attended a banquet and ball that continued well into the early hours of the morning. When it was finally over and dawn was fast approaching, the new rulers departed to their beds, and it seemed that not even the sight of the dilapidated and vermin-ridden National Palace—midway through a hasty renovation—could dampen their spirits. The empress declared herself enchanted with the whole experience, while the emperor expressed delight at being so joyously welcomed far away from the stuffy atmosphere of the courts of Europe.[1]

All was not as it seemed, however. As Maximilian and Carlota's procession had weaved its way through the city streets, commanders of the French expeditionary force, troops representing France's emperor Napoleon III, had led it. In fact, Napoleon had handpicked Maximilian to become the new ruler of Mexico, and Napoleon's forces had planned the celebrations of his coronation, ensuring that the crowds were suitably jubilant in their response. The French government had carefully stage-managed the whole event to give an impression of unity at a time of conflict. Napoleon had even organized the plebiscite to make it appear that the Mexican people had elected Maximilian.[2]

The beginning of Maximilian's rule as head of the Second Mexican Empire was in fact the culmination of a broader Napoleonic project to reestablish European rule in the Americas and Asia. The French emperor had sent forces to intervene in Mexican affairs in late 1861, initially alongside those of Britain and Spain, with the ostensible goal of recovering debts owed by the republican government of Benito Juárez. Yet, it quickly became clear that Napoleon had broader aims to oversee the formation of an imperial state in Mexico. Because of this, the British and Spanish governments withdrew from the enterprise in April 1862, leaving France on its own. Napoleon's reasons for pursuing this plan were complex, but they included a desire to revive French influence in Central America and the Caribbean and to limit the growth of the United States, perhaps by expanding into its southwestern territories, and he took advantage of Washington's preoccupation with its own civil war to launch his quixotic scheme.[3]

As Napoleon may have expected, many people in the United States reacted furiously to his actions. These Americans considered them a direct imperial challenge to the republican nations of the Americas and thus a contravention of the Monroe Doctrine, as well as a flagrant attempt to take advantage of the United States during a moment of extreme but temporary weakness: "The Mexican Republic has been extinguished and an empire risen on its ruins. But for this wicked rebellion in our country this calamity would not have occurred" fumed Secretary of the Navy Gideon Welles.[4] Some even feared that Napoleon's Mexican policy foreshadowed other major European powers intervening militarily in the United States' civil war. Even if it did not, the mere presence of foreign forces so close to the United States was a worrying sign of potential interference in the Union war effort, including its blockade of the eastern seaboard. Napoleon's moves also appeared to destroy the notion that the liberal triumph of President

Benito Juárez in Mexico and the election of Abraham Lincoln in the United States heralded an era of improving relations between the two countries after decades of civil strife.[5]

Because it was in the midst of fighting its own civil war, the United States government could do little to end the venture. Many sympathetic United States citizens gave financial and military support to the republican cause in Mexico, encouraged by representatives of Juárez. Although some members of the Lincoln administration, acting as private individuals, were complicit in these schemes, the Washington government was also constrained in terms of what it could do.[6] Aside from its limited military means, its desperation to avoid European military involvement in its own war and maintain diplomatic ties with France and Britain also ensured that it would not act. The leadership did not therefore invoke the now revered Monroe Doctrine, and while some at the cabinet level advocated a military response to drive the French out, successive presidents Abraham Lincoln (1861–1865) and Andrew Johnson (1865–1869) largely disavowed them.

Less explicit but no less important were the ideological implications of Napoleon's actions, and the United States' response. This imperial maneuver by a European power was a direct challenge to the authority of the United States in the Americas. It caused alarm among the American population and officials in Washington not only because it resonated with their preconceptions about European imperialism and the long history of European interference in the Americas, but also because it appeared to be a challenge to the growing regional power of the United States, even if it was curtailed at this moment. Therefore, while this episode was a vital one in the development of American foreign relations with Europe and other nations during the Civil War, it was also crucial in exposing American attitudes toward European empires, and aspects of the United States' own developing imperial identity.[7]

In the North, there was generally severe antipathy to the French interference in a neighbor, but it is hard to discern more than a broad, incoherent discourse about empire at this time. Partially, this was because of the schisms within the United States and the relative power of a divided nation. But it was also due to the emerging pattern of empire that the United States confronted. As Don Doyle has pointed out, one strand of the regional and global significance of the American Civil War was that it threatened the existence of the longest-lived and most successful republic on earth at a time when a number of countervailing forces, notably slavery and imperialism, appeared to be thriving.[8] For their part, Southern secessionists believed that the strength of slavery was evident in its regional economic success in the United States, Brazil, and Cuba and that the British had erred in abolishing it within their empire.[9] While there was a lack of agreement about how to respond to these threats, the eventual Union victory, the triumph of republicanism, and confirmation of the United States as republicanism's foremost exponent signaled a growing sense of regional dominance that, ironically, saw the United States becoming more like the powerful European empires its leaders sought to expel from the Western Hemisphere.

As emperor of Mexico, Maximilian was certainly not Napoleon's stooge and tried his best to enact liberal political and social reforms that would benefit the people, but the Second Mexican Empire ultimately proved to be as ramshackle as the National Palace in which the emperor and empress spent their first night.[10] The Mexican civil war continued, Maximilian lost ground, and he eventually fled from the capital before Juárez's forces quickly captured him. By this time, Napoleon had effectively withdrawn his support and was in the process of removing his army from Mexico. In June 1867, just over three years after his triumphant entrance to Mexico City, republican troops executed Maximilian along with two of his loyal generals.

The French Empire and Mexico

Napoleon's scheme for Mexico was the culmination of a long history of interference in the country by European powers, as well as by the United States. While some Mexicans welcomed the potential benefits that direct American involvement in their country might have brought, there was also considerable interest in returning the country to European rule. Decades of civil unrest following independence from Spain had resulted in the establishment of rival conservative and liberal governments by the late 1850s and, in 1858, a formal request by conservative leader General Felix Zuloaga for European powers to intervene in order to establish a protectorate. While neither the French nor British would accept such a proposition at that time, European concern at the continuing turmoil in Mexico ensured that this idea persisted. Mexicans who entertained such thoughts based them on a desire for stability in their country, but they also rightly feared that if they didn't have protection, the United States would press south,

DESIGN FOR A *MODERN HISTORICAL* PICTURE.
Napoleon III. crossing the American Continent on his Mexican Mule.

Figure 2.1 This depiction of Napoleon III references Jacques-Louis David's famous 1801 painting of Napoleon Bonaparte heroically crossing the Alps. The cartoonist's view of the wisdom of Napoleon III's venture in Mexico, and of the emperor himself, is easy to discern (note the skulls on the ground beneath him).
Source: Anonymous, "Design for a *Modern Historical Picture*: Napoleon III Crossing the American Continent on His Mexican Mule," *Harper's Weekly*, March 7, 1863.

exploiting Mexico's resources and perhaps taking parts of its territory as it had done in the 1840s.

All of these pressures converged when the liberal government of Benito Juárez, which had consolidated its position by capturing Mexico City at the beginning of the year, voted to suspend payments on debts to foreign governments in July 1861, just as in the American Civil War the Union experienced a humiliating defeat at the First Battle of Bull Run, portending the possibility of the European powers recognizing the Confederacy. The Juárez government owed money to France, Britain, and Spain, which together determined to send a combined military force across the Atlantic to seize ports and oversee payment of reparations. In response, the U.S. State Department and Senate Foreign Relations Committee explored taking on some of Mexico's debt using claims on public lands and mineral rights in the Mexican states of Lower California, Chihuahua, Sonora, and Sinaloa as security, although the Senate eventually rejected the proposal.[11] By this time, the three European powers had formalized their agreement in the Treaty of London—signed in November 1861, at the height of the *Trent* crisis, when Britain and the United States seemed close to war over a captured American vessel—and the force arrived in early December. This soon became a unilateral expedition when France moved to install an emperor, while Britain and Spain withdrew.[12]

As we saw in the previous chapter, responses to French imperialism in the nineteenth century ranged from modest approval to outright hostility, and this continued into the Civil War period. Preacher and writer John S. C. Abbott, for example, called for his compatriots to understand the connections between Americans and Europeans in terms of their national characteristics: "England loves her monarchy; America loves her republic; France loves her empire . . . Each of these governments has its merits and its defects. . . . It is surely the teaching of wisdom that they should respect each other, and that they should regard with courtesy the institutions under which each has risen to greatness."[13] Conversely, many elite Americans remained skeptical about France and its newfound imperial zeal under Napoleon III. Napoleon, the nephew of Napoleon Bonaparte who had spent time in the United States, was a complex and contradictory figure who had exploited a prolonged period of political turmoil in France to his own ends. Involved in coup attempts in the 1830s and 1840s, he was elected as the president of the second republic in 1848 before staging another coup to ensure that he remained in power before declaring himself emperor. In doing so, as the sociologist and free trader William Graham Sumner pithily put it, he "gave the French democracy, under his own despotism."[14] Napoleon also resolved to restore France's colonial empire, which had been decimated through war with Britain and others since the late eighteenth century. He continued the long process of aggressive expansion in Algeria that had begun in earnest in the late 1820s and established a colony in Senegal in West Africa. He also struck out into East Asia and the Pacific, notably Indochina (to support Catholic missionaries there) in the hope of exploiting the much-prized markets of China.[15]

While most remained ignorant about these developments, concerned Americans responded to them in different ways.[16] Some believed that the spread of European civilization, including by France, promised new opportunities to indigenous populations and adventurous Americans alike. The

French conquest of Algeria and growing European influence in the Barbary States had, for example, allowed more Westerners to explore the area and offer what one American traveler called "some faint glimpses of this strange and mysterious region."[17] Others could be scathing about these actions, suspecting that Napoleon only took part in them to join the ranks of the other imperial nations. Sumner, for example, believed that French possession of Algeria was "the best example of a colony for the sake of a colony," and that "the longing of these countries for 'colonies' is like the longing of a negro dandy for a cane or a tall hat so as to be like the white gentleman."[18] An editorial in *Harper's New Monthly Magazine* took particular issue with Napoleon's hypocrisy when it came to empire building: "Having . . . begun to plant his colonies around the world, he smiles benignly, and says, 'Let every body be content with what he has, and let naughty war cease!' He seized his throne by terror, and, as he seated himself, said politely, 'This means peace.' "[19]

Napoleon's actions in Mexico and his implicit threat to the United States only reinforced such views, and many commentators on both sides of the Atlantic were damning. Writing in the *Westminster Review* in October 1863, journalist and poet Charles MacKay attacked what he saw as regressive policies that were analogous to the conquests of Cortez in the sixteenth century. Calling Napoleon's intervention "the most extraordinary event of our day," MacKay claimed that it was "strictly and simply a war of aggression and conquest."[20] The same year, an American writing as "Vine Wright Kingsley" (almost certainly a play on the idea of the divine right of kings) published a pamphlet in a similar vein. The author claimed that France was troubled by internal woes and had decided on empire building as the best way to deal with them. He was in no doubt that the responsibility for this foolish course lay with the French leader himself, who had "subverted liberty in France and erected an Empire," and now "performs the same labour for Mexico today."[21] For Congregationalist minister and writer Joshua Leavitt, Napoleon's scheme represented a conspiracy with the other imperial powers to carve up different areas, in this case a plot to revive Catholic fortunes in the New World, to which the British were acceding. Like Kingsley and others, Leavitt saw Napoleon's attempt to compensate for weaknesses at home by expanding abroad to gain strategic and economic advantages and win the favor of the French population. The auspices were not good, however, and the very fact that Napoleon was trying to recapture lost former glories should have told him something:

The experiments and failures of three hundred years, in Canada, Louisiana, the West Indies, Southern America, India and Africa, have not taught France that her people are not natural colonizers. With Algeria staring her in the face as virtually given back to the culture of the Moslem inhabitants, she longs to make another trial in Mexico, with some new schemes of subjugation and colonization, in which blunders of past attempts are to be avoided by the superior sagacity of Napoleon III. It is easy enough to predict the inevitable ultimate failure of the scheme, because Frenchmen have not the power of self-control and self-government necessary for success in creating new nations by colonization.[22]

An editorial in *Harper's* expressed similar sentiments, contrasting France's misplaced foreign adventurism with the successes of the British Empire. Once again, Napoleon was diverting attention from his weaknesses at home by making the spurious claim that he was head of the "Latin race" in the Americas. His position was tenuous, however—"new imperial dynasties are not founded in the nineteenth century," and so he was "playing a desperate and hopeless game against civilization"—and in Mexico in particular he was "engaged in the unpromising enterprise of balancing a pyramid upon its point." This was especially troubling because he was effectively interfering in the internal struggles of the United States. In contrast, although Great Britain had "growled and snapped like an ugly mastiff guarding its own bone of aristocratic privilege," Americans effectively knew where they stood with them. France, however, was watching and waiting "like a tiger."[23]

The famous New York–based scientist and historian John W. Draper saw Napoleon's duplicity toward his allies—Britain, Spain, and the Confederacy—over Mexico as a "mask" that he suddenly threw off. Writing in his multivolume history of the American Civil War, published in the late 1860s, Draper suggested that the French emperor had particularly beguiled the leaders of the Southern states, who favored an alliance with a European power and a potential union with a southern neighbor that might be susceptible to the reintroduction of slavery: "An empire was established in Mexico. Well might the leaders of the Southern Confederacy be thunderstruck . . . Yet no one in America, either of the Northern or the Southern States, imputed blame to the French people in these bloody and dark transactions. All saw clearly on whom the responsibility rested . . .

the Republic of the West was forever alienated from the dynasty of Napoleon."[24]

There were a few exceptions to this condemnation of France's actions in Mexico. Even during Maximilian's final days, historian and travel writer William V. Wells admiringly described the mixture of Mexican and European dignitaries at the court in the *Overland Monthly*, calling it "a miniature picture of Mexican Imperial Life at its best." Many had grown rich, he said, and many Mexicans appeared to accept that they would be ruled from now on by a European prince.[25] Similarly, in a series of essays on the emperor published shortly after Napoleon's fall, Californian lawyer John W. Dwinelle noted the regular opprobrium heaped on the emperor over his failed expedition. Dwinelle, however, argued that the scheme did not originate with Napoleon, nor did it necessarily contravene the wishes of the Mexican people. In fact, Dwinelle believed that the United States bore the responsibility "of preventing the Mexicans from 'choosing an empire, which they prefer, and forcing upon them a republic, which they detest.'" The French established this monarchy in the face of a "brigand republic" that "pretends to be civilized" but was in fact "barbarous and savage." This was evidenced now by the continued disorder in the country, which had terrible consequences for Americans there.[26]

All these responses were influenced and infinitely complicated by the enormous civil strife in the United States. There is no doubt that Napoleon took advantage of the chaos and violence in North America to enact his Mexican scheme, seeking to exploit divisions and weaknesses in both sides. The Southern leadership's desperate bid for diplomatic recognition from the two biggest powers of Europe, Britain and France, would, it believed, ensure survival and victory. It approached the problem primarily through an economic policy, "King Cotton," predicated on the idea that Britain, and to a lesser extent France, could not live without a cheap high-quality cotton supply to keep its mills operational. Indeed, these leaders believed that Britain's moving toward free trade policies was a sign of this.[27] But it combined this approach with a specifically ideological appeal: that it was an independent nation seeking to determine its own future against an aggressive, bullying northern neighbor.[28] Initially, this pitch seemed to offer promise, but it was short-lived. Britain's early declaration of neutrality may have come from a genuine desire to remain out of the conflict, but it also alienated Washington because it showed the London government leaning toward the Confederacy and giving it legitimacy. Although Paris essentially followed London's lead in withholding recognition, Napoleon dangled the prospect of recognizing the Confederate States in front of leaders in Richmond as he intervened, initially with Britain and Spain, in Mexico.[29]

As time went on and Napoleon's plans for an empire in Mexico became clearer, Confederate leaders were in some ways encouraged, notably Judah P. Benjamin, who became secretary of state in March 1862, just as the tripartite alliance was collapsing. Benjamin was perhaps the most capable Confederate cabinet member and he attempted to craft a more sophisticated approach to foreign policy than his two predecessors. But even he still relied on cotton to do most of the work, continuing to believe that a lack of supply would draw in the great powers. French adventurism in the Americas reinforced the sense that Napoleon could be separated from Britain because the fledgling Mexican empire needed a strong regional ally in order to survive.[30]

Overseeing Washington's response to France's actions was the architect of United States Civil War–era foreign policy, Secretary of State William Henry Seward, who served for all of presidents Lincoln's and Johnson's terms of office.[31] A leading Republican and a strong advocate of American economic expansionism who had vied with Lincoln for the party's presidential nomination in 1860, Seward was a compelling and somewhat controversial figure. Like many Americans, he and his colleagues viewed European intervention in Mexico with alarm, but, perhaps more than any other person in Washington, the secretary of state recognized that he had to moderate the American response according to the prevailing conditions of the day. He therefore constructed a careful response that demonstrated his deep dissatisfaction with France's actions while simultaneously ensuring the maintenance of positive relations with Paris at a time of great uncertainty. In particular, Seward was concerned about the possibility of France recognizing the Confederate States of America, and thus undermining a key plank of Union foreign policy, while he was aware that France prized potential U.S. recognition of its regime in Mexico.[32] Seward also faced the broader ideological implications of the intervention for the United States, and so, while he grappled with the diplomatic considerations, it is significant that he couched his complaint to the French in terms of the threat they posed not just to the United States, but to all American nations. In making their statements in such terms, Seward and others in Washington set out the United States' case for leadership within the Americas as a successful, republican, and increasingly powerful nation.

While he maintained diplomatic pressure on France and Austria throughout this episode, Seward did not intend to provoke conflict with them. He focused his efforts on Paris, needling the government for answers about their intentions in Mexico, particularly following the end of the U.S. Civil War in 1865, when Austria threatened to send troops to replace those withdrawn by France.[33] Whether this had any significant effect is open to debate. As might be expected, many American commentators at the time believed it did. In his contemporary study of Napoleon III, published shortly after the withdrawal from Mexico, John S. C. Abbott opined that "the attitude assumed by the United States undoubtedly had a powerful influence" upon Napoleon because it threatened war.[34] More recently, Mary Ann Heiss has argued something similar.[35] It seems, however, this may be overplaying Washington's part, and Michelle Cunningham has convincingly suggested that the United States had a largely peripheral role. The French decision to withdraw, she argues, had more to do with the lack of popularity of the venture in France and the ineffectual nature of Maximilian's rule—particularly its inability to ameliorate the suffering of the people while simultaneously dealing with the republican military threat—than it was to do with American diplomatic pressure. Ultimately, she concludes, Paris welcomed the chance to withdraw its forces in 1866 and 1867.[36] So while Seward's State Department has, perhaps rightly, received praise for its careful diplomatic handling of the French-Mexican crisis, it seems that its response was less important in expelling France than the chronic problems within the Mexican empire itself.

Slavery and Empire

From the beginning, the gravity of the French action in Mexico was clear to many Americans, especially Northerners, who saw the domestic ramifications of this external threat. They were concerned that Napoleon had enacted his scheme during a period of extreme vulnerability in the United States, an existential threat with both internal and external ramifications. In practical terms, this threat was particularly acute on the border, exacerbating longstanding tensions between the two nations and fomenting further violence between indigenous groups and American settlers on the frontier.[37] From Seward's perspective, the various groups vying for dominance in the borderlands contributed to "anarchy," which in turn operated "as a seduction to those who are conspiring against the integrity of the Union to seek strength and aggrandizement for themselves by conquests in Mexico and other parts of Spanish America."[38] The regional position of the United States was thus being challenged internally by those who opposed the imposition of what they believed was a tyrannical regime threatening the institution of slavery, and externally by a European imperial power. The latter sought not only to change government structures in a neighboring authority, but also to build alliances with native tribes as they had done many times before during periods of conflict. Further, the Lincoln administration worried that Confederates would take advantage of this disorder to the south and west to expand the institution of slavery, perhaps by incorporating the border states of northern Mexico into the Confederacy.[39]

The intimate connections between slavery and empire carried various ideological implications and lessons for advocates and abolitionists. Former slave and social reformer Frederick Douglass was bleak in his prognosis that the United States faced a long-term struggle to overcome a slave state on its southern border, wondering whether, as it approached its centenary, "this great Republic" would sink into perpetual civil war like "unhappy Mexico," or "become like old Spain, the mother of Mexico, and by folly and cruelty with its renown among the nations of the earth, and spend the next seventy years in vainly attempting to regain what it has lost in the space of this one slaveholding rebellion."[40] In drawing comparisons to other empires, Radical Republican Thaddeus Stevens offered a more legalistic—and more positive—approach. He was optimistic about the lack of international political legitimacy of rebellions such as the one currently underway in the United States and proposed an alternative of repealing laws designating southern points of entry. In doing so, he drew comparisons between the Confederates and other recent insurgents around the world: the Taipings in China, the Sepoys in India, and the Irish fighting against British rule. In all cases, Stevens noted, the established powers had refused to go through ports in the rebels' possession. A strong moral position on the part of the United States would also bolster this, as "Christian nations—civilized nations, whether Christian, Mohammedan or Pagan, do not sympathize with slave-mongers."[41]

In contrast, for pro-slave Southerners looking at the modern empires of the world, this morality meant nothing. For them, there was more than a hint of hypocrisy both about these empires' exploitation of colonies for

Figure 2.2 As secretary of state for all of the Civil War, William Henry Seward was a careful reader of the French threat in Mexico and had to calibrate his response with the ongoing domestic catastrophe in the United States.
Source: Library of Congress, undated.

profit, and their willingness to overlook slavery in different parts of the world when it suited them. The European nations condemned slavery in the United States, noted Leonidas W. Spratt, a member of the Succession Convention from South Carolina, but they often chose to "trade in Coolies" in their own empires, and ignored the continuing practice of slavery in others. "There is a mode upon the subject of human rights at the moment, and England, France and other States . . . are leaders of the mode," he continued. Nevertheless, these states traded in and profited from cotton produced by slaves and, fearing the growing power of American cotton, would "crush" their own colonies in places such as India and Algeria to ensure they maintained their supply.[42]

In the early stages of the struggle, one of Seward's chief concerns was that the issue of slavery, rather than disunion, would become the defining domestic issue of the war. In this respect, as Kinley Brauer has argued, slavery was an important practical as well as moral consideration, and Seward's approach to it was complex and changed over the course of the war. While Seward may have seen slavery as a moral blight on the United States, he conceived of it more as a part of an inefficient labor system, and regarded its gradual abolition as bound up in the development of the American empire. If the United States had been aggressively expansionist in the past, Seward reasoned, it was because the institution of slavery had made it so. Now, only a free system of labor would allow the United States to fulfill its promise to become a major power, but this could not, according to the secretary of state, be forced, and slavery would naturally die out over time.[43]

Seward thought that because slavery was an internal matter—and one that, early in the war, he believed was for individual states and not the federal government to decide upon—the European nations had no right to intervene, and indeed that no one, including the European governments themselves, would benefit from such an action. If they did so, he reasoned, they would be unable "to suppress wars of ambition" that would "inevitably break out" in North America, perhaps threatening other European colonies.[44] Seward believed that far from benefitting from two divided and antagonistic American republics, Britain in particular would find building strong diplomatic links with both sides problematic, especially if the South continued to uphold the peculiar institution. Establishing relations with the Confederate South would raise questions about slavery in colonies controlled by European powers, especially in the Caribbean, threatening at least to postpone emancipation if not further extend the practice of slavery.[45]

So while French intervention was deeply troubling in itself, it also exposed the intimate links between the Confederate and European challenges. It was significant that Seward's famous April 1861 memorandum to President Lincoln, in which he called for a more "vigorous continental spirit of independence on this continent against European intervention," and argued for a declaration of war against France and Spain if adequate answers about their intentions were not forthcoming, also focused on what he believed to be the lack of a clear articulation of the Union's domestic policy.[46] As Seward subsequently suggested, what he called the "equilibrium of the nations" with the United States on one side of the Atlantic and the European states on the other would be gone if the Confederacy were successful in its quest for independence. He wrote, "the struggles of nations in that system for dominion in this hemisphere and on the high seas, which constitutes the chief portion of the world's history in the eighteenth century, would be renewed."[47] Early in the war, Washington feared that France would follow Great Britain if London decided to recognize the Confederate States, and newspapers even reported that Paris was moving toward recognition in return for the Richmond government handing over Texas and perhaps Louisiana to either France or Mexico.[48] Later, American leaders came to believe that the new regime in Mexico might also acknowledge the Confederate States; indeed, they even thought that recognition was a sine qua non for Maximilian accepting the throne.[49]

One of the many problems for the Confederacy, however, was that the issue of slavery exposed the tensions in Napoleon's plans to colonize Mexico. Napoleon wanted to avoid charges that French imperialism in the New World was regressive. He sincerely held the belief that his intervention would provide social improvements to the people of Mexico and potentially others, however much he tried to deny his intentions early in the venture and later to assuage fears with an assurance that he would withdraw the French presence once Maximilian was safely installed as emperor. But this expansion, almost by definition, limited Southern aspirations for growth (tempered while fighting the Union) and potentially threatened their new Confederacy, perhaps even by attempting to dismember it to create buffer states. Furthermore, Napoleon's supposedly benevolent imperialism was predicated on one crucial element: the end of slavery over time in all parts of the Americas. This notion was given greater scope after the Emancipation Proclamation came into effect at the beginning of 1863, just as he was maneuvering to place Maximilian on the Mexican throne and still considering the possibility of recognizing the Confederacy. In their desperation for recognition from at least one powerful European ally, the Confederate leadership consistently had to put concerns about such matters aside.[50] But recognition never came.

Monarchy and Empire

For the leadership in Washington, the ideological and practical considerations of slavery and empire grew as they faced the prospect of the imposition of a European emperor in neighboring Mexico. While the governments of France, Great Britain, and Spain had been primarily interested in debt collection in 1861, and the Treaty of London that had established their alliance specifically renounced the acquisition of Mexican territory or other internal interference, the Lincoln administration quickly and correctly came to suspect that the Europeans tacitly sought to impose a longer-term solution to deal with Mexico's financial woes, a prospect that augured ill for Europe's imperial ambitions elsewhere in the region. Specifically, France wanted to impose a foreign emperor on Mexico.[51] If it succeeded in doing so, it would, in U.S. minister to Mexico Thomas Corwin's words, "henceforth be a European colony in fact."[52] Certainly, all three nations believed at that juncture that a change in government of some sort, preferably to a monarchical one, might well be necessary. However, the British government soon changed its mind, almost certainly under pressure from the United States, reaffirming that the European powers had no right to interfere in the internal affairs of Mexico.[53]

By this time, Spain had also altered its position. This was brought about in part because it was already involved in the recolonization of Santo Domingo in the Caribbean—which, like the Mexican venture, caused anguish but little action in the United States—as well as the fact that France had clearly taken the lead in the Mexican expedition. Spain sought to reassert its much-reduced authority in the region by landing troops, and supporting a sympathetic Santo Dominican leader, although it faced stiff internal and regional resistance and ultimately withdrew in 1865. In 1864, Spain also intervened in Peru, seizing its Chincha Islands, and then went to war not just with Peru, but also Chile, Ecuador, and Bolivia the following year. While this gave rise to a measure of Pan-American solidarity in the face of Spain's aggression, the United States was once again too preoccupied with its own affairs to organize any significant response, and it did not want to break with its traditional policy of avoiding entangling alliances. As a result, the United States was not even invited to an eight-nation conference intended to deal with region's problems in 1864.[54] By this point, and despite growing antipathy between Washington and Madrid, Spain was long absent from the Mexican venture.

In contrast, the realization that France had decided to install a monarchy in Mexico was deeply troubling to the United States government—a retrograde step that seemed out of keeping with recent experience and the promise of liberal revolutions in Europe.[55] From the beginning, Washington was clear that France had the right to make war against Mexico if it had a genuine grievance, but it worried that Napoleon's intention was at least partially to encourage anti-republican and anti-American feelings there.[56] In early 1862, President Lincoln therefore sought assurances that none of the European powers involved was contemplating an intervention that would involve altering the present form of government or any other political change in Mexico "in opposition to the will of the American people."[57] In response, the French government insisted that it had no broader interests, and its political attentions merely focused on the need for a stable government, regardless of whether it was a monarchy or a republic.[58]

It soon became clear that this was not the case, and Americans reacted with consternation to the revelation—seen in a letter to the commander of French forces that was published in the *New York Times*—that in establishing a monarchy in Mexico, Napoleon was trying to limit growth of the United States in the Americas. Apparently fearing that the American republic would swallow various other nations and territories in the Caribbean and Central and South America, the French emperor said he sought to ensure Mexican independence and territorial integrity, and the restoration of the "Latin race" in this region. However sincere these sentiments, Napoleon conceded that taking this action would establish French strength and influence in Central America, also supposedly ensuring Mexico's gratitude and its harmony with the other European powers. "Today, then, our pledged military honor, the exigency of our policy, the interests of our industry and of our commerce, all make it a duty to march upon Mexico, and boldly plant there our flag; to establish a monarchy, if it is not incompatible with the national sentiment of the country, or, at all events, a Government which promises some stability."[59]

This was unconvincing to most concerned Americans. Seward complained that the French government had departed "very materially" from its previous assurances, and expressed fears that undermining republican institutions in a neighbor threatened them in the United States.[60] He and his colleagues insisted that it was not the idea of monarchy itself to which they objected—because they claimed they would have done nothing to prevent the Mexican people from developing their own monarchical system if they so desired—but rather the imposition of a foreign prince upon a neighbor.[61] Whether Napoleon could really gauge Mexico's national sentiment regarding monarchy was open to question, however. How, asked the American minister in Paris, could Mexicans choose not to be ruled by a monarch with the French army camped on their territory?[62]

Beyond his adherence to republicanism, Seward's attitudes were linked to his ideas about the expansion of the United States.[63] While it is difficult to discern consistent patterns in his statements on American expansion, it is clear that Seward increasingly prioritized economic over territorial growth while aspiring to a form of what Walter Sharrow has called "democratic imperialism" to incorporate new land if propitious conditions prevailed, and as long as he believed it was not imposed on unwilling populations. Sharrow suggests that Seward believed the United States was superior to all other nations and therefore perfectly placed to conduct this form of imperialism, although he ultimately concludes that Seward implemented it quite carefully. Indeed, for all of Seward's talk of an expanding United States in the period before he became secretary of state, his record once in office was modest, and his most notable achievement was the acquisition of Alaska from Russia in 1867.[64] Seward was certainly selective in his interpretation of past U.S. expansionism, seeing it (as many of his contemporaries and forbears did) as largely peaceful and altruistic, except where settlers had used it to expand slavery. As he later explained to the U.S. minister in France, John Bigelow, the imposition of rule by France on Mexico was different from expansion by the United States, which was "domestic and republican." American territorial increase, Seward insisted, had occurred largely without military conquest, because it had involved "the annexation of adjacent peoples, who have come into the Union through their own consent as constituent republican states under the Constitution of the United States." While this statement ignored the huge numbers of Native Americans and others for whom this was clearly not the case, and conveniently glossed over the vexed issue of slavery, for Seward this characterization had important implications for the body politic, because it meant the United States was able to maintain its democratic character, and because it also allowed the nation to forge cordial relations with the other American states. Concerning the latter, however, the secretary of state believed that "the advance of civilization in this hemisphere" was more likely to be secured "when the other American states assimilate to our own."[65]

Similar complexities and contradictions can be discerned in Seward's attitudes toward European empires themselves. He was often suspicious about the motives and policies of the imperial nations, but also, like many of his contemporaries, he demonstrated a fascination with and grudging admiration for the great powers of the day. His opposition toward many European activities in the Americas, his claims of support for the independence of subjugated peoples there, and his aspirations for the growth of American power had led him to make a number of provocative statements decrying European imperialism during the 1840s and 1850s, while also predicting that the United States would inevitably and rightly inherit the mantle of the European empires.[66] Despite this early high-blown rhetoric, Seward generally adopted a quite different tone once he became secretary of state, and took a more generous view of the European imperialism that he had previously railed against, especially the British Empire. Notably, however, he drew at least tentative comparisons between potential problems for the cohesion of the British Empire and the American Union that was presently unraveling.[67]

Seward also spoke favorably of Russia, which he claimed had been "a constant friend" of the United States. While acknowledging that the two nations were "so remote and so unlike," their relationship had, he suggested, also generated much interest. The reason for this was "obvious":

Russia, like the United States, is an improving and expanding empire. Its track is eastward, while that of the United States is westward. The two nations, therefore never come into rivalry or conflict. Each carries civilization to the new regions it enters, and each finds itself occasionally resisted by states jealous of its prosperity, or alarmed by its aggrandizement. Russia and the United States may remain good friends until, each having made a circuit of half the globe in opposite directions, they shall meet and greet each other in the region where civilization first began, and where, after so many ages, it has become now lethargic and helpless.[68]

Such views had important implications for the imperial nations themselves, but also the areas they had colonized, and especially for the United States' southern neighbor, Mexico. For Seward, the key traits of Spanish imperialism—"African slavery, colonial restrictions, and ecclesiastical monopolies"— were almost entirely negative and had enduring legacies, making Mexico "a theatre of conflict between European commercial, ecclesiastical, and political institutions and dogmas, and novel American institutions and ideas." But he could acknowledge that in the years since independence, it was Spain's former colony and not the United States that had abolished slavery, and suggested that the internal strife in Mexico was necessary in order "to lay sure foundations of broad republican liberty."[69] At other times, however, Seward expressed exasperation that the former Spanish colonies had simply not achieved that of which they were capable, because the legacy of colonial rule still hung heavily over them. "The very mention of a South American state suggests always the same inquiry: why a people so free, so virtuous, so educated, and so emulous, are not more secure, fortunate and happy," he complained in 1861. Although he claimed that everyone in the United States wanted the best for the Spanish American states, "everybody loses patience with them for not being wiser, more constant, and more stable." Many of Seward's cabinet colleagues supported the idea that, however bad Spanish colonialism had been, the Mexicans had done little to improve their own fortunes. Secretary of the Navy Gideon Welles put it starkly: "Torn by factions, down-trodden by a scheming and designing priesthood, ignorant and vicious, the Mexicans are incapable of good government, and unable to enjoy rational freedom." Secretary of the Treasury Hugh McCulloch simply called Mexicans "worthless."[70]

This chimed with broader prejudices that saw elite Americans struggle to reconcile their desire to celebrate Mexico's republicanism with their racist views. Historian John S. C. Abbott blamed Mexico's troubled history on its complex racial heritage, which to him meant that "the masses of the people were in a very low state of ignorance and debasement."[71] Such views were evident in the South as well as the North. The Confederate minister to Mexico City, John T. Pickett, from Virginia, with one eye on southern expansion into the north of the country, saw foreign intervention in

Mexico as inevitable, because the Mexican people ("if Mexico may be said to have a 'people'") consistently displayed "gross ignorance and super-stition."[72] Looking back on Mexican history, Frederick Douglass was often more generous. He praised Juárez and his republican movement, recognizing the "disadvantages and drawbacks" that Mexico experienced.[73] Douglass was fully aware that recent administrations in the United States had justified grabbing Mexican territory at least in part by suggesting that Mexicans were "an inferior race, that the old Castilian blood had become so weak that it would scarcely run down hill, and that Mexico needed the long, strong and beneficent arm of the Anglo-Saxon care extended over it." This, Douglass suggested, made the United States little different from Russia in its designs on the Ottomans, or the English in their attitudes toward the Irish.[74] At other times, however, he reinforced these very views. People in the United States wondered why Mexicans were so different from them, Douglass suggested. "Their comparatively low state of civilization" and the "demoralizing influence of long contin-ued Spanish tyranny" were two reasons for this, he claimed in 1871, but he conceded that "perhaps a deficiency inherent in the Latin races" could also account for their inability to come to a "full comprehension of the principles of republicanism."[75] Somewhat in contrast, the New York Times suggested that a despite "all their ignorance," Mexicans were "as thor-oughly democratic in all their feelings as the people of our own republic." But it also believed that the French could not maintain a monarchy there for long, because the country was too poor and the cost of keeping an empire was much greater than a republic.[76]

These sometimes contradictory views and impulses converged, leading many American leaders to call on the United States government to sup-port its republican neighbor. Some prominent ones even wanted the United States to declare war, or at least to forcibly eject France from Mexico, and perhaps occupy Mexican territory itself. In 1863, prominent Republican Party member Joshua Leavitt published a plea for the Lincoln administra-tion to publicly restate the Monroe Doctrine and, in effect, call France's bluff.[77] Throughout the war, many political elites supported schemes to help Mexican republicans, and Congress passed a number of often strongly worded resolutions on the issue. In February 1863, California senator James A. McDougall's request for a debate about the French installation of an emperor met with the approval of a majority of his colleagues, and the Senate then tabled a resolution condemning the French government for its actions and calling on the Lincoln administration to convey these views to Paris.[78] In April 1864, the House passed a resolution stating its rejection of "any monarchical government erected on the ruins of any republican government in America under the auspices of any European power."[79] And in the wake of the Union victory in April 1865, and with Maximilian becoming more repressive in Mexico, the two houses also passed a more strident joint resolution, which included the accusation that Maximilian's rule as emperor had "practically established slavery in his dominion," and that in denying the republican fighters in Mexico their rights as belligerents and executing them if they were captured, he had "violated the usages of civilized warfare."[80]

Ironically, for all the potential challenges that monarchical forms of government brought to the Americas at this time, they also proffered the potential for reform and progressive change. As the Civil War in the United States dragged on, a Union loyalist in Louisiana worried about reports that the new Mexican regime would offer inducements to free peoples in the United States. Writing from Union-occupied New Orleans in 1864, Alfred Jervis told his ally Thaddeus Stevens that there were now rumors of the European emperor in Mexico guaranteeing to freed people in the United States "that which *France* and some other Despotisms, concede to all their citizens, but which we prohibit: to wit: *'Equality to all casts before the Law.'*" Jervis even worried that Maximilian might hold out the possibility of black recruits crossing the border to fight against the United States in an unlikely alliance with Confederates and imperialists. The "French and other influences" in Louisiana could easily undermine the support of "our colored inhabitants" if "their reasonable demands are not secured to them."[81]

A Question of Territory

At the end of the Civil War, Ulysses S. Grant, the commanding general of the United States Army and already the likely Republican nominee for the next presidential election, proposed seizing the opportunity of General Philip Sheridan's position on the border with some 50,000 Union men to invade Mexico and drive out the French imperialists.[82] Mexico with its emperor supported by French troops was a tempting proposition for many disillusioned Confederates. The Confederacy's president Jefferson Davis planned to escape there following the Union victory, and John Wilkes

Booth attempted to flee into Mexican territory following his assassination of Lincoln.[83] Grant became progressively more bellicose, informing the cabinet that it needed to act, because defeated American rebels were crossing the Rio Grande to enter the service of the Austrian emperor in significant numbers, taking weapons and slaves with them. In response, commanding major general John M. Schofield began recruiting veterans to help with a possible invasion, a task made easier as many recently demobilized military personnel were already responding to calls from Juárez's representatives to volunteer, while Sheridan placed arms in the borderlands region for the use of Mexican republican forces.[84] Numerous Americans supported the United States Army taking such action, and Gideon Welles noted that many in the army were "chafing to make war on the imperial government and drive the French from that country" despite the "exhausted state of our affairs."[85] Even Andrew Johnson had expressed his admiration for the idea before becoming president, and with the end of the conflict in the United States and the changing dynamic of the conflict in Mexico—as well as his rapidly deteriorating domestic political position—he came under considerable pressure to exploit America's position to gain territory.[86] Influential Ohio Republican and Johnson confidante Lewis D. Campbell advised the president not to violate the traditional policies of the United States and to time carefully any measures he took to prosecute the Monroe Doctrine, but simultaneously argued that if the Mexican people were compelled to change their form of government "at the point of the French and Austrian bayonet," then it would "become a high duty we owe to our historic record and to the integrity of our policy long since enunciated, and on all proper occasions re-iterated, to interfere, even though war ensue."[87] Another correspondent told President Johnson, "Any movement towards the occupation of Mexico by our Government would meet with a hearty & cordial approval not only from the American people, but from every European Government also. The administration which acquires Mexico will be the most popular one which has ever controlled the destinies of the nation, and there would be no more certain and surer road to political ruin than opposition to such a measure."[88]

Others sought moderation, however, particularly because of the potentially negative repercussions for Franco-American relations at a time when the United States was in such a precarious position. From the beginning of the crisis, the French government knew that the United States could not cope with a foreign war in addition to a domestic one, and that Washington would, in the words of the American minister in Paris William Dayton, "submit to much rather than incur that hazard."[89] In response to Senator McDougall's call for action in 1863, the powerful chairman of the Senate Foreign Relations Committee, Charles Sumner, complained that even having such discussions about whether to censure the French only served to "embarrass" the United States government and "give aid and comfort to the rebellion." Although Sumner had been a vociferous opponent of the Mexican War in the 1840s and expressed continued sympathy for the Mexican Republic, he suggested that taking any kind of measure risking war with France was "madness" when French power "cannot be doubted," and he would rather "carefully cultivate" its friendship, concluding that the United States should focus on fighting the present war rather than beginning a new one.[90] Sumner acknowledged, however, that recognizing the new regime probably offered few advantages in diplomatic relations with the French and what he called its "new-fangled imperialism."[91] Seward himself also expressed concern and frustration that actions taken toward Mexico might not only have repercussions at home but also abroad, while in private he fumed that what he called the "complication" of France's interference in Mexican affairs sometimes led him to believe "that they would have no serious objection if they could exasperate us, in our present crippled condition, into an attack of some kind on them."[92]

In private, Seward was sympathetic to those in the United States who wanted to uphold the Monroe Doctrine, and noted the French affront to the doctrine in correspondence with close associates. He admitted that intervention by the United States to prevent the establishment of a monarchy (or to remove it once it had been established) "would be just and wise in itself," but justifying such an intervention was challenging "in the absence of any direct wrong committed against the United States."[93] He suggested that in seeking to impose an emperor on an unwilling population in this way, France was likely to "scatter seeds which would be fruitful of jealousies, which might ultimately ripen into collision between France and the United States and other American republics." While he wanted the French to know that the United States government did not support those who called for a more vigorous response, he also warned the authorities in Paris that many in the United States and elsewhere who were far less well disposed toward France than he was did hold such views, and that these rumors of war would eventually have consequences.[94] Privately, he told Dayton that, in keeping with the tenets of Monroe's

Doctrine, he wanted to separate the American and European theaters so that Britain and France would "soon come to the conclusion that it is wise to remit American affairs exclusively to the government of the United States."[95]

Yet, Seward resisted discussing the Monroe Doctrine with foreign governments or in public, refusing to risk a diplomatic spat with France or any other European power. Under Seward's direction, the Lincoln administration refused to use the term "Monroe Doctrine" at any point during the crisis.[96] As Napoleon's real intentions became apparent, Seward saw the difficulties of a public affirmation of the doctrine that Washington could not or would not support by attendant military action. As Seward put it to Postmaster General William Dennison, the United States government could not simply invoke the doctrine without being "prepared to maintain it." His memories of the war with Mexico in the 1840s made him cautious, especially because Sheridan's actions on the Mexican border were so reminiscent of those employed by United States forces some twenty years before. Furthermore, Seward knew that intervention in Mexico almost certainly meant supporting some kind of United States military presence there, and he could not countenance this. In mid-1865, Welles noted that the secretary of state "was emphatic in opposition to any movement [into Mexico]. [He said] the Empire was rapidly perishing, and, if let alone, Maximilian would leave in less than six months, perhaps in sixty days, whereas, if we interfered, it would prolong his stay and the Empire also."[97] Even as the war scare persisted, Seward supported Bigelow in resisting calls from his cabinet colleagues to put the Monroe Doctrine into effect, instead placing his faith in Napoleon to remove French forces as quickly as he could.[98] He did not want to antagonize Paris more than he felt was necessary, and he was therefore careful to reassure the French about American intentions, while Napoleon declared himself broadly appreciative of the "conduct and loyalty" of the United States regarding Mexican affairs.[99] Moreover, as Secretary of the Treasury Salmon P. Chase—no ally of Seward's— suggested to Joshua Leavitt, Seward himself did not actually renounce the Monroe Doctrine, even during the Civil War, "he only forebore [sic] to insist on it, when to insist on it would only have been counted a menace and would have precipitated recognition of the rebel Confederacy—and that recognition would have been followed by war."[100]

Nonintervention

As when Grant threatened invasion, Seward was central to maintaining the impression of impartiality and noninterference throughout the Mexican crisis, in both the Lincoln and Johnson administrations. From its earliest stages, the U.S. government established precedents for such a policy. When the allied powers first intervened, for example, they offered for the United States to join with them in seeking reparations. Caleb Cushing—former attorney general, future minister to Spain, and close friend of the secretary of state—even recommended that Seward should accept the offer of joining with the Europeans to reclaim American debts, but Seward refused.[101] Meanwhile, the Senate's attempt to forestall European involvement in Mexican affairs by taking on some of the country's debt was made "with the explicit understanding that the United States declines any territorial acquisition, and seeks the consolidation of Mexico without dismemberment of any kind."[102] These kinds of reassurances continued over the years that followed. Echoing the Senate's sentiments, Seward told Lewis Campbell, who briefly became the American minister to the Juárez government, in 1866:

> What the government of the United States desires in regard to the future of Mexico is not the conquest of Mexico, or any part of it, or the aggrandizement of the United States by purchase of land or dominion, but, on the other hand, they desire to see the people of Mexico relieved from all foreign military intervention, to the end that they may resume the conduct of their own affairs under the existing republican government, or such other frame of government as, being left in the enjoyment of perfect liberty, they shall determine to adopt in the exercise of their own free will, by their own free act, without dictation from any foreign country, and, of course, without dictation from the United States.[103]

Seward followed a similar line toward Paris, informing the French government that the United States would maintain the policy handed down from George Washington not to interfere in the internal affairs of any other state, because, as Mexico was both a neighbor of the United States and had a similar system of government, the United States had "naturally benevolent sentiments for that Republic, and are interested in her security, her prosperity and her welfare."[104] The primary aim of the United States toward Mexico, he later summarized to William Dayton, was simply "for the restoration of peace within her borders."[105]

Ironically, in making such a claim, Seward even attempted to draw out some of the similarities between the positions taken by Washington and Paris in order to appeal to the French authorities. Neither nation, he suggested, in fact wanted to annex Mexico or any part of it, nor did either want "any special interest, control, or influence" over it; rather, both sides wanted to see "the reëstablishment of unity, peace, and order" there. Seward suggested to Dayton that President Lincoln "unhesitatingly believes that they are the sentiments of the Emperor [Napoleon] himself in regard to Mexico."[106]

Seward's realization that Napoleon sought to install a European emperor may have tempered such feelings, but they did not alter his stance on non-interference. He told United States diplomats in various capitals around the world to stress that the principles the government followed in regard to Mexico were the same as it did for all the other nations; namely, that it had "neither a right nor a disposition to intervene by force in the internal affairs of Mexico, whether to establish and maintain a republic or even a domestic government there, or to overthrow an imperial or a foreign one, if Mexico chooses to establish or accept it."[107] Such interference, he suggested later, "would be only to reverse our own principles, and to adopt in regard to that country the very policy which in any case we disallow."[108] Instead, the United States offered only "moral support" to those who looked to establish and preserve republican systems.[109] Seward genuinely believed that the Mexicans wanted and needed a republican form of government, and that the United States would benefit from a close neighbor maintaining one, but stressed that Washington could not insist on them adopting it. Washington would, he said, rather allow it "to exercise the freedom of choosing and establishing institutions like our own, if they are preferred."[110] "Our policy of non-intervention, straight, absolute, and peculiar as it may seem to other nations, has thus become a traditional one," he told Dayton in 1863, "which could not be abandoned without the most urgent occasion, amounting to a manifest necessity."[111] Moreover, despite his own views on the subject, President Johnson deferred to Seward on this issue. In his first annual message to Congress, Johnson spoke from Seward's script to claim that the United States government had "wisely and firmly" refused to promote republicanism abroad: "It is the only government suited to our condition; but we have never sought to impose it on others; and we have consistently followed the advice of George Washington to recommend it only by the careful preservations and prudent use of the blessing."[112]

Seward explicitly contrasted this apparently exemplary set of U.S. policies with the actions of the European imperial powers in the Americas, implicitly reiterating the benign nature of American leadership in the face of such challenges, and at a time of acute weakness. As he put it in July 1862 at the height of the American Civil War:

> We have so conducted our affairs as to deprive it of all pretense of right or of provocation. We have interfered with the dominion or the ambitions of no nation. We have seen Santo Domingo absorbed by Spain, and been content with a protest. We have seen Great Britain strengthen her government in Canada, and we have approved it. We have seen France make war against Mexico, and have not allied ourselves with that republic. We have heard and redressed every injury of which any foreign states has complained, and we have relaxed a blockade in favor of foreign commerce that we might rightfully have maintained with inflexibility.[113]

Those who, like Lord Russell, claimed the United States was in fact "fighting for empire" in the south were correct, but the empire already belonged to the United States and it had been lawfully acquired and held: "We defend it, and we love it with all the affection with which patriotism in every land inspires the human heart," as Seward put it.[114] Seward also criticized those European empires that were unable to accept the fact that they were no longer able to maintain "parental" control over the former American colonies.[115] This became even more important as the Civil War ended and the State Department remained concerned that the European powers were looking to exploit continued U.S. weakness to gain new influence and territory. Rumors swirled that Great Britain might even attack the United States from the north, although more realistic and pressing were fears that the French and British were independently seeking new alliances in the Americas, in the French case through an extension of Maximilian's Mexican empire into Honduras, and in the Sandwich Islands in the case of Britain.[116] Both were worrying, but officials in Washington particularly feared that growing British influence in Hawaii threatened the expansion of U.S. missionary interests there. The Johnson administration also communicated with Britain about Haiti, agreeing that both nations should strive to keep the island country independent and self-ruling, while hinting that the United States might take action if that nation came under the control of another state.[117]

American Republicanism

In addition to maintaining a policy of nonintervention, Seward appeared to suggest that a form of exemplary republicanism at home would have benefits in the international sphere and he wanted to ensure that other nations understood the role the United States would play after the war had ended. When the minister in Nicaragua, Charles N. Riotte, enquired about possible U.S. interest in acquiring Costa Rica in 1863, Seward assured him that there was no thought of annexation at that time, "however desirable such an extension of our republican empire may once have seemed and whatever may be the sentiments of this country in regard to it hereafter." In a classic articulation of democratic imperialism, the secretary of state suggested that for the present moment and for what he called "the period which bounds the responsibilities of American Statesmen, the first and supreme need is to perfect proper self discipline so as to secure everywhere the stability and peaceful operation of the Federal Republican system of Government."[118] Thus, the United States would avoid territorial acquisitions and foreign interventions in favor of building up the nation at home. While there seemed to be at least a hint that Seward wanted the United States to bide its time, this was because of the difficult conditions in which it found itself. Yet, in defining American actions in this way, Seward implicitly acknowledged the leading diplomatic *and* ideological role that the United States now played in the Americas in spite of the domestic depredations of the Civil War.

Because of its growing material power and regional hegemony, both Britain and France believed that the United States was the key player in the resolution of the Mexican crisis. Paris had constantly sought American approval for its actions, and the French foreign minister, Édouard Drouyn de Lhuys, suggested that the United States was "entitled" to a greater say in Mexican affairs than "distant European countries."[119] The United States was fully aware of the French public's deep dissatisfaction with its government's imperial adventures in Mexico, and when Napoleon announced his troops' withdrawal during the winter and spring of 1866—to be carried out in three stages over the following year—European calls for the United States to intervene in Mexico to stabilize the country increased.[120] Members of the British government supported the expansion of the United States into Mexico as a way to check French power. Following Maximilian's death, the new minister in London, Benjamin Rush, reported that British Foreign Secretary Lord Clarendon had said, "It was our destiny, so I understand him, to have Mexico, and that it would be the best thing that could happen for Mexico, and I think he added—the World."[121] Moreover, as one American commentator noted, Britain had chosen to do nothing about the French intervention in part because seeing Napoleon tied down in the Americas suited its objectives, although it could also be said to show Britain's relative weakness.[122]

Seward had no such intention. The Johnson administration's disastrous Reconstruction policies certainly contributed to this reluctance. However, he also spurned seeking opportunities to gain new territories to the south of the United States, believing that the admission of Cuba, Santo Domingo, and Saint Thomas to the United States was "ultimately inevitable," because the populations of these islands would see the value of joining the United States.[123] Instead, he focused on rehabilitating the Southern states based on their rights as self-governing entities, which had existed in embryonic form since they had been British colonies, and had to be reintegrated as soon as possible, a process that could not be forced by an "imperial hand."[124] Seward supported and even encouraged President Johnson to reintegrate the South to the benefit of whites and at the expense of blacks, and did so in explicitly imperial terms. He reportedly told his allies in April 1886 that the North had "nothing to do with negroes [sic] . . . I have no more concern for them than I have for the Hottentots . . . They are not of our race."[125] It was therefore almost impossible for him to contemplate integrating other apparently alien people from Mexico at this particular time, aside from the country's association with the growth of slavery and its connections to the erstwhile Confederacy, and it reinforced his ideas about the precedence of commercial rather than territorial expansion.

While the government in Washington resisted calls from different quarters for territorial enlargement into Mexico, however, American leaders increasingly "claimed the undoubted right to regulate the affairs of the American Continent," as the author Vine Wright Kingsley had put it in

1863.[126] In this sense, the Monroe Doctrine was becoming an assertion of American regional control. It is significant, for example, that this era of emancipation saw growing agitation for female political involvement. One of the leading suffrage campaigners, Victoria Woodhull, also espoused a vision of global government modeled on the United States. Despite the evident shortcomings of its political system, Woodhull, who would go on to be the presidential candidate for the Equal Rights Party in 1872, believed that the United States would become "a Universal Republic of the United States of the World." In doing so, Woodhull hoped to create a more equal and peaceful society through elements of redistribution and international arbitration. It was also notable that in developing this system, she thought the United States would "compel every State to maintain within its limits a republican form of government upon all matters in all its legislation and administration."[127]

Even radicals who espoused a vision of republican unity in the Americas also assumed that the United States would have a leadership role within it to ensure the long-term security of the continent. To this end, and despite his opposition to the United States government taking direct action against France, Charles Sumner was clear that the reestablishment of an explicitly republican form of government in Mexico was necessary. In a special session of Congress in 1867, he suggested that the United States was "bound by neighborhood and republican sympathies to do all in their power for the welfare of the Mexican people," and proposed that it should offer its good offices to mediate between the various factions "in order to avert a deplorable civil war, and to obtain the establishment of republican government on a foundation of peace and security."[128] This echoed an earlier statement that Seward had made in 1863, opining that the United States government "knows full well that the inherent normal opinion of Mexico favors a government there republican in form and domestic in its organization, in preference to any monarchical institutions to be imposed from abroad." He continued:

This government knows, also, that this normal opinion of the people of Mexico resulted largely from the influence of popular opinion in this country, and is continually invigorated by it. The President [Lincoln] believes, moreover, that this popular opinion of the United States is just in itself, and eminently essential to the progress of civilization on the American continent, which civilization, it believes, can and will, if left free from European resistance, work harmoniously together with advancing refinement on the other continents. This government believes that foreign resistance, or attempts to control American civilization, must and will fail before the ceaseless and ever-increasing activity of material, moral, and political forces, which peculiarly belong to the American continent. Nor do the United States deny that, in their opinion, their own safety and the cheerful destiny to which they aspire are intimately dependent on the continuance of free republican institutions throughout America.[129]

In making this final observation, Seward acknowledged his belief that republicanism had to exist and grow in the Americas for it to continue to thrive in the United States. It was also telling that he espoused growing confidence about republicanism at home as the United States slowly began to emerge from its prolonged existential crisis.[130] He may well have been right about popular opinion in Mexico favoring republican institutions, but Seward's logic was that the United States would lead them toward such institutions, and that they would welcome this leadership. Nonetheless, his suggestion that if France withdrew and agreed not to intervene further in Mexico, this would "thereafter relieve both France and the United States of all concern about her affairs, and resume with motivated spirit her progress toward well-organized and discreet self-government" seemed somewhat optimistic and even disingenuous.[131]

Despite the often ignoble history of relations between the United States and Mexico in the preceding decades, therefore, in the 1860s the administrations of Abraham Lincoln and Andrew Johnson attempted to offer a coherent vision of Mexico as a fellow republic that had been usurped by a European colonial power. While the exigencies of its own Civil War seriously limited Washington's response to the French intervention, it was significant that it couched its justifications for noninterference in another nation's political affairs and its refusals to countenance the acquisition of additional Mexican territory in terms of the republican values that it claimed to uphold. On the surface at least, Mexico was a test case about the need for all American nations to decide their own fate and their own form of government. As Seward wrote to Henry E. Peck of the U.S. legation in Port-au-Prince during a period of tension between Haiti and Santo Domingo, he could do no better to explain the U.S. position toward disputes such as these than to point toward "correspondence that has recently taken place between the United States and some European powers with regard to Mexico."[132] Washington's form of exemplary republicanism, both at home and abroad, was thus intended to serve as a beacon for other regional powers, and to define more sharply the American nation and its role in the world at a time when republicanism was under severe threat, blending the principle of nonintervention with the reality that a more proactive policy would have been difficult at this time. Rhetorically at least, the United States saw the benefits of portraying itself in opposition to European colonial practices in the Americas and around the world, even as it developed more assertive regional economic policies and increasingly dominated its neighbors.[133]

Thus, while the French challenge in Mexico posed a serious threat to the United States, American opposition to it both reinforced a sense that the United States was an anti-imperial nation, *and* simultaneously bolstered what many saw as its natural leadership role, and even its dominance, in the Americas. The notion that republicanism was particularly well suited to the Western Hemisphere set the nations of the region against Europe, augmenting negative conceptions of monarchy in contrast with republicanism. This also suggested that as the most advanced republican nation, the United States should be at the vanguard of guiding other American nations and shaping regional policies. In presenting their policies merely as a response to an imperial threat in the Americas from Europe, leaders in Washington largely failed to acknowledge the growing similarities between their own outlooks and those of the European powers.

Conclusion

As part of his diplomatic appeal to France during the Civil War, Seward privately admitted that the United States and European governments were often closely aligned on issues of Mexican politics. All sides agreed that the Europeans had genuine grievances against the government of Mexico, and all wanted to find a solution to their outstanding financial claims. Moreover, all genuinely desired a long-term, stable resolution to the Mexican crisis that would not only ensure that nothing like this happened again, but would also see positive developments for the Mexican people. However wrong-headed Napoleon and Maximilian were, and however understandable American dissatisfaction with the European response to their actions, both France and the United States claimed to have the interests of the Mexican people at heart.

Yet, American leaders did not see any tension in condemning France's contravention of the Monroe Doctrine and the doctrine's own assertion of U.S. leadership, and even dominance, of the American republics. Because the United States largely disavowed taking Mexican territory and espoused republicanism for Mexico, it could only see that it wanted to help its neighbor. It therefore could be nothing like France or any of the other imperial nations of Europe that apparently wished the fledgling nation ill, or at least were willing to exploit it for their own ends. To them, the benefits of American republicanism were clear, while the growing strength and regional authority of the United States would bring more American nations within its orbit, augmenting its existing commercial power and perhaps even its territory as a result. This was part of a natural process, and nothing like the aggression of France and other European nations in the Americas.

While the French intervention was undoubtedly a challenge to the United States' growing power within its sphere of influence, Seward's articulation of nonintervention and hemispheric unity was also part of a trajectory in which he looked to expand the United States' regional and global outlook. His determination to press into the Pacific saw him attempt a number of maneuvers after the Civil War ended, the most famous—and infamous—being his successful purchase of Alaska from Russia, as well as annexing the tiny Midway Islands. Both occurred in 1867 in an attempt to expand America's commercial reach. Moreover, while he largely failed in his other schemes—in Hawaii, the Danish West Indies, and Santo Domingo—he signaled the intent to extend the country's influence through the acquisition of naval coaling stations in the Caribbean and then the Pacific. The administration regarded this as part of a sensible strategy without any of the negative connotations of formal imperialism. As Gideon Welles put it at the end of 1865, neither the American government nor people wanted to buy the French out of Mexico, because they did not want those "possessions." If offered a chance to get French islands in the Caribbean, such as Martinique or Guadeloupe, however, "we should embrace the opportunity of getting either," because this made good commercial sense. This need had only become more acute, President Johnson explained to Congress at the end of 1867, because of the recent Civil War, in which Confederate rebels and European antagonists operating from Caribbean ports had exposed the relative weaknesses of the Union lacking any such bases. Thus, Johnson reasoned, continental American nations, including the United States, might one day absorb the colonies in the West Indies, although he thought it wise to leave questions about this to what he called the "process of natural political gravitation."[134] The United States also increasingly operated on the basis of competition and cooperation with the European powers in Asia, an area one prominent government supporter predicted would soon be "of more importance to us than the trade we now carry on with the nations of Europe."[135] In this respect, political leaders modeled their approach to expansion on "Wise Old England," as Seward called it near the end of his life, in that they prioritized commercial expansion, alongside a search for the acquisition of suitable naval bases, both to improve their long-term international position and challenge the European powers themselves. While this did not mean that Seward had thrown off all his suspicions about the United States' erstwhile imperial master, it did mean that he recognized the value of following some of the precepts of British foreign policy. While Britain continued to pose a threat to U.S. interests in both the Americas and Asia, it also pointed the way for America and even provided a target for the United States to aim at, suggesting that the United States could one day take its place.[136]

The Mexico case tested American reactions to imperial challenges in the Americas. Emerging from the turmoil of the Civil War, the United States would face a new test stemming from European colonial practices close to the shores of the United States, albeit one that it had been confronting in different guises for decades. This time it concerned Spain and its brutal colonial policies on the island of Cuba.

CHAPTER III

Spain and the Ten Years' War in Cuba

In the early hours of a November morning in 1873, Spanish guards rounded up four men from the jail in Santiago de Cuba and took them to meet their deaths. The nationality of each man remained unclear to the authorities, and none was a bigger mystery than a tall, clean-shaven individual who claimed to be called George Washington Ryan. Despite knowing his imminent fate, Ryan had dressed elegantly in a white undershirt and blue vest on which was pinned the star of a brigadier general in the Cuban rebel army. He had also donned his trademark wide-brimmed hat. The previous evening, the Spanish authorities had allowed Ryan to write letters to his loved ones and to compose his will. Now, as the group moved through the streets of Santiago, Ryan nonchalantly lit a cigar. When he reached the place of the execution, a wall outside the local slaughterhouse, he continued smoking as the first two of his companions were forced to kneel with their backs to the guards before they were shot. Ryan and his remaining companion, Pedro de Céspedes, brother of the president of the provisional Cuban republic, refused to let the guards dispatch them in such a manner, and there was something of a scuffle before they submitted. Yet, as their time came, these two, like the pair before them, faced their demise and those who would administer it with a quiet, even confident dignity. Only in the last few seconds before the troops fired their weapons did Ryan finally throw away his cigar.[1]

Ryan, whose real given name was William, was in fact an Englishman who had moved to Canada and then the United States, where he had fought for the Union in the Civil War. Following the end of the conflict, he lived in New York, where he had decided to accept a commission in the army of the Cuban junta, which was rebelling against Spanish rule and looking to recruit able, battle-hardened Americans to fight. As an ex-solider, Ryan fit the bill well. By this route, Ryan had ended up on the steamer *Virginius*, a blockade-runner bought by an American on behalf of members of the junta, which operated for several years in the seas around the United States before the Spanish finally caught up with it a few miles off the coast of Cuba at the end of October 1873. While some members of the captured ship's crew stood trial, a Spanish court had already convicted Ryan and his three mercenary companions of piracy and sentenced them to death in absentia. Now all that a hastily convened court-martial had to do was iden-tify the men for the sentence to be carried out. Despite the protests of the American vice-consul, in the days that followed, the local Spanish com-mander in Santiago, General Don Juan N. Burriel, oversaw more execu-tions of the *Virginius* rebels, including the captain, Joseph Fry, a former commodore in the Confederate navy. In total, fifty-three men died in early November on Burriel's orders.

While initial reactions in the United States to the deaths of Ryan and his companions were relatively muted, news that such a large number of men had been killed soon caused uproar. It was unclear as to the number in the group who were American citizens, but for many people the sheer scale of the action was an affront to the nation, especially because the ship was registered in New York and flying an American flag (which the Span-ish forces had reportedly trampled at the time of its capture). This was the closest point at which the United States and Spain came to war before 1898.

This incident took place in the middle of a period of intense and brutal fighting, later known as the Ten Years' War (1868–1878), between groups of Cuban insurgents and forces of the colonial Spanish regime. It broadly coincided with the eight years of the Ulysses S. Grant (1869–1877) admin-istration and therefore occupied a great deal of its attention.[2] Inter alia, Cuba's location, its close trade association with the United States, and long-standing American interests in acquiring (or at least economically controlling) the island, as well as the brutal nature of the war itself, were all important factors in generating this intense scrutiny that strained rela-tions with Spain on numerous occasions and brought them close to breaking over the *Virginius* affair. As with the Mexican debacle during and after the Civil War, the United States Congress, sections of the American press, and members of the public placed great pressure on the government in Washington to take some kind of action. This ranged from recognizing that a state of war existed through to military intervention. Some even suggested using this turmoil as an opportunity to end Spanish rule in the Americas and seize Cuba for the United States.

Yet, the Grant administration largely resisted pressure to support the insurgency, and its criticism of Spanish rule was consistently muted as important figures in Washington sought to modify rather than end Spanish colonial practices. Their primary objective was to alter what they saw as the autocratic and at times barbaric nature of Spanish control, especially the continuation of slavery (a particular point of contention among members of the Republican Party after 1865), and to challenge the exclusion of the United States from open trade with Cuba. However, perhaps even more than in the case of French intervention in Mexico, the Grant administration did very little to pursue an overtly anti-colonial agenda and at times even supported the continuation of Spanish sovereignty over the Cuban population as part of a drive to enhance its own material interests in Cuba. It thus prioritized positive diplomatic relations with Madrid while conforming to the tenets of the Monroe Doctrine.

The doctrine was not threatened by Spain's actions in Cuba, because it was an existing colony. Somewhat like the Mexican episode, diplomatic inaction from the United States was in part because of its relatively weak position following the Civil War and during the domestic trauma of Reconstruction. It was also because of the numerous contradictions contained in its position on imperialism in the Caribbean. While there was broad sympathy in political circles and among the population for the rebels who were fighting for freedom from colonial control in Cuba, and Washington no longer saw independent nations in the Americas as incipient threats to American Union, its response to the Cuban crisis was always limited and formulated within the confines of broader concerns about ideology and U.S. regional power.

Specifically, it was constructed in a racial and racialized context. As Eric Love has convincingly argued, racial paradigms based on notions of the superiority of white Americans (as they saw themselves) over others were actually a brake on American imperialism in the postbellum period, because few of these Americans wanted to incorporate peoples they believed were inferior into the body politic of the United States. Love argues that this should be understood as *racism*, because it privileged a group of people who defined themselves as "white" and who thought others unfit for the freedoms afforded by independent democratic institutions, effectively consigning them to the margins. Racism and imperialism thus went hand in hand. Love also contends that race was not a defining theme of the rhetoric of those who wanted to annex new territories during this period, but rather for the leaders who resisted such annexations. In fact, policymakers and others who pressed for the territorial expansion of the United States actually downplayed the need to uplift "inferior" races abroad, because they knew it would not play well with domestic audiences. This was especially important at a time when Americans were engaging in profound and divisive debates about the future of race relations in their own nation. Therefore, American elites used racist tropes learned and implemented at home—in the South *and* North of the United States—to oppress groups considered nonwhite, extending these tropes into the international sphere.[3] This elite group included such leading figures as the secretary of state, Hamilton Fish, who served President Grant for all of his term and oversaw Washington's policy toward Cuba, and even Radical Republicans such as Charles Sumner, a vociferous opponent of bringing Caribbean lands into the Union because of the ethnic makeup of their populations.

Such racist assumptions applied particularly to Cuba, which, even more than Mexico, had long captured the imagination of the American people, but which also often deeply troubled them. Cuba's ethnic makeup, its continued rule by colonial Spain, and the prolonged grip of slavery on the island were just some of the problems, but these did not prevent many American journalists, policymakers, and others from looking longingly at it with a view to a much closer relationship. Cuba was alluring not just because it was close—so close they often referred to it as "contiguous" territory—but because it was simultaneously exotic and alien. Its proximity meant many of these Americans thought the United States inevitably had a role in its future, and some believed that it was destined to become a part of the United States.[4] As Louis Pérez suggests, such lines of thought—and especially the idea of Cuba as a "neighbor"—provided a moral veneer to an essentially self-interested stance on the part of the United States.[5] This self-interest dictated the policy during the Ten Years' War. Cuba's very otherness, especially its racial differences, made interference in the colony more difficult to justify, so the prospect of Cuban accession to the United States was abhorrent to many, including Fish and Sumner. The result was effectively an affirmation of the status quo, including the continuation of Spanish rule. In one of Pérez's many metaphors, Cuba may have been "ripe fruit" but it was not yet ready for picking.[6]

Spanish Imperialism

Throughout the nineteenth century, interested Americans were suspicious of Spanish imperialism. They generally saw it as stifling and regressive, despite Spain's increasingly diminished status as an imperial nation. Its colonial holdings were minuscule in comparison to those it had controlled before the revolutions at the beginning of the century. From the 1820s, it still occupied a few important outposts, such as Cuba and Puerto Rico, both of which were close to the United States and therefore considered by many American leaders to be prime candidates for incorporation into the Union. This caused some considerable tension between Washington and Madrid over successive decades.[7] Spain also ruled its empire by giving local governors and commanders huge amounts of control, and during the middle of the nineteenth century it embarked on a renewed surge of attempted empire building, not just in the Americas but also North Africa and Southeast Asia.[8]

Cuba in particular had a greater symbolic power for many Americans than its political or diplomatic status warranted. The United States government had essentially always been caught in the same dilemma in that it desired autonomy for Cuba because of its broad support for independent (and preferably republican) nations in the Americas, but it also wanted to develop greater trade links with, and perhaps ultimately dominate, the island.

Here, Americans' preponderant belief in Anglo-Saxon forms of rule had significant consequences. Firstly, it meant that they were often especially scathing about Spanish control of Cuba. Following her trip there in 1859, for example, the poet and activist Julia Ward Howe observed: "The past history of Spain shows to what a point that nation can carry insensibility to the torment of others . . . The Spanish race is in the saddle, and rides the Creole, its derivative, with hands reeking with plunder."[9] Secondly, because of this enervating form of Spanish rule, American leaders were also consistently suspicious of the Cuban population's ability to rule itself, and fearful that the end of the Spanish era might herald a new period of domination by another European country, probably Great Britain.[10] As a result, for most of the nineteenth century, successive U.S. governments were largely indifferent to Cuban independence and thus effectively supported Spanish colonialism on the island, despite their prevailing attitudes toward it.

Before the American Civil War, Cuba's position as a slaveholding colony as well as its proximity to the south of the United States complicated this. As part of efforts to free it from Spanish rule, some private U.S. citizens conducted "filibustering" expeditions to the island. These illegal attempts to interfere in another nation or colony in the region were widespread. They had reached something of a peak in the 1850s, captivating the attention of many Americans despite their ultimate futility. Citizens of the United States often resented foreigners singling out their country for censure over these filibustering ventures when, to them, many nations appeared to be conducting very similar practices. They saw British policies in India and the activities of Robert Clive and the East India Company as particularly relevant here, at least in part because of the tendency of many English commentators to decry these private American overseas endeavors. As one commentator noted on the eve of the Indian rebellion, while "only a private corporation" in Britain, in India and the rest of Asia the East India Company "exercised all the powers of a great nation," because it had acquired India by military force and maintained a huge, regional army.[11] Even newspapers in northern cities such as New York and Philadelphia cited the activities of the East India Company as effectively being filibustering. Indeed, to them Britain's colonial ventures and the absorption of vast territories into its empire were far worse than the often minuscule and underfunded expeditions that Americans undertook.[12] But there was no doubt that many filibusters looked at the Caribbean and South America as potential outlets for slavery and as something that would help secure the institution in the south of the United States. Cuba's status as a slaveholding colony after the American Civil War meant that these associations continued in the years that followed, as did some American filibustering campaigns in Cuba during the Ten Years' War.[13]

Even those Northerners and Midwesterners who opposed the incorporation of Cuba into the Union as a slaveholding state sometimes believed that its future outside of colonial control and beyond the grip of slavery would inevitably mean a much closer association with the United States. Prominent German émigré Carl Schurz, who had left Europe following the failed 1848 revolutions there, wrote in the 1850s that he was concerned about the American interest in Cuba when it was so closely associated with slavery. He therefore had no desire for the United States to acquire it at that time. Yet Schurz, who would briefly serve as ambassador to Spain and go on to be one of the staunchest opponents of President William McKinley's expansion in the Caribbean and Pacific in the late 1890s, said that if the Spanish government were willing to seize the opportunity and emancipate the black population, then "Cuba would be welcome" to join the United States.[14]

The prospect of reform in Cuba thus excited many more progressive minds in Washington because they could read it as part of a broader liberalization of imperial rule around the world. When U.S. newspapers reported in the late 1850s that the Spanish authorities were moving toward abolishing slavery on the island, leading antislavery Republican Charles Sumner declared that its realization would be the most important event in the Americas since the declaration of independence eighty years before. Sumner speculated that a number of different global movements had contributed to this possibility, including Spain's need to keep American filibusters out and its response to the emancipation of territories in other empires around the world. Yet, he suggested that the single most important factor was the new regime of Tsar Alexander II in Russia, whose move toward the emancipation of the serfs would finally be realized a few years later as the United States was descending into civil war.[15]

The end of slavery in the United States changed the nature of these discussions, but debates about annexation continued after the Civil War. Although the United States government still held no territorial possessions in the Caribbean, its growing economic power increasingly saw it vying for commercial and trading influence with the European colonial powers in such places as Haiti, Santo Domingo (the Dominican Republic), and Cuba. From the 1870s, burgeoning global demand for sugar, especially in Western Europe and North America, and the high capital costs of investing in the industry gave first Cubans and then capitalists from the United States increasing access in Santo Domingo, although U.S. domination of sugar markets there was not complete before the 1890s.[16] Similarly, in Haiti, investors and traders from the United States dominated only staple goods, while Europeans—and especially those from Great Britain—did so in other areas.[17] But the influence of the United States was rising, a fact aptly illustrated by events in Cuba following the end of the American Civil War when a new repressive ministry in Spain imposed a set of protectionist policies to which the United States responded by placing tariffs on numerous Cuban goods. These moves coincided with a drop in sugar production and prices that brought disaster to the Cuban economy and further exposed the problems of Spanish rule. So too did the conservative Spanish government's response, setting off calls for revolution that resulted in the start of ten years of fighting.[18]

The Cuban Rebellion

The rebellion in Cuba that began in October 1868 was based, at least in part, on ideas about progressive reform. A collection of different groups— farmers, free blacks, and others—worked together to oppose Spanish control, but also to improve the lives of Cubans and end the institution of slavery. However, as this movement grew, its leader, Cuban planter Carlos Manuel de Céspedes (brother of Pedro, who would be executed with William Ryan), recognized that in order to garner and maintain support from across Cuban society, he needed to proceed with great care. He thus prioritized the expulsion of Spain over freeing slaves. Céspedes and his fellow rebels only achieved modest success in attracting the planter class, however, because planters feared that rebellion was bad for business and anyway doubted whether revolutionaries were capable of achieving wide-reaching reforms. Moreover, Céspedes's stance exposed deep fissures within the independence movement between the fighters who saw issues of abolition as being intimately linked with ending Spanish rule and civilians in positions of authority who did not. This directly affected the conduct of the war, which was mostly fought in the east of the island because the rebel leaders did not want to disrupt sugar production in the west and so alienate affluent planters who were potential allies.[19]

Such issues also influenced the diplomacy of the war. In part this was because some of the independence leaders saw the importance of the regional dynamics of the struggle and wanted to attract the attention and support of the United States. They based their conservative stance concerning abolition in part on their fear that anything that smacked of inciting a race war in Cuba would alienate the United States government and its people. For many Cubans, the idea of independence was notional, because they ultimately wanted Cuba to join the United States in some form. From

Figure 3.1 Like his friend Henry Seward with France and Mexico, Hamilton Fish maintained a cautious approach to Spain's position in Cuba. In part, he based this on his negative view of Cubans, whom he thought incapable of good self-government.
Source: Library of Congress, undated.

the earliest days of the conflict against Spain, this was an explicit aim of the rebels, and early in their struggle they appealed directly to outgoing secretary of state Seward on this issue but with no success.[20] With Seward leaving his post during the first months of the conflict, it fell to Ulysses Grant's secretary of state, Hamilton Fish, in office from 1869 to 1877, to deal with these issues.

Fish had to balance Washington's desire to see Cuba escape the confines of colonial rule against the need to maintain diplomatic relations with Madrid. Somewhat like Seward in the years before, Fish dominated American diplomacy during a decade of hesitancy in the 1870s. Succeeding his much better-known friend, he preceded those who built on Seward's legacy, and who began to flourish in the 1880s, to advocate building up U.S. naval power, developing island coaling stations, and negotiating new customs treaties as a means to attain greater regional influence. Fish served in the role for all of Grant's term of office and thus oversaw the policymaking process during almost all of the Ten Years' War. A former Whig, he was a rather colorless figure (especially in comparison to Seward), and because of this, he has been marginalized in the historiography of U.S. foreign relations in spite of his length of service and relative importance.

Of those who have written about Fish, all emphasize his inherent conservatism but they disagree on whether this allowed him to conduct his diplomacy successfully or whether it led to stagnation in the Department of State.[21] Despite such disagreements, it is clear that he essentially plotted a middle course between isolationism and interventionism, unilateralism and multilateralism, suspicion of the imperial powers and recognition that their geopolitical power necessitated their involvement in the hemisphere. Furthermore, he exemplified the tension in American diplomacy between a desire for global influence and one for clear limits on territorial acquisitions, and, very much like Seward, saw the advantages of a European-style informal empire for the United States, especially British free-trade imperialism.[22]

On Spain and Cuba, however, Fish knew he had to be cautious. In principle, it seems that he opposed Spanish rule and supported Cuban independence, at least eventually. At the beginning of his tenure in 1869, Fish noted the "sympathy which Americans feel for all people striving to secure for themselves more liberal institutions and that inestimable right of self-government which we prize as the foundation of all progress and achievement."[23] He later noted that the American people were more sympathetic to nations that moved toward what he called "our simpler form of Government" and said the "sympathies of the world . . . were gradually becoming more interested in behalf of a people who were claiming relief from an oppressive Government, and that the whole tendency of the world was towards the abandonment of distant Colonial possessions."[24] Yet Fish, like many of his contemporaries, perceived political and social advancement in the Caribbean nations to have been slow. The first black republic, Haiti, continued to be wracked by civil instability, and President Andrew Johnson had summarized the feelings of many when he commented in late 1868 that the attempt to establish republics throughout the West Indies had encountered "many obstacles, most of which may be supposed to result from long-indulged habits of colonial supineness and dependence upon European monarchical powers." Johnson suggested that the situation was becoming so acute that it would not be long before the United States would have to take action in Santo Domingo and Cuba.[25] Fish wanted to resist making such bold moves, however, and continually defined his objections to colonial control narrowly, focusing on the worst excesses of Spanish rule in Cuba. He thus reflected a deep conservatism in the administration's politics, but also a desire for the United States to have greater influence in the hemisphere.

Fish's racial attitudes also animated his approach to the desperate struggle in Cuba, and these gave him further caution, particularly regarding the possibility of the incorporation of Cuba into the United States. He had visited Cuba in 1855 and, while he liked much of what he saw there, the population repelled him because of its racial makeup.[26] He believed the black Cuban to be inferior to the black American and therefore rejected the idea that Cuba could be brought into the Union. This was an especially important consideration in his mind when he became secretary of state, as the United States had just ratified the Fourteenth Amendment. As he told the Prussian minister in Washington, Friedrich von Gerolt, "the people are of a different race & language; unaccustomed to our institutions or to self-government; we would not wish to incorporate them with us." However bad Spanish dominion over the island was, though, he was clear that "under no circumstances" would the United States allow the island to become a possession, or fall under the control, of any other European government after Spain left.[27]

Other key republicans shared Fish's racial attitudes, which were particularly apparent in the negative reactions to President Grant's failed attempt to purchase Santo Domingo early in his presidency.[28] Grant tried to portray his proposed acquisition of the republic on the island of Hispaniola as adhering to the Monroe Doctrine. He argued that its annexation would not only enhance the ability of the United States to trade with Europe and Asia, but that it would also encourage the abolition of slavery in its last outposts in the Americas—Cuba, Puerto Rico, and Brazil—while settling "the unhappy condition of Cuba," and ending its "exterminating conflict."[29] Persisting with such arguments throughout his presidency, Grant's interest in Santo Domingo at times appeared to be something of an obsession, and he was deeply disappointed that more of the American people did not support him in his endeavor to acquire it.[30] He also saw intimate connections between the domestic opposition to Santo Domingo and some of his other policies, particularly in Cuba. At a time when there were deep fissures within the Republican Party, and indeed in his own cabinet, over both issues, he worried that he looked weak to many members of the Senate. He believed that many senators who might otherwise support the annexation of Santo Domingo could oppose it if he did not come out in favor of the revolutionaries in Cuba, although in this area he was also disappointed.[31]

While the objections of notable Republicans such as Justin S. Morrill, Carl Schurz, and Charles Sumner to the Santo Domingo purchase were wide-ranging, in part they based them on the potential difficulties they envisioned with integrating people of color into the United States' system of government at a time of great domestic turmoil in race relations. This mirrored Fish's stance on Cuba. Sumner, as chairman of the powerful Senate Foreign Relations Committee and therefore the most prominent of Grant's opponents, was particularly forthright on this issue. A radical Republican, Sumner believed that, despite being equal, different races were destined to inhabit separate geographical areas. Arguing that the United States could cope with expansion to the north, he had tentatively supported Seward's purchase of Alaska in 1867. But he did not hold that the same could be said of its growth into the tropics. As he told one correspondent, he had "always thought that the West India Islands belonged to the blacks," because of, as he told another, their "climate, occupation, and destiny under Providence," and so "we should not take them away."[32]

Furthermore, in his famous speech of December 1870 denouncing Grant's policies, Sumner noted the wider implications of American activities in the Caribbean, which he equated with imperialism. His "Naboth's Vineyard" address was an excoriation of the foreign policy of Grant, whom Sumner later said he believed was "unfit" for the office of president.[33] It seemed to the senator that the United States was acting just as an imperial European power would do to gain control of a territory. Sumner had previously rehearsed the long struggles between France and Spain over Santo Domingo and suggested that in interfering in its affairs now the United States was becoming like them. He had found evidence, for example, that the support of the U.S. government and its navy had effectively kept the Santo Dominican leader, Buenaventura Báez, in power, and this deeply disturbed him. On this point, Sumner even drew a comparison with the ongoing situation in Europe, where the struggle between France and Germany had seen Napoleon III lose power and then advancing Prussian forces capture him. Rumors were now emerging of a plan to put Napoleon back on the throne in order to make him sign an agreement with the chancellor of the North German Federation, Otto von Bismarck, something the new French republican government had refused to do. Yet, Sumner thundered to his fellow senators, "this was the very part played by the American government. Baez has been treated as you fear Bismarck may treat Louis Napoleon. You call him 'president;' they call him there 'dictator;' better call him 'emperor' and the comparison will be complete."[34]

Other leading social and political reformers supported Sumner's position. Linking the situations in Cuba and Santo Domingo, former abolitionist William Lloyd Garrison believed that it was not America's place to expand its territory when it had so many problems at home. Garrison argued that it was "not the province of the American Government to leave its own domains in quest of opportunities to put down factious disturbances or to establish free institutions in other lands." Such moves would, Garrison contended, have repercussions in the United States, accelerating what he called "national decadence . . . in proportion as we grasp at foreign colonial possessions." He also saw the likelihood that this would only be a first-step on the road to further acquisitions in Mexico, the Caribbean, and beyond.[35] Garrison's close associate and leading suffragist Lydia Maria Child agreed, decrying the current "insane rage for annexation" and "national greed for territory." Child explicitly linked the current struggle for women's political freedom in the United States with Dominican independence, although while she—like Sumner—balked at the prospect of bringing Santo Domingo into the Union, in her case it was not because its inhabitants were black, but rather because they were Catholic. The long-term legacies of Spanish colonialism thus meant they were unprepared to embrace republican institutions, a fact that she believed had been borne out over the previous decades in Catholic Haiti.[36]

For Sumner, who corresponded with Child on these issues, it was the prospect of interference in Haiti that was his overriding concern about the San Domingo debacle and that dominated his rhetorical attacks on Grant's policies. As the first black republic in the Americas occupying the western side of the island of Hispaniola, Haiti had struggled for years for recognition from the United States. Sumner, who had long been associated with the Haitian government, was dismayed that it had taken until 1862 for the United States finally to recognize it (a move he had helped to facilitate). European powers also threatened Haiti's territory, and the United States had engaged in discussions with Spain about upholding its neutrality.[37] Now, as Sumner reported in 1870, the Haitian minister in Washington was "much disturbed by the attempt of our govt. to establish itself on their island."[38] Like Garrison, Sumner was particularly fearful that Grant's play for Santo Domingo was the first step toward further annexation in the Caribbean, and he believed that Haiti, already wracked by instability and war, would be next on Grant's list. In one of the most striking passages of the "Naboth's Vineyard" speech, he explicitly—and misleadingly—compared what he called "the spirit" with which Grant was pressing for Santo Domingo to the Kansas-Nebraska Act and the Lecompton Constitution of the mid-1850s, signal moments in the United States' descent into civil war, "by which it was sought to subjugate a distant Territory to slavery."[39]

The debates over Santo Domingo thus illustrated the complexity of American attitudes toward expansionism during the transitional decade after the Civil War, particularly with regard to culture and race. In striking contrast to figures like Sumner, the brief moment of optimism about the possibilities of emancipation at home actually encouraged African American political activists such as Frederick Douglass to support Pan-American ideals as a way to advance the lives of African Americans in the

United States and elsewhere in the Americas. Despite rejecting arguments in favor of the forcible acquisition of territory, and his opposition to later schemes such as the purchase of a naval base at Môle St. Nicholas in Haiti, Douglass utilized the idea of black Pan-Americanism to support President Grant's policy of annexing the Dominican Republic. There was a range of reasons for Douglass backing Grant, including his loyalty to the Republican Party and to the president personally, because he believed them both to be the champions of African American civil rights at home. Douglass also hoped that control by the United States would improve the lives of Santo Domingo's inhabitants by offering them technological and moral development. This effectively brought him to support American informal imperialism and territorial acquisition predicated on United States exceptionalism, even as he condemned historical and modern forms of European empire. Thus, while he could be deeply critical of British, French, and Spanish imperialism in places such as Ireland, Mexico, and Cuba, Douglass remained convinced that the leadership of the United States in the Americas could unite peoples of different races and bring them up to higher forms of modernity.[40] As he put it in making the case for Santo Domingo, the people there apparently wanted "Saxon and Protestant civilization. They have tried the Latin and Catholic rule, let them have a chance to try free thought and free religious opinions . . . Let us lift them up to our high standard of nationality."[41] As we shall see, he could also take a generous view of European forms of empire if he believed they advanced Western forms of civilization. Douglass was not a lone African American voice in this regard; other activists supported him in taking such views, including the first black member of the United States Congress, Senator Hiram Revels (R–MS).[42]

Fish, however, entertained no such ideals when it came to Cuba. He based his views on racial stereotypes suggesting that the Cuban forces were unable to organize themselves politically, which reinforced his belief that Spanish rule remained the least bad option for the present time. In following this line, the United States government during the 1870s largely accepted Spanish contentions that because of Cuba's racial makeup and history, in Ada Ferrer's words, it "could not be a nation."[43] Perhaps based on his skepticism about the abilities of the Cuban population, Fish was unconvinced about the insurgency's chances of success. In discussions with the president early in the war, Fish thought the Spanish would eventually regain control of the island, claiming the insurgents would fail, because they were "inefficient, & have done little for themselves."[44]

Instead of interfering directly in Cuban affairs, Fish preferred the idea that when Spain eventually did grant it independence, Cuba would have a "guardianship or trusteeship," in other words that it would become a protectorate of the United States.[45] This would take time, however. The first time Grant's cabinet met to consider the Cuba problem, Fish observed that the United States should permit the "madness and fatuity of the Spanish Dominion in Cuba" to continue until other nations would come "to regard the Spanish rule as an international nuisance, which must be abated, when they would all be glad that we should interpose and regulate control of the island."[46] In another irony, however, Fish's notion of guardianship spoke to broader concerns about the racial problems of expansion into the Caribbean: in rejecting annexation of Santo Domingo, Sumner instead suggested some form of protectorate as an alternative.[47]

Pressure for Intervention

Despite—or perhaps because of—Fish's caution, the Grant administration experienced similar domestic pressures over Cuba to those felt by the Lincoln and Johnson governments over Mexico. In the Cuban case, this pressure was primarily aimed at encouraging it to recognize the belligerency. In fact, President Grant was highly sympathetic to the Cuban cause, especially in the early stages of the fighting, and he expressed a belief that the Cubans would succeed, as well as publicly raising expectations that he would help them to do so.[48] Other influential Americans supported him. Long before the war, prominent African American activists such as Martin Delany had seen the challenges of slavery in Cuba as an opportunity for black Cubans to rise up and follow the Haitian path: "Cuba must cease to be a Spanish colony and become a negro government," as he put it at the end of the 1840s.[49] Now within Grant's government, Secretary of War John A. Rawlins, who had close links with the Cuban rebels, and Daniel E. Sickles, U.S. minister to Spain during the first half of the war, both expressed their belief that the Cubans deserved independence and encouraged the president and secretary of state to aid the insurgency in order to achieve this.[50] A lower-ranked official went further. As Grant was taking office, Henry R. de La Reintre, the U.S. vice consul in Havana, resigned his position in protest against Spanish actions toward American citizens and urged Grant to recognize the resistance.[51] Simultaneously, the

THE SPANISH BULL IN CUBA GONE MAD.
It must be stopped. If Spain can't do it, WE MUST!

Figure 3.2 Public pressure on President Ulysses S. Grant and his secretary of state, Hamilton Fish, to take action over the conflict in Cuba was immense, particularly during the *Virginius* episode, when *Harper's* published this cartoon. In Nast's view, the president and secretary of state seem willing to bend to this pressure. In the cartoon, Fish helps Uncle Sam over the fence, and Grant hands him a weapon to fight the bull, while other Americans rush to join the fight.

Source: Thomas Nast, "The Spanish Bull in Cuba Gone Mad," *Harper's Weekly*, November 29, 1873.

House of Representatives was debating a resolution passed down from the Committee on Foreign Affairs noting that the people of the United States were in sympathy with the people of Cuba "in their effort to secure their independence," and would "welcome to the family of independent nations a republican government that guarantees the liberty of all persons." It authorized the president to recognize the independence of Cuba "whenever in his opinion a republican form of government shall have been in fact established." The vote passed on April 9, 1869, by 98 to 25, with representatives from both parties voting in favor.[52]

Grant also received correspondence from U.S. citizens in support of the rebellion, and various groups around the nation passed resolutions favoring the Cuban cause.[53] William Greenleaf Eliot's views on the affair were typical. Greenleaf was an influential minister and president of Washington University in St. Louis, Missouri. In a missive to Grant in early 1873, Eliot acknowledged the difficulties of interfering in another nation's affairs but argued that Cuba was a unique case in the Americas, not just because the island was close to the United States but also because its predicament touched on fundamental issues. Eliot compared Washington's refusal to help Cuba with Britain's nonintervention in Poland's uprising against the Russian Empire in the early 1860s, inverting some of the more positive views that other Americans had of the rule of the tsars. Like the Polish situation, Cuba's was "a struggle of freedom against tyranny," he argued, and, "as a free nation," the United States "ought not to stand coldly looking." He suggested that in Cuba there were "great principles of humanity" at stake, and that if the United States "permit that old oppressor, Spain, to tread down the hopes of freedom in that beautiful land, History will surely punish us for our neglect."[54]

Others wanted the United States to do more than simply aid the insurgents. Looking back on decades of violence from the vantage point of the 1890s, suffrage campaigner Elizabeth Cady Stanton said she had "long felt" that the United States government should intervene when "Spain had proved that she is incompetent to restore order and peace."[55] Other voices echoed Frederick Douglass's in arguing that Caribbean islands should be brought into the Union to improve the lot of their black populations that had struggled under European dominion. Indeed, like Stanton, Douglass himself wanted direct—military if necessary—intervention in Cuba to help "those heroic and noble Cubans, who are now defending the cause which this Society and all America [sic] have sworn to support." In doing so, the

United States could help Cuba achieve what Haiti had done, without its assistance, at the beginning of the century.[56] Writing to President Grant from Kingston, Jamaica, James Hall of Baltimore, Maryland, told the president that he should hold steady on his policy to annex Santo Domingo in order to ensure that the people of the region had access to a system of "free labor, which they do not [have] & cannot enjoy under European rule." Hall complained that, in Jamaica, the English provision of one shilling per day for workers was "barely enough to sustain life," nor was the six quarts of meal and two pounds of meat or fish a week provided for inhabitants of the Danish islands adequate for their needs. The writer thus urged Grant to look for acquisitions across the West Indies "solely for the benefit of the African race in these islands."[57]

Fish understood that the popular mood in the United States was probably in favor of the Cuban rebels and against the Spanish regime, and thus had to convince the Spanish government that Washington was not about to recognize a state of belligerency in Cuba.[58] As he told Lopez Roberts, the Spanish minister in Washington, "the sympathies of large portions of the people of the United States naturally became interested in the struggle to throw off a political connection which had entailed upon Cuba an onerous system of taxation and which had deprived it of its autonomy." The feeling that the insurgents were also struggling for a cause—"the abolition of African slavery"—for which the United States had recently suffered only enhanced the feeling, he said.[59] The ongoing war between Spain and two South American nations, Chile and Peru, further complicated Fish's efforts. The United States could only view this development with mistrust, although it had refused to help republican Chile (Seward had declared that the United States could not become involved in every regional conflict, had no army to take on such a role, and its constitution was "not an imperial one") and instead attempted to mediate in the conflict. Somewhat understandably, Spain was suspicious of this move and treated it as part of an attempt by Washington to assert itself in the Americas, and perhaps to acquire Cuba.[60]

American citizens living in Cuba also faced threats to their lives and property because of the war, another significant factor in relations between Washington and Madrid. While it allowed Grant and Fish to focus directly on misconduct against United States citizens, gaining any kind of recourse proved problematic because of the nature of Spanish rule. As Fish put it to Sickles: "The Spanish authorities in Cuba seem to be [clothed?] with absolute power for the commission of such acts as are now complained of; but when redress is sought, we are referred to the distant Cabinet of Madrid, where it is often found necessary to refer again to Cuba for information; and the case is then suspended and delayed to the grievous injury of the parties."[61]

Resisting Pressure

While Fish recognized that United States commercial interests in Cuba complicated Washington's diplomatic position, he was largely able to resist domestic pressures to take firmer action against Spain and avoid deeper entanglements with the Cuban insurgents by using recent precedents.[62] Although a number of issues dominated his refusal to recognize the rebels, early British, French, and Spanish recognition of the Confederacy during the American Civil War through their declarations of neutrality was the most important. In that instance, declaring neutrality gave effective legitimacy to both sides, thus providing tacit European recognition of the Confederacy, a move that had infuriated Lincoln and Seward. Grant apparently believed that Washington would have been justified in making a declaration along the lines of the one that the Spanish had made at the beginning of the Civil War. However, Fish knew it was very difficult for the United States to contemplate acknowledging the belligerency of the Cuban rebels without being seen as hypocritical.[63] Compounding such concerns, U.S. objections to these actions were a part of the ongoing Alabama Claims arising out of the Civil War, when the British government had allowed the building and outfitting of Confederate vessels in its shipyards. More than this, as Fish explained to the Spanish authorities, he was satisfied with Spain's adherence to

the doctrine that in time of war it is as well the right as the duty of the non combatant powers to maintain a neutral position—a doctrine of which the United States were the earliest, and have remained the most consistent, advocates. In the first stage of their national history, they suffered from the unlawful attempts of other belligerent powers to force them from the neutral attitude which they had the right to maintain. In a later and more trying period, they were injured by the neglect of other powers to preserve their neutrality when they themselves were in a state of war.[64]

Commenting on the House resolution of April 1869, the *New York Times* concurred: "Any plea now presented for acknowledging the Cuban insurrection, or for hastily recognizing any body purporting to be a Government which the insurrection may produce, may be urged with greater force by Great Britain and France in justification of their conduct toward the Confederacy." It suggested that if the House was right to argue for belligerent rights during the present struggle in Cuba, which was "trifling," then the European powers were correct to grant the privileges of belligerency in 1861 to "a rebellion which by comparison was gigantic."[65]

Many Republicans were also sympathetic to Fish's position and particularly worried that the conflict in Cuba could be exacerbated by the involvement of other European powers, perhaps even in concert with one another, if the United States made any kind of intervention of its own. Early in the conflict, Charles Sumner said that he wished "the Cuba question looked clearer, & nearer a solution. Spain must go, & the sooner she sees it the better for all."[66] Still, he thought that recognizing the insurgency "would be a wrong to Spain; therefore I cannot consent to it." Sumner particularly detested the idea that the United States might be drawn into war, although he admitted that this was also because it would divert attention from his goal of wresting Canada from the British, a policy he and others supported as part of the Alabama Claims.[67] He was therefore sympathetic to the Cuban rebels, but repelled by the idea that the United States might actually try to control Cuba as a colony. Instead, he believed that it was the duty of the United States to convince liberals in Spain that "the day of European colonies has passed—at least in this hemisphere" and that Cuba, as well as other Caribbean island nations, would move into the United States' orbit and become protectorates. As with Santo Domingo, he could not countenance the thought of bringing Cubans into the Union.[68] Similarly, future president James A. Garfield argued in the House of Representatives that it was not the moment to "increase our complications with foreign nations." He continued: "I hope our government will be very slow in taking any measures in relation to Cuba, in relation to Spain, in relation to Great Britain and in relation to any other nation with whom we are now at peace to deepen the angry feelings which already exist."[69]

LET US THINK TWICE BEFORE WE LET LOOSE THE DOGS OF WAR.

Figure 3.3 As Nast illustrates in another of his takes on the war, published just two weeks after the previous one, many Americans also urged caution. Here, the female figure of Columbia sits with the eagle of war and the dove of peace, the issues of "Cuban slavery" and "Spanish atrocities" beneath her feet, with the dogs of "Death" and "Destruction" held at bay for now. Behind her are reminders of the legacies of the Civil War in the United States, both economic and human. In the caption, the cartoonist paraphrases Mark Antony in Shakespeare's *Julius Caesar*, echoing, among others, abolitionist William Lloyd Garrison.

Source: Thomas Nast, "Let Us Think Twice Before We Let Loose the Dogs of War," *Harper's Weekly*, December 13, 1873.

The constraints of Reconstruction and its domestic consequences also influenced such attitudes. At the start of the conflict, the *New York Times* had noted that while the idea of incorporating Cuba into the Union might initially be appealing, the domestic question of what to do with the freedmen in the United States demanded far more urgent attention. Moreover, like Sumner and Garfield, the *Times* complained that those who were now giving aid to the insurgency and attempting to persuade them to call for annexation "implie[d] hostility to Spain and its Government." The newspaper saw notable signs that a more liberal government in Spain heralded the prospect of positive reforms: "Instead of plotting and planning for the annexation of Cuba let us wish for it peace and prosperity under the new era which dawns upon it."[70]

Few in positions of authority therefore moved to outline or enforce strict anti-colonial principles. In public, leaders presented their views as part of broader framework that titled toward ideological support for anti-colonial causes but resisted calls to interfere in the affairs of European nations in the Americas, as set out in the Monroe Doctrine. Prefacing comments on Cuba in his first annual message to Congress, for example, Grant (in a passage written by Fish) explained that because the United States was "the freest of all nations," its people sympathized with those who struggled for "liberty and self-government." But such sympathy had its limits, as he noted that "we should abstain from enforcing our views upon unwilling nations and from taking an interested part, *without invitation,* in the quarrels between different nations or between governments and their subjects." Grant further said that the United States had "no disposition to interfere with the existing relations of Spain to her colonial possessions on this continent." The United States, he continued, believed that "in due time Spain and other European powers will find their interest in terminating those relations and establishing their present dependencies as independent powers— members of the families of nations."[71]

Washington would have been pleased to see Spain voluntarily grant independence to the island, but Fish especially believed that pressure to achieve this could not be applied precipitously if it risked alienating such an important European ally and one, moreover, which had helped the fledging United States gain its own independence from a colonial oppressor almost a century before. Norman Graebner suggests that Fish saw the insurgency in Cuba "as an imperial affair, and thus outside the legitimate concerns of American policy." In Fish's words, it was "a purely domestic question . . . [and] the United States have no other right to interpose than that growing out of friendly relations which have always existed between them and Spain . . ."[72] Despite deep divisions in the cabinet, Fish stood firm on this and was even willing to offer his resignation over the issue.[73]

Instead of making any move toward recognizing that a state of war existed in Cuba, the United States government therefore decided that it would "exert its friendly influence" to try to "bring this unhappy strife to a close." Early in Grant's first term, the president authorized the U.S. minister in Madrid, Daniel E. Sickles, to offer the good offices of the United States to the Cabinet in Madrid on the following terms: the independence of Cuba would be acknowledged by Spain; Cuba would pay compensation to Spain in recognition of her interests in the island, although this might be paid in installments; the abolition of slavery in Cuba; and the arrangement of an armistice pending the agreement of terms.[74] In drawing up such an offer, Fish must have been aware of the slim chances of success and he remained skeptical of similar approaches throughout the war.[75] Crucially, however, he refused to renounce the right to recognize a new government if Washington felt it was able to do so.[76]

"Uncivilized" Warfare

Washington's prioritization of diplomatic relations with Madrid continued, despite growing misgivings over Spain's prosecution of the war in Cuba and the success of the rebels there.[77] It quickly became apparent that Spanish forces were willing to employ extreme methods to suppress the rebellion and, to American eyes, the refusal to change course was difficult to understand. The earliest reports suggested that the war was "being waged by the Spaniards in the most cruel manner; the rule being that all persons captured in arms are immediately shot," as *Harper's* magazine put it in 1869.[78] In telegrams to his superiors, Sickles did much to emphasize these vicious tactics, augmenting them with cuttings from Spanish newspapers showing the devastating effects of the government's military policies. The Spanish press reported on the "utmost barbarism" being practiced in the colony as well as the great success that some of the guerilla forces were having against troops. Some journalists and diplomats began speculating that Spain would lose the war, or at least that it would be years before it brought the rebellion under control.[79] Such reports had an impact. Later in the war,

Fish complained that while Spanish diplomats had often acknowledged the oppression—as part of which prisoners were "constantly garroted or shot" and extreme punishments "inflicted on mere suspicion of sympathy with people struggling for liberty"—Madrid had done nothing of any significance to deal with it. As the secretary of state acknowledged, the United States could not ignore this, because of the island's proximity, and so had to press for "a more humane and Christian mode of warfare" there.[80] By the end of 1873, Fish was complaining to the Spanish minister in Washington that because of its actions in Cuba, relations with Spain had become "seriously embarrassing and critical."[81]

In fact, pressure from groups within Spain to attenuate their rule in Cuba was widespread, and successive governments in Madrid attempted to make reforms throughout the conflict. For example, some in the Spanish military offered concessions to those who surrendered—General Arsenio Martínez Campos, whose activities in central Cuba from 1876 combined renewed military vigor with promises of pardons or even money if rebels turned themselves in.[82] This is not to suggest that Spanish conduct in the war was commendable—far from it—but rather that Fish and some of those around him generally did not (perhaps could not) recognize the changes that were taking place. Even after the accession of more liberal regimes in Madrid and, from February 1873, a republican government, Washington apparently saw little moderation in Spain's brutal oppression.[83]

Moreover, and somewhat ironically, Washington could maintain its distance more easily, because the guerrillas were also perpetrators of extreme violence. As Fish summarized in the president's message to the Senate in 1870: "On either side the contest has been conducted, and is still carried on, with a lamentable disregard of human life and of the rules and practices which modern civilization has prescribed in mitigation of the necessary horrors of war. The torch of Spaniard and of Cuban is alike busy in carrying devastation over fertile regions; murderous and revengeful decrees are issued and executed by both parties."[84] In part, both Fish and Grant objected to these practices, because they threatened U.S. economic interests on the island and the well-being of many United States citizens who lived there.[85] But these comments were also significant in that they outlined a set of norms and standards to which "civilized" nations were supposed to conform and which both the imperialists and aspiring republicans had failed to do.[86] Thus, the terrible measures the insurgents were taking against Spanish forces suited

Fish to an extent, because they relieved pressure on him to favor one side over another.[87]

The perceived inability of the Cuban forces to organize themselves politically played into the racial stereotypes that dominated perceptions of the islanders in the United States, and reinforced a belief that Spanish rule remained the least bad option for the present time. The Spanish military force was superior to that of the insurgency in almost every respect, and Spanish troops continually held almost every major port and town. The rebels were thus restricted to forests and mountains, relying on destroying the economic infrastructure of the Spanish forces and their supporters to achieve their ends.[88] Therefore, the administration's public position was always that the rebellion had not proved sufficiently advanced to establish a government, so the United States could not recognize Cuban independence or even that a state of war existed.[89] As President Grant summarized in a special message to Congress of June 1870 (written, of course, by Fish), neither side seemed likely to win, and therefore it was very difficult for the United States to declare for one or the other. The American people were naturally sympathetic to those were struggling for "liberty and self-government," he said, but it seemed unlikely that they would be in a position to triumph at any point soon.[90] In private, Fish was even starker in saying that any recognition of Cuban independence by the United States "would really be a stultification of ourselves and a falsification of facts."[91] Charles Sumner agreed that there was "nothing to justify this great concession to insurgent Cubans" when they had "not reached that point of reasonable certainty for the present & future, which alone can justify such a step on our part, unless we accept the hazards of war with Spain." Sumner claimed that he wanted only two things for Cuba: "(1) Independence & (2) Emancipation." Both, he said, would come "very soon." Yet, he wondered, "why should we assume needless responsibilities of money or arms?"[92]

The Grant administration also urged the Spanish government to move toward what Fish called "efficient and practical" abolition of slavery on Cuba.[93] This was certainly a delicate enterprise. The end of slavery at home meant that the United States government felt bolder about asserting its moral authority to propose abolition to Madrid.[94] However, from the late 1860s, the main impetus for a closer association with Cuba came increasingly from radical Republicans such as Nathaniel P. Banks, Orville Babcock, and Benjamin Butler. They saw abolition as an achievable outcome of the Cuban struggle and even suggested going to war with Spain in order to achieve it.[95] Furthermore, emancipation in the United States encouraged Cuban reformers to seek a closer association with the United States, perhaps even annexation to rid the island of slavery.[96] This gave Fish cause to worry that any statement the president made could be seized upon by those in the United States who supported recognition of the belligerency, and thus allow the nation to "drift" into war.[97] Yet, many moderate Republicans remained resistant to anything that would bring Cuba closer. Certainly the history of filibustering being so intimately associated with Democrats and slavery was a factor, but Fish's view of the Cubans' abilities were far from unique, and the problem of imposing any solution on Spain without seriously jeopardizing relations remained.

Perhaps because he did not know about them, Fish also largely failed to acknowledge the tentative steps that Spain was taking toward abolition, as well as the effects these changes were having on the ground. As Rebecca Scott has shown, very gradual emancipation began during the Ten Years' War, a highly complex and challenging process. From early in the war, the insurgency in some parts of the country, especially in the east, where they were doing the majority of the fighting, encouraged what Scott labels "nominal" abolition that saw some slaves freeing themselves and fighting for independence. These developments placed pressure on the metropolitan center and, in response, the Spanish Cortes introduced the so-called Moret Law of 1870, which gave freedom to very young and old slaves, but also held out the promise of emancipation to others, thus changing the parameters of the debate about slavery and offering the possibility of ending it. Such moves were certainly limited, because, as Christopher Schmidt-Nowara argues, planters resisted such reforms and so slavery largely continued as before, but these attempts were largely lost on Washington.[98] Caleb Cushing lamented that he could do little regarding reform in Cuba, for example, because no Spanish leader was politically strong enough to make sufficient concessions.[99] "Thus far all the efforts of Spain have proved abortive," stated Grant in the section of his 1875 address, "and time has marked no improvement in the situation."[100]

The Grant administration followed this line and, sometimes in conjunction with the British, urged Spain to reform and particularly to move toward abolition.[101] How serious it was about this remains open to debate, however. Philip Foner has argued that Fish did so little to press the Spanish that successive governments in Madrid knew they only needed to make minor concessions, such as ending slavery in Puerto Rico, where it was not particularly widespread anyway, while maintaining the prospect that they would push for abolition in Cuba in the future.[102] Certainly, many Cuban reformists were relatively conservative, and, if the U.S. government had so wished, they could have tapped into a movement that sought to effect social change and develop a version of Cuban autonomy along the lines of the dominion of Canada, rather than annexation by the United States.[103] However, throughout the war, Washington confined most of its diplomatic pressure to political rhetoric with the occasional volley of dispatches to the U.S. minister in Spain. By the time of Grant's 1875 message to Congress, the president and secretary of state had to acknowledge the effective failure of their approach. In the message, Grant covered broad and familiar themes, namely that he had hoped "Spain would be enabled to establish peace in her colony, to afford security to the property and the interests of our citizens, and allow legitimate scope to trade and commerce and the natural productions of the island." Because of this, "and from an extreme reluctance to interfere in the most remote manner in the affairs of another and a friendly nation, especially of one whose sympathy and friendship in the struggling infancy of our own existence must ever be remembered with gratitude," he had "patiently and anxiously waited the progress of events." Grant also noted that the U.S. Civil War was "too recent for us not to consider the difficulties which surround a government distracted by a dynastic rebellion at home at the same time that it has to cope with a separate insurrection in a distant colony."[104] The president then introduced a major multilateral initiative to involve the European powers in the conflict, a significant shift in policy representing complex and competing pressures, while Fish's State Department attempted to inaugurate a coalition of nations to persuade Spain to end the war.[105]

The Grant administration's determination to be seen as even-handed ultimately only served to benefit Spain, and even give the impression that Washington supported continued Spanish rule in its colony. As the United States was emerging as the most powerful nation in the Americas, its actions could have profound effects on both sides. Recognizing the Cuban rebels as belligerents would have given them access to resources that were previously unavailable, most notably shipments of arms from the United States, as well as holding out the possibility of eventual diplomatic recognition, and perhaps hastening the end of slavery. Yet, the stance that the Grant administration took—namely, holding off on recognition until there was a stable form of government, a highly unlikely proposition—had the effect of backing Spain, which was abusing its authority in a way the U.S. government apparently found abhorrent and contrary to its guiding principles in international affairs. Moreover, as Foner points out, for the rebels to reach a position where the U.S. government considered recognition would have involved them changing a strategy that was proving to be reasonably successful in disrupting Spanish colonial rule and its ability to wage war.[106]

It seems that Fish went as far as he could to dampen support for the Cuban insurgents. In January 1870, he even planted a story in the *New York Herald* saying that the rebellion was effectively over, although he knew that this was definitely not the case, to try to reduce the clamor for recognition.[107] Two years later, a ship, the *Pioneer*, arrived in Rhode Island with its captain claiming to represent the Cuban navy and requesting official recognition from the secretary of state.[108] Fish demurred, declaring that he could not officially receive him, even as a private citizen, a line he held despite the captain's appeal to the precedent of the American Revolution, when France recognized the independence of the United States while other countries did not. Grant, under the influence of Fish, was also clear that Spain was "a nation with whom the United States are at peace" and so gave the marshal of the District of Rhode Island permission to take possession of the vessel. In response, the captain complained of a conspiracy between the United States and Spain.[109]

Even the *Virginius* affair, with its mass executions and domestic uproar, failed to produce any meaningful change in the U.S. government's attitude toward Spanish colonial rule.[110] Washington may have been distracted by the burgeoning domestic economic crisis brought about by bank failures and the bankruptcies of numerous railroad companies, resulting in a depression that would be felt for the rest of the decade.[111] But it certainly did nothing to encourage Americans to think differently about the Cuban people: "We do not want Cuba with her ignorant population of Negroes, mulattos . . . alien to our population," as William Cullen Bryant, editor of *New York Evening Post*, told a no doubt sympathetic Fish at the height of the crisis.[112] While the Grant administration seemed to be moving toward a position where it might actually recognize the insurgents, it refused to press even for the abolition of slavery or the independence of Cuba as part of its claims over the *Virginius*. Therefore, despite its prominence in Spanish-American relations during this period, the incident had little impact on the broader parameters of Grant and Fish's Cuban policy.

In addition to racial prejudice, Richard Bradford suggests that a number of different factors, including the lack of public and political desire for war, an uninfluential press, and the relatively poor state of U.S. forces following the end of the Civil War all helped to prevent a declaration of war on Spain. Racial attitudes were of particular importance, he argues, because of the dim view Fish and his colleagues still took of the black population in Cuba, and the deep divisions in the United States over issues of race following the conclusion of the Civil War. The *Virginius* affair also led to the removal from office of Daniel E. Sickles, the ambassador to Madrid, primarily because of his attempt to steer the United States toward war with Spain through his aggressive diplomacy.

It was significant that his replacement, the moderate Caleb Cushing, reinforced Fish's racial views. Cushing complained to Fish, for example, that the rebels could "produce no man of commanding military talent," because "otherwise they would find something better to do than merely to burn and murder, and would be commanded by Cubans, not by Dominicans and Mexicans."[113] On another occasion, he claimed that there was a greater threat to the Creoles than to Spain in Cuba, because the insurgency sought to eliminate the white race there. He drew parallels with the Haitian revolution at the turn of the previous century, and suggested that the current state of affairs promised "to carry Cuba for generations to come into the same series of military usurpations, sanguinary civil wars, [and] sterile revolutions, with their accompanying barbarism, which have characterized independent Hayti."[114]

Bradford also notes the importance of relations with Spain, in particular because at the time of the incident Spain was a republic, and the U.S. government saw this as a potentially more liberal regime that chimed with American values and held out the possibility of reform in the colonies.[115] More than this, influential public figures such as Sumner, Schurz, and Oliver P. Morton continued to urge caution and emphasized their respect for Spain.[116] Even reformer William Lloyd Garrison complained about the press in the United States drumming up war fever, "crying 'havoc,' to 'let slip the dogs of war.'" Garrison was extremely sympathetic to the republican government in Madrid, calling its president a "sublime genius" who would deal with the mess in Cuba in good time and eventually end slavery there. Garrison could see little evidence that the *Virginius* affair was an insult when so many people from the United States had interfered in Cuba affairs, either to promote slavery there before the Civil War or now, supposedly, to abolish it. He expressed skepticism about the insurgents' purported aims to emancipate Cuba, based on their violent methods and willingness to foment anti-Spanish sentiment in the United States. Spanish-American relations had been "shamefully violated again and again," he concluded, "and it will require no little 'cheek' on the part of our Government to call Spain to account for anything pertaining to the Cuban imbroglio."[117] It therefore did not change U.S. attitudes toward either the Spanish colonial regime or those who were fighting against it. Furthermore, in coming to such conclusions about the supposed inability of Caribbean peoples to look after themselves, Fish, Cushing, and others were, ironically, reinscribing arguments made by slaveholders from the south. From her new home in Cuba on the eve of the Ten Years' War, former Louisiana slaveholder Eliza McHatton wrote to her sister: "The more we see of the Cuban character, the more convinced we are that a military government is what they need. They are totally unfit for freedom & the pusillanimous puppies will never have it unless some strong nation fights for it, for them."[118]

By 1876, both sides in the Cuban struggle had come to recognize that neither could win outright victory. The war had been a debilitating experience, with tens, perhaps hundreds, of thousands of casualties and little sign of a conclusion. As a result, tentative negotiations began. These coincided with the presidential election in the United States, which turned out to be one of the most controversial and disputed in United States history. Madrid considered the eventual winner, Rutherford B. Hayes, a fortuitous choice, because it believed he was better disposed toward Spain than his opponent, Samuel Tilden, who drew more support from the Southern states. By early 1878, enough rebels had been convinced they should end their struggle that they agreed to sign the Pact of Zanjón. Although it brought peace, it really represented something of a hiatus in the struggle and did little to change relations between the United States and Spain; indeed, in some ways it exacerbated tensions, because the number of American claims against Spain arising from the war increased.[119] But American attitudes toward Spanish rule in Cuba largely remained the same.

Conclusion

As during the Mexico intervention, Washington felt there was relatively little—diplomatically at least—that it could do about the war in Cuba.

Despite Spain's terrible treatment of the Cuban population, Washington had to maintain strong links with Madrid, because its material capabilities were not sufficient for it to do otherwise. The stakes were somewhat different to the Mexican episode in that Spain had been established in Cuba for centuries and so, however unpalatable this was, there was no possibility of raising the issue of the Monroe Doctrine in response. Although Washington was concerned about the prospect of another major power stepping into the turmoil and gaining control—formal or informal—of Cuba if Spanish rule collapsed, it was also difficult to envision it being able to take action to prevent this. During the continuing social and political turmoil of the Civil War and Reconstruction, the United States could therefore offer little to induce Spain to follow its preferred course of reform leading to independence for Cuba.

The great sympathy many Americans felt for the island's population in effect meant little, because, regardless of the United States' material condition, Hamilton Fish refused to countenance the possibility of U.S. involvement in the Cuban cause. What was striking about the episode was the remarkable consistency with which the Grant administration stuck to its course of neutrality. The secretary of state maintained the possibility of recognizing an independent Cuba, but acquiesced to Spanish rule for the foreseeable future. While he may have held out hope for a favorable solution, the fact that the war persisted for so long appeared to give him little cause for doubt. It seems that the racial predisposition of Fish against the Cuban population allowed him to rationalize a policy that appeared to be at odds with the administration's declared objectives and the will of many Americans. While this might not seem remarkable, it is striking that many others in Washington accepted the continued subjugation of Cuba to Spain if it meant that Cuba remained outside of the United States but the possibility was kept open for U.S. protection or even domination of the island in the longer term. Such views were often grounded in deeply racists attitudes. The 1870s thus proved a transitional decade in American thoughts on empire and imperialism in the hemisphere as the United States contemplated, but generally did not act on, interventionist impulses, preferring to see the maintenance of the status quo. This would begin to change over the next two decades as the government drew on more imperialist ideas and language to justify its decisions and moved toward some more assertive forms of foreign policy, including military intervention and deeper engagement with the imperial powers.

This did not mean that it was not assertive in the 1870s. Perhaps most obviously, Fish had sent a naval expedition to Korea in 1871 seeking to ensure the protection of American citizens in the region and possibly open it up for trade. Ultimately, this party attacked fortifications on the Yomha River and slaughtered hundreds of Korean defenders. Among other things, this terrible episode was a signifier of an American belief system that placed the United States alongside the European imperial powers, ideologically pitting them against what they considered to be the "uncivilized" regions of the world. This was based on racial and cultural assumptions about the inhabitants of these areas. In the case of Korea, the reticence of officials there to engage with American military and diplomatic representatives reinforced this sense of difference, as did the tenacious and ultimately futile way the Koreans fought. Echoing some of the ways observers in the United States discussed the nature of combat between the Cubans and Spanish, the Koreans' violent response to being attacked confirmed contrasts between "Anglo-Saxons" and others (in this case, "Orientals") that was cohering at home and leading to growing anti-immigration sentiment there.[120]

It is striking that the 1871 Korean conflict took place far from the United States. This was indicative of a broadening of American horizons, and the very distance allowed more freedom of action. The violence gained some press coverage in the United States, which generated an amount of dissent as well as celebration there. But this military action was of little significance or controversy to most Americans when compared to the protracted warfare taking place so close to the U.S. mainland. Fish could have contemplated no similar action in Cuba even if he had wanted to do so.

As the Cuban episode demonstrated, the United States was still not consistently assertive on the world stage, but Washington's responses to the processes of global empires bolstered its traditional stance of opposition to formal colonialism alongside its sense of self-awareness as an international power. In regard to the latter, the Mexican and Cuban episodes starkly illustrated the growing challenges of what became known as the "new imperialism" around the world, in which the European powers asserted their claims to control and administer foreign territories. Increasingly, this centered on Africa. One of the most striking examples of this in the years that followed the end of the Ten Years' War concerned the United States' former colonial master, Great Britain, and its Near Eastern and North African interests in Egypt.

CHAPTER IV

Britain and the Occupation of Egypt

I n 1882, protracted violence erupted on the streets of Alexandria. On June 11, Egyptians—including police and soldiers—commenced what the *New York Times* described as "the burning and sacking" of the city and "the brutal massacre of the Christians who were left within its walls."[1] The authorities could not establish exactly how the riots began: there were rumors they were sparked by a disagreement between a Maltese trader and a boy with a donkey, while another account said there had been a break-in at the shop of a European merchant. The cause or causes remained—and remain—unknown, but large numbers were killed: at least fifty Europeans and probably many more Egyptians who were the subject of European reprisals.

By early July, the situation in the city had become critical. Tensions brought about by the riots were exacerbated by the presence in the harbor of a British naval squadron, which had begun arriving in May and now comprised some fifteen vessels, including eight powerful ironclads. Egyptian rebels had begun building up coastal defenses against potential attack, and, as the days went by, the British government tested their resolve. The commander of the Royal Navy force, Admiral Beauchamp Seymour, made it clear to the military commandant of Alexandria that if Egyptian forces resisted British passage into the harbor, then he would have no option but to attack. While the commandant sought to reassure Seymour that Egypt's military preparations were purely defensive—and indeed they were not a direct threat to the admiral's ships at all—Seymour was apparently unconvinced. He and his superiors in London had decided to make war.

At 7 a.m. on July 11, a single shell from HMS *Alexandra* gave the signal to the other vessels, the start of a planned two-wave assault from both inside and outside the confines of the harbor. Over the course of the next few hours, British ships and Egyptian forts exchanged fire in a devastating display. Massively outgunned, the Egyptians fought on as the British launched wave after wave of attack. The morning air was so still that the smoke from the British cannons hung in the air, and so, despite their numerous advantages, the ships struggled to direct their fire. Thus, a combination of luck and fortitude meant that the Egyptians were able to defend their forts— making tactical retreats before returning to their posts to reopen fire— for longer than the British expected.

By early afternoon, the relentless British bombardment was beginning to take its toll as more and more Egyptian guns on the shore fell silent. While sporadic fighting went on throughout the evening and into the next day, the result was no longer in doubt, if indeed it had ever been. The Egyptians had fought determinedly and lost hundreds, including civilians, with hundreds more wounded, while the Royal Navy counted thirty-three casualties, only five of whom died. Meanwhile, fires spread across the city of Alexandria and burned for days afterwards, mostly in the European quarter. An American soldier on the scene visited the shattered forts shortly afterward and saw dead soldiers still under the cannons. In the city itself, he found the hospital had just three doctors desperately trying to treat the wounded and dying, many of whom were lying on hard stone floors.[2] Observing the scene some months later, an American Pentecostal minister compared it to Liberty Square in Boston after the terrible fire that had destroyed it ten years before. The fortifications built by the Egyptians were "all banged to pieces," and their guns were "standing on their heads." "[There] must have been some wonderful firing on the Englishmen's part," he said.[3]

This bloodshed effectively marked the end of a movement against foreign domination in Egypt led by the minister of war, Colonel Ahmed Urabi.[4] An officer who, unusually, had risen from the peasant classes, Urabi resented that so many high-level positions in Egyptian public life went to foreign-born people, and thus not to Egyptians who struggled to break free from a restrictive class system. As war minister in the government of Mohammed Tewfik Pasha, Urabi was hugely influential and pressed for political and social reform while leading the rebellion against Britain.

The British military action against Urabi's revolt also marked the culmination of one period of European interference in Egypt and the beginning of another. Egypt was part of the Ottoman Empire, but had gained semiautonomous status as a vassal state, or khedivate, in the mid-nineteenth century. During the 1870s, the powers of Europe had steadily gained influence at the expense of Egypt's nominal Ottoman rulers as its debts grew. Especially significant was the Franco-British acquisition of the Suez Canal, the vital artery built by the French and opened in 1869, which provided access to Asia and political influence in North Africa. The British government's purchase of a controlling share in the canal in 1875 further deepened its Egyptian interests.[5] Egypt served as the gateway between Europe and Asia, and Britain's military intervention was as much to ensure continued access to the Indian subcontinent as it was to protect its burgeoning private commercial and philanthropic interests in Egypt itself.[6] Following its military action in 1882, London moved toward unilateral control of Egyptian affairs—sometimes by stealth and often at the expense of nascent Egyptian nationalism—mirroring some of the bureaucratic institutions they had developed in India.[7] This unusual form of governance that one scholar has called "hesitant imperialism" lasted for decades, but Britain would never officially rule Egypt.[8] The intervention was also part of a broader reorientation of European colonialism during the 1870s and 1880s. This process saw mid-Victorian "informal" imperialism, in which powers sought to control regions and trade routes through commerce, shift toward greater military and bureaucratic interventionism, most notably in Africa. Some have even suggested that the Egyptian episode set off the so-called Scramble for Africa, in which the major nations of Europe fought each other for control of much of the African continent in the late nineteenth century.[9]

Political leaders in the United States stood apart from these developments, even as violence erupted in Egypt.[10] At least in part, this stance can be attributed to the American belief that the Mediterranean and Africa were regions of European concern. Relations between Washington and Constantinople, then the capital of the Ottoman Empire, remained relatively muted and sometimes poor, marked particularly by a tense diplomatic standoff over the killing of two American missionaries in 1883. Yet, studying responses to the unrest in Egypt reveals a strand of American thinking that is only recently being excavated in relation to this period: the influence of non-state actors, or at least those who were on the periphery of the state. In this chapter, many of these actors were in the United States consular service, which regulated the flow of trade and people outside of the diplomatic system. As Nicole Phelps has recently noted, members of the consular service in places such as the Ottoman Empire relied on European imperial partners to maintain a dominant position and advance the nation's commercial interests.[11] In observing the views of consular officials and others who were enmeshed in policy and practice but not at the center of them, we can get a sense of the emerging sense of American power and the prospects of empire.

In contrast to Washington's relative indifference, some United States citizens were also keen observers of Egypt. Americans were fascinated not just because it was distant, exotic, and troubled, but because it was home to the Suez Canal, a technical marvel that offered a model for the long-held dream of a similar waterway in the Americas. Moreover, the bombardment of Alexandria elicited much editorial comment. Some condemned the brutal attack, conducted as it was by an empire Americans usually regarded as being more benign than that of Spain or France, although others saw Britain's actions as a necessary response to a rebellious mob.

American elites also took great interest in what followed as the British extended their influence into more areas of Egyptian life. While many commentators adopted a critical attitude to these developments, historians have noted that the limited bureaucratic structures of the British protectorate in Egypt would also stand as a model for American empire builders after 1898.[12] Writing as the United States stood on the cusp of these colonial ventures, a prominent American commercial agent in the Congo, Richard Dorsey Mohun, viewed British rule in Egypt and elsewhere, which was advancing so rapidly, with some considerable admiration. Despite taking charge of troubled and sometimes anarchic areas, the British, he believed, had been nonetheless quite successful in developing the region's resources and in bringing order. "Her possessions are never encumbered with large numbers of military and civil officials," he said, "and she does everything in her power to foster and develop trade on strict lines of partiality to none."[13]

British imperialism was thus becoming a more acceptable model for the United States to consider and observe in relation to its own power. This was based on a number of different factors, including a strengthening of the notion of Anglo-American brotherhood, improving diplomatic relations, and converging global interests. It was also predicated on declining Anglophobic sentiment among some sectors of the American population amid a growing sense of "Anglo-Saxon" racial superiority.

The relative influence and reach of the British Empire did sometimes cause Americans to hesitate about the prospects for U.S. power, but it also motivated those who sought to exploit that power. As Elizabeth Kelly Gray has shown in her study of American antebellum literature and as Frank Ninkovich has argued in his account of post–Civil War periodical culture, a growing literary public, including some assertive policymakers, paid particular attention to developments in the British Empire, which appeared to serve as both an example and a warning to the United States.[14] During the 1880s the United States still did not have an overseas empire of its own, yet for influential Americans the experiences of the British Empire often provided useful insights, albeit sometimes negative ones.

Britain and Its Empire

In the decades that followed the Civil War, the turbulence of wartime diplomacy gave way to a quarter century in which no great issues troubled relations between the United States and Great Britain. From the settling of the Alabama Claims in 1871 to the mid-1890s, a growing understanding saw diplomatic accommodation rather than the threat of conflict. These were, in the words of one scholar, "the Quiet Years" of nineteenth-century Anglo-American diplomacy,[15] and the beginning of the so-called Great Rapprochement before the First World War.[16]

The generally conservative approach of successive U.S. secretaries of state undoubtedly helped this. To a greater or lesser degree, the tenures of Hamilton Fish (discussed in chapter 3), William M. Evarts, who served under President Rutherford B. Hayes, and President Chester Arthur's appointee, Frederick T. Frelinghuysen, all emphasized United States expansion while avoiding antagonizing the great powers. The exception to this was Anglophobic firebrand James G. Blaine, whom President James Garfield appointed and whose short term ended when Arthur replaced him with the patrician conservative Frelinghuysen after Garfield's death in late 1881. Frelinghuysen had previously turned down Ulysses Grant's offer to serve as the minister at the court of St. James in 1870, supposedly because he did not believe he was well suited to dealing with the complexities of Anglo-American relations at such a delicate time.[17] Although his plodding diplomacy as secretary of state may have frustrated many members of the United States Congress, it smoothed relations with London during potentially turbulent episodes, such as the arrest of Americans in Ireland agitating against British rule there, and Washington's effective abrogation of the 1850 Clayton-Bulwer Treaty concerning the building of an isthmian canal in the Americas.[18] As scholars have pointed out, it also signaled a growing assertion of U.S. power based on a sense of internationalism and the need for trade.[19] This meant that by the 1880s the U.S. diplomacy was gaining a "wider acceptance and a more influential hearing" in Britain, as Washington came to be seen to be more traditionalist in its foreign policy, and certainly more than it had been in the period before the Civil War, when the British believed that slavery was the driving force behind much of its diplomacy.[20]

While there remained something of an instinctive, popular Anglophobia in the United States, Stephen Tuffnell has convincingly argued that much of this was for the purposes of domestic consumption, as opposition to Britain united disparate groups and helped define United States nationalism more distinctly. Tuffnell notes that even James Blaine moderated his views as he faced the practicalities of foreign policymaking.[21] Americans' suspicions of the effects of British power on the United States as well as the differences between the British and American political systems were therefore offset by a growing sense of commonality brought about by the end of slavery in the United States and political reform in Great Britain that meant, as one American editor put it at the time, that Britain was "nearly as much entitled to be called a republic as she ever will be."[22] In particular, many American journalists and politicians appreciated British Liberal leader William E. Gladstone, whose zeal for reform contrasted with the increasingly murky world of American pork barrel politics.[23]

Although attitudes toward Gladstone's liberal social reforms garnered near universal praise, commentators were generally more guarded about his economic policies. Certainly, a group of enthusiastic free traders in the United States looked to their British counterparts for inspiration. Led by New England economist Edward Atkinson, who became best known for his anti-imperialist activities after 1898, they consistently promoted tariff reform by building links with English allies and they lobbied American political elites, including Hamilton Fish and Frederick Frelinghuysen, to do so.[24] Despite such efforts, however, most members of the Republican Party, including successive secretaries of state, broadly continued to support high tariffs, which they believed protected American farmers and manufacturers. British free trade policies were therefore generally seen as damaging to the United States as well as to the international economy, and at their most extreme as a form of imperialism imposed on the United States to limit its regional expansion, an argument made most prominently by historian and politician Henry Cabot Lodge.[25] Others were less severe but nonetheless unsure that free trade was the panacea its advocates claimed. In 1881, the *New York Tribune* referred to reports in the British press "that British manufacturers are declining, and that foreigners are competing successfully, even in the English markets, in consequence of the system of free trade." Noting that the United States was now in a highly advantageous position because it had paid off almost all of its Civil War debts, it suggested that England was "by no means in the same hopeful condition." Although the newspaper acknowledged that free trade had had some benefits, it believed the system had been "pressed too far."[26]

Americans had had mixed feelings about the international policies of Gladstone's predecessor, Benjamin Disraeli, the Earl of Beaconsfield. While some admired his robust approach to foreign affairs, this view was far from universal and there was often open hostility to him.[27] Disraeli's aggressive approach during his second administration in the 1870s had seen him give Queen Victoria the title "empress of India" and oversee a major war in Afghanistan. This coincided with a global drought and subsequent devastating famine across large parts of the globe that British imperial policies only exacerbated.[28] Disraeli's reputation therefore came to be that of the arch-imperialist, and Americans were resistant to praise such actions or associate too closely with them. "For God's sake let us avoid the imperial diplomacy of Beaconsfield," Vermont senator Justin S. Morrill implored James Garfield in reaction to renewed calls for the United States to intervene in Cuba in the wake of the Ten Years' War. "It is enough to be President of the U.S. without being Emperor of Cuba."[29]

Of particular importance to understanding the British Empire— although appearing the year after the Egyptian intervention—was the publication of *The Expansion of England* (1883), a popular bestseller by Cambridge professor John Robert Seeley. For American readers, there was much to admire in Seeley's thesis that British expansionism in the white settler colonies had been a "natural" process. While Seeley claimed he did not subscribe to the school of thought that deified the British Empire, he regarded most of its growth as "a mere normal extension of the English race into other lands, which for the most part were so thinly peopled that our settlers took possession of them without conquest." Seeley urged his readers not to think of it as an empire at all, but rather "a very large state" that he called "Greater Britain."[30] While this may have had some appeal to Americans seeing the "natural" expansion of the United States across continental North America, others urged caution. A review of the book in the *Atlantic Monthly* stated that although a "federation of separated countries may be possible in a Greater Britain," there was no direct parallel with the integration of territory in the United States. Such a federation of states in a "Greater Britain" could not, in the long term, prevent "the perfect autonomy of Australia or Canada."[31] This mirrored the thoughts of many others who believed that the British Empire was under strain around the world and could not continue indefinitely, at least in its present forms and especially in the white settler colonies. This was, presumably, in contrast to the United States, which ensured the continued vitality of the nation by incorporating new territories.

Suffrage campaigner Victoria Woodhull was concerned that decline was evident in both the British and American empires. Woodhull's concern for female equality and understanding of some of the connections between the treatment of blacks and women nonetheless evinced increasingly racist views. By the time she moved to Britain in the 1880s, she had developed a fierce outlook predicated on readings of Charles Darwin's *On the Origin of Species* (1859) and later work by Francis Dalton on eugenics. In an 1891 essay entitled "The Rapid Multiplication of the Unfit," Woodhull set out her thinking on the population growth of people of different classes and races, suggesting not only that the "right-minded" married too late and did not have enough children, but also that races that were "lower in the scale of development" were growing so quickly that they would soon take over the "more advanced races." Here, she drew attention to what she saw as the burgeoning black population in the United States, which, she believed, would soon "outnumber and overrun the whites if the rapid increase be not checked." She also feared that the Indian and Chinese were producing "vast hordes" that could soon "overrun and wipe out Western civilization."[32] Somewhat similarly, Elizabeth Cady Stanton increasingly praised Anglo-Saxon values that she saw in white Americans, in contrast to the growing immigrant communities in major U.S. cities.[33]

As this suggests, many whites like Seeley, Woodhull, and Stanton believed in the innate superiority of the Anglo-Saxon people, and thus often appreciated what they perceived to be the civilizing processes evident in British imperial rule. Surveying the international scene at the time of the British invasion of Egypt, Charles Dudley Warner—who ten years earlier had coauthored with Mark Twain the book that gave a name to the Gilded Age—saw in Britain's growth the rise of a benign giant. The "small, originally infertile island," as he called it, had become the most powerful influence on the globe. It was now comparable only to Rome in ancient times, and even this did not do it justice, because Rome's was "an empire of Barbarians," whereas the "marvelous achievements of England" had been attained in competition with the empires of Spain, Portugal, and others. Britain now stood at the center of the "solid civilization" of the world, he said.[34] Many American elites increasingly felt part of this world and, in historian Frank Ninkovich's words, "basked in the reflected glory of the Anglo-Saxon civilizing mission as expressed in the success of the settler colonies."[35]

Evidence for this could be seen in the publication of theologian Josiah Strong's *Our Country* in 1886.[36] A Midwesterner and Congregational minister, Strong saw the traits of Christian Anglo-Saxonism as the most potent of any people. This was not only because these people were the godliest, but also because, in contrast to Woodhull, he believed they were the most rapidly growing. As he noted, most Anglo-Saxons now lived outside of Great Britain, in its other colonies and in the United States, and it was in the latter that they were expanding most quickly. They were therefore in a unique position, never before known in the world, having "the greatest numbers, *and* the highest civilization," alongside an instinct for colonization. Strong also drew different lessons from the emergence of social Darwinism. With the United States benefiting from the results of "natural selection" and "survival of the fittest"—improving its people's mental and physical conditions while also becoming enormously wealthy—it was, he thought, soon bound to dominate the earth. "If I read not amiss, this powerful race will move down upon Mexico, down upon Central and South America, out upon the islands of the sea, over upon Africa and beyond," he concluded.[37]

Even campaigners for black rights like Frederick Douglass could claim that British imperial policies needed to be set in context in order for Americans to understand them. Douglass may have been suspicious of claims about the United States' "Anglo-Saxon" heritage, but he adopted some of the same language in thinking about the British contribution to global civilization. Here, Great Britain's leading role in promoting abolition of the slave trade and then slavery had given it a particular claim. Douglass had visited Britain after gaining his freedom and "tasted the sweets of liberty" that were denied to him in the United States. And while many Americans scoffed at the very idea of Britain being *Great*, Douglass thought the name well deserved:

Great Britain is great in fact as well as in name. She is great in her knowledge, great in her industry, great in her civil and social order, great in her wealth, her power, her progress and her prestige. She is great in her men, than whom no nations has raised up greater. In respect to territory she is simply magnificent . . . the sun never sets on her dominions, and her drum beat is heard all round the world . . . none stand in advance of her, in mental, moral and human civilization. We may not approve her rule in Asia, or Ireland; we may not approve her haughty self-assertion, or her grasping ambition, encompassing sea and land; we may deplore and detest her wars in Africa and Egypt, and declare that she has no business in either, and yet we can never forget or cease to applaud her rich contribution to the cause of justice and philanthropy wherever she has established her dominion. In this, her example is high, noble and grand.[38]

The growing connections people saw between Britain and the United States were thus due not only to a shared history but also to similar patterns of growth and development that these elites believed spread democracy and civilization over vast areas to the benefit of their populations.[39] Calling Great Britain the "nursery" of the Anglo-Saxons, journalist J. E. Chamberlain suggested that the strength of this race was its ability to adapt to diverse conditions without changing its essential character. The United States was clearly the heir to this British legacy, he suggested, because "the history of the United States is but the history of the acquisitions of England over again." The difference between the two, however, was that the United States had "improved on the original." He proudly noted that while the British had been unable to "Anglo-Saxonize" Ireland, the United States had successfully done so in California, Louisiana, and Texas.[40] Historian Eben Greenough Scott talked similarly of an "Anglican notion of a colony" in which a group of people occupied a new territory containing "all the germs of a future state" that would grow while retaining "all the characteristics of the original stock, modified only by the new conditions of existence." This racially charged definition also set the British model against that of other imperial nations, in this case the French, which did "not conform to its requirements." After the disastrous Mexican expedition under Napoleon III, the French Third Republic's reinvigorated colonial policy saw it acquire new territories in the Pacific, West Africa, and Indochina in the 1880s, piquing significant American interest.[41] Yet, according to Scott, French imperialism was still built on weak foundations, because its focus was military occupation rather than civilian government—ultimately, it seemed, because it did not have "fixity of governmental principles" to bestow upon the colonial population.[42]

Not all could be so sanguine about British rule, however, especially when considering conditions outside of the settler colonies. India was a particular source of fascination and sometimes repugnance—both of India itself and British rule there. Although the small number of Americans in India generally sided with the British in their view that Indians were unfit for self-government, many back home had been appalled at the immense cruelty meted out by the British during the rebellion of 1857, when Indian soldiers had become involved in a major revolt against imperial rule that resulted in a further tightening of the British grip on the subcontinent.[43] In the aftermath of the mutiny, one writer expressed his dismay at the "despotic rule" of the East India Company and its "oppressive and cruel exactions."[44] Similarly, John Russell Young, accompanying former president Ulysses S. Grant on a mammoth round-the-world trip between 1877 and 1879, saw British rule in India as "mighty, irresponsible, [and] cruel" despite his sense that it had ultimately grown "more and more beneficent" since the imposition of British government rule following the terrible events of 1857.[45] Campaigner Lydia Maria Child focused on the hypocrisy of imperialists who complained about the savagery of indigenous populations around the world when their methods were at least as bad. In her famous

1868 treatise about the treatment of Native Americans, Child complained about the characterization of American tribal warfare and methods of torture as "barbarous" when many Christian peoples had engaged in equally appalling practices. Her "An Appeal for the Indians" noted that while the British may have ended the most egregious forms of torture and execution for their own subjects at home, they had now effectively exported them to their colonies, placing "Hindoo rebels before the muzzle of a cannon" and scattering "the blood and brains of the poor wretches in all directions." That the British press and even leading religious figures had endorsed their government's violent response to the mutiny only reinforced her belief that Anglo-Saxon moral superiority was misplaced.[46] Child's views reflected the growing internationalism of American suffrage campaigners, as they increasingly associated their cause not just with other nations in the West, but also those women whom men oppressed in Eastern cultures in Turkey, China, India, and elsewhere.[47]

The editor of *Harper's New Monthly Magazine*, Alfred H. Guernsey, noted the particular ignorance of many of the young British administrators in India, who in the years before the mutiny had prioritized their own wealth and the East India Company's profits over the welfare of the people. The "poor natives were ground to a powder, as between the upper and nether millstones," he complained, because their well-being had been left "in the hands of the servants of a soulless corporation on the opposite side of the globe, whose predominant feeling was contempt for the people over whom they were placed." For Guernsey, this helped explain the rebels' actions.[48] He joined with others to predict the end of British dominion there—primarily because of diplomatic and military pressure from Russia in central Asia—and suggested that the British should relinquish their hold before they were forced to do so:

> Whether British rule in India is, upon the whole, a blessing or a curse
> to the natives is a matter of grave doubt; that it is most unwillingly
> borne, is beyond question. It is a despotism pure and unmixed, and
> a despotism of the most galling kind—a despotism exercised by a
> horde alien in race and religion, alien in habits and modes of thought,
> in life and manners, in customs and ideas . . . To maintain this des-
> potism, even against the feeble natives alone, imposes a heavy strain
> upon the British government. The British empire in India is only a
> thin crust overlying a bottomless quagmire, into which it is in peril

of sinking at any moment by a force from above or an upheaval from below. How nearly this came to pass during the accidental Sepoy mutiny of twenty years ago, is known to all men. Had that mutiny chanced to have broken out three years before, during the Crimean War, it is safe to say that the course of the world's history would have taken a different turn. Since then Great Britain has apparently somewhat consolidated this crust, but it is yet thin, and the weight of Russia thrown upon it could scarcely fail to break it through.[49]

Guernsey's sense that British rule was so fragile in South Asia suggested that others might challenge Great Britain's authority elsewhere.

The failures of colonial administration also explained why the natives remained so downtrodden. Travelers who visited India often recoiled from what they saw as the enervating effects of British rule, the enormous costs of which fell largely on the Indian people. The celebrated American journalist Thomas W. Knox, for example, reported on the increasingly desperate state of the natives. India was "every year poorer and poorer," he told his readers in 1879, and most of people remained "in a condition of the most wretched poverty" that was simply impossible to ignore. "Of all the countries of the globe I have ever visited," he said, "India is the one I least care to see again." Ultimately, like Guernsey, he predicted that foreign rule could not last there.[50]

Views of British imperial activity in East Asia were similarly divided. As Gordon Chang has noted, although the United States did not participate in the imposition of the treaty port system in the wake of the Opium Wars in China (1839–1842 and 1856–1860), it broadly supported and benefitted from it. However, because the United States did not seek territory in China or elsewhere in Asia, many Americans believed it was much friendlier to Chinese interests than the European powers were.[51] Like others, Augustine Heard, nephew of his more famous entrepreneurial namesake who had traded extensively in China in the preceding decades, agreed with Eben Greenough Scott in comparing the British favorably against the French in Asia. Considering the frequent political and social turmoil in metropolitan France, Heard found French international enterprise in Asia surprising. Also like Scott, he thought French actions in Indochina remained "uncertain and groping," in contrast to those of the British in nearby Burma. While Britain had initially hesitated to colonize Burma, he suggested, its rule there proved "a triumphant justification of its final decision."[52] Else-where, however, prominent Americans were less sure about British poli-cies in the Far East. During the Civil War, radical Republican Thaddeus Stevens openly decried British actions in China. The Chinese authorities had sensibly excluded opium from its borders, he said. Forces of the British Empire had then waged war against "the most innocent people in the world." In doing so, "England violated every law of nations and every principle of morality by compelling the people, at the mouth of the cannon, to swallow $80,000,000 worth of it per year."[53] In the early 1880s, California business-man Charles Wolcott Brooks agreed, explicitly contrasting British policies with those of the United States, which he believed to be a superior moral force in the international sphere. Brooks, who had traveled extensively in Asia, saw the approach of the United States there as "humane, just and righteous," while Britain's was "dark indeed."[54] Overall, therefore, opin-ions of British imperialism, especially in Asia, were decidedly mixed.

The United States and Egypt

The influence of the United States in Egypt remained limited in the years that followed the Civil War. Unlike other areas of the Ottoman Empire, American protestant missionaries had struggled to establish a foothold there in the early nineteenth century, because of opposition from Muslims and Coptic Christians.[55] American commercial and diplomatic interests also remained relatively few. Perhaps the most significant decisions taken in the United States relative to Egypt, and which continued to have an impact during the 1870s and 1880s, concerned the Union blockade and Confeder-ate cotton embargo during the Civil War. These actions forced the British to search for alternative cotton supplies within its orbit, resulting in a fivefold increase in Egyptian cotton production and Egypt's growing dependence on a single export commodity.[56] Elsewhere, however, there were few connections. In 1880, the U.S. consul in Cairo noted that the government in Washington continued to have a "reluctance to interest itself, or have anything to do with" the details of Egypt's "internal affairs."[57] Between 1879 and 1881, the tonnage of vessels passing through the Suez Canal doubled, but in that time only one U.S. ship navigated it.[58] In early 1882, the U.S. consul general Simon Wolf complained he had not seen a

Figure 4.1 Simon Wolf served briefly as U.S. consul general in Egypt (1881–1882), and was an astute observer of the worsening situation there.
Source: Library of Congress, c. 1915–1920.

single American vessel at Port Said despite the harbor being crowded with many other nations' ships. Wolf implored his superiors to take a greater interest in the region. He wanted Washington to build on the United States' fast growing political and cultural capital in Egypt. Feelings toward the United States were "friendly and generous," he said, and had never been more so. For his part, Wolf had been striving "against great odds" to promote the interests of the United States and to reassure the native population that—by implication, unlike the European powers—it was "their friend, [and] that we are not here to plunder and oppress but to aid and encourage." This feeling, he suggested, ought to be "taken advantage of not only for the interest of Egypt but also our own."[59]

Wolf's characterization of Egyptian attitudes appears to be generally accurate, because influential Egyptians tended not to regard the United States in the same way as they did imperial Europe. In 1879, for example, Mohammed Tewfik Pasha, the khedive or ruler of Egypt from 1879 to 1882 under the authority of the Ottomans, told U.S. officials that he wanted them to become more heavily involved in Egyptian matters, especially on questions concerning its foreign debts.[60] In a sign of this growing rapport, in May 1879 the new khedive gave the United States an ancient Egyptian obelisk, generically known as Cleopatra's Needle, for transportation to New York. The other two cities with such obelisks were London and Paris and, as a U.S. official reported, Britain and France had obtained them under very different circumstances. It was, therefore, "a very great mark of favor on the part of the Government of Egypt towards that of the United States" that it made such a bequest.[61]

Elsewhere during the 1860s and 1870s, a few select Americans gained political influence because of the growing interest of Tewfik's predecessor, Ismail Pasha, in expanding his kingdom. While this kingdom was at the cusp of a series of overlapping imperial interests, Ismail (khedive from 1863 to 1879) and other influential Egyptians coveted territory in the interior of Africa that they regarded as part of a greater Egypt. This endeavor placed Egypt in the position of being what one writer has called the "colonized colonizer," experiencing the limits of exogenous control while looking to extend its own regional sovereignty over others.[62] Egypt's attempt to create this "great African empire" involved a small group of Americans who worked in the khedive's government and military.[63] These men, mostly Civil War veterans, conducted missions into the Sudan and

Uganda seeking, among other things, to build land and sea defenses against possible attack, to construct railways, and to search for gold.

Egypt was also fascinating to many American travelers who went there in increasing numbers as the century ended, often as part of a pilgrimage to the Holy Land. Travelers' tales were the main way most Americans discovered anything about the Orient, and prominent visitors to the region included former president Ulysses S. Grant, scholar Henry Adams, poet and journalist William Cullen Bryant, and socialite Sarah Haight, as well as numerous American writers, including Ralph Waldo Emerson, Mark Twain, and Herman Melville.[64] Visiting Egypt became as important to Americans "as the pilgrimage of good Mohammedans to Mecca," reported the former consul general in the 1890s. By this time, half the foreign visitors to the country during the winter months came from the United States. Americans were just like any other tourists, experiencing Cairo's mix of cultures, staying in its "conspicuously modern" hotels, and helping to drive a growing demand for the exploitation of ancient sites and the sale of historical artifacts as souvenirs.[65]

Because of the increasing number of Americans in Egypt, most official U.S. attention in the years that followed the Civil War focused on what they perceived to be the weak legal regime that left foreign victims of crime in the Ottoman Empire without justice.[66] This was especially important in a country where Egyptians and foreigners worked so closely together in government and business.[67] In order to deal with this problem, from the mid-1870s, Khedive Ismail established the so-called mixed courts system. Based on British and French law and incorporating local customs, the mixed courts were intended to make the administration of justice in Egypt simpler and clearer in cases between Egyptians and foreigners, and between foreigners living in Egypt. Successive U.S. administrations enthusiastically supported these courts and participated in the process, seeing the development of an efficient legal system as a vital component of government reform and "one of the principal factors in promoting the advancing civilization in Egypt."[68] Americans particularly appreciated the British influence on the mixed courts system, because British and American legal traditions were so similar.[69]

The U.S. consular authorities also took some interest in the continuing problem of slavery and slave trading. Although it was technically illegal to own slaves in Egypt, many prominent Egyptians did so with little or no prospect of punishment. The authorities dealt more harshly with trafficking in slaves, but many men, women, and children continued to be forcibly brought north from Abyssinia and sold in Egypt. Perhaps because of their own country's recent history, American officials made personal efforts to help purge this practice, with one consular official suggesting that if the United States government was reluctant to be involved in other areas, it was "all the more fit and proper that our best efforts be here in this land thrown in with those of Great Britain in the cause of freeing the enslaved."[70]

European Influence in the Ottoman Empire and Egypt

Although American diplomatic interests in Egypt remained slight, the growing encroachment of the European powers on Egyptian sovereignty increasingly troubled Washington's regional representatives. By the 1870s, amid burgeoning economic pressures, the Ottoman sultan was losing control of parts of his vast and diverse empire in the Balkans and North Africa, including Egypt. In spite of the efforts of successive sultans at social and political reform, Americans in the region observed that Britain, France, and an increasingly assertive Germany were assuming the empire's debts and making large capital investments in infrastructure projects such as railways.[71] Moreover, putative European attempts to protect the empire foundered as different countries were either given, or asserted their claims over, various parts. Agreements made in Berlin gave Cyprus to Britain and saw the main European empires carve up the Balkans in order to prevent Russian dominance there, while France gained Tunisia, which it forcibly took control of in 1881. These developments provoked a range of responses in the United States, from dismay at the sometimes naked displays of imperial power to appreciation at the advance of what some saw as European "civilization" in the region.[72] A particularly strident view castigated the "civilized powers of Europe" for brokering a treaty in Berlin "upon precisely the same principles as those which justified the crusades of the middle ages, directed against the same religion, and involving an equal amount of bloodshed and misery in almost the same region."[73] Regardless of Americans' views of the Ottoman Empire, it was clear to all observers of these developments that the empire was in decline. As Ulysses Grant's minister in Constantinople, George H. Boker, saw it, European encroachment not only sapped the Ottoman Empire of its power but also reinforced its image as the sick man of Europe: "So odious and dependent a state of tutelage would not be borne by the humblest recognized government among the European states . . . Why the Ottoman Empire submits to this slur upon its sovereignty, this denial of right of self-government, this continual and vexatious interference with its internal affairs, can only be accounted for by supposing that it is easier for an indolent people to endure an abuse that has obtained the force of habit than to redress it by means that might require a violent exertion or a proud appeal to the justice of nations." But despite his view of the Ottomans as "indolent," Boker believed that the empire was "sufficiently liberal and enlightened to conduct its international relations upon a footing of equality, and, as between nations, to be entitled to receive all that it is willing to concede." He also argued against the United States becoming involved in the kind of interference in Ottoman affairs in which the Europeans were now engaged.[74]

Sympathy for the Ottoman plight, however, had been dealt a blow by reports that leaked out of a mass slaughter in Bulgaria in 1876 in response to an uprising there. Americans in the region did much to publicize the atrocity, including in Britain, where the government of Benjamin Disraeli was dismissive of such reports. In particular, the work of journalist Januarius Aloysius MacGahan raised the profile of the Bulgarians' plight in both the United States and Britain when his work appeared in British newspapers. Published reports by the U.S. consul in Constantinople, Eugene Schuyler, also encouraged then leader of the British opposition William Gladstone to write his famous pamphlet, *Bulgarian Horrors and the Question of the East*, in September 1876, a condemnation of the Ottoman regime as well as the failure of Disraeli's government to deal with it.[75]

The attitudes of most interested Americans toward the Ottoman Empire were generally predicated on their views of its allies, Britain and France, as well as its enemy, Russia.[76] Many continued to see Russia as a progressive force, a view that was boosted by the Russian Empire's support for the Union during the American Civil War. In a telling summary written in the early 1870s, for example, Thomas Knox implicitly contrasted what he saw as the genius of benign Russian growth—which he almost certainly associated with the territorial expansion of the United States—with the regressive practices of the European imperial powers.[77] Others who followed in the tradition of the Young Americans of the 1840s and 1850s, however, opposed Russian expansionism, particularly after it appeared to lead to the outbreak of war with the Ottomans in 1877, which in turn led to the Berlin agreements.[78] Writing at the start of this conflict, Alfred H. Guernsey predicted dire international consequences if Russia gained Constantinople, because it would give the Russians a "fearful preponderance" of power in the region and foreshadow a terrible "collision" with Britain.[79]

Observers were aware that the Ottoman Empire's decline was of particular importance to Egypt, which was also becoming indebted to the major powers of Europe. Egypt's strategic position and fertile lands made it "a constant temptation to some of the Great Powers," as Simon Wolf put it, where on a "limited chess board . . . [the] game of European diplomacy is more or less played."[80] On the one hand, American officials broadly agreed with the Europeans that Egyptian rulers should prioritize economic and social stability over political autonomy and religious unity, and industry and commerce over territorial expansion. They therefore appreciated the efforts of successive Egyptian khedives to modernize their country and deal with its debts.[81] In February of 1882, Khedive Tewfik, who had now replaced Ismail, assured Wolf that the new cabinet "had no disposition to evade or disturb Egypt's obligations towards foreign power but simply to assert and insist upon control of the interior affairs of the country."[82] Wolf therefore seemed to be optimistic that the wisdom of Egyptian leaders augured well for the future of the country, which in his view lay in the education of its population and being able to govern its own affairs.[83] On the other hand, American officials worried that these reforms relied too heavily on European models that "dazzled" Egypt's leaders into believing that France under Napoleon III had been "the highest expression of the world's civilization" and that allowed the European powers too great an influence in the process.[84]

Such fears had only been amplified by Khedive Ismail's effective withdrawal from public life in 1878 and then his removal from power the following year, a "grave proceeding" according to the U.S. consul in Constantinople.[85] Ismail had, in American eyes, generally been a force for progress in the previous years, and his fall was deeply troubling. The consul general in Cairo, Elbert E. Farman, who would go on to serve as a judge in the mixed courts, noted:

> However much may be said against him, one thing is beyond dispute: Egypt, during the sixteen years of his reign, has advanced more in all that pertains to modern civilization than in the hundred, or

perhaps five hundred, years next preceding, and more than it will be likely for a long time to come; and for this advancement the country is almost wholly indebted to him.

Unfortunately for His Highness personally and perhaps for his country, he had seen too much of Europe, and conceived the idea that a great African state, perhaps empire, could be established on the European model on the banks of the Nile, and extending from the Mediterranean to the Equator.

He learned too late that the engrafting of European civilization upon the old Oriental system is expensive and ruinous. It is easy, as the world's history shows, to successfully plant new colonies: but to create new and vigorous states by engrafting modern civilization on the stocks of old ones, is an experiment the possible success of which remains to be demonstrated.[86]

By the time Tewfik was installed as Ismail's replacement in mid-1879, European powers were effectively directing Egyptian affairs.[87] Farman commented that with the Europeans struggling for control, "very little power" was left to the new khedive.[88]

American observers also saw first-hand the impact of such an uneasy mixture of Egyptian reform and European encroachment on the people. From the late 1870s, changing climate conditions meant that the Nile failed to rise, causing starvation across Egypt.[89] As the country descended into disorder and violence, a nationwide outbreak of cholera brought further misery. Despite much evidence to the contrary, the British insisted that the disease was caused by local conditions in places such as India and Egypt and could not be carried from place to place, concluding that quarantining people was therefore an ineffective containment tactic. This stance was heavily influenced by their fears that global commerce would be curtailed by limits on the movements of ships and sailors passing from India through the Suez Canal. Therefore, the British moved to exclude from the policy debates those who argued that cholera was caused by human intercourse.[90] One of Farman's successors, George P. Pomeroy, noted the disastrous effects this had in Egypt: the disease had run rampant because the British "never permitted any restrictions to be used by the Egyptian Sanitary Authorities, which would interfere with their Indian trade," he said, and, as a result, "the Government of Egypt was compelled to allow the free passage of vessels, engaged in this trade, through the Suez Canal, and to stop at its different ports."[91] Moreover, under pressure from London, the Egyptian authorities had increasingly excluded other nations' medical experts who disagreed with the British position on the spread of the disease from the International Quarantine Board, which monitored ships passing through the canal for signs of cholera and other diseases.[92] Pomeroy shrewdly noted the relatively limited impact of cholera in Alexandria, ostensibly because it had the greatest European influence, including the headquarters of the International Quarantine Board, and had organized committees to deal with the outbreak. He also suggested that the British government had actively opposed projects of the Egyptian sanitation authorities to prevent the spread of the disease in Egypt itself.[93]

Britain in Egypt

Engaged Americans thus struggled to reconcile their admiration for Britain's "civilizing" influence and dominant position over its European rivals with their unease at its growing role in the administration of Egypt. This tension notably increased after 1875, when the Disraeli government purchased Egypt's shares in the Suez Canal, beginning a decade-long process in which London took control of the company as well as the country.[94] At first, U.S. consul Richard Beardsley praised Britain's "decisive move" on the canal. It was "a wise and judicious" decision for Britain to gain a share of the enterprise (French business interests still had the controlling stake), he said, and it demonstrated that London was both dealing with the Eastern question and ensuring its own continued access to India. The French government's failure to seize the initiative and purchase the shares for itself, Beardsley told Hamilton Fish, was symbolic of its declining regional ambition and influence. While he recognized that Britain was "aiming to establish a protectorate over Egypt," he seemed unconcerned by this. "Her policy," he concluded, "is to strengthen herself here by every possible means, and this she seems to be doing as rapidly as is consistent with good policy."[95]

Others were not so sure. Farman suggested that rather than bolstering its own financial position, Britain's power in the Mediterranean could instead be used to free Egypt from the loosening grasp of the Ottoman

Empire. He astutely observed that Britain chose not to help in this way for two main reasons: firstly, because it wanted to strengthen the Ottoman Empire "as a bulwark against Russian power and influence in the Orient," and, secondly, because Egypt's "tribute" to its rulers in Constantinople in fact went directly to the sultan's creditors in Britain.[96] Farman complained that, regardless of who sat on the commission set up to oversee Egypt's debts, it had been established "simply [as] an instrument to carry out projects that have already been decided upon in London and Paris."[97] And while the European governments made much of Khedive Ismail's years of supposed profligacy in incurring his country's debts, especially his building of palaces, it was clear that this was a relatively minor factor. Much more significant, Farman wrote in August 1880, was "the official and officious

WHERE IS EGYPT LEADING THEM?
"Go slow, young man, please."

Figure 4.2 In another Thomas Nast cartoon, an Egyptian man drags a corpulent John Bull and a backward-facing British officer out into the dessert, and ultimately to war. It was prescient—just three days after it was published, British naval forces attacked Alexandria.
Source: Thomas Nast, "Where Is Egypt Leading Them?" *Harper's Weekly,* July 8, 1882.

interference of certain foreign powers and of their subjects sustained by official influence."[98] Even Beardsley later somewhat modified his upbeat assessment of British investment in the Suez Canal when he acknowledged that Britain and France had forced Egypt to make "great sacrifices" that were "out of all proportion to her interest in the work and her resources, and she alone has reaped the fewest benefits from the success of the great work."[99]

Long before the British military action, Americans were aware that this growing British interference in Egypt's affairs caused resentment among the population, most of which lived in penury.[100] As Farman put it in 1877, "If the people of the United States had to pay in proportion to their resources a tithe of the taxes paid by the Egyptians, they would think they were oppressed beyond endurance."[101] Despair at the draining of Egypt's wealth continued as the British grip tightened. In a scathing summary after the bombardment, one official said he was fully convinced that the British "occupation" meant "nothing but the transfer of Egyptian wealth to the pockets of Englishmen, to be thus wholly removed from the country of its production." Britain's policy was, he said, designed "to give Elbow room for the grasping propensities of a money loving people." This accretion of power meant that the British took all the best jobs in the government at inflated salaries. Because they placed "a low estimate upon the ability of Americans," it also meant removing from their posts almost all U.S. citizens in Egyptian government service. Thus, the Egyptian treasury effectively paid for the British occupation of its country as its money went to British officials, while its wealth was exported back to Britain, and the burden of Egypt's debts fell on the general population. Although the European countries had the potential to do something about this, Americans were pessimistic that they would. The "British right to prey upon the weak may probably be sustained," the official concluded.[102] Free trader Edward Atkinson called this situation "a disgrace."[103]

In the months before the British military campaign, this oppression led directly to the emergence of an anti-foreign movement agitating to expel external influences. The group, which in part blamed the Muslim nations for allowing this situation to develop, looked to the Egyptian intelligentsia and the Chamber of Deputies to address its concerns.[104] It targeted not just the British and French, but also the Turco-Circassian elite, whose origins were in the Northwest Caucasus on the Black Sea and who held great influence in Egyptian politics as an ostensibly distinct and socially privileged class (successive khedives, including Ismail and Tewfik, were of Circassian heritage).[105] The group's figurehead was Colonel Ahmed Urabi—"the champion of Egyptian rights against foreign aggression," as Wolf called him—whose support in the interior of the country grew rapidly in the early 1880s.[106] As Egypt's problems mounted, Urabi told the Americans that he believed the interference of the European powers was not just an end in itself, but was also a pretext for them to invade and annex it.[107] He said that he would resist any such moves, and vowed never to give in to British and French demands for him to leave the country.[108]

Commentators struggled to comprehend the possible economic and social consequences of these perilous circumstances.[109] Writing in August 1881, Vice Consul N. D. Comanos said he believed that the growing rebellion in the army led by Urabi was not representative of broader discontent among the Egyptian people, and there would be "no great crisis."[110] In a more discerning assessment two months later, however, Simon Wolf admitted that while he simply could not know the extent to which resentment in the military was reflected in the population at large, he saw that there was developing discontentment among the Moslem population, and that "the moment the Egyptians think that the army is strong and will be successful, they will gladly range themselves on its side."[111] As early as March 1879, the ever insightful Farman had drawn the attention of his superiors to the "danger of open revolt" against foreign influence.[112]

Because of the United States' affinity with struggles to throw off foreign rule, there was some considerable American sympathy for the Egyptian plight. Comanos recognized that the officers involved in anti-foreign protests had valid claims to be what he called "the last remaining bulwark of 'Egyptianism' against Christendom." These officers did not want the army's affairs to be "liquidated" in the same way that the finances of the country were "in behalf of London and Paris Bondholders," he said.[113] Somewhat similarly, Wolf believed that growing anti-European sentiment, while concerning, was a reasonable response to serious long-term grievances against the Egyptian government and people. Reporting on Egyptian calls to expel a French newspaper editor accused of blasphemy in the fall of 1881, Wolf contended that a foreigner who insulted Catholicism in "enlightened Germany" would experience the same kind of treatment, or perhaps even worse. He concluded: "The Egyptians have a right to their belief; they do not disturb us in ours; they are the natives and the owners of the soil, and have been under the oppression of Europe for ages. The cup is full to overflowing, and he who sows the wind reaps the whirlwind."[114]

Observers generally became more skeptical about this burgeoning Egyptian nationalism as they became more fearful of its potency. Part of the problem was with Urabi himself, who, while charismatic, was too radical for many American tastes. In the weeks leading up to the riots, Comanos reported on divisions in the cabinet between the European-backed khedive and many of his other ministers, led by Urabi. While Comanos believed the ministers would ultimately have to back Tewfik in order to keep the peace, he remained concerned that the events might take what he called "another course."[115] Such fears appeared to be confirmed when the outbreak of violence occurred in Alexandria, a development the American officials generally blamed on Urabi.[116] The riots briefly and uncharacteristically galvanized Secretary of State Frelinghuysen into diplomatic action as he enthusiastically agreed to Constantinople's suggestion that the United States might mediate with the British on how to deal with Urabi. The sultan consulted with the American minister to Turkey—Lew Wallace, Civil War general and author of the novel *Ben Hur*—about this, but, despite Frelinghuysen's backing, the proposal came to nothing amid the ruins of the British bombardment.[117]

Even in the aftermath of Britain's brutal military action, the American focus largely remained on Urabi and his violent response. Comanos reported on Urabi's retreat across the country, destroying parts of Alexandria, burning villages in the interior, and killing any Christians, Europeans, or Egyptians who opposed him. If he was allowed to continue, Comanos told Frelinghuysen, "Egypt would soon disappear, and all inhabitants and their properties would be completely ruined."[118] Frelinghuysen's indifference to what he referred to merely as the "recent events in Egypt" continued, however, with Washington's main diplomatic action consisting of its participation in an international commission on claims arising out of the unrest.[119]

This did not mean that Americans supported the British use of force. The bombardment shocked and angered many commentators, some of whom were at least modest admirers of the British Empire and expected better from it. One American newspaper noted the absurdity of the foremost global power pounding a small, underdeveloped nation into submission. However, several other publications supported the intervention at least as a necessary evil, as did former president Grant, who had visited Egypt during his post-presidential world tour and claimed that the lot of the Egyptian people would improve under British rule.[120]

Such disagreements over whether to embrace or reject British gunboat diplomacy were reflected among those who had much greater knowledge of the region. Some directed their anger at the risk the British attack had placed on U.S. citizens and their property, although an American naval presence in Alexandria harbor, requested by Comanos and ordered by Frelinghuysen, somewhat mitigated this.[121] People also voiced their dismay at the brutal and arrogant manner of the operation. One of the most prominent critics was Charles Pomeroy Stone, longstanding chief of the general staff in Egypt and the only American not expelled from the Egyptian army as part of the khedive's cost-cutting measures. Writing in *Century* magazine two years after the events, Stone contrasted the British authorities' actions with those of the participants in the Alexandria riot. Calling the June disorder a "so-called 'massacre,'" he claimed the participants had only attacked European men, and not women or children. Then, in addressing the violent British response to it, Stone decried the short notice (just twenty-four hours) that the British authorities had given foreigners to leave—and after the last train had left the city, he claimed. This "barbarous disregard on the part of the British of the lives of citizens of all other nationalities" had led to a "horrible death" for many Europeans, he said, as well as for the "hundreds of Egyptian women and children who perished in the bombardment." Stone compared the British action to the United States' attack on Vera Cruz in 1847 in the Mexican-American War, during which, he claimed, the American authorities had given the few neutral parties there ample time to escape before the assault began.[122]

Stone had reason to treat the British action with contempt. He had stayed in Alexandria to defend the khedive, while his wife and daughters remained in Cairo. He had also spent the eve of the bombardment trying to dissuade the British from attacking the city. He not only failed but also claimed that he had found those who were about to commence the action nonchalantly eating and joking about it. When the attack came, he joined other Americans in tending to the wounded and dealing with the terrible aftermath. Later, Stone's daughter Fanny published poignant and at times harrowing extracts from her diary, detailing her family's struggle to reach Alexandria from Cairo following the bombing in order to meet up with her father.[123]

Some saw the British action very differently. Lieutenant Commander Charles F. Goodrich of the U.S. Navy, who had been in Alexandria at the time of the events, contradicted Stone's account. Goodrich censured Stone for making light of the massacre in the city in June. Moreover, he denied that hundreds of women and children died in the naval attack and claimed that the British had given foreigners ample time to leave the city beforehand. The fact that they had managed to remove all their own subjects only served to prove "that other governments are less solicitous than the British for the welfare of their citizens."[124] American Protestant missionaries also often celebrated the bombardment and subsequent occupation, in part because of their affinity with their British counterparts, but also because they believed that these developments demonstrated the inherent superiority of civilizing Christianity over barbarous Islam.[125]

Union general–turned–Democratic politician George B. McClellan had another perspective. Although, like Stone, McClellan was disillusioned with Britain's role in Egypt, he blasted the British not for their militarism but for their timidity. Arguing that they should have acted far more decisively against the rebellion, he was concerned that the response to Urabi had actually weakened Britain's authority in the country and so, regardless of the success of the military enterprise, their position was now seriously— perhaps fatally—compromised. McClellan—who, like Grant, had also visited Egypt in the 1870s—argued that Urabi's "insolence . . . should have been promptly and decisively rebuked," even if this meant landing a military force in Egypt at the first signs of trouble rather than when the situation had descended into chaos. Moreover, France should also have seen the value of joining with its European neighbor and "nipping this difficulty in the bud by combined action."[126]

Similar tensions animated American officials' reactions. Aaron A. Sargent, head of the U.S. legation at Berlin, was perhaps the most enthusiastic in praising Britain's "prompt and effective military operations," which he believed had enhanced its influence in the region and bolstered its reputation in Europe. The empire had "engaged in a great enterprise for the protection of its interests, and the honor of its flag," he said, and had "shrunk from no sacrifice to attain its object."[127] Comanos struck something of a contrasting tone: although he blamed Urabi for the initial outbreak of violence, he said that Britain had acted "very imprudently" in deciding to bombard Alexandria "without any serious reason," and its failure to prepare fully for a military occupation had led to further turmoil in the country.[128] He later reported that the British had set about ending the war and restoring order, but it was clear that he found the methods the British had employed to do this to be troubling.[129]

Pomeroy also objected to the high-handed British response to the revolt, suggesting that Urabi's actions had provided the perfect pretext for the assertion of British control. Following the bombardment in July and Urabi's surrender in September, the British tried the rebel leaders at the end of 1882. During this process, they effectively blamed Urabi for the entire breakdown in law and order, and thus placed on him all responsibility for their subsequent intervention. The fact that the British then persuaded the khedive to commute Urabi's sentence from execution to a life in exile on Ceylon, Pomeroy argued, suggested that the process was political rather than judicial. The British needed to make an example, without making a martyr, of Urabi, but in the process of being seen to administer justice, they undermined the khedive's authority. Thus, Pomeroy wrote, "The reports of the burning and pillage of Alexandria and the murder of many innocent victims [by Urabi], seem to have been drowned in London by political considerations . . . even incendiarism and murder may be condoned and forgotten if they can be made subservient to the political exigencies of the hour."[130]

Race and Rule in British Egypt

In the months that followed, Pomeroy's replacement, John Cardwell, saw the effects of the British military presence firsthand and decried its disruption of the fabric of Egyptian society. He complained that drunkenness among British troops had become "a very customary thing" in Alexandria and other areas of Egypt, where it had been previously unknown. Soldiers were "disgracefully disorderly at times," he reported, but the authorities rarely, if ever, took any action. In one particularly egregious case in Port Said, British soldiers wrecked an American drinking house, stealing goods and furniture without even being reprimanded.[131] By 1887, Cardwell reported, there were now some four hundred "grogshops" in Cairo alone. Not only was the drunkenness associated with these establishments a problem, but so too was the prostitution that many of them supported, with "women of ill-fame" very often available to serve British soldiers. Numerous drinking houses were also close to mosques, and alcoholism was

BRITISH BENEVOLENCE.
"It is painful to be obliged to use force against the weak."—*Earl Granville in House of Lords.*

Figure 4.3 Aside from the folly of Britain's enterprise in Egypt, its brutality in putting down Ahmed Urabi's rebellion shocked American elites. Many of them expected better from the British Empire, although this *Puck* cartoon from shortly after the Alexandria assault acknowledges Britain's aggression elsewhere against weaker opponents (note the caricature of an Irishman pulling on a small glove labeled "Fenian" in the bottom right corner). The quotation from British foreign secretary Lord Granville reads: "It is painful to be obliged to use force against the weak."
Source: Joseph Keppler, "British Benevolence," *Puck*, July 19, 1882.

becoming such a problem among the native population that temperance societies were now working in the country.[132]

At its worst, this British presence had devastating effects on the native population. Cardwell said that because the occupying British forces had so little to do, their chief occupations were drinking and engaging in sports: "They go shooting in the cultivated fields of Egyptians, riding and walking down growing and nurturing crops; they fire off their guns anywhere and everywhere, regardless of people on the highways and in the fields; they devote a great part of their time to grooming ponies and running races with them, to games of polo and other outdoor amusements, to crowding the drives and rides, to showing themselves in all public places, and last, but by no means least, to the grogshops." Such activities could have very dark consequences. He detailed an incident in which British soldiers out hunting had become involved in an altercation with two young boys, culminating in the soldiers shooting both and killing one. Instead of punishing the soldiers, an overzealous colonel chastised the devastated villagers for interfering with British military personnel. Some were sent to jail while others were publicly whipped with a cat-o'-nine-tails in front of their neighbors. Cardwell was appalled at "this most cruel punishment, in satisfaction of outraged English sentiment" and believed that it was out of step with a "civilized" power.[133]

While Cardwell and others may have expected better from the British and expressed sympathy for the Egyptians, who bore the brunt of their actions, American observations continued to be shot through with racialized language and attitudes. Partially, these were based on the complexities of nineteenth-century theories of race. The Egyptian population was in the middle of the scale of racial hierarchy as perceived by white Westerners, somewhere between the paramount white man and his black counterpart at the bottom. These racist views arguably became more fixed in the age of science, despite emancipation, as white Westerners sought a concrete basis for their existing views. Increased contact between Americans and others around the world challenged and complicated their outlook as they encountered peoples—like Egyptians—who were neither "black" nor "white," but who still seemed to their eye less "civilized" or "progressive" than Americans or Britons.[134] Such tensions were evident in Comanos's categorization of the Arabs and Bedouins who began the assault in Alexandria in June 1882 as being "all of the lowest class," capturing something of his attitudes toward them. That he contrasted them with the "Europeans" who "had no other defense but to use their revolvers" reveals more, as he told Frelinghuysen that the Europeans "fired at the Arabs and the trouble became terrible," leading to a "dreadful butchery."[135] While Comanos's fear that the turmoil would spread across the country to Cairo and lead to reprisals against Americans was understandable, he also reported that the Muslim population had become "very insolent: they insult, threaten and curse the Christians in the streets."[136]

General McClellan was starker. In his view, "Orientals" were completely different to North Americans and Europeans. The inhabitants of the upper Nile were "a gentle, amiable race, child-like in their ignorance and simplicity," who had historically been kept "in the greatest poverty" by a "capricious and unjust government." The European influence had only served to moderate this kind of rule and improve the lot of the Egyptian people, he believed. Although McClellan acknowledged that Britain had intervened for economic rather than altruistic reasons, he contended that Anglo-French rule had relieved the Egyptian people of many of their former "evils" and brought benefits, such as lower taxation and a viable justice system.[137]

These racial views had an impact on Pomeroy, who was skeptical about the prospects for significant change under British rule. He recognized the need for reform and, at least in the months that followed the attack, genuinely appeared to believe that the British offered the best chance to achieve it. He largely agreed with Lord Cromer, British consul general in Cairo, who argued that British control was necessary because Egypt was "too civilised and too closely connected with Europe to be able to fall back into the tranquil oriental barbarism of former days" but not yet "civilised enough to walk on its own."[138] During a "pleasant and interesting" meeting in May 1883 with Lord Dufferin, the British ambassador to the Ottoman Empire, Pomeroy discussed Britain's plans for the reorganization of Egyptian political affairs, including the gendarmerie, judiciary, legislative chamber, and local government. If properly implemented in Egypt, Pomeroy commented, these changes would "assuredly turn to the account and benefit of its Government and people."[139] At this stage, he believed British claims that they wanted to enact far-reaching reforms that were "worthy of a great nation and liberal statesmen."[140] Yet, because of the limitations he saw in the native population, Pomeroy was increasingly cynical that meaningful political and social reform was possible. Two years into the British occupation, he dismissed London's attempts to implement a written constitution, because the Egyptian people were unprepared—and perhaps ultimately unsuited—for it. In an echo of McClellan, he said that the fault of the British was in treating the Egyptians "not as children, but as full grown people." This meant that they had "showered upon them all the modern blessings of free institutions, civil rights, electoral franchise, equality before the law, etc. etc. etc. forgetting that Egypt is to day less advanced than Europe was in the Middle Ages, and that the Fellah [peasant] [refuses?] to be educated in order to be prepared and fitted for the rights and duties of a citizen."[141]

Indeed, however cynical he might have been about aspects of British colonial rule, Pomeroy believed that Britain was too reticent to embrace the role of imperialist.[142] London's refusal to annex the country showed its unwillingness to deal with the central issue of Egypt's poor financial state, because if Britain took control of the country, it would have to guarantee the payment of interest on Egyptian loans. The British therefore decided on half measures that suited neither them nor the Egyptian people. Because they could not live with the existing system but did not want to introduce a British one, they developed something of a hybrid: "Egyptian in form, English in spirit—in fact, English conceptions with an Egyptian label."[143] Pomeroy thought the British were not being honest about their intentions, something he attributed to the Liberal Gladstone and his reservations about imperialism. The Egyptian debacle had posed ideological dilemmas for Gladstone's government, which had previously opposed the imperial policies of the Conservatives and now struggled to reconcile its liberal domestic program with greater control of parts of the empire.[144] Exactly what the current British policy was "would be difficult to define," Pomeroy said, "for what is done by the English here, and their whole action, is diametrically opposed to the repeated declarations of Mr. Gladstone and [Foreign Secretary] Lord Granville."[145]

In a suggested break with U.S. diplomatic tradition, his solution was joint European-American intervention in Egypt to achieve a more stable economy. He said that the "presence of the United States might be wholesome, for, thoroughly disinterested politically and otherwise, our meditations would undoubtedly have a conciliatory effect. We would be able to tone down the too ambitious views of other Powers, and oppose any and every attempt at annexation or a protectorate." Indeed, he suggested that the United States could even take a lead on some issues.[146] Despite his previous interest, Frelinghuysen did not countenance such a move, nor did his successor, Thomas F. Bayard, as Washington maintained its position of detachment, leaving the British to continue their muddled rule alone.

Conclusion

Because of the lack of United States' diplomatic engagement in Egypt, it was left to American citizens to record their observations and opinions about what Pomeroy variously called this "unhappy" and "ill-fated and barely governed country."[147] Only in exceptional circumstances did Washington become directly involved in either Egyptian or broader Ottoman Empire affairs, and rarely did the secretary of state give his views or engage in dialogue on the region and the European impact on it. Evidently, successive administrations felt that developments in the Ottoman Empire were outside of their sphere of influence, a reflection of the perceived alien nature of its political landscape and the growing domination of the European nations over it, as well as the fact that American interests—trade and otherwise—remained much closer to home. The United States was therefore a genuine observer of Egypt rather than the participant it was becoming in the affairs of countries such as Mexico and colonies like Cuba.

Broad concern in the United States about the encroachment of the European empires on Egypt was tempered somewhat by the belief that action needed to be taken to deal with the nation's chronic economic and social problems. Of course, there was recognition that the Europeans had accelerated many of these problems themselves, but there remained a nagging sense among many engaged Americans—whether they lived in the country, had visited it, or viewed it from afar—that Ottoman and Egyptian rulers possessed limited abilities to govern, and that European powers being able to promote their own interests so successfully in these areas was, in part, a testament to this fact.

Reactions to the British intervention in Egypt were therefore mixed. Britain was, after all, an imperial power, and while Americans considered the British to govern well, they also saw that they governed "in the imperial interest."[148] Some supported the action in Egypt, while others opposed it; some deplored its belligerent nature but backed its overall aims; some became disillusioned with it over time. Still, there was a widespread belief among Americans in the country and those watching on from back home that action needed to be taken to deal with a purportedly failing state. While Pomeroy's views that the British were foolhardy to portray themselves as benign patriarchs rather than colonial rulers may have been expressed more forthrightly than most, many elites thought that the imposition of a European imperial framework was necessary for Egypt to reach modernity and for it to ultimately become "civilized." They also frequently suggested that Britain had generally proved itself to be the most able of the European powers to undertake this task.

Growing rapprochement with Britain and an understanding of its global role during this period dovetailed with a sense of burgeoning American power. In a sign of the United States' growing assertiveness, domestic disquiet over the condition of the United States Navy, which in effect governments had left to rot since the end of the Civil War twenty years before, was beginning to emerge. Politicians had raised the issue of the navy's precipitous decline during the tension with Spain and Cuba in the previous decade, but by the 1880s, as the technological prowess of the other nations grew, more Americans sensed that the geographical isolation of the United States was fast receding, and proponents of a stronger navy, including Admiral Stephen B. Luce and Secretary of the Navy William E. Chandler, found greater support for their cause in Congress and beyond.[149] Tentative signs of this change could even be seen in Egypt, where Simon Wolf had once decried the lack of American commercial engagement. In early 1886, John Cardwell reported to Washington with some satisfaction that the United States Navy now had two vessels in Alexandria's port, including the flagship USS *Pensacola*. This had, he said, "started the impression in the minds of some people, that the United States of America maintains a *real navy*."[150]

As part of this—albeit hesitant—assertion of its power even outside of the Western Hemisphere, the Arthur administration agreed in 1884 to become involved in multilateral discussions over the status of the Congo in West Africa. It did this for various reasons, including trade and its interest in promoting what it saw as "civilization" in Africa, as well as concerns that the European powers sought to carve up various areas of the world to suit their interests. This development, focusing as it did on an area from which the United States had traditionally remained aloof, was in many ways an aberration—but one that initiated a dialogue with the European powers on their colonial ambitions in West Africa, providing insights into American attitudes toward them.

As in their observations of European involvement in Egypt, American elite opinions of the imperial powers in West Africa, outside of the traditional geographic areas of U.S. interest, open up opportunities to understand their views of empire without these views being clouded by diplomatic exigencies or Washington's own regional hegemonic ambitions. Even in an era of relative passivity in the conduct of U.S. foreign policy, the growing interest American leaders—both in the government and outside of it—took in the ways that the great powers of the day were shaping the world tells us much about developing conceptions of the international sphere among elites in the increasingly powerful United

States. Certainly, views of how U.S. power should be used were often deeply divided, but the growing sense that its affinities lay with the Europeans, not with those whom they colonized, was becoming more discernable, even if it did not yet mean that policymakers in the United States saw themselves as colonizers. As we shall see in the final chapter, American involvement in the Berlin West Africa Conference brought these ideas into sharper relief.

CHAPTER V

Germany and the Berlin West Africa Conference

W illard Parker Tisdel was an American in Africa. He had made his way to the west coast of the continent from the United States in September 1884 via London, Brussels, Berlin, and Lisbon. He then spent the first weeks of 1885 traveling from the port of Banana at the mouth of the Congo River to Vivi, slightly upstream, and on to reach what Europeans then called Stanley Pool. Although notionally on a one-man trek, he was far from alone on his journey. Accompanying him were fifty-six porters—each of whom carried a load of some seventy pounds—plus twelve armed guards, four servants, a chef, and an interpreter. The secretary of state, Frederick Frelinghuysen, had tasked Tisdel with seeking out opportunities in "the Congo," the vast region of West Africa still largely unknown to Europeans, which promised industrial prizes such as rubber, ivory, and palm oil, and which had already started to be the subject of fierce competition among Europe's imperial powers. Frelinghuysen required Tisdel to report on the climate, agriculture, and people of the region, and what commercial opportunities might be available to American manufacturers, businessmen, and entrepreneurs. Tisdel did this in a number of missives written during his time in Africa and afterward. By the time Tisdel had come back downriver in March, he believed he had valuable information for his superior. He returned to Europe the same month and then, after a brief stop there, back to the United States.[1]

Frelinghuysen had sent Tisdel on his mission at that particular time because of growing American interest in the region. As Tisdel was beginning his expedition, representatives of almost all the major nations of Europe were in Berlin at the request of the German leader Otto von Bismarck to discuss the future of the Congo. Americans were also there. The United States minister in Berlin John A. Kasson led a U.S. delegation accompanied by Henry Morton Stanley—soldier, adventurer, and writer—whose fame and expertise on Africa, along with the fact that he claimed to be a United States citizen, had led Kasson to demand that he be included in the party. Also present was Henry S. Sanford, a businessman and diplomat from Connecticut with close links to the government who had achieved stunning personal success in persuading the administration of Chester Arthur to recognize the International Association of the Congo, under the auspices of which many of the European claims for control of African territory had already been made. Tisdel also briefly attended the conference in Berlin on his way to Africa.[2]

Not present in Berlin was the man who had brought all these men together and who oversaw the International Association, Leopold II, king of Belgium, whom Tisdel had also seen before his departure. Leopold had ambitious plans for the development of large swathes of the African continent through his Association. Despite his absence from Berlin, he had established the terms of the meeting, which Bismarck set out in his opening remarks. These included aiming to expand commerce in the region as well as attempting to eliminate slavery and other ills, although exactly which areas were under discussion and how these objectives were to be achieved at this stage remained unclear.[3]

Also absent were any representatives from Africa itself. As the British delegate Sir Edward Malet noted in his response to the German chancellor's comments, this meant the Europeans could not hear African views. Malet suggested that unfettered commercial access to the region was likely to have negative consequences on the native population, something the various members of the delegations had to consider.[4] While there was more than a hint of hypocrisy in this declaration given Britain's recent and ongoing actions in Egypt, Malet's comments proved to be prophetic. The Congo Free State, a political and commercial entity that emerged from the International Association of the Congo shortly after the Berlin conference and which Leopold also controlled, proved to be a humanitarian catastrophe for its inhabitants. Hundreds of thousands, probably millions, died as a result of unscrupulous slavers and rubber traders who advanced a rapacious system of exploitation, violence, and cruelty that engulfed the region.[5] Eventually, the Belgian state intervened and took direct control. In the years after the conference, a few Americans were central figures in revealing the dire situation in the Congo. Mark Twain memorably captured the suffering endured by its inhabitants in his biting satire *King Leopold's Soliloquy* (1905), although it was the work of African American journalist and lawyer George Washington Williams that first exposed Western public opinion to these horrors.[6]

Washington's recognition of Leopold's Association, and its decision to send a delegation to Berlin and Tisdel to the region, raises many questions about its attitudes toward European colonialization during this period. Both actions seem out of keeping with many of its other pronouncements and principles, not least the Monroe Doctrine, which many furious Americans claimed its government had now abandoned, because it had become involved in affairs outside the Western hemisphere. This break with diplomatic tradition can be partially explained by the apparently genuine belief that it was engaged in a humanitarian exercise designed not just to promote commerce and prevent conflict between the European powers, but also to improve the lives of the inhabitants of Africa. Historians have also seen the decision as being as much about the personal ambitions and lobbying efforts of Sanford, effectively Leopold's personal representative, as it was about U.S. diplomatic relations with Europe or even its commercial interests in Africa. Indeed, much of the academic attention to American participation in the conference has focused on whether the U.S. delegation was too close to Leopold, and perhaps in effect working for him rather than the president.[7]

However, the United States' presence in Berlin also represented its increasingly evident assertiveness on the international stage and its sense of growing power, even outside of the Western hemisphere. Diplomatic participation at such a convention, however much of an anomaly at this stage of its international career, could not have been contemplated a generation before, and its invitation to attend by the major imperial nations represented perceptions in the capitals of Europe of Washington's growing diplomatic heft. Moreover, reactions of the various U.S. officials and participants, both in Berlin and Washington, reveal American views of the so-called Scramble for Africa and the rise of a new imperial power, Germany, which would also become a diplomatic rival.

Because the United States Congress repudiated the Berlin protocol when it was presented to them at the beginning of the administration of Arthur's successor, Grover Cleveland, historians have often overlooked the significance of the American presence in Berlin and the United States' growing interest in African colonialism. Regardless of the diplomatic and humanitarian outcomes, which were clearly significant and severe, the dialogue among Americans revealed a segment of the political classes that was not just engaged with such issues but adopted a language of imperialism, albeit one that sought to balance American principles with the world it encountered. To be sure, Washington remained reserved and somewhat on the periphery; it coveted no territory for itself and gained none. But the Scramble for Africa did not pass it by.

This episode illustrates the developing dynamics of American imperial thought and action at this time. Led by a small group of elites, the United States was increasingly competing with other empires as its own power grew. In many cases, this meant gaining greater access to markets and resources as it sought out what is commonly known as an Open Door for its commercial interests. This allowed it to continue to portray itself as exceptional and outside the realm of the other empires. Yet, it also built on long-term trends in American thinking about territorial acquisition and violence that had been clear since before the beginning of the republic. Now, entangled with empires in an increasing variety of ways, leaders were also gaining a deeper understanding of the essential malleability of ideas about imperialism and anti-imperialism. They could change according to circumstances, the empires involved, and the people they dominated. The ebb and flow of its interactions with empire during the 1880s saw the United States become further embedded in concepts of race and rule that would be discussed much more widely in the decade that followed, and ultimately acted upon in multiple arenas.

The United States, Africa, and the European Powers

The participation of the United States government in the Berlin conference built upon its growing, but still limited, interests in sub-Saharan Africa in the years after the Civil War. Even by the 1880s, it had relatively few commercial or diplomatic concerns on the continent outside of Liberia, although there were some interactions between Americans and Africans.

Missionaries who spent time in Africa in increasing numbers had long been concerned with Christianizing the millions of "heathens" that populated it; indeed, a key theme of the Berlin conference endorsed the idea that only by adopting Christianity could a country become "civilized" and put on the road to modernization. Such aims were also bolstered by the work of the American Geographical Society, which enthusiastically supported American expeditions about a whole range of humanitarian and commercial concerns. Because Africa remained largely unknown, however, especially in its interior, this also gave it an allure, as more Americans both in government and among the public regarded it with growing enthusiasm.[8]

Somewhat like American interest in Egypt, a significant reason for this was Americans' exposure from the mid-nineteenth century onward to African travelers' tales via newspapers and popular journals. Many became fascinated by this "dark continent" that was full of "savages" beyond the reach of civilization, and they were united with their European counterparts in admiring the exploits of the explorers who sought out danger and hardship in the hostile environment of the African interior. Judging by the numbers of articles published during this period, readers devoured accounts of these long treks through the stifling heat and humidity of the jungle as travelers faced threats from exotic wild animals, hostile tribes, and crippling diseases.[9] Perhaps the apogee of this excitement was *New York Herald* editor James Gordon Bennett's commissioning of Henry Morton Stanley to find the lost British missionary David Livingstone, which led to the famous Stanley–Livingstone encounter at Lake Tanganyika in late 1871. Bennett's scheme made Stanley an international celebrity who was feted when he returned to the United States, whetting the appetites of Europeans and Americans alike for more such tales. By the early 1880s, this craze had gone so far that one commentator complained he had become "rather tired of African travellers" with their familiar stories of struggles with lions and narrow escapes from murderous native chiefs. Readers now "easily anticipated" all such tales, he said.[10]

While the American government continued to remain largely aloof from political developments in Africa, there were tentative signs of change. Its links with Liberia—a nation of free black Americans founded by the American Colonization Society (ACS) in the 1820s that had become an independent republic in the 1840s—grew in the years after the abolition of slavery in the United States.[11] While maintaining close ties to Liberia in the period before the Civil War through the ACS, American policymakers hesitated to recognize it in part because of the increasingly fractious debates about domestic slavery. When Washington did finally extend formal diplomatic recognition in 1862, it was at a highly symbolic moment—at the height of the war and shortly after it had recognized Haiti, another black republic with which it had close ties. As scholars have noted, Liberia's founders were able to establish their nation because of a unique set of circumstances during the early and mid-nineteenth century. These conditions included not only the United States government's willingness to work with and through the ACS, but also that the European powers had yet to make significant inroads into African territory. Indeed, this allowed the American settlers in Liberia to practice their own forms of settler colonialism. Growing fears of European encroachment into Liberia increasingly shaped U.S. interests there, and Washington's concerns only grew as the government in the capital, Monrovia, became indebted to banks in London. British, French, and German bids for Liberian territory continued in the final years of the nineteenth century and into the twentieth, periodically drawing in the United States government and encouraging it to take a degree of financial responsibility for Liberia, short of establishing a protectorate. Early in the Grant administration, for example, Hamilton Fish helped to resolve—at least temporarily—a boundary dispute between Liberia and British Sierra Leone.[12]

American interests in Liberia also encouraged some broader attention to West Africa. In 1878, as part of a voyage to the Far East (including a more peaceful and far more successful overture toward Korea than the one in 1871), Secretary of State William Evarts sent Commodore Robert W. Shufeldt to Liberia. Shufeldt's reports emphasized not only the great potential wealth of the land and possibilities for trade with West African natives, but also the dangers of losing out to other powers if the government did not do enough to support commercial ventures. Indeed, Shufeldt helped to promote an increasingly widespread view that Africa's primitivism and lack of development were some of its most important qualities, rendering it full of untapped potential and ripe with possibilities: a clean slate on which the language of Western civilization could be written.[13] Such views were only reinforced as the recession of the early 1880s hit and Americans searched for new markets for their goods.[14]

The desire to engage was also given added urgency by the sense that the European powers were closing areas off to free trade as the Scramble for Africa took hold. Much of the continent remained uncharted as

Germany, Britain, and France vied with each other for dominance in the final decades of the nineteenth century. Indeed, Steven Press contends that Bismarck decided to hold the international conference that included several smaller powers in part because he wanted to promote Germany's power and legitimize its claims in Africa.[15] Simultaneously, Leopold II of Belgium was moving behind the scenes, positioning his private organizations to take advantage of the changing political landscape. Elites in Washington were well aware of this new strident "policy of colonial extension," as the minister in Paris Levi P. Morton called it, and they tended to base reactions to it on their predispositions to the particular European country involved and their attitudes toward its perceived abilities as a colonizer.[16]

As usual, American elites generally had a cynical view of French policy. In a long, fascinating exposition of the relationship between the United States and the colonial powers written while he was at the conference in Berlin, John Kasson gave a startling assessment of French ambitions. France was still smarting from its losses in the Franco-Prussian War and the realization that it would never regain its territories of Alsace-Lorraine, and Kasson suggested that politicians in Paris had "sought to satisfy the restless ambitions of the French by an enlargement of their colonial possessions." As a result, France had recently acquired territories in North Africa and Southeast Asia while involving itself in quarrels with China and with the British in Egypt, he said. Although Kasson was concerned about this in the broadest terms, his specific objection was that the Paris government would not be content with a limited number of new possessions, meaning that when French acquisitions in Africa and Asia had reached their limit, its intentions would be diverted west to the Americas and would only be stopped by adverse public opinion in France or opposition from a greater power. Kasson concluded that this present assertion of French imperial interests was "more dangerous" than it had been under Napoleon III because it was now "more insidious."[17]

The Arthur administration had already experienced some of this renewed imperial French ambition on the island of Madagascar, where the United States had significant interests. A commercial treaty brokered by the Johnson administration in 1867 had led to a boom in trade, with estimates that the island imported about $1 million of American goods annually, about half the island's total. During 1882 and 1883, French aggression had led to some calls at home for the United States to take a more interventionist position to protect American interests, although in the end Frelinghuysen resisted.[18] Moreover, Washington had observed France's attempts to undermine Portuguese territorial claims in West Africa. In late 1881, Morton informed the secretary of state of an agreement the Italian-born French representative Pierre Savorgnan de Brazza had recently brokered on behalf of the government in Paris with a chief of the Makoko tribe close to the Congo River. It established a settlement that was already being called "Brazzaville," giving the French a commanding position on the waterway. Although he reported that the chief had made the agreement voluntarily, Morton conceded that the treaty itself appeared to have been written in deliberately vague language, and its geographical limits were "so meager" that its exact location remained uncertain.[19] Similar reports of assertive French colonization in 1883—including the landing of a ship at Ponta Negra (Pointe-Noire) on the Congo coast and a declaration that it was now French rather than Portuguese territory—prompted the American minister in Lisbon, John M. Francis, to complain about the current spirit of competition between the colonial powers. While Portuguese domination of the region had been longstanding, he noted, Portugal was now relatively weak and its ambitions contained. In contrast, the establishment of a great power like France in the Congo River basin was likely to impact negatively on commerce in the region for the other interested powers, he said.[20]

As in other cases, American observers generally treated Britain more favorably, in part because they often did not perceive it to be as strident in its quest for territory. Even after the British government's crushing of the resistance in Egypt, many continued to take its preeminence to be indicative of inherent virtue and saw growing signs of kinship between Britain and the United States based on shared heritage and American aspirations to emulate their Anglo-Saxon cousins. To others, Britain's burgeoning role in Africa made it seem too much like any of the other European colonial powers. The African American newspaper the *New York Freeman*, for example, saw England as "a sly, grasping, avaricious bully," greedily eying the Congo River and its basin.[21]

Of greatest interest was the newest European imperial power, Germany. American shock at Prussia's ability to vanquish France in 1870 and unite the German nation gave way to an ambivalent and sometimes contradictory relationship with the new state. The United States government tended to regard Germany favorably, building on the close connections it had established with Prussia during the American Civil War, a position that was itself helped in no small part by their shared antagonism toward France. The extraordinary rates of economic and territorial growth in both countries during the years that followed also reinforced some of their natural affinities. Previously, Germans had admired U.S. expansionism across the North American continent, seeing it as a form of "liberal imperialism" that they could emulate in Europe or in building settler colonies in the Americas. Following unification and the increasingly enthusiastic search for overseas colonies, some of these connections continued to have resonance. In particular, German liberals were united with their American counterparts in believing that control of the American West and colonial conquest in Africa could both be progressive if done properly. While such actions might involve the destruction of native habitats, and regrettably even the loss of lives, this was a price worth paying if it meant the improvement (in other words, westernization) of the society in question.[22] However, in other areas relations became strained, most notably over the issue of the importation of American pork products to Germany and the subsequent protests of the minister in Berlin, Aaron A. Sargent. Frelinghuysen, under pressure from Bismarck, agreed to replace Sargent with Kasson a few months before the Africa conference began.[23]

American elites' feelings about Germany's global ambitions were more mixed than those concerning its economic and territorial growth in Europe. In part, this was because one of its colonial schemes directly challenged the United States in its own growing sphere of interest. The Pacific Islands of Samoa bore the brunt of this competition between the United States, Germany, and Britain.[24] More generally, however, Americans were undecided about the prospects of German colonialism. Sargent, for example, was stark in his assessment that Germany simply did not have the requisite qualities to become an imperial power like Britain or France. Although he saw that growing numbers of Germans advocated a strong colonial policy based on their perception that the country needed new markets and land, Sargent suggested that there were "peculiar reasons" why Germany could not gain and hold onto distant territories. These included its lack of a long coastline, weak navy, and the continued threat from its neighbors in Europe.[25]

His successor Kasson took a wholly different position. Kasson was a great admirer of Bismarck, calling him "the most illustrious figure of the nineteenth century."[26] He recognized that the Iron Chancellor had already made Germany an important European player and saw that his aspirations for colonial glory were producing results in Africa and the Pacific. But far from regarding these moves as a threat to the United States, he believed Germany was establishing these colonies with an "intelligent and resolute purpose" and its government appeared to have "uniformly respected the rights of the weak" (an obvious allusion to the characteristics he believed it shared with the United States). Yet even he recognized that these features could change and was troubled by the prospect of a powerful German state acting more like Britain or France. While he recognized that Bismarck's colonial policies were ambitious and believed his plans for the creation of a strong German navy were purely for defensive purposes, a powerful, selfish, militaristic Germany was an "alarming" short-term prospect.[27] Such views were only heightened as Kasson reported on diplomatic spats over British and German colonial policies in the weeks after the Berlin conference, including in Samoa.[28] No sooner had the summit ended than the German government claimed sovereignty over areas to the west of the Zanzibar coast on behalf of the Society for German Colonization.[29] "The movements of the European powers, especially of Germany and France, for colonial acquisitions in Africa are so active that no publication of maps can keep pace with them," Kasson reported at the beginning of March 1885.[30]

In an article published the following year, socialist Daniel De Leon was more forthright. In stark contrast to Kasson, De Leon already saw Bismarck as a dangerous figure in European affairs, promoting an "aggressive attitude of Germany upon the seas" and a "peculiar colonial campaign" in Africa and beyond. De Leon did not appear to believe that this campaign was for the large-scale acquisition of territory; rather, he saw it as Bismarck's effort to stimulate trade outside of Europe to the exclusion of other powers in order to sell German goods and so bolster living standards. The British ("with praiseworthy tenacity and energy") were attempting to keep the Germans out, but Bismarck persisted, seizing the opportunities offered to him, De Leon reported.[31]

Washington responded to these challenges from France, Britain, and Germany in Africa within the range of its limited means. Sometimes this involved demonstrations of military power. As early as the mid-1870s, it had considered sending a naval squadron to Liberia to deal with possible threats from the European powers during a period of insurrection there, and by the 1880s it was increasingly directing its naval vessels stationed in the Mediterranean to operate off the west coast of Africa.[32] However, its navy was still small and it could do relatively little. Moreover, it remained cautious about further involvement in African affairs for fear of becoming like one of the colonial powers, or at least being seen to be like them. It was as part of the United States' new approach toward Africa that Frelinghuysen sent Willard Tisdel upriver in order to provide a first-hand account of the region and its possibilities, although the government did not accredit him as its official representative to the Congo Association. Tisdel's remit was thus limited to being "geographical rather than political."[33] Even as it approached the discussions in Berlin, the Arthur administration was desperate to avoid what David Pletcher has characterized as "anything that smelled political."[34] Despite this reticence, in late 1884, Arthur and Frelinghuysen agreed to send a delegation to Bismarck's conference.

Colonization and Imperialism

In addition to the modest growth of American interests in Africa during this period, the Arthur administration's decision to recognize the International Association of the Congo was the result of the personal diplomacy of several key individuals. The most prominent of these was Henry S. Sanford, but Sanford had assistance from a number of others, including Kasson and John Tyler Morgan. The influence of these men suggests that the decision for the United States to participate in Bismarck's conference had less to do with a lack of leadership on the part of President Arthur and Secretary of State Frelinghuysen (although this may have been an element of it) and more to do with Washington's interest in a scheme that appeared to blend the two elements it believed its foreign policy promoted: humanitarianism and commercialism. However, the imperial aims set forth during the conference, which Leopold and Bismarck downplayed and the American participants often overlooked, had important implications for Washington's relationship with the European powers, as well as its own sense of imperial identity.

Sanford's direct access to the White House allowed him to persuade President Arthur to provide official recognition to Leopold's Association in the spring of 1884, making the United States the first nation to do so. As minister to Belgium under Lincoln and Johnson, Sanford had been a crucial player in the delicate diplomacy of the Civil War as well as in American opposition to the accession of Maximilian—whose wife Carlotta was

Figure 5.1 John Kasson was the U.S. minister in Berlin and led the American delegation at the conference. He was an avid supporter of U.S. expansionism and disappointed
with the Cleveland administration's repudiation of the meeting shortly after its
conclusion.
Source: Library of Congress, undated, c. 1865–1880.

Leopold II's sister—to the Mexican throne. Sanford had established a rapport with Leopold from the beginning of the latter's reign in part based on
what both men perceived to be the shared interests of Belgium and the
United States.[35] Later, in promoting Leopold's plans for the Congo, Sanford emphasized the Belgian monarch's inherently humanitarian nature
while playing on American sympathy for the people of Liberia. He also
trumpeted the continued prospects for settling free blacks there, as well as
the region's commercial possibilities and the need to prevent the European
powers from closing it to free trade. He had, in fact, begun this process in
the late 1870s, working on successive secretaries of state (William Evarts
and then James Blaine) to try to ensure that the United States developed
its own claims in the region. He then wooed the next president directly.
In 1883, Arthur stayed at Sanford's mansion in Florida, and at the end of

the year the two men met, Sanford having returned to the United States to outline Leopold's plans to the president in detail. Sanford's lobbying worked spectacularly. Not only did Arthur study the proposals carefully, he endorsed them, adopting Sanford's language to promote the organization in his message to Congress at the end of the year.[36]

Kasson in effect followed Sanford's lead, although Leopold's plan dovetailed nicely with his passionate desire for a more proactive American foreign policy. A strident American nationalist, Kasson saw a future for the United States as a great world power. He had been a longtime participant in American politics, having served in the Lincoln administration and then been elected as a representative for Iowa. Like Sanford, he had vehemently opposed the French intervention to place Maximilian on the throne in Mexico and quietly worked with Maryland representative Henry Winter Davis on the April 1864 resolution condemning the French government's actions.[37] A close friend of Frelinghuysen (although far more strident in his foreign policy views), he had served in Vienna as minister to Austria-Hungary prior to his re-election to the House in 1880, and then agreed to replace Sargent in Berlin. As a passionate advocate of U.S. naval expansion, Kasson decried the low levels of interest he believed many of his fellow Americans had in foreign affairs. He was particularly fierce about the need to uphold and extend the Monroe Doctrine, seeing an opportunity to do so at a time when the United States was becoming more powerful and had relatively positive diplomatic relations with the other important powers.[38] This advocacy was, however, also because he believed the nation faced continued threats from those powers, especially because of the prospect of a French transoceanic canal in the Americas. Kasson suggested that such a canal constructed by Frenchmen, as at Suez, would be like "ripening fruit, waiting to be picked by an ambitious French Government." Predatory political interference from Paris was inevitable, whether it was done by purchasing shares or finding a pretext for invasion. Either way, the United States would be excluded and face the possibility of "the utter and ignominious abandonment of the Monroe Declaration."[39] As his biographer observes, Kasson effectively argued that the United States should contain such imperial threats from the European powers by becoming more imperial itself, and Kasson argued that the United States should act more forcefully on the global stage, even suggesting "a change in our territorial policy" to take possession of islands in the West Indies and Pacific Ocean in order to lead it toward markets in East Asia and Australia.[40]

As his close associate and friend, Kasson was highly influential in persuading Frelinghuysen to accept Stanley as part of the United States' delegation in Berlin. Kasson saw Stanley's expertise as an essential component of American efforts to promote the territorial integrity of the region and recognition of tribal rights in any agreement (although Stanley received no payment for his efforts).[41] In this sense, Kasson's erroneous belief, along with many others, that Stanley was a citizen of the United States—because he had fought in the Civil War and taken an oath of allegiance to the republic—was crucial. This, along with the idea that Stanley had made "discoveries" in the African interior, led to Kasson arguing that the United States had a "special influence" at the conference, and that it should be involved in exposing Africa "to the light of civilization" while simultaneously remaining disinterested in its exploitation as a colony.[42] During the first days of the conference, Kasson wrote with some apparent satisfaction that the arrival of someone with Stanley's international stature had "awakened the public interest in Berlin" because of his high profile, which Stanley himself did nothing to resist.[43] Stanley was also something of a celebrity at the convention itself. At one point, as its members discussed the geographical limits of the Congo basin, Kasson offered Stanley's expertise to the other delegates. As someone who passed up no opportunity to be the center of attention, Stanley responded enthusiastically, crossing to the large map of Africa on the wall and proceeding to give a lecture containing "vivid description of the features of the Congo basin" that according to Kasson "engrossed" every dignitary there.[44]

John Tyler Morgan also encouraged the Arthur administration to support Sanford. Morgan, the bullish senator from Alabama, was a member (and later the chair) of the Senate Foreign Relations Committee, and his brand of Southern ambition and deep-seated racism was perfectly realized in Leopold's plans for the Congo. A Southern loyalist and Alabaman to his core, Morgan believed that the Northern states controlled the South as an imperial power ruled its colonies, but he also supported an aggressively expansionist foreign policy for the United States in part as an attempt to escape from this. Morgan argued that the South's path to recovery after the Civil War lay in rapid commercial growth, and during the 1880s and 1890s he vocally advocated for such measures as the creation of strong merchant and military navies, the building of a canal in Nicaragua under U.S. control, and the annexation of Hawaii. His sense that Reconstruction had failed the South was also based on a belief that it had focused too much on

Figure 5.2 Kasson lobbied for the State Department to add Henry Morton Stanley to the American delegation because of Stanley's knowledge of West Africa and because he claimed to be an American. In fact, Stanley's presence in Berlin was probably as much to do with his celebrity status as it was about his African expertise, while his claims of U.S. citizenship were spurious.

Source: Bibliothèque Nationale de France, 1884.

the status of blacks rather than whites. What he saw as the attempts by Congress to "elevate the negro race in the States" had encouraged blacks to "wage a conflict" against whites and stimulated African Americans to demand a social equality that he argued they were simply "not prepared to enjoy." He was explicit about his fears that the black population was growing at such a rate that blacks would soon outnumber whites, while racial mixing would rapidly become commonplace throughout America. His answer was repatriation to Africa, the black man's "native land," as he called it.[45]

Frelinghuysen's decision to send Stanley and Sanford to accompany Kasson has led Sybil Crowe to contend that, despite his own absence from the conference in Berlin, Leopold was represented not just by Belgian diplomats but also by three American ones (Stanley's questionable citizenship notwithstanding). For her, American participation in the proceedings "explains why it is so often possible during its discussions, simply to read for the words 'International Association' those of the 'United States.'"[46] On one level, Crowe's view is entirely understandable, as Sanford reported to Brussels constantly throughout the proceedings. However, it also overlooks the fact that Kasson and Sanford were representatives of a more robust and outward-looking *American* foreign policy evident by the early 1880s. As George Shepperson has argued, the three representatives from the United States—Kasson, Sanford, and Stanley—were not Leopold's stooges in the way that other commentators, including Crowe, have suggested. Instead, they were precursors to the expansionists of 1898 and advocates of what would become known as the Open Door policy—a new, muscular Americanism that saw opportunities for the United States to take its place alongside the other great powers of the world.[47] To Sanford and Kasson, the decision to recognize Leopold's Association and then to participate in the Berlin conference was entirely consistent with this. Indeed, Leopold's desire for the affirmation of the U.S. government was that it would, among other things, strengthen his relatively weak position as the head of a small state with few global interests compared to the other powers, a sign of the United States' growing global influence.[48]

While Sanford remained loyal to Leopold until close to the end of his life, only turning against him when he saw that the Belgian king was restricting free trade and effectively supporting slavery in his colony, he also remained resolute in his belief that the Congo offered untold opportunities for the United States. In the years that followed the conference,

Sanford persisted with his claim that the United States would be a significant trading power in the region and that Africa would become "the greatest market for our domestic cotton goods outside our own domains."[49] Kasson went even further. While he believed that the United States was different from the major colonial powers in Africa because it joined the conference while coveting no territory there (a tacit admission that other powers did), he revealingly noted that the United States was "not *yet* a colonizing power."[50] As this implied, it might become one in the future, and he also believed it should be in the Caribbean and Pacific, even if he might have thought this would be to prevent other powers from closing off territory to trade. During the conference, Kasson also pushed U.S. interests further than Frelinghuysen was willing to go. In late 1884, he suggested dispatching "one or more naval vessels" to the mouth of the Congo to search for "a healthful point" from which the United States could launch its commercial ventures in the region and help the Americans to establish a coaling station there. He asked of his superior in Washington: "Would it not be worthy of consideration by the President to send orders to our Diplomatic Agent in the Congo, or a naval vessel with orders, to negotiate with the local chief for the best district on the lower Congo for a coaling station, contracting for exclusive jurisdiction along the best stretch of river coast?" Frelinghuysen made it implacably clear that this—effectively a form of gunboat diplomacy—was against the spirit of American participation.[51] Perhaps because of this, Frelinghuysen demanded assurances from him that Kasson was not participating with the other members in making agreements on rival claims for territory. Kasson hastily responded that no such undertaking had occurred.[52]

Frelinghuysen resisted becoming involved in European machinations as well as Kasson's worst excesses, yet even he became swept up in some of the ambitions and propaganda of Leopold's schemes amid the conference proceedings. He told Kasson he hoped that Washington's recognition of the International Association of the Congo would "give further shape and scope" to Leopold's project of creating what he called "a great state in the heart of Africa." Going further, he suggested that the organization of such a state would place it in a position in which it would be "held for all time, as it were, in trust for all peoples." Moreover, while he wondered whether it could achieve such noble ends, he still believed that the Berlin meeting "should be productive of broad and beneficial results."[53]

Commerce and Trade

By far the most important factor motivating Europe and the United States to become involved in African development at this time was trade. During the final decades of the nineteenth century, all the major nations of Europe experienced forms of economic depression that encouraged them to think about exploiting new, untapped markets, including those in the sub-Saharan region that to some appeared to offer almost limitless potential. While in reality returns from Africa were often modest, this increased fretting over apparently finite consumer markets in Europe dovetailed with a growing sense of what one author has called the "imperialism of prestige" to encourage national governments to seek economic preeminence and territory in Africa. By 1888, for example, the British government had decided to remain in Egypt for the foreseeable future, confirming its interest in Africa as well as India.[54]

The main aim of the Arthur administration was to ensure that these European powers did not close off opportunities for the United States on the African continent. As this implied, the U.S. government shared a belief with many in Europe that Africa offered not only raw materials but also potentially untapped markets for their own finished goods that would be lost if they did not participate in its development.[55] In making his decision to support the Congo conference, Frelinghuysen stated his belief that some kind of "enlightened" intervention was necessary to nurture this potential while also expressing his anxiety that the United States must ensure it obtained "its proper share of the commerce of the Congo."[56] Somewhat similarly, Kasson saw the United States being left behind if it did not participate. Believing Africa to be filled with the promise of both "civilization" and "enterprise," he compared the current American interest there to the bitter struggles of recent centuries for imperial influence. As he explained, in deciding to participate, the Arthur administration had addressed the question of Africa's future, and he asked:

> For whom should be opened the new markets of Central Africa, destined to be the next century's vast growth and development? Should Portugal make of it another of its closed colonies? Or Spain make another Cuba of it? Should France control it as a French market with another 60 per cent. discrimination against foreign goods

as in some other African colonies?. . . [H]ad we no interest in keeping open to American enjoyment the great country and the great river which an American had first opened to the world? In a word, should we leave to the next century a heritage of the same struggles for access to the African market which during the present century have characterized our separate struggles to obtain access to the West and East Indian colonies?[57]

Washington's presence in Berlin was therefore predicated on Leopold's assurances that free trade was at the heart of the European project in Africa. Indeed, the manifesto of the Association even claimed to have adopted the doctrine of the Manchester School promoted by Richard Cobden and John Bright. This move could have done little harm in the United States, despite its own domestic protectionist policies, because it promised the United States an equal footing with the European powers and perhaps gave advantages to the increasingly efficient American manufacturing sector.[58]

From the earliest stages of the negotiations in Berlin, Kasson prioritized the principles of free trade and the extension of the designated free trade area as far eastward as the other delegates would allow.[59] In one sense, this was a relatively uncontroversial position, especially because, as a non-colonial power, the United States saw itself as something of an honest broker between the rival imperial nations. Yet, this also meant that Kasson cast the United States as ideologically distinct from the other participants, a position that justified its joining in the first place. He suggested that there was "nothing embarrassing" about the United States attending such a meeting as it had done so at other international conferences (such as the recent one that had set the common meridian for measuring time) and as a burgeoning trading nation it should "naturally be represented" in a conference concerning trade in Africa.[60] As he put it:

> We cannot barter colonial privileges for the like in return, as can France, England, Germany, Holland, and even Portugal. These powers could close every colony against trade but their own, as was the usage of the last century, and may be again the usage in the next. . . .
> It is in our interests to prevent any single flag, or adverse combination of flags, from controlling the avenues to the heart of that continent [Africa]. As our Government seeks no possessions there, our whole practical interest is in opening to American enterprise, upon

the freest possible and equal terms, the present and prospective possessions appropriated by other nations, and to keep the Congo country and its outlets as far as possible from such appropriation, and from every needless burden on commerce and intercourse with them.[61]

This early example of what would later be categorized as the Open Door policy was striking.

So too was Kasson's discussion of European expansion in Africa as "the valve to relieve the compression" caused by overproduction at home. Here, his arguments were something of a rehearsal of those that would become so prominent during the following decade to explain and justify American commercial and imperial expansion in the Caribbean and the Pacific. He believed that European colonialism in Africa during the 1880s was driven by more than just a lust for power and international prestige, arguing that "the material forces of popular necessity" were responsible. According to him, the three most powerful nations of the time—France, Great Britain, and Germany—had a surplus of population, production, and energy that was beyond anything that their domestic markets could consume. This inevitably led to the search for foreign markets and the acquisition of new territories. Kasson therefore appeared to suggest that colonial expansion was almost inevitable, serving the same purpose war had done in previous decades.[62]

This led to what was perhaps the most significant American intervention at the conference, in which Kasson proposed various measures to prevent conflict between the European powers and to neutralize the whole Congo basin in the event of a war. He connected this idea explicitly to the need for open, unrestricted trade in the various territories and the maintenance of peace: "As regards their usefulness in time of war, what would be the good of possessing for the purpose of military operations abroad, a dependent Colony above the falls of the Yellala [in other words, in the interior]? From the moment when possession of a Colony does not take for granted its commercial monopoly, it ceases to have any value for a foreign Government. The revenues which it would bring to the mother country would never be equal to the expenses which its maintenance would require." Although the logic of this intervention was questionable—if the European powers believed their territories would become worthless if they engaged in war, then they would almost certainly not engage in it—he had other motives. His expressed belief that such a war would bring "universal ruin" to the interests of neutrals also suggested that he was probably more concerned with the United States being shut out in the event of such a conflict than he was about its impact on the Europeans or indeed the natives.[63] Freedom of trade alone was thus not enough, or at least it had to be forged within a broader framework of conflict prevention among the great powers.

Augmenting this desire for peace in the region, Kasson also sought "to steadily encourage productive labor" among the native tribes of Africa, "thus increasing the means to buy the merchandise of the civilized nations."[64] In doing so, he built on Stanley's claims that the African coast and interior were filled with people ready to embrace the process of civilization, to trade with Europeans, and to grow any crop that (by implication) the European consumer desired. In his numerous speeches in England, Stanley appealed to various manufacturers' fears that during this period of intense competition and economic stagnation their livelihoods would be threatened unless they sought out alternative markets. He virtually promised them infinite economic rewards if they grasped the opportunities presented in bounteous Africa. In one particularly egregious speech in Manchester, he claimed to have calculated that if the entire population of the Congo basin were to buy just "one Sunday dress each," this would equate to the production of three hundred million yards of Manchester cloth![65] The rapturous reception the crowd gave to this most dubious of assertions may have been very much misplaced, but the cotton producers and manufacturers of the United States could understand the message equally well: Africa was open for business.

Stanley's optimistic view was not universally supported in either Britain or America, however. The *Glasgow Herald* gave it an especially frosty reception and questioned whether his vision was of any "practical value."[66] In the United States, perhaps the most prominent critic was the government's Congo agent, Willard Tisdel. Frelinghuysen had asked him to report as widely as possible on the political, geographical, and commercial situation he found in the Congo Valley.[67] Initially at least, Tisdel was eager to support his government, and he threw himself into the mission. But his rapid realization that Americans were far behind the Europeans in the race for commercial influence tempered his enthusiasm. He cautioned that any citizen of the United States thinking of setting up an enterprise in the lower Congo or any region of West Africa would need to have substantial amounts of capital and a realistic view that the British, Dutch, and Germans already controlled the east coast. Furthermore, representatives from these nations—and others—already had considerable experience of operating there, another disadvantage for American entrepreneurs.[68]

Tisdel's voyage up the Congo River only served to dampen his zeal further. Initially, much like Stanley, he emphasized the wonders of the African climate, soil, and vegetation, and the potential of the natives for trade. Indeed, his early reports even echoed those of Stanley himself, stressing the untapped potential of the countless Africans whom Americans could surely persuade to buy their fine products. He also played on Stanley's theme that such enterprises would be particularly attractive for those manufacturers who were experiencing economic uncertainty because of diminishing domestic markets.[69] However, he gradually modified his views. In fact, he found little there to suggest that Stanley's wild estimates of the amounts of money to be made by selling natives cotton goods or cutlery were likely to be correct.[70] The general air of excitement felt by those who were presently engaged in plans to establish commercial ventures was because of faulty intelligence from traders and missionaries who were rushing into the country, he said.[71] The inhospitable climate, lack of infrastructure, and low levels of interest among the inhabitants he found saw him argue with a growing passion against further American activism there.[72] "The reported wealth of the up country has, in my opinion, been greatly exaggerated," he stated at the end of his journey in March 1885, "and admitting for a moment that all glowing reports of good climate, fertility of soil, wealth of mineral deposits, and inexhaustible stores of ivory are true, it would still be an undesirable and unprofitable country for the white man to make his home, or to embark on any business enterprise."[73]

Civilization

As Roger Louis has put it, at almost no other time before or since did Europeans (and, one could add, Americans) approach their relations with Africa with such "confidence, enthusiasm and idealism" as they did during the Berlin Congo conference.[74] Indeed, Leopold's assurances that he would prioritize infrastructure projects was designed to show that although he was concerned with European investment opportunities, he recognized that these could not be realized without sufficient attention to the impact on the region and its people.[75] From the beginning, such humanitarian concerns had been central to Washington's decision to support Leopold's venture.[76] Arthur's message to Congress advocating recognition all but adopted Sanford's language outlining the International Association's supposed mission:

> Large tracts of territory have been ceded to the association by native chiefs, roads have been opened, steamboats placed on the river, and the nuclei of states established at twenty-two stations under one flag which offers freedom to commerce and prohibits the slave trade. The objects of the society are philanthropic. It does not aim at permanent political control, but seeks the neutrality of the valley. The United States can not be indifferent to this work nor to the interests of their citizens involved in it. It may become advisable for us to cooperate with other commercial powers in promoting the rights of trade and residence in the Kongo Valley free from the interference or political control of any one nation.[77]

In giving its assent, the Senate Foreign Relations Committee used a similarly effusive tone, citing the program of internal improvements that it believed the International Association was making while claiming that the association's flag of blue with a gold star was "the symbol of hope to a strong but ignorant people."[78]

African Americans had particular praise for this supposed altruism, with many believing that their African heritage meant they were well placed to participate in it. Before the Civil War, African American groups sought to build on what they saw as the success of the Liberian model by transplanting large numbers of people from the new world to West Africa to build a black, westernized, Christian empire there.[79] As Sylvia M. Jacobs has shown, middle-class black Americans generally supported the Europeans' proclaimed civilizing mission in Africa. Even those who attacked what they saw as Europe's attempted exploitation of the continent, a feature of African American comment that became more prominent as the century ended, could largely agree that Africa needed to be developed and exposed to Christianity.[80] These commentators—clergymen, journalists, educators, and others—were broadly supportive of the aims of the Berlin conference when it met.[81] Notable black lawyer and activist David Augustus Straker, for example, applauded the work of the Association.

In early 1884, he wrote that African Americans had an especially great interest in the future of the dark continent, accepting the arguments of Stanley and others that, despite its perceived present backwardness and the history of exploitation of its native peoples, Africa held untold potential for Africans, Europeans, and Americans alike.[82] Straker was supported by such figures as Alexander Crummell, an Episcopalian clergyman who had spent time in Liberia and who believed that educated black Americans would go to Africa in significant numbers to help the population there, and George Washington Williams, author of *History of the Negro Race in America* (1883), who would later expose many of the horrors of Leopold's regime. In 1884, Williams met the Belgian king and then testified before the Senate Foreign Relations Committee in support of the United States' participation in the work of his Association.[83]

Ironically, these men professed broadly similar views to some of their white counterparts, who also believed that African Americans could—and should—build a special relationship with Africa. The foundations of such racialized and culturally reductionist views were that, as people of color and the descendants of Africans, American citizens had a natural connection and empathy with distant cultures on the African continent. Tisdel held such an outlook when he began his mission, claiming that blacks in the United States had it within their power to "educate and civilize" fifty million Africans once the continent had reached a sufficient level of political organization.[84] In a more extreme version, John Tyler Morgan, who heard George Washington Williams's testimony to the Foreign Relations Committee, also supported the notion that the United States had an "exceptional" relationship with Africa, because a significant minority of its population was "descended from the negro races in Africa."[85] Morgan's support for this position was, however, because he saw Liberia as the model to be emulated. In this respect, his racist views were congruent with the work of the ACS, which still officially represented Liberia in Washington and had largely recast itself as a humanitarian organization in the years after the Civil War. Even in the 1880s, its members continued to harbor a desire to repatriate black Americans to what they believed to be their homeland.[86]

Other organizations were also captivated by the prospects of this great civilizing work. The *New York Times* argued that on the evidence it had seen, the European approach to Africa was different from its colonial projects in the rest of the world. Although the processes by which these nations organized peoples, most of whom had never heard of Europe, was "arbitrary," it said, they were still better than those seen in Europe's usurpation of India or even the European conquest of North America. In expressing such views, the *New York Times* argued that contact with the occident was likely to yield predominantly positive results for those groups experiencing it: "Certainly the native Africans are not likely to suffer, and their descendants must gain greatly by the definite application to their future intercourse with Europeans of the principle that all alike shall share in whatever trade may be established, and no one nation shall practice in Africa the grasping monopoly and the unchecked exactions known on this continent and in Asia." Somewhat ironically, the paper particularly lauded "a singular revival of the old American spirit" captured in Sanford's dream of building a railroad around the great falls of the Congo, which promised to open up the area to commerce in the region and germinate the seeds of progress.[87] In this instance, taking a technical innovation that had played its part in further marginalizing and decimating the native population of America was recast as a way to bring Africans along the path of "civilization." Several philanthropic groups in the United States supported such views. In line with their existing presence in Africa, Christian missionary organizations applauded the work in which they believed the Berlin conference was engaged. The American Baptist Missionary Union of Boston expressed its "sincere gratification" that the United States government had made the decision to participate with the European nations in the cause of "civilization, humanity and religion" in Africa.[88] So too did the National Temperance Society and the Peace Society, both of which also saw benefits to their respective causes in it.[89]

Some commentators were more cautious, however, expressing concerns about the timing of any measures and the potentially negative impacts on the native population. In the *Chicago Daily Tribune*, journalist Charles G. Leland evinced some skepticism when he wrote that the great endeavor currently underway to divide up what he called "the waste land of the world," including Africa, was being done by governments "of those races which *conceive themselves* to be civilized or enlightened." In expressing such views, Leland was also downbeat about their chances of success, suggesting that the task was "as great an undertaking as was ever recorded in history."[90] And while diplomat John M. Francis, somewhat like Kasson, worried

European rivalries were likely to lead to war and devastation in the region, his concern was not primarily that it would diminish the influence of Europe in Africa but that it would further tarnish the reputation of those who meddled, disgracing "the European element—the white element—in the minds of blacks."[91]

Despite such warnings, the delegates carried their sense of idealism into the conference itself. Sanford and Kasson in particular reveled in the participation of the United States in what Sanford described as the "great civilizing work" of Leopold II.[92] Because of this, Sybil Crowe is critical of the American approach, suggesting that the United States delegation's proposals were "too Utopian to be of any practical importance."[93]

Was this the case? Certainly, those who were intimately involved in the United States' effort appear to have had a genuine desire to help the African people and sought to promote humanitarian causes that had deep resonance in American life. Most significantly, Kasson pressed for a clearer declaration against the slave trade, which he claimed was "the grossest of existing crimes against humanity," in Central Africa. The European proposition that it was merely "the duty of all nations to suppress it as far as possible" was simply not enough for him, and he urged his colleagues to make a more "effectual declaration," pledging to employ "all administrative means in its power" to end the practice and punish anyone who participated in it.[94] Ultimately, the conference adopted something close to his language, combining it with British proposals, even if its impact on the ground was negligible.[95] Like others at the conference, Kasson also wanted to suppress the African natives' access to alcohol. Once again, he connected this to the American historical experience, supporting strong provisions for the prevention of its use as a means of payment in exchange for goods, as had been so prevalent in commerce between Europeans and Native Americans over the centuries. He cited current U.S. laws prohibiting its use for trade among American tribes to support his arguments.[96] He even promoted religious freedom in order to allow different missionaries to operate in the regions overseen by the European powers, drawing more comparisons with the United States. It was, he said, "but one step in logic" from a general admission that if the principle of religious freedom was just for Central Africa, it was "also just for Europe, and for all the people of the Earth."[97] Promotion of these causes has led his biographer to argue that Kasson was the champion of native rights at the conference.[98]

However idealistic some of the American schemes may have appeared, Washington's primary concern was the economic exploitation of the region and its people, and Kasson's interest in the process of civilization was offset by his admission that Americans and Europeans had to encourage "productive labour" among the Africans and ensure the safety and security of the "white race." Building on his proposals to restrict warfare among foreign nations, he expressed particular fears of conflicts in "a country which is full of savages thirsting for the plunder of the white men's property."[99] Kasson's highly racialized views of the Africans equated them with other groups that white Americans generally regarded as inferior, most notably Native Americans. To Kasson, it was obvious that the circumstances to be found in central Africa were "now, to a great extent, the conditions of America when first opened to the European world." And because— augmenting his general fears about the introduction of European wars—he believed that these lesser peoples had a natural proclivity for war, he feared that the racial mix would be combustible. As he saw it, the European powers' search for alliances with various tribes in North America in past centuries had unleashed "frightful barbarities and massacres, sparing no age nor either sex," because of the Natives' "natural love of violence and pillage." And like the Native Americans, black Africans were also "always easily aroused to barbaric strife." Such comparisons not only contrasted both these groups with white Europeans (ignoring that one of the underlying reasons for holding this conference, and, indeed, for him making this intervention during it, was to prevent war between the powers of Europe), but also propounded the paternalistic notion that in doing "the work of reducing Africa to civilization, it is our duty to save them from a repetition of the fatal experiences which characterized the like conditions in America."[100] In this way, the presence of Westerners in Africa helped to create the conditions that required them to remain there.

Such views of the African tribes were not restricted to men like Kasson who had never been to Africa, or even to those who supported American civilizing projects there. After observing the population of the interior, Tisdel broadly agreed with Kasson's assessment. Noting that these tribes often went to war with each other "upon the most trifling pretext," he claimed they were generally "a cruel, treacherous, thieving set," which meant it was not safe for white men to travel there. (He did, however, reveal some of the methods of controlling them with the admission that "the certain fatal result" of a rifle shot would "strike the native with terror.")[101] Although he found those tribes living upriver from Stanley Pool (Pool Malebo) to be slightly more palatable than those further downstream, he saw little reason to believe that they wanted contact with white men at all, or that this contact would bring them along the path of progress. Variously calling them "shrewd, cunning, and thoroughly unprincipled" and "wild, savage, and cruel," he concluded: "Their population is too great, and as they live now so they have lived for ages past. Their morals are of the lowest type. They have no regard whatever for virtue, and their immoral practices place them quite as low in this respect as are the apes or monkeys of the low countries. Disorders of the most loathsome character are rife and apparent everywhere."[102]

The key difference between Kasson and Tisdel was that where Kasson took the apparently base state of Africans to be an opportunity to impose European-style "civilization" on them, Tisdel saw no such prospects. Even during the early stages of his mission when he was still imbued with a sense of optimism, he was already concerned that it was "next to impossible" to get them to appreciate the value of work.[103] While he suggested that some of this may have been brought about by the provision of gin, which he noted was the primary unit of trade, worth many times more than cloth or any other product, this carried the implication that their low morals made them particularly susceptible to its temptations and effects. Traders without alcohol to offer often could not do business, he said, and Africans could sometimes only be induced to work with the promise of a drink at the end of their labors. Tisdel was notably far more complimentary about the women, who he said did most of the hard work and without whom sales to foreign merchants would have been impossible. In contrast, the men "lounge about, drinking, gossiping, fighting, or hunting, as it may suit their tastes."[104]

As his mission progressed, Tisdel's views only hardened. Because education was "in any sense of the word . . . wholly unknown," he perceived the natives to live "like brutes" who seemed to have "no idea above the brute creation." Although, again, he acknowledged that there were exceptions to this and some of the people he had encountered "here and there" showed "signs of intelligence far above the ordinary run of people," especially in the way they bartered and traded, he appeared to believe that large-scale education was impossible. Some of the missionaries had established schools and claimed to be actively engaged in teaching young children, but he said this must be untrue: "I have yet to see a Congo man, woman, or child with whom the missionaries have made any progress."[105]

The Monroe Doctrine and Domestic Reactions

Before the Berlin conference began, Washington was deeply concerned about harmonizing its participation in the conference on West Africa with the United States' policy of noninterference in other nations' affairs. The necessity of doing so was amplified by the fact that the delegates mostly represented the countries of Europe, the main focus of the 1823 Monroe Doctrine. Washington insisted that its recognition of the International Association of the Congo was in keeping with traditional aims of seeking out commercial opportunities for its citizens without becoming involved in foreign alliances.[106] Symbolic of its residual reticence to involvement in such pacts, it reserved the right to decline the subsequent conference's conclusions.[107]

This position was influenced not just by the long-standing debates about the virtues and potential risks of multilateralism, but also by recent experience. During the Garfield administration, Frelinghuysen's predecessor James G. Blaine had proposed holding a Pan-American conference in Washington with representatives from all American nations, a policy Frelinghuysen and his deputy J. C. Bancroft Davis opposed in line with their opposition to Blaine's broader approach. This had led to the Arthur administration withdrawing the invitations to the conference in late 1882, after Garfield's death and Blaine's departure from the State Department.[108] Now, in apparent contrast to this move, Frelinghuysen and Arthur had agreed to involve the United States not only in an international summit but also one that was overseen by European powers and about a third continent, Africa. In addition to the other factors motivating him, Frelinghuysen's concession was an attempt to steer a course between the Half-Breed faction of the Republican Party, which could be regarded as the more liberal wing, led by Blaine, and his own more conservative Stalwarts.

This supposed sop to internationalism was too much for some. Democratic House members Hilary A. Herbert of Alabama and New York's Perry Belmont tabled resolutions of enquiry about the instructions Frelinghuysen had given to Kasson. While they worried about the potential contravention

Figure 5.3 These two Thomas Nast cartoons from the time of the Berlin West Congo Conference in January 1885 demonstrate concerns about Germany's growing power, including in the Americas, and its potential threat to the Monroe Doctrine. The quote under the cartoon on the right reads "In all that concerns Panama and Nicaragua, Germany has quite as important interests at stake as England or France." In the background of the cartoon on the left, note also the figure of Uncle Sam "nosing" in the Congo, hinting at a potential complication of the United States government's involvement in African (and European) affairs.
Source: Thomas Nast, "The Penalty of Over-Officiousness Abroad" and "Bismarck Nosing," *Harper's Weekly*, January 17, 1885.

of the Monroe Doctrine, they were especially concerned that involvement in Africa could provide a pretext for European interference in the Americas—the memory of France in Mexico still fresh in the collective memory—and they were openly skeptical of administration claims that such involvement advanced the interests of the United States. Giving interviews to the *New York Times*, they argued that Leopold had effectively duped the United States government into becoming involved in the division of African territory under the auspices of the International Association. Herbert went so far as to say that he saw the United States becoming one of the sponsors of the construction of a great state in Africa by way of a "joint stock enterprise" along the lines of the East India Company.[109]

Some newspapers attacked the venture on similar grounds, with the *New York Herald* turning from support to open hostility. As the conference began, the *Herald*'s backing was predicated on the notion that United States involvement was designed to break up imperial monopolies. It chided the

European powers, and especially Britain and Portugal, for having practiced the "traditions of colonizing of which the cardinal principle was to seize everything and defy everybody else to approach." The Congo meeting was, it said, going to teach these European nations that this "principle of colonizing" was now "altogether out of date." By January 1885, however, the *Herald* was calling the meeting "a side show," because, it argued, the diplomats were more concerned with the frivolous trappings of summitry—including attending balls and parties—than they were about negotiations. Because of this lack of focus, it feared the outbreak of a major war in Africa. Other publications, including the *Nation* and the *New York Tribune*, also questioned how the United States had come to participate in such an event, and worried that the country would be dragged against its will into an African conflict started by the Europeans.[110]

Such discontentment was not helped by the great interest in Europe generated by the American agreement to attend. British newspapers in particular celebrated what they saw as a change in the direction of U.S. foreign policy and the potentially stronger alliance between the two English-speaking nations that could result.[111] This celebratory air and the lack of European reciprocity was one of the reasons that Daniel De Leon decried the Arthur administration's engagement. He argued that Bismarck had artfully pushed Washington into attending, while forcing the United States and the other nations to acknowledge new precedents in international law that worked only to the advantage of Germany. And, like Congressman Herbert, De Leon claimed the United States was effectively involved in the "carving of a new state on the Congo." Ironically, this saw him supporting what he believed were the legitimate and long-held claims of colonial Portugal in the Congo basin over those of Germany.[112]

The increasingly cynical Tisdel also condemned American entanglements with the European powers over what he called the Congo "fraud," although he looked further back to place the blame on men such as Stanley and Sanford for duping Leopold in the first place.[113] Both men responded to these charges, and Stanley and Tisdel became involved in a bitter war of words. For his part, Sanford praised Leopold's "munificence" in opening up the region to progress while refuting the notion that he was involved in a German plot to exploit the region for its own ends. The results of U.S. participation had been "of practical value and of importance," which would in time "speak for themselves," he said.[114]

Like Sanford, Kasson replied publicly to answer critics who had attacked him. Writing in the *North American Review* at the beginning of 1886, he argued that the United States had contravened no tradition in its foreign policy by attending the Berlin summit. Rehearsing the usual arguments about the American "discovery" of the West African region (he was referring to Stanley) and the need to protect it from marauding colonialists, he said the conference had focused on commercial rather than political interests, while its general act had ensured the progress of civilization and the maintenance of regional peace. He even claimed that the agreement on freedom of trade was "the very substance of the American Constitution extended to the heart of Africa," eviscerating opponents—most notably the incoming Cleveland administration—in the strongest terms for their flagrant misunderstanding of the situation, which he declared to be "so stupendous as to be incredible."[115]

A year before, Kasson had set out his views concerning the Monroe Doctrine in private correspondence with Frelinghuysen and incoming secretary of state Thomas F. Bayard. The influence of President's Monroe's pronouncement had been evident at a number of points during the conference, and several of the other participants, including Britain, alluded to the necessity of developing a similar doctrine for Africa.[116] Yet, Kasson maintained that the meeting had not sought to do this. Monroe's declaration had been "a protest and a warning" to the governments of Europe not to intervene in the affairs of the Americas and to alter the forms of government there, he said. In the present instance, he optimistically asserted, there was "no question" of a change of government or territory. Nor did it foreshadow entangling alliances with the European powers, as Washington had made clear to the other participants from the start.[117] In participating as a full member, the United States had merely assumed its "rightful place in this consultation of civilized nations." All conference members held a veto and had observed strict rules and restrictions on their discussions, while he, as its lead delegate, had focused on preserving the "perfect independence" of the United States by scrupulously avoiding any commitment to combined actions or statements.[118] However, Kasson hinted at the real motive of many European participants when he subsequently argued that not to have accepted Bismarck's invitation and to wait until the other powers had carved up the region would have been "an abdication" of the government's duties, requiring "a timidity, even cowardice, rarely seen in America."[119] In addition, in gendered language, he revealed his growing frustration with continued adherence to Monroe's Doctrine as U.S. power grew, suggesting it was now time to "raise the question" of whether "the rules given for the guidance of childhood will be equally profitable if applied to all the stages of strong manhood."[120]

Unfortunately for Kasson, there had been a distinct shift of mood in Washington as the new administration of Grover Cleveland took office. Perhaps sensing this, and certainly attuned to Kasson's overenthusiasm, Frelinghuysen did not deem it "advisable" to accede to a formal treaty and continued to promote the administration's right to reject any final agreement.[121] New secretary of state Bayard was not satisfied with this, however, informing the German government that the previous administration had entered into the conference "in a merely consultative capacity, and with a distinct reservation of its liberty of action with respect to such recommendations as the conference might adopt." Going further, Bayard rejected the idea that the United States would enter into any political arrangements in "so remote and undefined a region as the Congo Basin."[122] He also refused to endorse, or even comment on, the new German acquisitions to the west of Zanzibar.[123] Although neither Kasson nor Sanford had been given plenipotentiary powers, he was nonplussed that both had signed the conference's general act. He insisted it had no bearing on the United States' continued reservations about the enterprise and on adherence to the constitutional authority of the Senate to approve the measure.[124]

In his first message to Congress at the end of 1885, Cleveland acknowledged the previous administration's position by recognizing the good work of the International Association of the Congo and the reservations that the U.S. delegates had taken into the Berlin conference. Still, he was clearly disturbed that those same delegates had effectively reneged on this in signing the general act. He concluded: "This Government does not . . . regard its reservation of liberty of action in the premises as at all impaired; and holding that an engagement to share in the obligation of enforcing neutrality in the remote valley of the Kongo would be an alliance whose responsibilities we are not in a position to assume, I abstain from asking the sanction of the Senate to that general act."[125] Despite Kasson's pleading, the new administration was not to be swayed.

Conclusion

The final session of the Berlin Congo conference was held on February 26, 1885, just a few days before Grover Cleveland became president of the United States. Bismarck delivered a closing address, before the participants, in alphabetical order by country, signed the general act. In keeping with the grand scale of the meeting and its lofty intentions, each copy was printed in vellum with a red cover.[126] As the conference was nearing its ending, colonial fervor had been further stoked by the news that the long siege of Khartoum in the Sudan, brought about by a religious uprising against foreign rule there, had ended with the city being overrun and its British leader, General Charles Gordon, killed. Intriguingly, Gordon had been recalled to the Sudan to deal with this crisis despite his prior agreement to work for Leopold's new Congo Free State, while the British and Egyptian troops in Khartoum had been left exposed in part because the main forces of the army were still dealing with continuing unrest in Egypt. The *New York Times* reported from London with no little hyperbole that the siege and Gordon's death had generated even more excitement than the Indian mutiny almost thirty years before.[127]

Despite this interest, as we have seen, the newly elected administration in Washington had taken a decidedly different turn. Suspicious of European power and reticent to be seen to embrace U.S. imperial ambitions, Cleveland and Bayard effectively rejected the findings of the Congo conference and the Arthur administration's decision to participate in it. As this suggests, Arthur and Frelinghuysen's response to Bismarck's invitation can be seen as something of an anomaly—the result of a peculiar set of circumstances, including the enthusiastic lobbying of Henry Sanford and the consistent support of John Kasson, rather than as part of a concerted effort for the United States to take a greater international role. The dedication and purpose with which Kasson and Sanford in particular applied themselves to the cause of Africa and Leopold's plans for its development can thus be seen to have diverted American foreign policy and led to a clearer association of the United States with internationalism than most elites were willing to contemplate.

Yet, the U.S. delegation's presence in Berlin was also part of a pattern of experimentation with, assertion, and retraction of American power that was becoming more pronounced by the mid-1880s. Arthur and Frelinghuysen had, after all, also reneged on U.S. involvement in a multilateral exercise, Blaine's Pan-American conference (which Blaine would realize just a few years later when he returned to the State Department), just as the Cleveland administration was now retreating from theirs. Moreover, they saw involvement in Africa in the terms that they saw many other aspects of their politics—as a limited and relatively conservative engagement that could enhance the power and prestige of the United States. And while the public reaction against the Congo conference and U.S. involvement in colonial affairs in Africa was sometimes pronounced, and this is of significance, it is perhaps surprising that there was not more opposition to these policies. Instead, many agreed with the broad thrust of the ideas that lay behind the decisions, even if they objected to some of the specifics of the Congo enterprise. These objections—whether from the *New York Herald* or Willard Tisdel—were therefore less about whether it was necessary to find new markets or even about potential contravention of the Monroe Doctrine, and more to do with whether African markets were actually of any potential value, or if diplomats were going about exploiting them in a useful way.

As this suggests, there was a tension at the heart of American participation in Berlin. In accepting that the European powers could meet in such circumstances and then in agreeing to participate, the United States was engaging in an imperial project. The State Department broadly agreed with its European counterparts in placing faith in the power of trade and commerce to stimulate "civilization." Its ambitions were thus bolder and more like the missions of the European nations and the International Association than it conceded publicly, regardless of whether it sought its own colonies or territorial rights. While many of the Americans who supported Washington's decision applauded the apparently humanitarian motives that lay behind it, to them civilization was always partnered with commercialization and usually seen as a means to an end rather than an end in itself. This opened up possibilities for terrible exploitation of the native populations as well as the further development of burgeoning international rivalries it was intended to preclude, implicating the United States in both.

Undoubtedly more sensitive to such conditions, it was often African Americans who raised these concerns, and sought to expose the fallacy of the Western civilizing mission in Africa. George Washington Williams finally visited the Congo in 1890 and was shocked at what he found, writing an open letter to Leopold expressing his "bitter disappointment" at

Belgian rule there, which was, he said, "cruel and arbitrary." Historian and activist W. E. B. Du Bois also changed his mind about the conference. Du Bois increasingly saw the struggle of African Americans in the United States as part of a global fight for labor rights and social justice amid the exploitative systems of European and American imperialism. Du Bois would go on to blame the meeting in Berlin, at least in part, for the outbreak of World War I.[128]

Conclusion

When Benjamin Harrison became president in 1889, he appointed James G. Blaine his secretary of state. This was Blaine's second time in the role. He had been James Garfield's secretary of state before Garfield was assassinated.

Blaine quickly resurrected an idea he had first floated in Garfield's cabinet: a Pan-American conference. This had been shelved in 1881, when Chester Arthur ascended to the presidency, but now, under Harrison, Blaine held the conference in Washington in 1890. On its eve, liberal journalist Albert G. Browne Jr. wrote an article in the *Atlantic Monthly* expressing his concerns. Partially, these were predicated on the United States government breaking George Washington's golden rule about avoiding diplomatic entanglements, but Browne also worried about the impact the conference would have on the other American states. Browne suggested that the conference signaled the U.S. government's desire to dominate its neighbors economically and diplomatically, and he was surprised that these other nations would send representatives to attend such a meeting.

This apparently sympathetic stance toward the United States' neighbors masked another concern for Browne: that he also saw little merit in a closer association between the United States and the other countries that just happened to share its hemisphere. In his article, he emphasized what he saw as the inherent differences between the United States and these American nations, based on their divergent histories. As he saw it, "the Spanish aristocracies" represented at the conference were "heirs of the glories of Old Spain as our democracy is of the glories of Old England." These, in turn, were "heirs of the Roman Empire" and the other empires of history. Because of this imperial lineage, Latin America was, Browne suggested, very different from "Saxon America" with its foundations in British political practice and law, and he argued that such differences impelled the United States to hesitate before it pursued an imperial role in the Americas. If this conference were to achieve anything positive, he suggested, it had to be to reassure the peoples of the Americas that the United States was no threat to their respective national independence. Primarily, however, this was because long-held traits made them unsuitable for conquest. He urged his fellow citizens to realize that their "Latin characteristics make them an acquisition to be shunned rather than solicited, and that, if destiny condemns us to absorb them as certainly we shall some day absorb Canada, the longer the day is postponed the better for us."[1]

As Browne's article suggests, many people in the United States viewed their neighbors to the south with suspicion. Partly this was based on colonialism and its legacies, partly on the racial makeup of their populations. For Browne, Canada was like the United States because it was predominantly white, but also because it too had been born of the British Empire. It therefore possessed desirable traits that made it an important neighbor and a potentially attractive acquisition. "Latin" countries possessed few such qualities because of their predominantly black and mixed-race populations, and their long history of denigration through Catholic (mis)rule. This did not mean that elite Americans were necessarily sympathetic to British dominion, but many continued to be influenced by it, and, paradoxically, saw it as, if not one of the best, perhaps one of the least worst systems of control—certainly better than those of the French or Spanish. If there had to be empires, including colonial ones, they preferred a British empire to any one run by a continental power.

Because Americans found it all but impossible to escape from European forms of empire, political leaders and other elites constantly compared the great empires of the day with each other. They also contrasted these empires against their own nascent political project. Despite their sometimes grudging admiration for Britain, they generally disliked imperial rule. These Americans found empires to be largely wanting, because they did not fulfill basic criteria they believed were signal features of the developing international environment: a system of democratic rule within a particular polity that encompassed all citizens. Most believed that the United States adhered to such principles, because their nation had grown only by incorporating territory to form a single nation-state, without the complication of overseas colonies.

But this was a questionable way of thinking, a "semantic sleight of hand," as Thomas Bender has called it. It was also a generous reading of the territorial growth and political development of the United States.[2] In fact, the westward movement that came to be called "Manifest Destiny" from the mid-nineteenth century was an integral component of the United States' system, and its political leaders expanded their nation in a conscious and determined manner from the beginning. This had manifold consequences for the people who were overwhelmed by this process—hundreds of Native American tribes, Mexicans, and many other groups—so although successive United States governments eschewed pursuit of overseas territories, the method and logic of their continental expansions bore a striking resemblance to the European powers from whom they were so often keen to distance themselves. These leaders largely erased the idea of conquest by developing narratives and myths about the natural expansion of the United States into contiguous territories that were either unoccupied or in need of modernization. The growing regional salience of the Monroe Doctrine also spawned an assertive nationalism that increasingly presupposed U.S. dominance at the expense of newly independent nations in the Americas, as well as an attempt to replace the imperial powers of Europe, whose preeminence it was initially intended to curtail. As Browne acknowledged in his 1889 article, "We are greatly in error if we suppose that the Latin nations of America in our time feel any gratitude to us for the Monroe Doctrine, or regard it with any respect."[3]

Despite this, the notion that this constitution of an American pattern of power was an *empire* remains highly contested even today. This is especially the case in public debates about United States history, but also surprisingly prevalent in American academia too.[4] Such debates are unlikely to be resolved anytime soon. A more fruitful form of engagement is to understand how American elites thought about the patterns and uses of power over time in the empires they observed.

The debates that took place in the very final years of the nineteenth century amplified and expanded those that occurred in the years and decades before. Elite Americans had always operated within an imperial and colonial world, and this encouraged them to deliberate about how strong states ruled in the international system and what this meant for them as an expanding power. In thinking so deeply about empires, Americans often drew starkly different conclusions. Some viewed with horror the possibility that their nation might try to copy the colonial empires of Europe. There was especially deep apprehension about the more formal patterns of rule, whereby European powers exerted their authority through rigid political, social, and economic structures. This explains why commentators were likely to be more sympathetic to European—and especially British—dominion in settler colonies like Canada and Australia. Browne termed these "Saxon" nations like the United States, and believed their peoples were developing their own political systems at this time. These commentators were much less sympathetic to the rule exercised in less autonomous societies such as India or Egypt, where people struggled under the yoke of British rule. It also helps to explain why there was such uproar in some quarters when the United States appeared to change course in 1898 and acquired new territories in a manner that was indistinguishable from its European colonial counterparts. As we have seen, however, these debates were not new to 1898. Opposition to empire predated the formation of the United States itself and propelled it into existence. These sentiments merely intensified at this time.

Others were more positive about aspects of European empire, and some saw a value in emulating elements of imperialism and even overseas colonialism. Even a repudiation of some forms of colonial control did not necessarily represent a rejection of empire per se. As the United States itself aptly demonstrates, there can be an array of different forms of rule within one empire, and people might admire aspects of a particular imperial polity while eyeing other elements with suspicion. Just as there was no overall imperial project in Europe—and no single British, French, or Spanish empire—so strands of imperial thought and practice could compete for prominence at particular times and in particular ways. Because imperialism was not monolithic or even consistent, neither was anti-imperialism.

Thus, the development of United States international power involved exploring ideas about jurisdictions and processes of control, as well as putting such ideas into practice. Understanding the study of American global influence like this reveals the ways in which the United States was "thinking like an empire." That is, it confronted fundamental questions about how peoples under different administrative structures should be treated by the metropolitan center. In this formulation, groups of people could at once belong within the same empire while also often being governed by it in different ways.⁵ Of all the cases examined in this book, this could be seen perhaps most clearly in relation to the Berlin West Africa Conference. Here, the United States government and press struggled to balance fundamental arguments about the extent to which an imperial space—in this case the region they called "the Congo"—should be a site for material gain *and* humanitarian imperatives. While Americans who were interested in the schemes of Bismarck, Leopold, and other European political leaders rebuffed the suggestion that the conference was concerned with the exploitation of African people, they implicitly recognized that the political order would be altered by their interference in the continent. Although Chester Arthur's administration was willing to entertain this change, the more outwardly critical government of Grover Cleveland that followed it was not. As this shows, an important element in the evolution of the United States on the international stage was the way in which it mirrored the European powers. Just like them, it considered, incorporated, and rebuffed ideas about the empires that it saw around it. Regardless of particular stances, the United States was therefore always intimately connected to the other empires of the day.

Controversy and disagreement about imperial processes usually focused on developments close to home. Such discord could often be seen in responses to the United States' own continental expansion. While some saw this growth as a natural extension of the American civilizing process, a minority recognized the terrible consequences—subjugation, control, and violence—for those it incorporated and banished. Because physical coercion and repression of people in foreign territories were at the heart of colonial encounters and often central to understandings of empires, this influenced the ways that these Americans conceived of the plight of Native Americans, black slaves, and others who bore the brunt of the rapid extension of U.S. control, even if they generally did not connect them explicitly in these terms. Many American leaders also remained fascinated and oftentimes concerned by the impacts of European imperial power around the world. Sometimes this was because these impacts were felt in areas that they believed were within the growing purview of the United States. In these cases, the actions of the European empires directly impinged on them, or at least threatened to do so. This was especially the case with the French intervention in Mexico, but also with prolonged Spanish rule in Cuba. Both posed a direct military and political threat to the United States, and raised fundamental ideological questions about racial difference and how America's burgeoning regional power would be used against peoples Americans considered as inferior. While there was growing interest in the Pacific region—Hawaii, China, Japan—there was generally less concern with territories and peoples far away, explaining the relatively muted and contradictory elite responses to violent British rule in Egypt.

By the 1890s, American elites were increasingly aping the European empires they observed as they absorbed lessons from them. In many cases, this meant spurning formal control while asserting economic dominance based on their understandings of the British model. In practice, this resulted in several territories coming firmly into the United States' orbit as the final decade of the century approached. For example, Hamilton Fish had overseen a reciprocity treaty with Hawaii, a feat his predecessor William Henry Seward had failed to achieve, preparing the islands for what Walter LaFeber memorably called "the hug of annexation."[6] This encouraged an influx of Americans to the islands, where they dominated the Hawaiian economy and its politics by the late 1880s. Frederick Frelinghuysen took a similar approach toward Cuba, drawing the colony ever closer to the United States. Spain's power was waning year by year, and the relative proximity of the United States to the island of Cuba gave it huge advantages. While successive U.S. government efforts expanded and contracted according to the prevailing circumstances and interests of those in power, over time they undoubtedly grew as Madrid's ability to maintain control over the island withered. As the industrialist Andrew Carnegie observed in 1890, when the Harrison presidency signed new treaties concerning Cuba and Puerto Rico, Cuba would soon be to Spain as Canada was to Britain—that is, of diminishing value and slowly slipping away.[7] The pace at which U.S. regional power grew quickened into the 1890s, and domestic concerns (largely misplaced) about the overproduction of agricultural and manufactured goods escalated. This drove a search for markets, especially with the onset of another significant economic downturn in the United States starting in 1893.[8]

The increasing interconnectedness of the United States' burgeoning regional power and its replacement of European hegemony was perhaps best illustrated by its long-held dream to build an isthmian canal connecting the Atlantic and Pacific Oceans.[9] Driven by the Californian gold rush of the late 1840s, American interest in such a canal produced the 1850

Clayton-Bulwer Treaty between the United States and Great Britain, promising neutrality and joint control of any future venture. The treaty represented an improvement in Anglo-American relations at that time and was a component in the already extant belief in inherent Anglo-Saxon superiority over other regional nations and imperial powers. Although French engineers led the way in the decades after 1850, it is significant that most American observers regarded these early efforts to develop the canal with singular skepticism.[10] Americans saw an intimate connection between the United States' right to build a canal and a broader assertion of its power. The reasons it wanted to control Hawaii in the Pacific were varied, but by the 1890s some American leaders saw the connections between acquiring the islands and building an isthmian canal as ways to prevent the European powers from expanding in the Americas and Pacific.[11]

This assertion of regional hegemony was undoubtedly made easier by the relative decline of European concerns in the Western Hemisphere. The French were no longer a force in the region. Spain's empire was in terminal decline. The other strong and rising powers had more important concerns elsewhere. As the century drew to a close, rivalries in Asia became more apparent, and the carving up of territories in Africa was reaching its crescendo. Because of this, the United States could press more of its own plans unilaterally. When Washington renegotiated the Clayton-Bulwer Treaty on Anglo-American relations in Central America in 1900, for example, it was aided in no small part by the British government's attention diverting to its conflict with the Boers in South Africa.[12] The United States' promotion of its regional economic power in turn discouraged European adventurism in the Americas, further reducing diplomatic friction.

There were exceptions. Although relations with Britain generally improved in the 1880s and 1890s, and London mostly approved of its Anglo-Saxon progeny squeezing out other diplomatic rivals, a significant moment of tension emerged over a disputed boundary in South America. In 1895, a long-simmering disagreement between Britain and Venezuela over the border of British Guyana erupted as Britain claimed more territory. As might have been expected, many Americans saw the British move as a contravention of the Monroe Doctrine, and they said so. This time the United States government agreed, making it the basis of its case in support of Venezuela. The disagreement eventually went to international arbitration.

Although the outcome largely favored Britain, the significance of the episode was that it demonstrated the increasing diplomatic decisiveness of the United States, and broad agreement across the American political spectrum about the need to defend and promote the Monroe Doctrine. Ardent expansionist senator Henry Cabot Lodge from Massachusetts, for example, believed that acquiescence to Britain on this issue had the potential to encourage renewed French and German adventurism in the Americas. "These powers have already seized the islands of the Pacific and parceled out Africa," he said. Now, he claimed, the American people were unwilling to "give up their rightful supremacy in the Western Hemisphere. On the contrary, they are as ready now to fight to maintain both, as they were when they forced the French out of Mexico. They are not now, and never will be willing to have South America, and the islands adjacent to the United States, seized by the European powers."[13]

Perhaps surprisingly, President Grover Cleveland agreed with him. Cleveland is often referred to as an anti-imperialist because he rejected the outcome of the Berlin West Africa Conference at the beginning of his first term, refused to sanction the annexation of the Hawaiian Islands when the American population there staged a coup in 1893, and then joined the Anti-Imperialist League when he was out of office at the end of the decade. But in this case, and indeed in others, he could be forthright in his expression of American power. In Asia, his administration did more than observe the machinations of the European empires. During the Sino-Japanese war of 1894–1895, for example, despite claims of indifference and neutrality, it tacked distinctly toward Japan, because it wanted to open up commercial opportunities in China and Korea and undermine Great Britain's regional influence.[14] Besides geopolitical calculations, this stance was also predicated on negative views of the Chinese, who were increasingly denigrated as an immigrant group in the United States. Many believed China was backward in comparison to modern Japan. Cleveland was also clear on the issue of the Monroe Doctrine and the need for the United States to assume a dominant regional role to resist the European powers. Observing that the doctrine was "of vital concern to our people and their Government," Cleveland believed Britain's claim of more territory in Venezuela was a sign that it might be more assertive elsewhere, which is just what President Monroe had warned Americans about in the 1820s.[15]

This increasing self-assuredness on the part of the United States government ultimately led to war with Spain over Cuba under Cleveland's successor, William McKinley. The eruption of another Cuban rebellion against Spanish rule in 1895, a generation after the Ten Years' War, was once again brought about in part by Cuba's economic dependence on the United States (which was this time much deeper), as the depression of the 1890s led to a new round of American tariffs that put the Cuban sugar industry into crisis. The uprising in Cuba against Madrid's rule was another brutal affair that renewed the chorus of anguished voices in the United States about what to do, this time louder than it had been during the 1860s and 1870s. Many of the elements in place a generation before were still evident as Americans surveyed the decaying Spanish empire in the 1890s. Commentary once again focused on the unsatisfactory nature of Spanish rule and Spain's brutal suppression of the insurgency. The key difference this time was that Washington would no longer accede to the perpetuation of Spanish colonialism. Moves toward limited autonomy were unacceptable in the bloody circumstances, and McKinley maneuvered the United States Congress to declare war against Spain in April 1898.

The war was decades in the making. It may have been triggered by short-term factors including growing jingoism in the U.S. press, especially over the sinking of the battleship USS *Maine* in Havana Harbor in February that year, and a downward spiral in diplomatic relations between Washington and Madrid. But it built on generations of developing American economic interests in Cuba and ideas in the United States about Spanish imperial decline, the inability of Cubans to rule themselves, and the perceived potential benefits of American civilization on the island. It was neither an aberration nor an accident, but rather a series of deliberate decisions to overthrow Spanish imperial rule and implement a new American one.[16]

In refusing to make Cuba a colony or to give it independence after it had defeated Spain, the United States government instead created what George Herring has called "a neo-colonial economic structure built around sugar and tobacco" that made Cubans dependent on the United States without officially being ruled by it.[17] It was a course chosen amid a dizzying period of changing ideas and influences and, in particular circumstances, one of the many variants that the United States had observed in other empires. But it was chosen. For comparison, Washington selected different forms of control in Puerto Rico, Guam, and the Philippines—all of which it also seized from Spain during the war—and for Hawaii, which it also finally annexed in 1898.[18]

The debates that raged after 1898 between imperialists and anti-imperialists were infinitely more intense than those that had taken place in the decades before, but the broad outlines of that debate were well established. To many anti-imperialists (although they were such a motley group it is hard to generalize), the policies toward Cuba and then the Philippines were folly, betraying the ideals on which the country was founded. Specifically, taking noncontiguous territories and ruling them was outside the realms of the constitution, and the United States was consciously becoming like nations of the Old World. In contrast, many who supported the imperial policies believed they illustrated exactly the opposite—that the United States was rightly joining the civilized nations of the world, particularly Great Britain, and bringing the benefits of Anglo-Saxon civilization to others. To them, the United States had to take up what Rudyard Kipling in 1899 famously called "The White Man's Burden." There were, in fact, more similarities than differences between these two camps. Racial concerns, learned at home and influenced by the international environment, presupposed the superiority of white, Anglo-Saxon rule. Imperialists used these ideas to advance an expansionist vision that sought to bring civilization to those who supposedly did not have it and who were incapable of ruling themselves. Meanwhile, anti-imperialists fretted that expansion would inevitably bring more "inferior" races closer to the United States, as the unprecedented influx of immigrants was doing. The anti-imperialists expressed little concern for those who bore the brunt of these expansionist ventures. White immigrant communities also participated in these debates, drawing on their own experiences and observations of imperial rule, and also often relying on familiar tropes of racial hierarchy and the inferiority of those presently being colonized to understand it.[19]

The continuity in comprehending the colonizer and colonized applied particularly to the Philippines, which the United States went on to rule for almost a half century after 1898. The American invasion led to a brutal guerilla war against an indigenous force from 1899 and the imposition of a system that drew on Spanish precedents but fundamentally rested on what various American rulers regarded as Anglo-Saxon rule. As *Century* magazine editor Richard Watson Gilder recognized, American interest in the British Empire was now at its peak. United States officials in the Philippines used examples of British control in Egypt and India to guide them, and while they did not always follow British blueprints, they broadly adhered to the maxim that Filipinos required tutelage in financial and bureaucratic affairs if they were to achieve modernity.[20] In doing so, they demonstrated the interconnectedness of the American colonial empire with other empires of the time. They also showed, albeit unwittingly, the need for modern-day observers to reconsider teleological assumptions about 1898 and American imperialism.[21]

Crucially, the debates that took place between people in the United States from the beginning of the republic about the uses of power—their nation's power and the power of others—encourages us to reconceive our understanding of the United States' international role in time and space. Temporally, Frederick Cooper's notion of "unbounding colonialism" in European history could also be applied to the United States. Just as Cooper suggests that scholars of empire often tend to think of European colonial projects as beginning in 1492 and ending at some point in the 1970s, so historians of the United States all too often situate the development of the United States' global role within a particular, bounded timeframe. Many continue to emphasize 1898 as a turning point, a signal moment in the emergence of an American Empire (if this is what they call it). But in fact so many of the elements of American imperial encounters—including colonial ones—were already in evidence long before.[22] Moreover, in terms of space, Cooper acknowledges the need to overcome the sometimes awkward ways scholars have explored the effects of European empires by juxtaposing a colonizing Europe with an ill-defined and generic "colonialism" outside of it. Similarly, scholars must also acknowledge the interrelationships between the United States and other nations and regions that they too often see as separate, breaking down existing dichotomies to better understand imperial and colonizing processes.[23] Perhaps the scholar who has captured this need most succinctly is Amy Kaplan in her 1993 essay on the absence of empire in the study of American culture. She writes about the "interdependence," as she calls it, between the United States and European colonialism in different settings and contexts. This interdependence applied to American actors within European empires who experienced the sensorial and material realities of these empires. Moving beyond this, such interdependence also applied to how elite Americans imagined empire in the period before 1898, including from observations made within the confines of the United States. Several of the actors in this book never set foot in what they would have regarded as an imperial or colonial setting, but still they responded to them. As Kaplan recognizes, imperial ideas and cultures rebounded at home, because they were discussed and contested there, shaping domestic narratives and debates.[24]

This illuminates—but also complicates—our understandings of the United States as an imperial, colonial, and postcolonial nation, and it has implications for the ways we consider the relationship between empire and U.S. national identity. Because the United States defined itself against what it was not, as well as what it was, leaders often compared their own actions and the U.S. system of rule to others. Most obviously, they contrasted the United States with nations and "races" they perceived to be less civilized, often in colonial or quasi-colonial spaces in the Americas, Africa, and Asia. They also compared themselves with other empires. This narrative was important in the development of American identity, suggesting that the United States and its people were almost the diametric opposite of the iniquitous European regimes that were carving up large sections of the world territorially and economically in the late nineteenth century. Moreover, in delimiting the United States in this way, such leaders broadly reinforced the image of the United States as a white, Christian, and often northern-dominated nation determined to survive any threat to its territorial integrity and national identity, especially after the Civil War. These could be from the imperial powers with the ideological and material threats that their rule posed, especially from nearby places such as Mexico and Cuba. They could also be from colonial subjects or former subjects from these empires, who might try to upset the racial and cultural equilibrium by coming to the United States, as they were doing in huge numbers at this time. But they could also be from within, whether this meant Southerners clinging to the institution of slavery, black former slaves, or the Native Americans who would bear the violent brunt of this development over the final decades of the century.[25]

Thus, because most leaders and many people in the United States generally thought of their nation as being fundamentally *unimperial*, this encounter with the empires of Europe reinforced a sense of American exceptionalism with long-term consequences. As we saw at the beginning of this book in the quote from President Obama (a man whose father grew up in Kenya when it was still part of the British Empire), a number of different historical elements have constituted this exceptionalist creed. These include the nature of the American founding, the tenets of the United States' political system, and the relative pacific geopolitical environment (especially compared to Europe) in which it expanded. More than this, it presupposed that the United States simply could not—and cannot—be an empire because its intentions and institutions are fundamentally different to the European empires of the nineteenth and twentieth centuries, which were the exemplars of modern imperialism. Implicit in this stance is the idea that despite the deeply intertwined histories of the United States and the rest of the world, the nation was always separate from and superior to the polities and populations of Europe's colonies and the empires that governed them. Even for those who acknowledge some of the similarities in imperial traits between the United States and these empires, it has always been clear which nation is at the top of the hierarchy of rule.

Yet, in responding in such ways, Americans have consistently confirmed their imperialist mindset and revealed parallels in their development with the other empires of the day. Indeed, their assessments of these empires were vital constituent components of this development during the nineteenth century. Like the progenitors of European empire, American commentators privileged what they thought of as universal concepts of civilization and modernity, and they promoted such ideas because they believed all peoples around the globe should aspire to them. For these leaders, modernity was an end, a natural terminus for social, political, and economic development. It was a state that the Europeans *and* Americans had largely reached, as evidenced by the very fact that they were able to engage in its international promotion to peoples who had not yet achieved it. Americans accepted this as much as Europeans did. So too did they generally accede to the notion that modernity, progress, and uplift could successfully be exported. This belief had profound political implications as U.S. economic and diplomatic power crested, because it presupposed that some interference in other nations and regions might be necessary to ensure their stability and to secure the interests of the United States. However much they may have balked at some of the methods of European imperialism, whether in the Americas, Africa or Asia, their mentality often increasingly mirrored it. Ultimately, like the British in India and Egypt, they valued what they saw as "good government" over "self-government," denying autonomy, reifying Western rule, and ultimately preempting Theodore Roosevelt's corollary to the Monroe Doctrine, promulgated following another dispute over European interference in Venezuela at the very beginning of the next century, which codified the preconditions for U.S. political intervention in the Americas.[26]

Placing the United States among the empires of Europe is not simply part of the current move toward transnationalism in U.S. history. It is an important process of drawing out the connections and collaborations that drove and limited the scope of its international growth. The United States was not at the vanguard of empire during the final decades of the nineteenth century. As Charles Bright and Michael Geyer have put it, it only "tangled with, but was not carried away with the 'new imperialism.'"[27] But its intellectual development was still deeply embedded in and influenced by these imperial processes and outcomes. Examining the ways that the United States approached empire in Mexico, Cuba, Egypt, West Africa, and elsewhere demonstrates the ambiguity of its position in the high imperial age, as it faced the great challenges of its rapid economic growth at home and the prospects of its burgeoning power overseas.

Notes

Introduction: The Challenge of the American Empire

The epigraph is taken from Barack Obama, Remarks at Fort Bragg, NC, December 14, 2011, *Public Papers of the Presidents of the United States: Barack Obama, 2011, Book 1* (Washington, DC: United States Government Printing Office, 2014), 1550.

1. James Bryce, "British Experience in the Government of Colonies," *Century: A Popular Quarterly* 57 (March 1899): 718–29. For a recent treatment of Bryce's views of the American government, see Frank Prochaska, *Eminent Victorians and the United States: The View from Albion* (Oxford: Oxford University Press, 2012), 96–121.

2. Frank Ninkovich, *Global Dawn: The Cultural Foundations of American Internationalism, 1865–1890* (Cambridge, MA: Harvard University Press, 2009). The most important study of ideology remains Michael H. Hunt, *Ideology and U.S. Foreign Policy* (New Haven, CT: Yale University Press, 1987).

3. See Amanda Foreman, *A World on Fire: An Epic History of Two Nations Divided* (London: Penguin, 2010), 10–13; Robert L. Beisner, *From the Old Diplomacy to the New, 1865–1900* (New York: Crowell, 1975), 28–31. On the consular service, see Nicole M. Phelps, "One Service, Three Systems, Many Empires: The U.S. Consular Service and the Growth of U.S Global Power, 1789–1924," in *Crossing Empires: Taking U.S. History into Transimperial Terrain*, ed. Kristin L. Hoganson and Jay Sexton (Durham, NC: Duke University Press, 2020), 135–58.

4. David Milne, *Worldmaking: The Art and Science of American Diplomacy* (New York: Farrar, Straus & Giroux, 2015).

5. For some of the ways that Americans saw their nation as non- or unimperial, see, for example, Mary Ann Heiss, "The Evolution of the Imperial Idea and U.S. National Identity," *Diplomatic History* 26, no. 4 (2002): 511–40.

6. Robert Buzzanco, "Anti-Imperialism," in *Encyclopedia of American Foreign Policy*, ed. Alexander DeConde, Richard Dean Burns, and Fredrik Logevall (New York: Scribners, 2002), 49–60; Ian Tyrell and Jay Sexton, eds., *Empire's Twin: U.S. Anti-imperialism from the Founding Fathers to the Age of Terrorism* (Ithaca, NY: Cornell University Press, 2015).

7. William Appleman Williams, *The Tragedy of American Diplomacy* (New York: Norton, 1991), 19–57. The quote is on 50.

8. On the Wisconsin school, see Emily S. Rosenberg, "Economic Interest and United States Foreign Policy," in *American Foreign Relations Reconsidered*, ed. Gordon Martel (London: Routledge, 2003), 37–51. The classic Wisconsin school text on the post–Civil War period is Walter LaFeber, *The New Empire: An Interpretation of American Expansion, 1860–1898* (Ithaca, NY: Cornell University Press, 1963).

9. See Samuel Flagg Bemis, *A Diplomatic History of the United States*, 5th ed. (New York: Rhinehart & Winston, 1965), 463–75; Julius W. Pratt, *America's Colonial Experiment: How the United States Gained, Governed, and in Part Gave Away a Colonial Empire* (New York: Prentice Hall, 1951).

10. Ian Tyrrell, "American Exceptionalism in an Age of International History," *American Historical Review* 96, no. 4 (1991): 1031–55; 1035. The literature on exceptionalism is huge. For a recent critique, see David Hughes, "Unmaking an Exception: A Critical Genealogy of US Exceptionalism," *Review of International Studies* 41, no. 3 (2015): 527–51.

11. Hunt, *Ideology and U.S. Foreign Policy*, 4–17.

12. Cushing Strout, *The American Image of the Old World* (New York: Harper & Row, 1963).

13. Hunt, *Ideology and U.S. Foreign Policy*, 46–58.

14. Richard White, *The Republic for Which It Stands: The United States During Reconstruction and the Gilded Age, 1865–1896* (New York: Oxford University Press, 2017), 172–212.

15. Matthew Frye Jacobson, *Barbarian Virtues: The United States Encounters Foreign Peoples at Home and Abroad, 1876–1917* (New York: Hill & Wang, 2000).

16. Jay Sexton, *The Monroe Doctrine: Empire and Nation in Nineteenth-Century America* (New York: Hill & Wang, 2011).

17. Eric T. L. Love, *Race Over Empire: Racism and U.S. Imperialism, 1865–1900* (Chapel Hill: University of North Carolina Press, 2004).

18. Edward P. Crapol, *America for Americans: Economic Nationalism and Anglophobia in the Late Nineteenth Century* (Westport, CT: Greenwood Press, 1973), 14.

19. For example, Charles S. Maier, *Among Empires: American Ascendency and Its Predecessors* (Cambridge, MA: Harvard University Press, 2006); Bernard Porter, *Empire and Superempire: Britain, America, and the World* (New Haven, CT: Yale University Press, 2006); Julian Go, *Patterns of Empire: The British and American Empires, 1688 to the Present* (New York: Cambridge University Press, 2011). For a recent interpretation exploring connections between nation and empire in the United States, stressing the ways it inherited its model of empire from the British, see Steven Hahn, *A Nation Without Borders: The United States and Its World in an Age of Civil Wars, 1830–1910* (New York: Viking, 2016).

20. For example, Kristin L. Hoganson, *Consumers' Imperium: The Global Production of American Domesticity, 1865–1920* (Chapel Hill: University of North Carolina Press, 2007); Hoganson and Sexton, *Crossing Empires*.

21. Alfred W. McCoy, Francisco A. Scarano, and Courtney Johnson, "On the Tropic of Cancer: Transitions and Transformations in the U.S. Imperial State," in *Colonial Crucible: Empire in the Making of the Modern American State*, ed. Alfred W. McCoy and Francisco A. Scarano (Madison: University of Wisconsin Press, 2009), 3–33.

22. In 2009, in front of an audience at Cairo University, President Obama declared: "Just as Muslims do not fit a crude stereotype, America is not the crude stereotype of a self-interested empire. The United States has been one of the greatest sources of progress that the world has ever known. We were born out of revolution against an empire. We were founded upon the ideal that all are created equal, and we have shed blood and struggled for centuries to give meaning to those words—within our borders, and around the world." Barack Obama, Remarks in Cairo, June 4, 2009, *Public Papers of the Presidents of the United States: Barack Obama, 2009, Book 1* (Washington, DC: United States Government Printing Office, 2010), 761.

23. For example, Jeremi Suri, *Liberty's Surest Guardian: American Nation-Building from the Founders to Obama* (New York: Free Press, 2011); Elizabeth Cobbs Hoffman, *American Umpire* (Cambridge, MA: Harvard University Press, 2013); A. G. Hopkins, *American Empire: A Global History* (Princeton, NJ: Princeton University Press, 2018).

24. Dane Kennedy, "The Imperial History Wars," *Journal of British Studies* 54, no. 1 (2015): 5–22.

25. Roger Owen, "Introduction," in *Studies in the Theory of Imperialism*, ed. Roger Owen and Bob Sutcliffe (London: Longman, 1972), 4.

26. David C. Hendrickson, *Union, Nation, or Empire: The American Debate Over International Relations, 1789–1941* (Lawrence: University of Kansas Press, 2009).

1. The United States and European Empires

1. See, for example, Kinley J. Brauer, "The United States and British Imperial Expansion, 1815–1860," *Diplomatic History* 12, no. 1 (1988): 19–37; Elizabeth Kelly Gray, "American Attitudes Toward British Imperialism, 1815–1860" (PhD diss., College of William and Mary, 2002); Reginald C. Stuart, *United States Expansionism and British North America, 1775–1871* (Chapel Hill: University of North Carolina Press, 1988). For British North American interests and their concerns about the rise of the United States, see Kenneth Bourne, *Britain and the Balance of Power in North America, 1815–1908* (London: Longman, 1967).

2. Robert Kagan, *Dangerous Nation: America and the World, 1600–1898* (London: Atlantic Books, 2006).

3. Peter S. Onuf, "A Declaration of Independence for Diplomatic Historians," *Diplomatic History* 22, no. 1 (1998): 71–83.

4. Neil L. York, *Turning the World Upside Down: The War of American Independence and the Problem of Empire* (Westport, CT: Praeger, 2003); Walter Nugent, *Habits of Empire: A History of American Expansion* (New York: Alfred A. Knopf, 2008), 3–40; William Earl Weeks, *Building the Continental Empire: American Expansion from the Revolution to the Civil War* (Chicago: Ivan R. Dee, 1996).

5. For a broader discussion, see Michael H. Hunt, *Ideology and U.S. Foreign Policy* (New Haven, CT: Yale University Press, 1987).

6. Eliga H. Gould, *Among the Powers of the Earth: The American Revolution and the Making of a New World Empire* (Cambridge, MA: Harvard University Press, 2012).

7. Peter S. Onuf, *Jefferson's Empire: The Language of American Nationhood* (Charlottesville: University Press of Virginia, 2000), 5.

8. Thomas Jefferson, *Summary View of the Rights of British America* (Williamsburg, VA: Clementina Rind, 1774).

9. Francis D. Cogliano, *Emperor of Liberty: Thomas Jefferson's Foreign Policy* (New Haven, CT: Yale University Press, 2014), 127.

10. Robert W. Tucker and David C. Hendrickson, *Empire of Liberty: The Statecraft of Thomas Jefferson* (New York: Oxford University Press, 1990), 108–17.

11. Alexander Hamilton, "Federalist no. 10," in *The Federalist Papers*, ed. Lawrence Goldman (Oxford: Oxford University Press, 2008), 60.

12. John Lamberton Harper, *American Machiavelli: Alexander Hamilton and the Origins of U.S. Foreign Policy* (Cambridge: Cambridge University Press, 2004), 47–49.

13. Tucker and Hendrickson, *Empire of Liberty*, 95–96.

14. John Gallagher and Ronald Robinson, "The Imperialism of Free Trade," *Economic History Review* 6, no. 1 (1953): 1–15; 8.

15. Brauer, "The United States and British Imperial Expansion," 24–25; Jay Sexton, "The United States in the British Empire," in *British North America in the Seventeenth and Eighteenth Centuries*, ed. Stephen Foster (Oxford: Oxford University Press, 2013), 318–45.

16. Matthew Karp, *This Vast Southern Empire: Slaveholders at the Helm of American Foreign Policy* (Cambridge, MA: Harvard University Press, 2016), 10–31.

17. See, for example, Drew R. McCoy, "Republicanism and American Foreign Policy: James Madison and the Political Economy of Commercial Discrimination, 1789–1794," *William and Mary Quarterly* 31, no. 4 (1974): 633–46.

18. John Adams to William Tudor, June 17, 1818, quoted in Edward Handler, *America and Europe in the Political Thought of John Adams* (Cambridge, MA: Harvard University Press, 1964), 202.

19. Henry Clay, "The American System" (February 2, 3, and 6, 1832), in *The Senate, 1789–1989: Classic Speeches, 1830–1993*, ed. Robert C. Byrd (Washington, DC: United States Government Printing Office, 1994), 83–116.

20. Karp, *This Vast Southern Empire*, 2–23; *Congressional Globe*, 26th Congress, 2nd Session, February 12, 1840, 171.

21. Samuel Flagg Bemis, *John Quincy Adams and the Foundations of American Foreign Policy* (New York: Alfred A. Knopf, 1949), 278; William Earl Weeks, *John Quincy Adams and American Global Empire* (Lexington: University of Kentucky Press, 1992), 41–45.

22. John Quincy Adams, quoted in Bemis, *John Quincy Adams*, 491.

23. Brauer, "The United States and British Imperial Expansion," 26–28.

24. John Quincy Adams, quoted in Weeks, *John Quincy Adams*, 44.

25. Bradford Perkins, *The First Rapprochement: England and the United States, 1795–1805* (Berkeley: University of California Press, 1967), 106–10. Perkins notes that ultimately the economic returns were quite limited.

26. John Quincy Adams, quoted in Weeks, *John Quincy Adams*, 97–98. Weeks suggests that Adams played up the potential problems of freeing large numbers of blacks in order to win over Southern congressmen who might otherwise have supported Henry Clay's interventionism in Latin America.

27. John Quincy Adams, quoted in Michael H. Hunt, *Ideology and U.S. Foreign Policy* (New Haven, CT: Yale University Press, 1987), 59.

28. John Adams to James Lloyd, March 27, 1815, quoted in Handler, *America and Europe in the Political Thought of John Adams*, 203.

29. Charles Gibson, *The Colonial Period in Latin American History* (Washington, DC: Service Center for Teachers of History, 1958), 13.

30. María DeGuzmán, *Spain's Long Shadow: The Black Legend, Off Whiteness, and Anglo-American Empire* (Minneapolis: Minnesota University Press, 2005); James W. Cortada, *Two Nations Over Time: Spain and the United States, 1776–1977* (Westport, CT: Greenwood Press, 1978), 17.

31. Thomas Jefferson to Alexander I, April 19, 1806, quoted in Cogliano, *Emperor of Liberty*, 5; *Niles Weekly Register*, quoted in Hiroo Nakajima, "The Monroe Doctrine and Russia: American Views of Czar Alexander I and Their Influence upon Early Russian-American Relations," *Diplomatic History* 31, no. 3 (2007): 439–63, esp. 458–59.

32. Hamilton, quoted in Kagan, *Dangerous Nation*, 118–19.

33. Henry Blumenthal, *France and the United States: Their Diplomatic Relations, 1789–1914* (Chapel Hill: University of North Carolina Press, 1970), 55.

34. Richard Koebner, *Imperialism: The Story and Significance of a Political Word, 1840–1960* (Cambridge: Cambridge University Press, 1964), 1–26.

35. W., "Styles, American and Foreign," *American Whig Review* 15 (April 1852): 354.

36. Tim Roberts, "Lajos Kossuth and the Permeable American Orient of the Mid-Nineteenth Century," *Diplomatic History* 39, no. 5 (2015): 793–818; Hamilton, "Federalist no. 30," in Goldman, *Federalist Papers*, 144.

37. Emily Conroy-Krutz, *Christian Imperialism: Converting the World in the Early American Republic* (Ithaca, NY: Cornell University Press, 2015).

38. Fuad Sha'ban, *Islam and Arabs in Early American Thought: The Roots of Orientalism in America* (Durham, NC: Acorn Press, 1990). While acknowledging that some American observers could take Islam seriously, Sha'ban suggests that Americans inherited European suspicions of it but blended them with their own particular cultural traits—Puritanism, millenarianism, and ideas of divine providence—leading them to develop Orientalist narratives about Muslims and Islamic cultures.

39. Karine V. Walther, *Sacred Interests: The United States and Islamic World, 1821–1921* (Chapel Hill: University of North Carolina Press, 2015), 1–29.

40. Walther, *Sacred Interests*, 6.

41. James A. Field Jr., *America and the Mediterranean World, 1776–1882* (Princeton, NJ: Princeton University Press, 1969), 237–42.

42. Field, *America and the Mediterranean World*, 248–49.

43. Hunt, *Ideology and U.S. Foreign Policy*, 102–6.

44. Timothy Mason Roberts, *Distant Revolutions: 1848 and the Challenge to American Exceptionalism* (Charlottesville: University of Virginia Press, 2009); Nicole M. Phelps, *U.S.-Hapsburg Relations from 1815 to the Paris Peace Conference: Sovereignty Transformed* (New York: Cambridge University Press, 2013).

45. "The English in Afghanistan," *North American Review* 55 (1842): 45.

46. Marc Egnal, *A Mighty Empire: The Origins of the American Revolution* (Ithaca, NY: Cornell University Press, 1988).

47. Benjamin Franklin, *Observations Concerning the Increase of Mankind, Peopling of Countries, &c.* (Boston: S. Kneeland, 1755).

48. Daniel Immerwahr, *How to Hide an Empire: A Short History of the Greater United States* (London: Bodley Head, 2019).

49. Richard H. Immerman, *Empire for Liberty: A History of American Imperialism from Benjamin Franklin to Paul Wolfowitz* (Princeton, NJ: Princeton University Press, 2010), 7; Michael Vlahos, *America: Images of Empire* (Washington, DC: Johns Hopkins Foreign Policy Institute, 1982), 1.

50. R. W. Van Alstyne, *The Rising American Empire* (Chicago: Quadrangle, 1960); Tucker and Hendrickson, *Empire of Liberty*; Michael P. Federici, *The Political Philosophy of Alexander Hamilton* (Baltimore, MD: Johns Hopkins University Press, 2012), 151; Harper, *American Machiavelli*, 164–65.

51. Quoted in Reginald Horsman, "Dimensions of an 'Empire for Liberty': Expansion and Republicanism, 1775–1825," *Journal of the Early Republic* 9, no. 1 (1989): 1–20; 6.

52. For differing views, see Tucker and Hendrickson, *Empire of Liberty*, 101–7; Lawrence S. Kaplan, *Thomas Jefferson: Westward the Course of Empire* (Wilmington, DE: Scholarly Resources, 1999), 134–39; Piero Gleijeses, "Napoleon, Jefferson and the Louisiana Purchase," *International History Review* 39, no. 2 (2017): 237–55.

53. Julian P. Boyd, "Thomas Jefferson's 'Empire of Liberty,'" *Virginia Quarterly Review* 24 (1948): 538–54.

54. Thomas Jefferson, Second Inaugural Address, March 4, 1805, in *A Compilation of the Messages and Papers of the Presidents*, ed. James D. Richardson (New York: Bureau of National Literature, 1897), 1:366–70.

55. Robert Lee, "Accounting for Conquest: The Price of the Louisiana Purchase for Indian Country," *Journal of American History* 103, no. 4 (2017): 921–42; Walter Johnson, *River of Dark Dreams: Slavery and Empire in the Cotton Kingdom* (Cambridge, MA: Belknap Press of Harvard University Press, 2013); Tucker and Hendrickson, *Empire of Liberty*, 145–47.

56. Troy Bickham, *The Weight of Vengeance: The United States, the British Empire, and the War of 1812* (Oxford: Oxford University Press, 2012); Richard W. Maass, "'Difficult to Relinquish Territory Which Has Been Conquered': Expansionism and the War of 1812," *Diplomatic History* 39, no. 1 (2015): 70–97.

57. Thomas Jefferson, quoted in Julius W. Pratt, *Expansionists of 1812* (New York: P. Smith, 1957), 153.

58. Hamilton, "Federalist no. 24," in Goldman, *Federalist Papers*, 120; Hamilton, "Federalist no. 25," in Goldman, *Federalist Papers*, 122. These factors bolstered Hamilton's case for strong federal political authority in the United States with a powerful treasury and a capable military.

59. Resolution Relative to the Occupation of the Floridas by the United States of America, 11th Congress, 3rd Session, January 15, 1811, quoted in Pratt, *Expansionists of 1812*, 68–74.

60. Weeks, *John Quincy Adams*, 19; Greg Russell, *John Quincy Adams and the Public Virtues of Diplomacy* (Columbia: University of Missouri Press, 1995), esp. 247–61.

61. Niall Ferguson, *Colossus: The Rise and Fall of the American Empire* (London: Penguin, 2004), 41.

62. David Mayers, *Dissenting Voices in America's Rise to Power* (Cambridge: Cambridge University Press, 2007), 109–37; Thomas R. Hietala, *Manifest Design: Anxious Aggrandizement in Late Jacksonian America* (Ithaca, NY: Cornell University Press, 1985).

63. Bemis, *John Quincy Adams*, 300–340. The quote is on 340.

64. Quoted in Sue Davis, *The Political Thought of Elizabeth Cady Stanton: Women's Rights and the American Political Traditions* (New York: New York University Press, 2008), 65.

65. Martin R. Delany to Frederick Douglass, February 19, 1848, in *Martin R. Delany: A Documentary Reader*, ed. Robert S. Levine (Chapel Hill: University of North Carolina Press, 2003), 83–85.

66. John Quincy Adams to Richard Rush, May 20, 1818, quoted in *Writings of John Quincy Adams*, ed. Worthington Chauncey Ford (New York: Macmillan, 1916), 6:321–22 (emphasis added).

67. *New York Morning News*, October 13, 1845, quoted in Frederick Merk, *Manifest Destiny and Mission in American History*, with a new foreword by John Mack Faragher (Cambridge, MA: Harvard University Press, 1995), 25.

68. David M. Pletcher, *The Diplomacy of Annexation: Texas, Oregon, and the Mexican War* (Columbia: University of Missouri Press, 1973), esp. 113–38; Sam W. Haynes, "Anglophobia and the Annexation of Texas: The Quest for National Security," in *Manifest Destiny and Empire: American Antebellum Expansion*, ed. Sam W. Haynes and Christopher Morris (College Station: Texas A&M University Press, 1997), 115–45.

69. Jackson to A. V. Brown, February 12, 1843, in *Life of Andrew Jackson*, ed. James Parton (New York: Mason Brother, 1861), 3:658–60.

70. Carroll Smith-Rosenberg, *This Violent Empire: The Birth of American National Identity* (Chapel Hill: University of North Carolina Press, 2010), esp. 17–18. Kariann Akemi Yokota, *Unbecoming British: How Revolutionary America Became a Postcolonial Nation* (Oxford: Oxford University Press, 2011), 12.

71. Anders Stephanson, "An American Story? Second Thoughts on Manifest Destiny," in *Manifest Destinies and Indigenous Peoples*, ed. David Maybury-Lewis, Theodore Macdonald, and Biorn Maybury-Lewis (Cambridge, MA: Harvard University Press, 2009), 21–49; Richard White, *The Middle Ground:*

Indians, Empires, and Republics in the Great Lakes Region, 1650–1815 (Cambridge: Cambridge University Press, 1991).

72. Gould, *Among the Powers of the Earth*, 4.

73. Gordon H. Chang, *Fateful Ties: A History of America's Preoccupation with China* (Cambridge, MA: Harvard University Press, 2015), 5.

74. Chang, *Fateful Ties*, 32–35.

75. Norman A. Graebner, *Empire on the Pacific: A Study in Continental Expansion* (New York: Ronald Press, 1955); Charles Vevier, "American Continentalism: An Idea of Expansion, 1845–1910," *American Historical Review* 65, no. 2 (1960): 323–35; Bruce Cumings, *Dominion from Sea to Sea: Pacific Ascendency and American Power* (New Haven, CT: Yale University Press, 2009).

76. Lawrence E. Gelfand, "Hemispheric Regionalism to Global Universalism: The Changing Face of United States National Interests," *Mid-American Historical Review* 76, no. 3 (1994): 187–203, 190; James E. Lewis, *The American Union and the Problem of Neighborhood: The United States and the Collapse of the Spanish Empire, 1783–1829* (Chapel Hill: University of North Carolina Press, 1998).

77. John Quincy Adams, *Address Delivered at the Request of the Committee of the Citizens of Washington, July 4, 1821* (Washington, DC: Davis & Force, 1821), 28–29.

78. James Monroe, Seventh Annual Message, December 2, 1823, in *A Compilation of the Messages and Papers of the Presidents*, ed. James D. Richardson (New York: Bureau of National Literature, 1897), 2:776–89; 786–87.

79. Jay Sexton, *The Monroe Doctrine: Empire and Nation in Nineteenth-Century America* (New York: Hill & Wang, 2011), 3.

80. Quoted in Bradford Perkins, *The Cambridge History of American Foreign Relations*, vol. 1, *The Creation of a Republican Empire, 1775–1865* (Cambridge: Cambridge University Press, 1993), 160–61 (italics in original).

81. Brauer, "The United States and British Imperial Expansion," 29–32.

82. Jesup, quoted in Bourne, *Britain and the Balance of Power in North America*, 55.

83. Dexter Perkins, *A History of the Monroe Doctrine* (Boston: Little, Brown, 1955), 67–70.

84. See, for example, Robert E. May, *Manifest Destiny's Underworld: Filibustering in Antebellum America* (Chapel Hill: University of North Carolina Press, 2002), 1–4; Robert E. May, *The Southern Dream of a Caribbean Empire* (Baton Rouge: Louisiana State University Press, 1973); Joseph A. Stout Jr., *Schemers and Dreamers: Filibustering in Mexico* (Fort Worth: Texas Christian University Press, 2002); Albert L. Hurtado, "Empires, Frontiers, Filibusters, and Pioneers: The Transnational World of John Sutter," *Pacific Historical Review* 77, no. 1 (2008): 19–47.

85. Aims McGuinness, *Path of Empire: Panama and the California Gold Rush* (Ithaca, NY: Cornell University Press, 2008).

86. On this point, see, for example, Thomas D. Schoonover, *The French in Central America: Culture and Commerce, 1820–1930* (Wilmington, DE: Scholarly Resources, 2000), esp. 1–54.

87. Louis A. Pérez Jr., *Cuba and the United States: Ties of Singular Intimacy*, 3rd ed. (Athens: University of Georgia Press, 2003); John Patrick Leary, "Cuba in the American Imaginary: Literature and National Culture in Cuba and the United States, 1848–1958" (PhD diss., New York University, 2009); Karl M. Schmitt, *Mexico and the United States, 1821–1873: Conflict and Coexistence* (New York: Wiley, 1974), esp. 27–29.

88. Jay Sexton, "'The Imperialism of the Declaration of Independence' in the Civil War Era," in *Empire's Twin: Anti-Imperialism from the Founding Era to the Age of Terrorism*, ed. Ian Tyrell and Jay Sexton (Ithaca, NY: Cornell University Press, 2015), 59–76.

2. France and the Mexican Intervention

1. This description is based on the following accounts: Richard O'Connor, *The Cactus Throne: The Tragedy of Maximilian and Carlota* (London: George Allen & Unwin, 1971); Joan Haslip, *Imperial Adventurer: Emperor Maximilian of Mexico* (London: Weidenfeld & Nicolson, 1971), 242–53; H. Montgomery Hyde, *Mexican Empire: The History of Maximilian and Carlota of Mexico* (London: Macmillan, 1946), 145–51; John S. C. Abbott, "Maximilian of Mexico," *Harper's New Monthly Magazine* 221 (October 1868): 667–83.

2. Halford L. Hoskins, "French Views of the Monroe Doctrine and the Mexican Expedition," *Hispanic American Historical Review* 4, no. 4 (1921): 677–89.

3. There is a huge literature on Napoleon III's intervention in Mexico. For works that focus on the U.S. role, see especially, Stève Sainlaude, *France and the American Civil War: A Diplomatic History*, trans. Jessica Edwards (Chapel Hill: University of North Carolina Press, 2019); Patrick J. Kelly, "The North American Crisis of the 1860s," *Journal of the Civil War Era* 2, no. 3 (2012): 337–68; Michele Cunningham, *Mexico and the Foreign Policy of Napoleon III* (Basingstoke, UK: Palgrave Macmillan, 2001); Thomas Schoonover, "Napoleon Is Coming! Maximilian Is Coming? The International History of the Civil War in the Caribbean Basin," in *The Union, the Confederacy, and the Atlantic Rim*, ed. Robert E. May (West Lafayette, IN: Purdue University Press, 1995), 101–30; Thomas Schoonover, *Dollars Over Dominion: The Triumph of Liberalism in Mexican-United States Relations, 1861–1867* (Baton Rouge: Louisiana State University Press, 1978); Alfred Jackson Hanna and Kathryn Abbey Hanna, *Napoleon III and Mexico: American Triumph Over Monarchy* (Chapel Hill: University of North Carolina Press, 1971); Arnold Blumberg, *The Diplomacy of*

the Mexican Empire, 1863–1867 (Philadelphia: American Philosophical Society, 1971); Paul H. Reuter Jr., "United States-French Relations Regarding French Intervention in Mexico: From the Tripartite Treaty to Querétaro," *Southern Quarterly* 6, no. 4 (1968): 469–89. For a useful contemporary perspective, see "The Mexican Question," *North American Review* 103 (1866): 106–42.

4. Diary entry, July 27, 1863, in *The Diary of Gideon Welles*, ed. Edgar T. Welles (Boston: Houghton Mifflin, 1911) (hereafter *Welles Diary*), 1:385.

5. Schoonover, *Dollars Over Dominion*, 13.

6. Robert Ryal Miller, *Arms Across the Border: United States Aid to Juárez During the French Intervention in Mexico* (Philadelphia: American Philosophical Society, 1973); Robert Ryal Miller, "Matias Romero: Mexican Minister to the United States During the Juarez-Maximilian Era," *Hispanic American Historical Review* 45, no. 2 (1965): 228–45.

7. For example, Lars Schoultz has noted the development of an "imperial mentality" toward Latin America after the Civil War. Lars Schoultz, *Beneath the United States: A History of U.S. Policy Toward Latin America* (Cambridge, MA: Harvard University Press, 1998), 78–90.

8. Don H. Doyle, *The Cause of All Nations: An International History of the American Civil War* (New York: Basic Books, 2015).

9. Edward C. Rugemer, "Why Civil War? The Politics of Slavery in Comparative Perspective," in *The Civil War as Global Conflict: Transnational Meanings of the American Civil War*, ed. David T. Gleason and Simon Lewis (Columbia: University of South Carolina Press, 2014), 14–35.

10. On Maximilian's attempts, and failures, to enact reforms, see Robert H. Duncan, "Political Legitimation and Maximilian's Second Empire in Mexico, 1864–1867," *Mexican Studies* 12, no. 1 (1996): 27–66.

11. Schoonover, *Dollars Over Dominion*, 60–64.

12. Spanish forces were the first to arrive at Veracruz on December 8, 1861. See Clifford L. Egan, "The United States and the Spanish Intervention in Mexico, 1861–1862," *Revista de Historia de América* 63, no. 4 (1967): 1–12; Schoonover, "Napoleon Is Coming," 101.

13. John S. C. Abbott, *The History of Napoleon III, Emperor of the French* (Boston: B. B. Russell, 1869), 7.

14. William Graham Sumner, "Republican Government" (1877), in *Essays of William Graham Sumner*, ed. Albert Galloway Keller and Maurice R. Davie (Hamden, CT: Archon, 1969), 2:193–212; 198.

15. Robert Aldrich, *Greater France: A History of French Overseas Expansion* (Basingstoke, UK: Palgrave Macmillan, 1996), 24–88.

16. See, for example, Garnier d'Abain, "Strange Scenes in a Strange Land," *Scribner's Monthly* 8, no. 3 (1874): 355

17. Samuel Williams, "Sahara and the Saharans," *Overland Monthly* 1, no. 5 (November 1868): 409.

18. William Graham Sumner, "Protectionism: The –ism Which Teaches Us That Waste Makes Wealth," 1885, in Keller and Davie, *Essays of William Graham Sumner*, 2:365–467; 415.

19. Editor's Drawer, *Harper's New Monthly Magazine* 28, no. 164 (January 1864): 279.

20. Charles MacKay, "The French Conquest of Mexico," *Westminster Review* 80 (1863): 313–44.

21. Vine Wright Kingsley, *French Intervention in America* (New York: C. B. Richardson, 1863).

22. Joshua Leavitt, "The Key of the Continent," *New Englander and Yale Review* 23, no. 3 (1864): 517–39; 531.

23. Editor's Easy Chair, *Harper's New Monthly Magazine* 26, no. 155 (April 1863): 709–10.

24. J. W. Draper, "The French Expedition to Mexico," *Harper's New Monthly Magazine* 37, no. 120 (September 1868): 520–25; 523.

25. William V. Wells, "A Court Ball at the Palace of Mexico," *Overland Monthly* 1, no. 2 (August 1868): 107–12; 109–10.

26. John W. Dwinelle, "Napoleon III. Second Period, 1865 to 1872," *Overland Monthly* 10, no. 4 (April 1873): 358–71; 364–65.

27. Matthew Karp, "King Cotton, Emperor Slavery: Antebellum Slavery and the World Economy," in Gleason and Lewis, *The Civil War as Global Conflict*, 36–55.

28. Doyle, *Cause of All Nations*, 27–49.

29. Howard Jones, *Blue and Gray Diplomacy: A History of Union and Confederate Foreign Relations* (Chapel Hill: University of North Carolina Press, 2010), 47–81.

30. Jones, *Blue and Gray Diplomacy*, 313–16; Amanda Foreman, *A World on Fire: An Epic History of Two Nations Divided* (London: Penguin, 2010), 271–72.

31. For a recent assessment of Seward's impact, see Walter Stahr, *Seward: Lincoln's Indispensable Man* (New York: Simon & Schuster, 2011).

32. Kathryn Abbey Hanna, "The Roles of the South in the French Intervention in Mexico," *Journal of Southern History* 20, no. 1 (1954): 3–21, esp. 12–14.

33. Nicole M. Phelps, *U.S.-Hapsburg Relations from 1815 to the Paris Peace Conference: Sovereignty Transformed* (New York: Cambridge University Press, 2013), 68–75; Stephen J. Valone, "Weakness Offers Temptation: William Seward and the Reassertion of the Monroe Doctrine," *Diplomatic History* 19, no. 4 (1995): 583–99.

34. Abbott, *History of Napoleon III*, 655.

35. Mary Ann Heiss, "The Evolution of the Imperial Idea and U.S. National Identity," *Diplomatic History* 26, no. 4 (2002): 511–40, esp. 523.

36. Cunningham, *Mexico and the Foreign Policy of Napoleon III*, 197–99.

37. Seward to Corwin, April 6, 1861, United States Department of State, *Foreign Relations of the United States* (hereafter *FRUS*), 1861 (Washington, DC: United States Government Printing Office, 1861), 65–66.

38. Seward to Corwin, April 6, 1861, *FRUS*, 1861, 65–66.

39. See, for example, Seward to Corwin, April 6, 1861, *FRUS*, 1861; Corwin to Seward, July 28, 1862, *FRUS*, 1862, 754–55. See also Charles S. Walker, "Causes of the Confederate Invasion of New Mexico," *New Mexico Historical Review* 8, no. 2 (1933): 76–97.

40. Frederick Douglass, "The Slaveholder's Rebellion," July 4, 1862, in *The Frederick Douglass Papers, Series One: Speeches, Debates, and Interviews*, ed. John W. Blassingame and John R. McKivigan (New Haven, CT: Yale University Press, 1985), 3:521–43; 522–23.

41. *Congressional Globe*, 37th Congress, 2nd Session, December 30, 1861, 180–81.

42. L. W. Spratt, "Slave Trade in the Southern Congress," *Southern Literary Messenger* 32 (June 1861): 409–20; 417–18.

43. Kinley J. Brauer, "The Slavery Problem in the Diplomacy of the American Civil War," *Pacific Historical Review* 46, no. 3 (1977): 439–69; Seward to Dayton, October 23, 1863, in *The Works of William H. Seward*, ed. George E. Baker (New York: AMS, 1972)(hereafter *Works of Seward*), 5:412.

44. Seward to Dayton, April 22, 1861, in *Works of Seward*, 5:224–25.

45. Seward to Pike, November 5, 1862, in *Works of Seward*, 5:367. See also Seward to Adams, July 30, 1863, in *Works of Seward*, 5:395.

46. Seward to Lincoln, "Some Thoughts for the President's Consideration," April 1, 1861, in *The Collected Works of Abraham Lincoln*, ed. Roy P. Basler (New Brunswick, NJ: Rutgers University Press, 1953), 4:316–18. Although Lincoln drafted a reply to Seward's message, it is unclear whether he ever sent it.

47. Seward to Clay, May 6, 1861, in *Works of Seward*, 5:251.

48. See, for example, "Relations of France with Mexico and the United States," *New York Times*, December 12, 1863, 2.

49. See Seward to Dayton, April 8, 1864, 524, Record Group 59, Records of the Department of State (hereafter RG 59), M77, Diplomatic Instructions of the Department of State, 1801–1906, France, 16, reel 57, National Archives and Records Administration, College Park, MD (hereafter NARA); Dayton to Seward, December 21, 1863, no. 388, 64, RG 59, M34, Despatches from United States Ministers to France, 1789–1906, reel 57, NARA.

50. Jones, *Blue and Gray Diplomacy*, esp. 309–11.

51. Doyle, *Cause of All Nations*, 117.

52. Corwin to Seward, March 24, 1862, *FRUS*, 1862, 732–33.

53. Lord Russell to Lord Crowley, September 27, 1861, quoted in Cunningham, *Mexico and the Foreign Policy of Napoleon III*, 48–49; Jay Sexton, *The Monroe*

Doctrine: Empire and Nation in Nineteenth-Century America (New York: Hill & Wang, 2011), 149.

54. See Wayne H. Bowen, *Shades of Blue and Grey: Spain and the American Civil War* (Columbia: Missouri University Press, 2011), 84–106; James W. Cortada, *Spain and the American Civil War: Relations at Mid-Century, 1855–1868* (Philadelphia: American Philosophical Society, 1980), 30–41; Robert W. Frazer, "The Role of the Lima Congress, 1864–1865, in the Development of Pan-Americanism," *Hispanic American Historical Review* 29, no. 3 (1949): 319–48; Schoonover, *Dollars over Dominion*, 153–57.

55. See Andre M. Fleche, *The Revolution of 1861: The American Civil War in the Age of Nationalist Conflict* (Chapel Hill: University of North Carolina Press, 2014).

56. Seward to Dayton, June 21, 1862, *FRUS*, 1862, 354–55.

57. Seward to William L. Dayton, March 3, 1862, 16, RG 59, M77, reel 56, NARA.

58. Dayton to Seward, April 22, 1862, no. 142; Dayton to Seward, June 5, 1862, RG 59, M34, reel 54, NARA.

59. "The Operations of France in America," *New York Times*, February 2, 1863, 8.

60. Seward to Dayton, February 13, 1864, 481, RG 59, M77, reel 57, NARA; Seward to Dayton, October 23, 1863, in *Works of Seward*, 5:410–11; Seward to Marquis de Montholon, December 6, 1865, in *Works of Seward*, 5:426.

61. Diary entry, July 27, 1863, *Welles Diary*, 1:385; diary entry, July 11, 1865, *Welles Diary*, 2:332–33; "Monthly Record of Events: The French in Mexico," *Harper's New Monthly Magazine* 193 (June 1866): 126–27.

62. Dayton to Seward, April 22, 1862, no. 142; Dayton to Seward, June 5, 1862, RG 59, M34, reel 54, NARA.

63. For different interpretations of Seward's imperial ambitions, see, for example, Frederic Bancroft, "Seward's Idea of Territorial Expansion," *North American Review* 167 (1898): 79–89; Gordon H. Warren, "Imperial Dreamer: William Henry Seward and American Destiny," in *Makers of American Diplomacy: From Benjamin Franklin to Alfred Thayer Mahan*, ed. Frank J. Merli and Theodore A. Wilson (New York: Scribner, 1974), 195–221; Richard H. Immerman, *Empire for Liberty: A History of Imperialism from Benjamin Franklin to Paul Wolfowitz* (Princeton, NJ: Princeton University Press, 2010), 98–127.

64. Walter G. Sharrow, "William H. Seward and the Basis for American Empire," *Pacific Historical Review* 36, no. 3 (1967): 325–42. For a somewhat similar interpretation, see Ernest N. Paolino, *The Foundations of the American Empire: William Henry Seward and U.S. Foreign Policy* (Ithaca, NY: Cornell University Press, 1973).

65. Seward to Bigelow, September 6, 1865, in *Works of Seward*, 5:423.

66. William H. Seward, "To the Chautauque [*sic*] Convention," March 31, 1846, in *Works of Seward*, 3:409; Seward, "Oration at the Dedication of Capital University, Columbus, Ohio," September 14, 1853, in *The Life of William H. Seward with Selections from His Works*, ed. George E. Baker (New York: J. S. Redfield, 1855), 328.

67. Seward to Adams, April 10, 1861, in *Works of Seward*, 4:199–213; Seward to Adams, July 28, 1864, in *Works of Seward*, 5:420–21. See Andrew Priest, "Imperial Exchange: American Views of the British Empire During the Civil War and Reconstruction," *Journal of Colonialism and Colonial History* 16, no. 1 (2015), for more on Seward's views of the British Empire at this time.

68. Seward to Clay, May 6, 1861, *Works of Seward*, 5:246.

69. Seward to Marquis de Montholon, February 12, 1865, in *Works of Seward*, 5:435.

70. Seward to Andrew B. Dickinson, June 5, 1861, in *Works of Seward*, 5:262; diary entry, July 27, 1863, *Welles Diary*, 1:385; diary entry, April 17, 1866, *Welles Dairy*, 2:485; Priest, "Imperial Exchange."

71. John S. C. Abbott, "Maximilian of Mexico," *Harper's New Monthly Magazine* 37, no. 221 (October 1868): 667.

72. John T. Pickett, quoted in Doyle, *Cause of All Nations*, 120.

73. "Our Southern Sister Republic," August 10, 1871, in *The Life and Writings of Frederick Douglass*, ed. Philip S. Foner (New York: International Publishers, 1955), 4:259.

74. Frederick Douglass, "What the Black Man Wants," January 26, 1865, in *The Frederick Douglass Papers, Series One: Speeches, Debates, and Interviews*, ed. John W. Blassingame and John R. McKivigan (New Haven, CT: Yale University Press, 1991), 4:59–69; 65–66.

75. Douglass, "Our Southern Sister Republic," 4:259.

76. "The Mexican Question," *New York Times*, June 8, 1865, 4.

77. Joshua Leavitt, *The Monroe Doctrine* (New York: Sinclair Tousey, 1863).

78. *Congressional Globe*, 37th Congress, 3rd Session, February 3, 1863, 694.

79. *Congressional Globe*, 38th Congress, 1st Session, April 4, 1864, 1408.

80. *Congressional Globe*, 39th Congress, 1st Session, December 11, 1865, 19; Marvin Goldwert, "Matías Romero and Congressional Opposition to Seward's Policy Toward the French Intervention in Mexico," *The Americas* 22, no. 1 (1965): 22–40, esp. 36–38.

81. Alfred Jervis to Thaddeus Stevens, April 8, 1864, in *The Selected Papers of Thaddeus Stevens*, ed. Beverly Wilson Palmer (Pittsburgh, PA: University of Pittsburgh Press, 1997), 1:452–55.

82. Bigelow to Seward, July 11, 1865; Bigelow to Drouyn de Lhuys, July 26, 1865; Drouyn de Lhuys to Bigelow, August 1, 1865, RG 59, M34, reel 61, NARA; Ulysses S. Grant, "A Threatened Invasion of California: Letter to Major

General McDowell by General U. S. Grant," *California Historical Society Quarterly* 13, no. 1 (1934): 38–42; William E. Hardy, "South of the Border: Ulysses S. Grant and the French Intervention," *Civil War History* 54, no. 1 (2008): 63–86.

83. Doyle, *Cause of All Nations*, 291.

84. Diary entry, June 16 1865; diary entry, November 23, 1866, *Welles Diary*, 2:317; 2:624–26; Henry Blumenthal, *France and the United States: Their Diplomatic Relations, 1789–1914* (Chapel Hill: University of North Carolina Press, 1970), 112–13; Miller, "Arms Across the Border," 34.

85. Diary entry, August 25, 1865, *Welles Diary*, 2:367.

86. Diary entry, August 25, 1865, *Welles Diary*, 2:366–67; Albert Castel, *The Presidency of Andrew Johnson* (Lawrence: University Press of Kansas, 1979), 40–42; Valone, "Weakness Offers Temptation," 598–59.

87. Campbell to Johnson, May 8, 1865, in *The Papers of Andrew Johnson*, ed. Paul H. Bergeron, LeRoy P. Graf, and Ralph W. Haskins (Knoxville: University of Tennessee Press, 1989), 8:46.

88. William W. Duffield to Johnson, July 15, 1867, in *The Papers of Andrew Johnson*, ed. Paul H. Bergeron, LeRoy P. Graf, and Ralph W. Haskins (Knoxville: University of Tennessee Press, 1995), 12:399–400.

89. Dayton to Seward, January 20, 1862, no. 104, RG 59, M34, reel 54, NARA.

90. *Congressional Globe*, 37th Congress, 3rd Session, February 3, 1863, 695.

91. Sumner to Nathaniel Niles, April 2, 1864, in *The Selected Letters of Charles Sumner*, ed. Beverly Wilson Palmer (Boston: Northeastern University Press, 1990), 2:232–33.

92. Bigelow to Seward, March 14, 1865, RG 59, M34, reel 59, NARA; Dayton to Seward, June 8, 1864, no. 483, RG 59, M34, reel 57, NARA; Seward to Geofroy, April 6, 1864, *FRUS*, 1865, 3:212–13.

93. Seward to Motley, April 14, 1864, reel 137, folder 5542, William Henry Seward Papers, Manuscript Division, Library of Congress, Washington, DC (hereafter Seward Papers).

94. Seward to Dayton, September 26, 1863, in *Works of Seward*, 5:403–4.

95. Seward to Dayton, October 23, 1863, in *Works of Seward*, 5:412.

96. Frederic Bancroft, "The French in Mexico and the Monroe Doctrine," *Political Science Quarterly* 11, no. 1 (1896): 30–43.

97. Diary entry, June 16, 1865; diary entry, July 14, 1865, in *Welles Diary*, 2:317; 2:332–33.

98. Diary entry, November 22, 1866; diary entry, November 23, 1866, in *Welles Diary*, 2:622; 2:624–26.

99. Dayton to Seward, January 29, 1864, no. 409, RG 59, M34, reel 57, NARA; Dayton to Seward, November 4, 1864, no. 557, RG 59, M34, reel 58, NARA.

100. Chase to Leavitt, January 24, 1864, in *The Salmon P. Chase Papers*, ed. John Niven (Kent, OH: Kent State University Press, 1997), 4:261–62.

101. Caleb Cushing, Draft Message on Mexican Affairs, undated, 1862, reel 187, folder 6442, Papers of William H. Seward, University of Rochester, NY.

102. *U.S. Senate Executive Journal*, 37th Congress, 2nd Session, February 19, 1862, 121–26.

103. Seward to Campbell, October 25, 1866, *FRUS*, 1866, 3:4–6.

104. Seward, quoted in Hoskins, "French Views of the Monroe Doctrine," 683.

105. Seward to Dayton, June 21, 1862, *FRUS*, 1862, 354–55.

106. Seward to Dayton, September 21, 1863, in *Works of Seward*, 5:399.

107. Seward to Dayton, September 26, 1863, in *Works of Seward*, 5:402.

108. Seward to Bigelow, March 17, 1865, *FRUS*, 1864–1865, 3:387.

109. Seward to Kirkpatrick, June 2, 1866, in *Works of Seward*, 5:444.

110. Seward to Bigelow, September 6, 1865, *FRUS*, 1864–1865, 3:413.

111. Seward to Dayton, May 11, 1863, in *Works of Seward*, 5:383.

112. Andrew Johnson, First Annual Message, December 4, 1865, in *A Compilation of the Messages and Papers of the President*, ed. James D. Richardson (New York: Bureau of National Literature, 1897), 8:3551–69; 3566.

113. Seward to Dayton, July 10, 1862, in *Works of Seward*, 5:332

114. Seward to Dayton, October 20, 1862, in *Works of Seward*, 5:362–63.

115. Seward to Adams, August 18, 1862, in *Works of Seward*, 5:353.

116. Seward to Adams, December 13, 1864, *FRUS*, 1865, 1:35; Seward to Adams, December 21, 1864, *FRUS*, 1865, 1:65–67; Seward to Adams, July 24, 1865, *FRUS*, 1865, 1:431.

117. Seward to Bruce, August 15, 1865, *FRUS*, 1865, 2:191.

118. Seward to Charles N. Riotte, undated [late 1863?], reel 137, folder 5549, Seward Papers.

119. Dayton to Seward, October 9, 1863, RG 59, M34, reel 56, NARA.

120. See, for example, George Bancroft to Johnson, January 14, 1866, in *The Papers of Andrew Johnson*, ed. Paul H. Bergeron, LeRoy P. Graf, and Ralph W. Haskins (Knoxville: University of Tennessee Press, 1991), 9:599–600; Bigelow to Seward, September 7, 1866, *FRUS*, 1865–1866, 1:340–41; H. A. Delille, "Napoleon III and the Press," *Galaxy* 3, no. 6 (March 1867): 677–82.

121. Rush to Johnson, September 10, 1867, in *The Papers of Andrew Johnson*, ed. Paul H. Bergeron, LeRoy P. Graf, and Ralph W. Haskins (Knoxville: University of Tennessee Press, 1997), 13:56. See also Adams to Seward, July 13, 1867, *FRUS*, 1868, 1:115–16.

122. S. J. Bayard, "The Decline of England," *Continental Monthly* 5, no. 1 (January 1864): 48–53.

123. Speech on his travels, undated, March 1870, reel 187, folder 6461, Seward Papers.

124. William H. Seward, "The President and His Cabinet," October 20, 1865, in *Works of Seward*, 5:520.

125. Seward, quoted in Walter LaFeber, *Cambridge History of American Foreign Relations*, vol. 2, *The American Search for Opportunity, 1865–1913* (Cambridge: Cambridge University Press, 1993), 10–11.

126. Kingsley also suggested that French interference in Mexico was meant not just to keep the American union apart, but also to prevent the United States from absorbing Mexico. Kingsley, *French Intervention in America*.

127. Victoria Woodhull, "Constitution of the United States of the World," in *Selected Writings of Victoria Woodhull: Suffrage, Free Love, and Eugenics*, ed. Cari M. Carpenter (Lincoln: University of Nebraska Press, 2010), 7–20.

128. *Congressional Globe*, Senate, 40th Congress, 1st Session, April 19, 1867, 851.

129. Seward to Dayton, September 26, 1863, in *Works of Seward*, 5:402.

130. Seward to Bigelow, September 6, 1865, in *Works of Seward*, 5:423.

131. Seward to Bigelow, June 30, 1866, *FRUS*, 1866–1867, 331.

132. Seward to Peck, May 11, 1866, *FRUS*, 1866–1867, 517–18.

133. See, for example, John Mason Hart, *Empire and Revolution: The Americans in Mexico Since the Civil War* (Berkeley: University of California Press, 2002). Of course, this did not prevent many Americans continuing to look toward Mexican territory with a view to acquiring it. David M. Pletcher, *The Diplomacy of Trade and Investment: American Economic Expansion in the Hemisphere, 1865–1900* (Columbia: University of Missouri Press, 1998), 84–85.

134. Diary entry, December 7, 1865, in *Welles Diary*, 2:393; Andrew Johnson, Third Annual Message, December 3, 1867, in *A Compilation of the Messages and Papers of the Presidents*, ed. James D. Richardson (New York: Bureau of National Literature, 1897), 9:3756–79; 3778.

135. Richard J. Hinton, "A Talk with Mr. Burlingame About China," *Galaxy* 6, no. 5 (November 1868): 613–23. See also Tyler Dennett, "Seward's Far Eastern Policy," *American Historical Review* 28, no. 1 (1922): 45–62; John Schrecker, " 'For the Equality of Men—For the Equality of Nations': Anson Burlingame and China's First Embassy to the United States, 1868," *Journal of American East-Asian Relations* 17, no. 1 (2010): 9–34.

136. Seward, quoted in Immerman, *Empire for Liberty*, 126. For a study of Seward's worldview and his travels after he finished his tenure as secretary of state, see Jay Sexton, "William H. Seward in the World," *Journal of the Civil War Era* 4, no. 3 (2014): 398–430.

3. Spain and the Ten Years' War in Cuba

1. This account is taken from Richard H. Bradford, *The Virginius Affair* (Boulder: Colorado Associated University Press, 1980); "Cuba: The Virginius Story as Related by the Tornado's Commander," *New York Herald*, November 18,

1873, 4; "The Virginius Massacre: Story of an Execution by an Eye-Witness," *New York Times*, December 5, 1873, 5.

2. On the United States and the Ten Years' War, see especially Jay Sexton, "The United States, the Cuban Rebellion, and the Multilateral Initiative of 1875," *Diplomatic History* 30, no. 3 (June 2006): 335–65; Lester D. Langley, *The Cuban Policy of the United States: A Brief History* (New York: John Wiley, 1968), 53–81; James B. Chapin, "Hamilton Fish and the Lessons of the Ten Years' War," in *Perspectives on American Diplomacy*, ed. Jules Davids (New York: Arno, 1976), 131–63. Chapin draws out some of the links between U.S. actions during the Ten Years' War and the war against Spain in 1898.

3. Eric T. L. Love, *Race over Empire: Racism and U.S. Imperialism, 1865–1900* (Chapel Hill: University of North Carolina Press, 2004), 1–26.

4. See Louis A. Pérez Jr., *Cuba in the American Imagination: Metaphor and the Imperial Ethos* (Chapel Hill: University of North Carolina Press, 2008), esp. 12–23.

5. Pérez, *Cuba in the American Imagination*, 34.

6. Pérez, *Cuba in the American Imagination*, 30.

7. Rodrigo Botero, *Ambivalent Embrace: America's Relations with Spain from the Revolutionary War to the Cold War* (Westport, CT: Greenwood, 2000), 70.

8. Stephen Jacobson, "Imperial Ambitions in an Era of Decline: Micromilitarism and the Eclipse of the Spanish Empire, 1858–1923," in *Endless Empire: Spain's Retreat, Europe's Eclipse, America's Decline*, ed. Alfred W. McCoy, Josep M. Fradera, and Stephen Jacobson (Madison: University of Wisconsin Press, 2012), 74–91.

9. Julia Ward Howe, *A Trip to Cuba* (Boston: Ticknor and Fields, 1860), 221–25.

10. Langley, *The Cuban Policy of the United States*, 5–19.

11. Review of *India, Ancient and Modern, Geographical, Historical, Political, Social, and Religious; with a Particular Account of the State and Prospects of Christianity*, by David O. Allen, *North American Review* 171 (1856): 417.

12. Robert E. May, *Manifest Destiny's Underworld: Filibustering in Antebellum America* (Chapel Hill: University of North Carolina Press, 2002), 59–62.

13. May, *Manifest Destiny's Underworld*, 286–91.

14. Schurz to Gottfried Kinkel, January 23, 1855, in *Speeches, Correspondence and Political Papers of Carl Schurz*, ed. Frederic Bancroft (New York: Negro Universities Press, 1913), 1:16.

15. Sumner to Wendell Phillips, April 20, 1858; Sumner to Theodore Parker, April 28, 1858, both in *The Selected Letters of Charles Sumner*, ed. Beverly Wilson Palmer (Boston: Northeastern University Press, 1990), 1:500.

16. Martin F. Murphy, *Dominican Sugar Plantations: Production and Foreign Labor Integration* (New York: Praeger, 1991), 11–13.

17. Brenda Gayle Plummer, *Haiti and the United States: The Psychological Moment* (Athens: University of Georgia Press, 1992), esp. 57–60.

18. Louis A. Pérez Jr., *Cuba and the United States: Ties of Singular Intimacy*, 3rd ed. (Athens: University of Georgia Press, 2003), 49–50.

19. Louis A. Pérez Jr., *Cuba: Between Reform and Revolution*, 4th ed. (New York: Oxford University Press, 2011), 89–92.

20. Pérez, *Between Reform and Revolution*, 92–93.

21. For generally positive perspectives, see, for example, Allan Nevins, *Hamilton Fish: The Inner History of the Grant Administration* (New York: Dodd, Mead, 1936); Justin Libby, "Hamilton Fish and the Origins of Anglo-American Solidarity," *Mid-America* 76, no. 3 (1994): 205–26; Clifford W. Haury, "Hamilton Fish and the Conservative Tradition," in *Traditions and Values: American Diplomacy, 1865–1945*, ed. Norman A. Graebner (Lanham, MD: Rowman & Littlefield, 1985), 1–27; Joseph V. Fuller, "Hamilton Fish," in *American Secretaries of State and their Diplomacy*, vol. 4, ed. Samuel Flagg Bemis (New York: Cooper Square, 1963), 125–214. A more negative portrayal can be found in James B. Chapin, "Hamilton Fish and American Expansion," in *Makers of American Diplomacy: From Benjamin Franklin to Alfred Thayer Mahan*, ed. Frank J. Merli and Theodore A. Wilson (New York: Scribner, 1974), 223–51.

22. Jay Sexton, "Toward a Synthesis of Foreign Relations in the Civil War Era, 1848–77," *American Nineteenth Century History* 5, no. 3 (2004): 50–73; Chapin, "Hamilton Fish and American Expansion," 244.

23. Fish to Sickles, June 29, 1869, Record Group 59, Records of the Department of State (hereafter RG 59), M77, Diplomatic Instructions of the Department of State, 1801–1906, Spain, 16, reel 144, 2, National Archives and Records Administration, College Park, MD (hereafter NARA).

24. Fish to Sickles, April 12, 1873, box 238, Hamilton Fish Papers, Manuscript Division, Library of Congress, Washington, DC (hereafter Fish Papers); diary entry, January 22, 1874, reel 4, Hamilton Fish Dairy, Fish Papers (hereafter Fish Diary).

25. Andrew Johnson, Fourth Annual Message, December 9, 1868, in *A Compilation of the Messages and Papers of the Presidents*, ed. James D. Richardson (New York: Bureau of National Literature, 1897), 9:3870–89; 3886.

26. Love, *Race over Empire*, 39.

27. Diary entry, October 28, 1869, reel 4, 153–54, Fish Diary.

28. For a contemporary account of the attempted purchase, see "Americus," "The Annexation of San Domingo," *Galaxy* 11, no. 3 (March 1871), 410–21. See also Nicholas Guyatt, "America's Conservatory: Race, Reconstruction, and the Santo Domingo Debate," *Journal of American History* 97, no. 4 (2011): 974–1000; Dennis Hidalgo, "Charles Sumner and the Annexation of the Dominican Republic," *Itinerario* 21, no. 2 (1997): 51–65.

29. Ulysses S. Grant, to the Senate of the United States, May 31, 1870, in Richardson, *A Compilation of Messages and Papers of the Presidents*, 9:4015–17.

30. Fish Diary, quoted in *The Papers of Ulysses S. Grant*, ed. John Y. Simon (hereafter *Grant Papers*) (Carbondale: Southern Illinois University Press, 1995), 20:123. Ulysses S. Grant, Eighth Annual Message, December 5, 1876, in Richardson, *A Compilation of the Messages and Papers of the Presidents*, 9:4365–67.

31. June 13, 1870 [1869?], Fish Diary, reel 4, 522–24. This appears to have been a difficult conversation between Grant and Fish, during which Fish directly confronted the president about whether he believed that Fish was opposed to Grant's policies on Cuba.

32. Sumner to Charles W. Slack, May 12, 1872, in Palmer, *Selected Letters of Charles Sumner*, 2:591; Sumner to Child, July 7, 1871, in *Memoir and Letters of Charles Sumner*, ed. Edward L. Pierce (Boston: Roberts Brothers, 1893), 4:448.

33. Sumner to Edward W. Kinsley, in Palmer, *Selected Letters of Charles Sumner*, 2:584.

34. Charles Sumner, *Naboth's Vineyard: Speech of Hon. Charles Sumner of Massachusetts on the Proposed Annexation of "The Island of Santo Domingo," Delivered in the Senate of the United States, December 21, 1870* (Washington, DC: F & J Reeves & Geo. A. Bailey, 1870), 7.

35. William Lloyd Garrison, "The San Domingo Question," *Independent*, April 13, 1871; "American Swagger and 'Manifest Destiny,'" *Independent*, April 27, 1871, both quoted in "Introduction," *The Letters of William Lloyd Garrison*, ed. Walter M. Merrill and Louis Ruchames (Cambridge, MA: Belknap Press of Harvard University Press, 1981), 4:5.

36. Allison L. Sneider, *Suffragists in an Imperial Age: U.S. Expansion and the Woman Question, 1870–1929* (New York: Oxford University Press, 2008), 37.

37. See Perry to Seward, March 11, 1865, United States Department of State, *Foreign Relations of the United States* (hereafter *FRUS*), *1865–1866* (Washington, DC: United States Government Printing Office, 1866), 1:514–15; Seward to Perry, April 4, 1865, *FRUS*, *1865–1866*, 1:521.

38. Sumner to Gerrit Smith, December 7, 1870, in Palmer, *Selected Letters of Charles Sumner*, 2:531–32.

39. Sumner, *Naboth's Vineyard*, 13.

40. Millery Polyné, *From Douglass to Duvalier: U.S. African Americans, Haiti, and Pan Americanism, 1870–1964* (Gainesville: University Press of Florida, 2010), esp. 25–44.

41. Frederick Douglass, "Santo Domingo: An Address Delivered in St. Louis, Missouri," January 13, 1873, in *The Frederick Douglass Papers, Series One: Speeches, Debates, and Interviews*, ed. John W. Blassingame and John R. McKivigan (New Haven, CT: Yale University Press, 1991), 4:342–55; 354–55.

42. Julius E. Thompson, "Hiram Rhodes Revels, 1827–1901: A Reappraisal," *Journal of Negro History* 79, no. 3 (1994): 297–303; 298–99.

43. Ada Ferrer, *Insurgent Cuba: Race, Nation, and Revolution, 1868–1898* (Chapel Hill: University of North Carolina Press, 1999), 8.

44. Dairy entry, December 13, 1869, reel 3, Fish Diary.

45. Fish to Alexander Hamilton Jr., March 13, 1870, quoted in Chapin, "Hamilton Fish and American Expansion," 245.

46. Diary entry, April 6, 1869, quoted in Philip S. Foner, *A History of Cuba and Its Relations with the United States* (New York: International Publishers, 1962), 2:202.

47. Guyatt, "America's Conservatory"; Hidalgo, "Charles Sumner and the Annexation of the Dominican Republic."

48. See, for example, Sumner to John Lothrop Motley, June 11, 1869, in Palmer, *Selected Letters of Charles Sumner*, 2:473. "Gen. Grant Said to Be in Favor of Cuban Independence," *New York Times*, January 18, 1869, 1.

49. Martin R. Delany, "Annexation of Cuba," April 27, 1849, in *Martin R. Delany: A Documentary Reader*, ed. Robert S. Levine (Chapel Hill: University of North Carolina Press, 2003), 160–66. Delany was almost certainly quoting a Spanish newspaper editor, José Antonio Saco.

50. Langley, *The Cuban Policy of the United States*, 61–62; James W. Cortada, *Two Nations over Time: Spain and the United States, 1776–1977* (Westport, CT: Greenwood Press, 1978), 94.

51. Henry R. de La Reintre to Grant, February 26, 1869, and March 13, 1869, in *Grant Papers* (1991), 19:351–52; Horace Greely to Grant, January 31, 1870, in *Grant Papers*, 20:46.

52. Appendix to the *Congressional Globe*, 41st Congress, 1st Session, April 9, 1869, 18–21; Foner, *History of Cuba*, 2, 200. This was the first of many congressional interventions. See Langley, *The Cuban Policy of the United States*, 66.

53. See, for example, "Cuban Independence, Immense Mass Meeting at Steinway Hall," *New York Times*, March 26, 1869, 8; "Cuba Independence, Large Meeting at Cooper Institute Last Evening," *New York Times*, May 5, 1869, 1; "The South Carolina Legislature—Cuban Recognition," *New York Times*, November 30, 1869, 1; "Cuba. Action Asked by Congress," *New York Times*, December 3, 1869, 2.

54. William G. Eliot to Grant, January 2, 1873, in *Grant Papers* (2000), 23:301–2.

55. Elizabeth Cady Stanton, *Eighty Years and More: Reminiscences, 1815–1897* (Boston: Northeastern University Press, 1993), 457.

56. Frederick Douglass, "Let the Negro Alone: An Address Delivered in New York, New York," May 11, 1869, in Blassingame and McKivigan, *Frederick Douglass Papers*, 4:199–213; 204.

57. James Hall to Grant, November 26, 1872, in *Grant Papers*, 23:454–56.

58. See, for example, Fish to Lopez Roberts, April 17, 1869; Fish to Roberts, October 13, 1869, box 224, Fish Papers.

59. Fish to Lopez Roberts, December 28, 1870, box 224, Fish Papers.

60. Seward to Kirkpatrick, June 2, 1866, *FRUS*, 1866–1867, 2:413–14. See also James W. Cortada, "Diplomatic Rivalry Between Spain and the United States over Chile and Peru, 1864–1871," *Inter-American Economic Affairs* 27, no. 4 (1974): 47–57; 56–57.

61. Fish to Sickles, June 24, 1870, box 225, Fish Papers.

62. Diary entry, July 3, 1869, reel 3, Fish Diary.

63. On Grant's linking of Spain's declaration of neutrality with the possibility of the United States following a similar course, see Charles Sumner to John Lothrop Motley, June 11, 1869, in Palmer, *Selected Letters of Charles Sumner*, 2:473. Sumner told Motley that he had advised Grant against it.

64. Fish to Lopez Robert, December 28, 1870, *FRUS*, 1871, 785–91. The quote is on 790–91. Libby, "Hamilton Fish and the Origins of Anglo-American Solidarity," 205–26; 218.

65. "The Demand for Cuban Recognition," *New York Times*, April 16, 1869, 4. See also "Foreign Policy of the Administration—the Cuban Revolution," *New York Times*, March 24, 1869, 6.

66. Sumner to Julia Kean Fish, September 29, 1869, in Palmer, *Selected Letters of Charles Sumner*, 2:491.

67. Charles Sumner, "Our Claims on England," Appendix to the *Congressional Globe*, 41st Congress, Special Session, April 13, 1869, 21–26; Sumner to Howe, March 16, 1870, in Pierce, *Memoir and Letters of Charles Sumner*, 4:426; Robert L. Beisner, *From the Old Diplomacy to the New, 1865–1900* (New York: Crowell, 1975), 40–41.

68. David Herbert Donald, *Charles Sumner and the Rights of Man* (New York: Da Capo, 1996), 416–17.

69. Theodore Clarke Smith, ed., *The Life and Letters of James Abram Garfield* (New Haven, CT: Yale University Press, 1925), 1:487. This was in early 1871. Garfield was responding to attacks on Britain and Spain in the House, and he expressed particular fears that the recently signed Treaty of Washington might be placed in jeopardy if relations with Spain deteriorated.

70. "Cuba and the United States—the Cry for Annexation," *New York Times*, November 18, 1868, 4.

71. Ulysses S. Grant, First Annual Message, December 6, 1869, in Richardson, *A Compilation of the Messages and Papers of the Presidents*, 9:3981–96; 3985–86 (emphasis in original).

72. Norman A. Graebner, "Introduction," in Graebner, *Traditions and Values*, xiv; Fish to Sickles, November 25, 1870, *FRUS*, 1871, 733–34. Later in the war, when Grant pressed again, saying that the United States could gain a "moral advantage" by recognizing the insurgents, Fish respectfully disagreed. See diary entry, August 5, 1873, reel 4, Fish Dairy.

73. Diary entries, October 21, 1873; April 21, 1874, reel 4, Fish Diary.

74. Fish to Sickles, June 29, 1869, RG 59, M77, 16, reel 144, 2, NARA; Fish to Motley, September 1, 1869, box 225, Fish Papers.

75. See, for example, diary entry, November 12, 1872, reel 4, Fish Diary; diary entries, July 21, 1873, and July 23, 1873, in *Grant Papers* (2003), 26:197. See also Fish to Cushing, February 6, 1874, *FRUS*, 1874, 859–63.

76. Haury, "Hamilton Fish," 7–8.

77. See, for example, Fish to Sickles, June 20, 1870, box 225, Fish Papers.

78. "Monthly Record of Current Events," *Harper's New Monthly Magazine* 232 (September 1869): 616.

79. Sickles to Fish, July 12, 1870, RG 59, M31, Despatches from U.S. Ministers to Spain, reel 49, NARA; Foner, *History of Cuba*, 2:196.

80. Fish to Sickles, April 19, 1872, *Grant Papers*, 23:73.

81. Diary entry, October 30, 1873, reel 4, Fish Diary.

82. See Rebecca J. Scott, *Degrees of Freedom: Louisiana and Cuba After Slavery* (Cambridge, MA: Belknap Press of Harvard University Press, 2005), 101–2; Ferrer, *Insurgent Cuba*, 60–67.

83. See esp. Fish to Sickles, April 23, 1873; Fish to Sickles, April 24, 1873, box 238, Instructions, Spain, Fish Papers; Fish to Sickles, August 27, 1873, *FRUS*, 1873, 1032–33. See also Haury, "Hamilton Fish," 11–12.

84. Ulysses S. Grant, To the Senate and House of Representatives, June 13, 1870, in Richardson, *A Compilation of the Messages and Papers of the Presidents*, 9:4018–23; 4018.

85. See, for example, Fish to Sickles, June 24, 1870, *FRUS*, 1871, 697–98; Sickles to Fish, July 26, 1870, *FRUS*, 1871, 701–5; Fish to Sickles, November 25, 1870, *FRUS*, 1871, 733–34; Fish to Lopez Roberts, December 28, 1870, *FRUS*, 1871, 785.

86. For similar expressions, see Ulysses S. Grant, Seventh Annual Message, December 7, 1875, in *A Compilation of the Messages and Papers of the Presidents*, ed. James D. Richardson (New York: Bureau of National Literature, 1897), 10:4286–310, esp. 4290.

87. Fish to Sickles, January 26, 1870, RG 59, M77, 16, reel 144, 26, NARA.

88. Foner, *History of Cuba*, 2:184–86.

89. Fish Diary, November 27, 1875, quoted in *Grant Papers*, 26:420.

90. Grant to the Senate and House of Representatives, June 13, 1870.

91. Diary entry, June 10, 1874, reel 4, Fish Diary.

92. Sumner to Cushing, July 10, 1869, in Palmer, *Selected Letters of Charles Sumner*, 2:482.

93. Fish to Sickles, August 31, 1872, box 229, Diplomatic Drafts, Fish Papers.

94. See, for example, Seward to Hale, May 23, 1866, *FRUS*, 1866–1867, 1:574–75.

95. See Sexton, "Multilateral Initiative of 1875," esp. 351–53; diary entry, November 6, 1875, reel 5, Fish Diary.

96. Luis Martínez-Fernández, "Political Change in the Spanish Caribbean During the United States Civil War and Its Aftermath," *Caribbean Studies* 27, nos. 1–2 (1994): 37–64.

97. Diary entry, November 5, 1875, reel 5, Fish Diary.

98. Rebecca J. Scott, *Slave Emancipation in Cuba: The Transition to Free Labor, 1860–1899* (Princeton, NJ: Princeton University Press, 1985); Christopher Schmidt-Nowara, *Slavery, Freedom, and Abolition in Latin America and the Atlantic World* (Albuquerque: University of New Mexico Press, 2011), esp. 147–50.

99. Cushing to Fish, November 4, 1874; Cushing to Fish, November 23, 1874, RG 59, M31, reel 64, NARA.

100. Grant, Seventh Annual Message, December 7, 1875, in Richardson, *A Compilation of the Messages and Papers of the President*, 10:4291.

101. See, for example, diary entry, January 2, 1873, reel 4, Fish Diary.

102. Diary entry, January 13, 1870, reel 3, Fish Diary; Foner, *History of Cuba*, 2:243.

103. J. C. M. Ogelsby, "The Cuban Autonomist Movement's Perception of Canada, 1865–1898: Its Implications," *The Americas* 48, no. 4 (1992): 445–61.

104. Grant, Seventh Annual Message, in Richardson, Richardson, *A Compilation of the Messages and Papers of the President*, 10:4290–91.

105. Sexton, "The United States, the Cuban Rebellion, and the Multilateral Initiative of 1875," 335–65.

106. Foner, *History of Cuba*, 2:203.

107. Foner, *History of Cuba*, 2:214–15.

108. On this point, see Foner, *History of Cuba*, 2:198.

109. Grant to James H. Coggeshall, July 24, 1872; Fish Diary, July 12, 1872; Fish Diary, July 20, 1872; *New York Tribune*, July 29, 1872, all quoted in *Grant Papers*, 23:209–10; Nevins, *Hamilton Fish*, 623.

110. For an overview of this episode, see Bradford, *Virginius Affair*.

111. Richard White, *The Republic for Which It Stands: The United States During Reconstruction and the Gilded Age, 1865–1896* (New York: Oxford University Press, 2017), 253–87.

112. Bryant to Fish, November 19, 1873, quoted in Nevins, *Hamilton Fish*, 162n19.

113. Cushing to Fish, May 24, 1876, RG 59, M31, reel 77, NARA.

114. Cushing to Fish, June 3, 1876, RG 59, M31, reel 78, NARA.

115. Movement toward a more liberal regime had been in evidence from the middle of 1872. See, for example, Sickles to Fish, July 11, *FRUS*, 1872, 561; Fish to Sickles, August 31, 1872, box 238, Fish Papers; Fish to Sickles, October 29, 1872, *FRUS*, 1872, 580–84. For Fish's optimism about the abolition

of slavery in Cuba, see Fish to Sickles, April 30, 1873, *FRUS*, 1873–1874, 966. For his frustration with the lack of rapid progress, see Fish to Sickles, August 27, 1873, *FRUS*, 1873–1874, 1032–33.

116. Bradford, *Virginius Affair*, 131–33.
117. Garrison to the editors of the *Boston Journal*, November 25, 1873, in Merrill and Ruchames, *Letters of William Lloyd Garrison*, 4:283–87.
118. Quoted in Matthew Pratt Guterl, *American Mediterranean: Southern Slaveholders in the Age of Emancipation* (Cambridge, MA: Harvard University Press, 2008), 101.
119. Cortada, *Two Nations over Time*, 98–100.
120. Gordon H. Chang, "Whose 'Barbarism'? Whose 'Treachery'? Race and Civilization in the Unknown United States–Korea War of 1871," *Journal of American History* 89, no. 4 (2003), 1331–65.

4. Britain and the Occupation of Egypt

1. "The Ruined Egyptian City: The Dreadful Scenes Enacted in Alexandria," *New York Times*, July 15, 1882, 1.
2. Fanny Stone, "Diary of an American Girl in Cairo During the War of 1882," *Century* 28, no. 2 (June 1884): 289–302.
3. Philips Brooks, "Philips Brooks's Letters from India," *Century* 46, no. 5 (September 1893): 754. For details of the background to the bombardment and British invasion, see, for example, Alexander Schölch, *Egypt for the Egyptians! The Socio-Political Crisis in Egypt, 1878–1882* (London: Ithaca Press, 1981); Charles Royle, *The Egyptian Campaigns, 1882 to 1885* (London: Hurst & Brackett, 1900), esp. 44–97; Afaf Lutfi Al-Sayyid Marsot, "The British Occupation of Egypt from 1882," in *The Oxford History of the British Empire*, vol. 3, *The Nineteenth Century*, ed. Andrew Porter (Oxford: Oxford University Press, 1999), 651–64.
4. In English, Urabi or 'Urabi is often rendered as "Arabi." For more on Urabi and his rise, see Donald Malcom Reid, "The 'Urabi Revolution and the British Conquest, 1879–1882," in *The Cambridge History of Egypt*, vol. 2, *Modern Egypt from 1517 to the End of the Twentieth Century*, ed. M. W. Daly (Cambridge: Cambridge University Press, 1998), 217–38.
5. Roger Owen, "Egypt and Europe: From French Expedition to British Occupation," in *Studies in the Theories of Imperialism*, ed. Roger Owen and Bob Sutcliffe (London: Longman, 1972), 200–203.
6. Alexander Schölch, "The 'Men on the Spot' and the English occupation of Egypt in 1882," *Historical Journal* 19, no. 3 (1976): 773–85; John Darwin, "Imperialism and the Victorians: The Dynamics of Territorial Expansion,"

English Historical Review 112, no. 447 (1997): 614–42. British interests in Egypt were longstanding, and there had already been much discussion of the possibility of occupation. See A. G. Hopkins, "The Victorians and Africa: A Reconsideration of the Occupation of Egypt, 1882," *Journal of African History* 27, no. 2 (1986): 363–91. A recent study has emphasized the humanitarian as well as economic factors behind Britain's extension of control in East Africa. Jonas Fossli Gjersø, "The Scramble for East Africa: British Motives Reconsidered, 1884–95," *Journal of Imperial and Commonwealth History* 43, no. 5 (2015): 831–60.

7. Harold H. Tollefson Jr., "The 1894 British Takeover of the Egyptian Ministry of Interior," *Middle Eastern Studies* 26, no. 4 (October 1990): 547–60.

8. James Sturgis, "Britain and the New Imperialism," in *British Imperialism in the Nineteenth Century*, ed. C. C. Eldridge (London: Macmillan, 1984), 85–105.

9. See Eric Stokes, "Late Nineteenth-Century Colonial Expansion and the Attack on the Theory of Economic Imperialism: A Case of Mistaken Identity?," *Historical Journal* 12, no. 2 (1969): 285–301.

10. For overviews, see James A. Field Jr., *America and the Mediterranean World, 1776–1882* (Princeton, NJ: Princeton University Press, 1969), 389–435; Michael B. Oren, *Power, Faith, and Fantasy: America in the Middle East, 1776 to the Present* (New York: Norton, 2007), 257–72.

11. Nicole M. Phelps, "One Service, Three Systems, Many Empires: The U.S. Consular Service and the Growth of U.S. Global Power, 1789–1924," in *Crossing Empires: Taking U.S. History into Transimperial Terrain*, ed. Kristin L. Hoganson and Jay Sexton (Durham, NC: Duke University Press, 2020), 135–58.

12. See, for example, Patrick M. Kirkwood, "'Lord Cromer's Shadow': Political Anglo-Saxonism and the Egyptian Protectorate as a Model in the American Philippines," *Journal of World History* 27, no. 1 (2016): 1–26.

13. R. Dorsey Mohun, "The Scramble for the Upper Nile," *Century* 56, no. 1 (May 1898): 59–62.

14. Elizabeth Kelly Gray, "American Attitudes Toward British Imperialism, 1815–1860" (PhD diss., College of William and Mary, 2002); Frank Ninkovich, *Global Dawn: The Cultural Foundation of American Internationalism, 1865–1890* (Cambridge, MA: Harvard University Press, 2009).

15. H. C. Allen, *Great Britain and the United States: A History of Anglo-American Relations, 1783–1952* (New York: St. Martin's Press, 1955), 518–45.

16. Bradford Perkins, *The Great Rapprochement: England and the United States, 1895–1914* (London: Victor Gallanz, 1969). While acknowledging this rapprochement, Charles Campbell has emphasized some of the continuing tensions during this period. See Charles S. Campbell, *From Revolution to Rapprochement:*

The United States and Great Britain, 1783–1900 (New York: John Wiley & Sons, 1974), 121–73.

17. David M. Pletcher, *The Awkward Years: American Foreign Relations Under Garfield and Arthur* (Columbia: University of Missouri Press, 1962), 61–62. There is no biography of Frelinghuysen. For an overview of his term as secretary of state, see Philip Marshall Brown, "Frederick T. Frelinghuysen," in *American Secretaries of State and Their Diplomacy*, ed. Samuel Flagg Bemis (New York: Cooper Square, 1963), 8:3–46.

18. David Sim, *A Union Forever: The Irish Question and U.S. Foreign Relations in the Victorian Age* (Ithaca, NY: Cornell University Press, 2013), 145–46.

19. Pletcher, *Awkward Years*; Edward P. Crapol, *America for Americans: Economic Nationalism and Anglophobia in the Late Nineteenth Century* (Westport, CT: Greenwood Press, 1973), esp. 119–41.

20. H. A. Tulloch, "Changing British Attitudes Towards the United States in the 1880s," *Historical Journal* 20, no. 4 (1977): 825–40.

21. Stephen Tuffnell, "'Uncle Sam Is to Be Sacrificed': Anglophobia in Late Nineteenth Century Politics and Culture," *American Nineteenth Century History* 12, no. 1 (2011): 77–99.

22. "Topics of the Time: Republicanism in France," *Century* 37, no. 6 (April 1889): 953–54.

23. See, for example, "Topics of the Time: The Lack of Earnestness in American Politicians," *Century* 26, no. 6 (October 1883): 949–50.

24. See, for example, Atkinson to Fish, March 11, 1876, folder: September 1, 1875–August 25, 1876; Atkinson to Carl Schurz, May 3, 1877, 479–80, folder: August 25, 1876–May 16, 1877; Atkinson to Gladstone, December 2, 1878, folder: May 16, 1877–February 11, 1879; Atkinson to Frelinghuysen, November 1, 1882, folder: May 13–December 21, 1882, box 16, Papers of Edward Atkinson, Massachusetts Historical Society, Boston.

25. Marc-William Palen, *The "Conspiracy" of Free Trade: The Anglo-American Struggle over Empire and Economic Globalisation, 1846–1896* (Cambridge: Cambridge University Press, 2016).

26. See, for example, "Free Trade Criticised," *New York Daily Tribune*, July 17, 1881, 1.

27. Writing from Meriden, Connecticut, Newton T. Hartshorn condemned Britain's global approach, but noted there were in the United States "a number of influential people who openly advocate a monarchical form of government," and many who greatly admired England and its foreign policy "as it was directed by Lord Beaconsfield." "Alarmed at Imperialism," *New York Daily Tribune*, May 24, 1881, 2.

28. Mike Davis, *Late Victorian Holocausts: El Niño Famines and the Making of the Third World* (London: Verso, 2001).

29. Morrill to Garfield, May 30, 1881, reel 98, vol. 142, Series 4, General Correspondence, James A. Garfield Papers, Library of Congress, Washington, DC (hereafter Garfield Papers).

30. J. R. Seeley, *The Expansion of England: Two Courses of Lectures* (London: Macmillan, 1914; first published 1883), 343–45.

31. "Seeley's Expansion of England," *Atlantic Monthly* 53, no. 316 (February 1884): 271–76.

32. Victoria Woodhull, "The Rapid Multiplication of the Unfit," in *Selected Writings of Victoria Woodhull: Suffrage, Free Love, and Eugenics*, ed. Cari M. Carpenter (Lincoln: University of Nebraska Press, 2010), 288–89.

33. Sue Davis, *The Political Thought of Elizabeth Cady Stanton: Women's Rights and the American Political Traditions* (New York: New York University Press, 2008), 208–9.

34. Charles Dudley Warner, "England," *Century* 25, no. 1 (November 1882): 134–42.

35. Ninkovich, *Global Dawn*, 257.

36. Josiah Strong, *Our Country: Its Possible Future and Its Present Crisis*, rev. ed. (Baker & Taylor, 1891; Cambridge, MA: Belknap Press of Harvard University Press, 1963). The citation, below, refers to the Belknap edition.

37. Strong, *Our Country*, 203–14.

38. "Great Britain's Example Is High, Noble and Grand: An Address Delivered in Rochester, New York," August 6, 1885, in *The Frederick Douglass Papers, Series One: Speeches, Debates, and Interviews*, ed. John W. Blassingame and John R. McKivigan (New Haven, CT: Yale University Press, 1992), 5:194–95.

39. George R. Parkin, "The Reorganization of the British Empire," *Century* 37, no. 2 (December 1888): 187–93. Yet this progress also brought the possibilities of the unraveling of the British Empire, leading to Parkin's conclusion that, rather than seeing Canada's incorporation into the United States, as many Americans wanted, a federation of Britain's settler colonies was required. For responses, see "Topics of the Time: Annexation, or Federation?," *Century* 37, no. 3 (January 1889): 471–72; Charles H. Lugrin, "Imperial Federation," *Century* 37, no. 6 (April 1889): 959; Arthur A. Loring, "Imperial Federation," *Century* 38, no. 3 (July 1889): 474–75.

40. J. E. Chamberlain, "A Dream of Anglo-Saxondom," *Galaxy* 24, no. 6 (December 1877): 788–91. See also John Fiske, "Manifest Destiny," *Harper's New Monthly Magazine* 70 (December 1884): 578–90.

41. James W. Gould, "American Imperialism in Southeast Asia Before 1898," *Journal of Southeast Asian Studies* 3, no. 2 (1972): 306–14; 313.

42. Eben Greenough Scott, "The French in Canada," *Atlantic Monthly* 64, no. 385 (November 1889): 602–11.

43. See Goberdhan Bhagat, *Americans in India, 1784–1860* (New York: New York University Press, 1970), 115–29; Paul A. Kramer, "Empires, Exceptions, and Anglo-Saxons: Race and Rule Between the British and United States Empires, 1880–1910," *Journal of American History* 88, no. 4 (2002): 1339; Gray, "American Attitudes Toward British Imperialism," 217–63.

44. "The Rebellion in India," *North American Review* 179 (1858): 488.

45. John Russell Young, *Around the World with General Grant* (New York: Subscription Book Department, 1879), 1:621–22.

46. Lydia Maria Child, "An Appeal for the Indians," in *A Lydia Maria Child Reader*, ed. Carolyn L. Karcher (Durham, NC: Duke University Press, 1997), 79–94; 84.

47. For example, Elizabeth Cady Stanton, *Eighty Years and More: Reminiscences, 1815–1897* (Boston: Northeastern University Press, 1993), 317–18. It should be noted, however, that Stanton was thinking primarily about educated women and objected to the fact that uneducated blacks were given the right to vote under the terms of the Fifteenth Amendment. She also objected to promotion of greater rights for Native Americans.

48. A. H. Guernsey, "The English in India," *Harper's New Monthly Magazine* 25, no. 149 (October 1862): 685–91.

49. A. H. Guernsey, "The Eastern Question," *Galaxy* 23, no. 3 (March 1877): 359–67.

50. Thomas W. Knox, "The English in India," *Harper's New Monthly Magazine* 58, no. 346 (March 1879): 568–75.

51. Gordon H. Chang, *Fateful Ties: A History of America's Preoccupation with China* (Cambridge, MA: Harvard University Press, 2015), 49.

52. Augustine Heard, "France and Indo-China," *Century* 32, no. 3 (July 1886): 416–21.

53. *Congressional Globe*, 37th Congress, 2nd Session, December 30, 1861, 181.

54. Brooks to Garfield, June 1, 1881, reel 99, vol. 143, series 4, Garfield Papers.

55. As several authors have noted, American missionary work relied heavily on the reach of the British Empire to spread its message. See, for example, Emily Conroy-Krutz, *Christian Imperialism: Converting the World in the Early American Republic* (Ithaca, NY: Cornell University Press, 2015); Field, *America and the Mediterranean World*, 272–74; 349–50; Heather Jane Sharkey, *American Evangelicals in Egypt: Missionary Encounters in an Age of Empire* (Princeton, NJ: Princeton University Press, 2008). For a recent interpretation of American missionary work elsewhere in the Ottoman Empire, especially Bulgaria, see Barbara Reeves-Ellington, *Domestic Frontiers: Gender, Reform, and American Intervention in the Ottoman Balkans and the Near East* (Amherst: University of Massachusetts Press, 2013). Although Reeves-Ellington's

primary focus is the cultural processes of American reform efforts, she also emphasizes that these efforts "proceeded initially under the protection of British imperial power" (5).

56. Owen, "Egypt and Europe," 200–203.

57. Farman to Evarts, February 14, 1880, United States Department of State, *Foreign Relations of the United States* (hereafter *FRUS*), 1880–1881 (Washington, DC: United States Government Printing Office, 1881), 999–1000. See also N. D. Comanos to Evarts, September 2, 1879, *FRUS*, 1879–1880, 1018–19.

58. Farman to Evarts, March 5, 1880, Record Group 59, Records of the Department of State (hereafter RG 59), T41, Despatches from US Consuls in Cairo, Egypt, 1864–1906, reel 8, National Archives and Records Administration, College Park, MD (hereafter NARA).

59. Wolf to Frelinghuysen, March 21, 1882, no. 62, reel 9, T41, RG 59, NARA.

60. Comanos to Evarts, September 1, 1879, *FRUS*, 1879–1880, 1018.

61. Farman to Evarts, May 22, 1879, *FRUS*, 1879–1880, 1003; Evarts to Comanos, August 1, 1879, *FRUS*, 1880–1881, 992.

62. Eve M. Troutt Powell, *A Different Shade of Colonialism: Egypt, Great Britain, and the Mastery of the Sudan* (Berkeley: University of California Press, 2003), 22.

63. Field, *America and the Mediterranean World*, 408.

64. Fuad Sha'ban, *Islam and Arabs in Early American Thought: The Roots of Orientalism in America* (Durham, NC: Acorn Press, 1990), 115–40, esp. 115–16. For an estimate of figures, see Cardwell to Reeves, February 12, 1888, *FRUS*, 1888–1890, 1631–32. For accounts of those who visited and lived there, see Cassandra Vivian, *Americans in Egypt, 1770–1915: Explorers, Consuls, Travelers, Soldiers, Missionaries, Writers and Scientists* (Jefferson, NC: McFarland, 2012).

65. See Frederic Courtland Penfield, "In Fascinating Cairo," *Century* 58, no. 6 (October 1899): 811–32; William W. Ellsworth, "Spoiling the Egyptians," *Century* 41, no. 1 (November 1890): 152–54.

66. Pletcher, *Awkward Years*, 219–22; Blaine to Wallace, June 29, 1881, *FRUS*, 1880–1881, 1184–86. This was exacerbated by Constantinople's attempt to withdraw its recognition of British representation on behalf of Americans in its territories. See Frelinghuysen to Wallace, January 7, 1882, *FRUS*, 1882–1883, 498.

67. Beardsley to Fish, October 2, 1875, *FRUS*, 1876, 595.

68. Farman to Fish, November 27, 1876, *FRUS*, 1877–1878, 618. See also Farman to Fish, August 10, 1876, *FRUS*, 1877–1878, 614–15; Farman to Fish, November 27, 1876, *FRUS*, 1877–1878, 618; Ulysses S. Grant, Annual Message to Congress, December 4, 1876, *FRUS*, 1876, vii; Farman to Evarts, July 10, 1878, *FRUS*, 1878–1879, 923; West to Frelinghuysen, December 13, 1883;

Frelinghuysen to West, December 17, 1883, *FRUS*, 1884–1885, 235; Frelinghuysen to West, January 8, 1884, *FRUS*, 1884–1885, 237.

69. Farman to Evarts, May 2, 1877, in *FRUS*, 1877–1878, 629.

70. Comanos to Evarts, August 20, 1880, RG 59, T41, reel 8, NARA.

71. Wolf to Blaine, October 17, 1881, RG 59, T41, reel 9, NARA; Marian Kent, "Introduction," in *Great Powers and the End of the Ottoman Empire*, 2nd ed., ed. Marian Kent (London: Frank Cass, 1996), 2–4.

72. Oren, *Power, Faith, and Fantasy*, 260–61.

73. "An Old Diplomat," "The Congress of Berlin and Its Consequences," *North American Review* 127 (1878): 395

74. Boker to Fish, January 29, 1874, *FRUS*, 1874–1875, 1148–50.

75. Field, *America and the Mediterranean World*, 364–68; W. E. Gladstone, *Bulgarian Horrors and the Question of the East* (New York: Lovell, Adam, Wesson, 1876).

76. Field, *America and the Mediterranean World*, 243–45.

77. Thomas W. Knox, "Russian Policy in Asia," *Harper's New Monthly Magazine* 47, no. 278 (July 1873): 214–25; 219.

78. See Evarts to Aristarchi Bey, May 3, 1877, *FRUS*, 1877–1878, 613–14.

79. Guernsey, "The Eastern Question," 359–67.

80. Wolf to Blaine, September 15, 1881, RG 59, T41, reel 9, NARA.

81. For example, Beardsley to Fish, November 10, 1873, *FRUS*, 1874–1875, 1178; Farman to Evarts, May 30, 1877, *FRUS*, 1877–1878, 630. In 1878, as part of these economizing measures, the khedive was forced to dismiss all but two of the U.S. officers in his army. See Farman to Evarts, July 3, 1878, *FRUS*, 1878–1879, 922–23.

82. Wolf to Frelinghuysen, February 6, 1882, RG 59, T41, reel 9, NARA.

83. Wolf to Frelinghuysen, March 21, 1882, no. 64, RG 59, T41, reel 9, NARA.

84. Maynard to Evarts, July 11, 1879, *FRUS*, 1879–1880, 982–83.

85. Maynard to Evarts, June 28, 1879, *FRUS*, 1879–1880, 979. See also Farman to Evarts, June 27, 1879, *FRUS*, 1879–1880, 1005.

86. Farman to Evarts, June 27, 1879, *FRUS*, 1879–1880, 1007.

87. Comanos to Evarts, August 19, 1879, *FRUS*, 1879–1880, 1016.

88. Farman to Evarts, March 18, 1879, *FRUS*, 1879–1880, 996.

89. Davis, *Late Victorian Holocausts*, 91–115.

90. Sheldon Watts, "From Rapid Change to Stasis: Official Responses to Cholera in British-Ruled India and Egypt: 1860 to c.1821," *Journal of World History* 12, no. 2 (2001), 321–74, esp. 337–39.

91. Pomeroy to Frelinghuysen, January 16, 1884, RG 59, T41, reel 11, NARA.

92. Watts, "From Rapid Change to Stasis," 357–59.

93. Pomeroy to Frelinghuysen, January 16, 1884, RG 59, T41, reel 11, NARA.

94. In 1885, the weakening French position and strengthening of the British one was exemplified by the increase in the number of directors in the Suez Canal Company from twenty-four to thirty-two, to accommodate British interests. This surprised Comanos, who noted that, after all, the Canal was "a great French enterprise." Comanos to Bayard, May 31, 1885, RG 59, T41, reel 12, NARA.

95. Beardsley to Fish, December 11, 1875, *FRUS*, 1876, 596–97.

96. Farman to Evarts, August 2, 1880, *FRUS*, 1880–1881, 1020–21.

97. Farman to Evarts, March 8, 1880, *FRUS*, 1880–1881, 1001–2.

98. Farman to Evarts, August 2, 1880, *FRUS*, 1880–1881, 1020–21.

99. Beardsley to Fish, December 13, 1875, *FRUS*, 1876, 598.

100. See, for example, Farman to Evarts, March 18, 1879, *FRUS*, 1879–1880, 996.

101. E. E. Farman to Fish, April 3, 1877, *FRUS*, 1877, 624–25. See also Field, *America and the Mediterranean World*, 423.

102. Cardwell to Porter, September 23, 1886, RG 59, T41, reel 13, NARA.

103. Edward Atkinson, "The Relative Strength and Weakness of Nations," *Century* 33, no. 4 (February 1887): 613–22.

104. Wolf to Blaine, October 22, 1881, RG 59, T41, reel 9, NARA.

105. Indeed, Farman reported that some rebels in the army focused their calls for reform more on the need to reduce the power of the Circassians rather than the Europeans. Yet Circassians had largely become integrated into Egyptian society over many generations and so had "no other home or country." Farman to Evarts, February 4, 1881, RG 59, T41, reel 8, NARA. Owen, "Egypt and Europe," 203.

106. Wolf to Blaine, October 17, 1881, RG 59, T41, reel 9, NARA.

107. Comanos to Frelinghuysen, May 25, 1882, RG 59, T41, reel 9, NARA.

108. Comanos to Frelinghuysen, May 25, 1882, RG 59, T41, reel 9, NARA.

109. See for example, Comanos to Frelinghuysen, June 19, 1881, RG 59, T41, reel 10, NARA; Wolf to Blaine, October 5, 1881; Wolf to Blaine, October 8, 1881, RG 59, T41, reel 9, NARA.

110. Comanos to Blaine, August 31, 1881, RG 59, T41, reel 9, NARA.

111. Wolf to Blaine, October 8, 1881, RG 59, T41, reel 9, NARA.

112. Farman to Evarts, March 18, 1879, *FRUS*, 1879–1880, 996.

113. Comanos to Blaine, August 31, 1881, RG 59, T41, reel 9, NARA.

114. Wolf to Blaine, October 29, 1881, RG 59, T41, reel 9, NARA.

115. Comanos to Frelinghuysen, May 21, 1882, RG 59, T41, reel 9, NARA.

116. Comanos claimed to have heard from "well-informed sources" that the disorder "was secretly prepared and organized previously to the cruel and horrible butchery." Comanos to Frelinghuysen, June 19, 1882, no. 86, RG 59, T41, reel 10, NARA. There is no evidence to support this view. See Reid,

"The 'Urabi Revolution," 231–32. Of course, if Urabi really did fear that the British were looking for a pretext to invade, then it seems highly unlikely that he would have encouraged this disorder and violence.

117. Justus D. Doenecke, *The Presidencies of James A. Garfield and Chester A. Arthur* (Lawrence: University Press of Kansas, 1981), 162–63; Pletcher, *Awkward Years*, 223–24.

118. Comanos to Frelinghuysen, July 28, 1882, RG 59, T41, reel 10, NARA. See also Comanos to Frelinghuysen, August 12, 1882, RG 59, T41, reel 10, NARA; Comanos to Frelinghuysen, August 21, 1882, RG 59, T41, reel 10, NARA.

119. Frelinghuysen to Lionel Sackville-West, undated, November 1882, Drafts: Diplomatic, 1882–1883, vol. 3, Frederick Theodore Frelinghuysen Papers, Manuscript Division, Library of Congress (hereafter Frelinghuysen Papers); Frelinghuysen to E. E. Farman, January 30, 1882, Drafts: Diplomatic, 1882–1883, vol. 4, Frelinghuysen Papers. See also Comanos to Frelinghuysen, June 10, 1882, RG 59, T41, reel 10, NARA; Chaille-Long to Frelinghuysen, September 8, 1882, RG 59, T41, reel 10, NARA; Frelinghuysen to West, September 22, 1882, *FRUS*, 1882–1883, 325.

120. Pletcher, *Awkward Years*, 224–25.

121. Comanos to Frelinghuysen, June 13, 1882; Comanos to Frelinghuysen, June 19, 1882, RG 59, T41, reel 10, NARA. In the second of his annual messages to Congress at the end of the year, Chester Arthur noted that these vessels "served as a protection to the persons and property of many of our own citizens and of citizens of other countries, whose governments have expressed their thanks for this assistance." Chester A. Arthur, Second Annual Message, December 4, 1882, in *A Compilation of the Messages and Papers of the Presidents*, ed. James D. Richardson (New York: Bureau of National Literature, 1897), 11:4715.

122. Charles Pomeroy Stone to the editor of *Century*, April 4, 1884, *Century* 28, no. 2 (June 1884): 288–89; Charles Pomeroy Stone, "The Bombardment of Alexandria. Rejoinder by Stone Pasha," *Century* 28, no. 6 (October 1884): 953–57.

123. Stone to the editor of *Century*; Stone, "The Bombardment of Alexandria"; Vivian, *Americans in Egypt*, 180–93; Oren, *Power, Faith, and Fantasy*, 265–68.

124. C. F. Goodrich, "The Bombardment of Alexandria," *Century* 28, no. 4 (August 1884): 635–36; C. F. Goodrich, "The Bombardment of Alexandria," *Century* 29, no. 5 (March 1885): 797–98.

125. Sharkey, *American Evangelicals in Egypt*, 49–50. In some ways, this mirrored missionary reaction to the Opium Wars in China, which many of missionaries condemned, but many also saw as a way to break down Chinese resistance to the West and open them up to Christianity. See Chang, *Fateful Ties*, 57–58.

126. George B. McClellan, "The War in Egypt," *Century* 24, no. 5 (September 1882): 784–89.

127. Sargent to Frelinghuysen, October 2, 1882, *FRUS*, 1882–1883, 172–74.

128. Comanos to Frelinghuysen, August 2, 1882, RG 59, T41, reel 10, NARA.

129. Comanos to Frelinghuysen, September 13, 1882; Comanos to Frelinghuysen, September 15, 1882; Comanos to Frelinghuysen, October 3, 1882, RG 59, T41, reel 10, NARA.

130. Pomeroy to Frelinghuysen, January 6, 1883, with enclosure from *Current News*, undated, RG 59, T41, reel 10, NARA; Schölch, *Egypt for the Egyptians*, 302–3.

131. Cardwell to Porter, September 6, 1886, RG 59, T41, reel 13, NARA.

132. Cardwell to Porter, printed enclosure, April 26, 1887, RG 59, T41, reel 13, NARA.

133. Cardwell to Porter, April 26, 1887, RG 59, T41, reel 13, NARA.

134. Michael H. Hunt, *Ideology and U.S. Foreign Policy* (New Haven, CT: Yale University Press, 1987), 36–38; 48–52.

135. Comanos to Frelinghuysen, June 12, 1882, RG 59, T41, reel 10, NARA.

136. Comanos to Frelinghuysen, June 13, 1882, RG 59, T41, reel 10, NARA.

137. McClellan, "The War in Egypt," 785–86.

138. Quoted in R. C. Mowat, "From Liberalism to Imperialism: The Case of Egypt 1875–1887," *Historical Journal* 16 (March 1973): 109–24; 120.

139. Pomeroy to Frelinghuysen, May 5, 1883, RG 59, T41, reel 10, NARA.

140. Pomeroy to Frelinghuysen, May 2, 1884, RG 59, T41, reel 11, NARA.

141. Pomeroy to Frelinghuysen, July 14, 1884, RG 59, T41, reel 11, NARA.

142. Pomeroy to Frelinghuysen, January 16, 1883, with enclosure from Dufferin to Foreign Office, RG 59, T41, reel 10, NARA.

143. Pomeroy to Frelinghuysen, May 2, 1884, RG 59, T41, reel 11, NARA.

144. Mowat, "From Liberalism to Imperialism."

145. Pomeroy to Frelinghuysen, July 14, 1884, RG 59, T41, reel 11, NARA.

146. Pomeroy to Frelinghuysen, July 14, 1884, RG 59, T41, reel 11, NARA.

147. Pomeroy to Frelinghuysen, January 6, 1883, with enclosure from *Current News*, undated, RG 59, T41, reel 10, NARA; Pomeroy to Frelinghuysen, May 2, 1884, RG 59, T41, reel 11, NARA.

148. Field, *America and the Mediterranean World*, 434.

149. John A. S. Grenville and George Berkeley Young, *Politics, Strategy, and American Diplomacy: Studies in Foreign Policy, 1873–1917* (New Haven, CT: Yale University Press, 1966), 1–38; Robert Seager II, "Ten Years Before Mahan: The Unofficial Case for the New Navy, 1880–1890," *Mississippi Valley Historical Review* 40, no. 3 (1953): 491–512; Pletcher, *Awkward Years*, 116–36.

150. John Cardwell to James D. Porter, May 21, 1886, RG 59, T41, reel 12, NARA.

5. Germany and the Berlin West Africa Conference

1. This account is taken from Andrew C. A. Jampoler, *Congo: The Miserable Expeditions and Dreadful Death of Lt. Emory Taunt, USN* (Annapolis, MD: Naval Institute Press, 2013), 31–59, esp. 49–54. Emory Taunt went to Africa shortly after Tisdel for two trips, becoming the State Department's resident official in the Congo. He died from Malaria in January 1891. Named after Henry Morton Stanley by Europeans, Stanley Pool is Pool Malebo.

2. For details of American participation, see David M. Pletcher, *The Awkward Years: American Foreign Relations Under Garfield and Arthur* (Columbia: University of Missouri Press, 1962), 308–24; George Shepperson, "Aspects of American Interest in the Berlin Conference," in *Bismarck, Europe, and Africa: The Berlin Africa Conference 1884–1885 and the Onset of Partition*, ed. Stig Förster, Wolfgang J. Mommsen, and Ronald Robinson (Oxford: Oxford University Press, 1988), 281–93.

3. Kasson to Frelinghuysen, November 15, 1884, Senate Executive Document 196, 49th Congress, 1st Session, *A Report of the Secretary of State Relative to the Affairs of the Independent State of the Congo, Part I, Correspondence Concerning the Berlin Congo Conference Together with the Protocols and General Act* (hereafter *Correspondence Concerning the Berlin Congo Conference*), 23–27.

4. Kasson to Frelinghuysen, November 15, 1884, *Correspondence Concerning the Berlin Congo Conference*, 27–30.

5. Adam Hochschild, *King Leopold's Ghost: A Story of Greed, Terror and Heroism in Colonial Africa* (London: Macmillan, 1999).

6. Hochschild, *King Leopold's Ghost*, 101–14; Sylvia M. Jacobs, *The African Nexus: Black American Perspectives on the European Partitioning of Africa* (Westport, CT: Greenwood, 1981), 85–87; Mark Twain, *King Leopold's Soliloquy* (Boston: P. R. Warren, 1905).

7. S. E. Crowe, *The Berlin West African Conference, 1884–1885* (Westport, CT: Negro Universities Press, 1970); Shepperson, "Aspects of American Interest in the Berlin Conference."

8. Harold E. Hammond, "American Interest in the Exploration of the Dark Continent," *The Historian* 18, no. 2 (1956): 202–29; Milton Plesur, *America's Outward Thrust: Approaches to Foreign Affairs, 1865–1890* (DeKalb: Northern Illinois Press, 1971), 144–56.

9. For a flavor of some of these accounts, see, for example, A. H. Guernsey, "Livingstone's Last African Expedition," *Harper's New Monthly Magazine* 32 (May 1866): 709–24; Helen S. Conant, "A Naturalist in the Heart of Africa," *Harper's New Monthly Magazine* 48 (May 1874): 772–86; S. S. Conant, "Last Journals of David Livingstone," *Harper's New Monthly Magazine* 50 (March 1875):

544–58; John Russell Young, "Through the Dark Continent," *Harper's New Monthly Magazine* 57 (October 1878): 667–86; "General Gordon at Kartoum [*sic*]," *Atlantic Monthly* 56 (September 1885): 415–19.

10. T. B. Aldrich, "A Day in Africa," *Harper's New Monthly Magazine* 63 (July 1881): 241–50.

11. Indeed, the American link with Liberia was one of the reasons the United States was invited to participate in the Berlin conference. See Kasson to Frelinghuysen, October 13, 1884, *Correspondence Concerning the Berlin Congo Conference*, 8–9.

12. Raymond W. Bixler, *The Foreign Policy of the United States in Liberia* (New York: Pageant, 1957), 12–36; M. B. Akpan, "Black Imperialism: Americo-Liberian Rule over the African Peoples of Liberia, 1841–1964," *Canadian Journal of African Studies* 7, no. 2 (1973): 217–36; Emily S. Rosenberg, "The Invisible Protectorate: The United States, Liberia and the Evolution of Neocolonialism, 1909–40," *Diplomatic History* 9, no. 3 (1985): 191–214.

13. Plesur, *America's Outward Thrust*, 147–48; Pletcher, *Awkward Years*, 225–26.

14. Charles S. Campbell, *Transformation of American Foreign Relations, 1865–1900* (New York: Harper & Row, 1976), 101–2.

15. Steven Press, *Rogue Empires: Contracts and Conmen in Europe's Scramble for Africa* (Cambridge, MA: Harvard University Press, 2017), 192–98.

16. Morton to Frelinghuysen, December 6, 1881, United States Department of State, *Foreign Relations of the United States* (hereafter *FRUS*), 1883 (Washington, DC: United States Government Printing Office, 1884), 259–61.

17. Kasson to Frelinghuysen, January 5, 1885, Record Group 59, Records of the Department of State (hereafter RG 59), M44, Despatches from U.S. Ministers to the German States and Germany, reel 55, National Archives and Records Administration, College Park, MD (hereafter NARA).

18. Pletcher, *Awkward Years*, 227–33.

19. Morton to Frelinghuysen, December 6, 1881, *FRUS*, 1883, 259–61.

20. Francis to Frelinghuysen, May 15, 1883, *FRUS*, 1883, 739–41.

21. "England on the Congo River," *New York Freeman*, April 26, 1884, in Jeanette Eileen Jones et al., "To Enter Africa from America: U.S. Empire, Race, and the African Question, 1847–1919," accessed July 26, 2016, http://greystoke.unl.edu/doc/llg.ber.035.01.html.

22. Jens-Uwe Guettel, *German Expansionism, Imperial Liberalism, and the United States, 1777–1945* (New York: Cambridge University Press, 2012); Raymond F. Betts, "Immense Dimensions: The Impact of the American West on Late Nineteenth-Century European Thought About Expansion," *Western Historical Quarterly* 10, no. 2 (1979): 149–66.

23. Pletcher, *Awkward Years*, 166–68.

24. Frelinghuysen to Kasson, February 17, 1885, no. 98, RG 59, M77, Diplomatic Instructions of the Department of State, 1801–1906, reel 68, NARA; Manfred Jonas, *The United States and Germany: A Diplomatic History* (Ithaca, NY: Cornell University Press, 1984).

25. Sargent to Frelinghuysen, March 12, 1883, *FRUS*, 1883, 349–55; Plesur, *America's Outward Thrust*, 131.

26. John A. Kasson, "Otto von Bismarck, Man and Minister," *North American Review* 143 (1886): 105–18.

27. Kasson to Frelinghuysen, January 5, 1885, RG 59, M44, reel 55, NARA.

28. See Kasson to Thomas F. Bayard, no. 197, March 9, 1885; Kasson to Bayard, no. 202, March 11, 1885, RG 59, M44, reel 56, NARA.

29. Baron von Alvensleben to Bayard, March 16, 1885, Senate Executive Document 196, 49th Congress, 1st Session, *A Report of the Secretary of State Relative to the Affairs of the Independent State of the Congo, Part II, Miscellaneous Correspondence Concerning the Independent State of the Congo* (hereafter *Miscellaneous Correspondence*), 324.

30. Kasson to Bayard, March 9, 1885, *Correspondence Concerning the Berlin Congo Conference*, 185–86; "Bismarck's Astuteness," *New York Herald*, February 27, 1885, 5.

31. Daniel De Leon, "The Conference at Berlin on the West African Question," *Political Science Quarterly* 1, no. 1 (1886): 103–39, esp. 119–27.

32. See Harvey Lindsey to Grant, November 23, 1875; Bishop Edmund S. James to Grant, November 30, 1875, Fish Diary, October 29, 1875, quoted in *The Papers of Ulysses S. Grant*, ed. John Y. Simon (Carbondale: Southern Illinois University Press, 2003), 26:546–47; James A. Field Jr., *America and the Mediterranean World, 1776–1882* (Princeton, NJ: Princeton University Press, 1969), 378–79; Walter LaFeber, *The New Empire: An Interpretation of American Expansion, 1860–1898* (Ithaca, NY: Cornell University Press, 1963), 52.

33. Frelinghuysen to Tisdel, December 12, 1884, *Miscellaneous Correspondence*, 357.

34. Pletcher, *Awkward Years*, 317–18.

35. Sanford to William H. Seward, September 29, 1866, *FRUS*, 1866–1867, 70–71; Joseph A. Fry, *Henry S. Sanford: Diplomacy and Business in Nineteenth-Century America* (Reno: University of Nevada Press, 1982), 66–111.

36. Chester A. Arthur, Third Annual Message, December 4, 1883, in *A Compilation of the Messages and Papers of the Presidents*, ed. James D. Richardson (New York: Bureau of National Literature, 1897), 11:4762–63; L. E. Meyer, "Henry S. Sanford and the Congo: A Reassessment," *African Historical Studies*, 4, no. 1 (1971): 19–39; Pletcher, *Awkward Years*, 310–12.

37. Thomas Schoonover, "John A. Kasson's Opposition to the Lincoln Administration's Mexican Policy," *Annals of Iowa* 40, no. 8 (1971): 585–93.

38. As Jay Sexton has pointed out, this brought Kasson into line with men like James Blaine. Jay Sexton, *The Monroe Doctrine: Empire and Nation in Nineteenth-Century America* (New York: Hill & Wang, 2011), 162–63.

39. Kasson to Frelinghuysen, January 5, 1885, RG 59, M44, reel 55, NARA; John A. Kasson, "The Monroe Doctrine in 1881," *North American Review* 133 (1881): 523–33.

40. Edward Younger, *John A. Kasson: Politics and Diplomacy from Lincoln to McKinley* (Iowa City: State Historical Society of Iowa, 1955), 293–95.

41. Kasson to Frelinghuysen, October 20, 1884; Kasson to Stanley, October 20, 1884; Frelinghuysen to Kasson, October 23, 1884, *Correspondence Concerning the Berlin Congo Conference*, 15–16.

42. Kasson to Frelinghuysen, November 3, 1884, *Correspondence Concerning the Berlin Congo Conference*, 20; Kasson to Frelinghuysen (with enclosure), November 20, 1884, *Correspondence Concerning the Berlin Congo Conference*, 33–34.

43. Kasson to Frelinghuysen, November 17, 1884, *Correspondence Concerning the Berlin Congo Conference*, 31–32.

44. Kasson to Frelinghuysen, November 24, 1884, *Correspondence Concerning the Berlin Congo Conference*, 42.

45. John T. Morgan et al., "The Future of the Negro," *North American Review* 139 (July 1884): 81–84; Joseph A. Fry, "John Tyler Morgan's Southern Expansionism," *Diplomatic History* 9, no. 4 (1985): 329–46.

46. Crowe, *Berlin West African Conference*, 96–97.

47. Shepperson, "Aspects of American Interest in the Berlin Conference," 284–88; George Shepperson, "The Centennial of the West African Conference of Berlin, 1884–1885," *Phylon* 46, no. 1 (1985): 37–48.

48. Crowe, *Berlin West African Conference*, 80.

49. Sanford, quoted in Meyer, "Henry S. Sanford and the Congo," 36.

50. Kasson to Frelinghuysen, October 18, 1884, *Correspondence Concerning the Berlin Congo Conference*, 14–15 (emphasis added).

51. Kasson to Frelinghuysen, November 3, 1884; Kasson to Frelinghuysen, December 22, 1884, no. 109, RG 59, M44, reel 54, NARA; Frelinghuysen to Kasson, January 15, 1884, RG 59, M77, reel 68, NARA; Pletcher, *Awkward Years*, 320. Although the rest of Kasson's message from November 3 is included in the published *Correspondence Concerning the Berlin Congo Conference*, his request for a naval presence is excised with no indication that this has occurred.

52. Kasson to Frelinghuysen, no. 138, January 17, 1885; Kasson to Frelinghuysen, no. 140, January 19, 1885, RG 59, M44, reel 55, NARA. Kasson's response also contains the text of Frelinghuysen's original message.

53. Frelinghuysen to Kasson, October 17, 1884, *Correspondence Concerning the Berlin Congo Conference*, 13–14.

54. G. N. Sanderson, "The European Partition of Africa: Origins and Dynamics," in *The Cambridge History of Africa*, vol. 6, *From 1870 to 1905*, ed. Roland Oliver and G. N. Sanderson (Cambridge: Cambridge University Press, 1985), 96–158, esp. 96–100.

55. Pletcher, *Awkward Years*, 308–9.

56. Frelinghuysen to Tisdel, September 8, 1884, *Miscellaneous Correspondence*, 347.

57. Kasson to Bayard, March 16, 1885, *Correspondence Concerning the Berlin Congo Conference*, 189.

58. Enclosure 5, Manifesto of the International Association, *Miscellaneous Correspondence*, 355–56.

59. Kasson to Frelinghuysen, November 17, 1884, no. 71; Kasson to Frelinghuysen, November 24, 1884; Kasson to Frelinghuysen, November 26, 1884, all in *Correspondence Concerning the Berlin Congo Conference*, 42–44. Kasson to Frelinghuysen, December 1, 1884, *Correspondence Concerning the Berlin Congo Conference*, 61–62.

60. Kasson to Frelinghuysen, October 15, 1884, *Correspondence Concerning the Berlin Congo Conference*, 10–11. See also Kasson to Frelinghuysen, October 10, 1884, *Correspondence Concerning the Berlin Congo Conference*, 8.

61. Kasson to Frelinghuysen, October 18, 1884, *Correspondence Concerning the Berlin Congo Conference*, 14–15.

62. Kasson to Frelinghuysen, January 5, 1885, RG 59, M44, reel 55, NARA.

63. "Statement Read by Mr. Kasson at the Sitting of the Commission, December 10, 1884," in *The Scramble for Africa: Documents on the Berlin West African Conference and Related Subjects, 1884/1885*, ed. R. J. Gavin and J. A. Betley (Ibadan: Ibadan University Press, 1973), 219–21.

64. Enclosure no. 2 to dispatch 95, *Correspondence Concerning the Berlin Congo Conference*, 63.

65. Stanley, quoted in William Roger Louis, *Ends of British Imperialism: The Scramble for Africa, Suez and Decolonization* (London: I. B. Tauris, 2006), 92–93.

66. Louis, *Ends of British Imperialism*, 93.

67. Frelinghuysen to Tisdel, September 8, 1884, *Miscellaneous Correspondence*, 346.

68. Tisdel to Bayard, April 25, 1885, *Miscellaneous Correspondence*, 358.

69. Tisdel to Frelinghuysen, November 23, 1884, *Miscellaneous Correspondence*, 349–50.

70. Tisdel to Frelinghuysen, November 23, 1884, *FRUS*, 1885–1886, 289.

71. Tisdel to Rear-Admiral English, March 29, 1885, *Miscellaneous Correspondence*, 378.

72. Tisdel to Bayard, June 29, 1885, *Miscellaneous Correspondence*, 375.

73. Tisdel to English, March 20, 1885, *Miscellaneous Correspondence*, 378.

74. Louis, *Ends of British Imperialism*, 124.

75. See Lambert Tree to Bayard, October 26, 1885, *FRUS*, 1885–1886, 63–64.

76. Frelinghuysen to John T. Morgan, March 13, 1884, *Correspondence Concerning the Berlin Congo Conference*, 168–69.

77. Chester A. Arthur, Third Annual Message, December 4, 1883, in Richardson, *A Compilation of the Messages and Papers of the Presidents*, 11:4762–63.

78. Senate Report no. 393, 48th Congress, 1st Session, *Correspondence Concerning the Berlin Congo Conference*, 161–67; 162.

79. Martin R. Delany, *Official Report of the Niger Valley Exploring Party* (London: Thomas Hamilton, 1861), esp. 52–55.

80. These views changed as African Americans became aware of the horrors members of Leopold's organization were perpetrating in the Congo, and some began to compare them to the poor treatment of blacks in the United States. Jacobs, *African Nexus*, 83–111.

81. Jacobs, *African Nexus*, 68–69.

82. D. Augustus Straker, "The Land of Our Fathers," *New York Freeman*, January 23, 1884, in Jones et al., "To Enter Africa from America," accessed July 27, 2016, http://greystoke.unl.edu/doc/llg.ber.036.01.html.

83. Shepperson, "Aspects of American Interest in the Berlin Conference," 288–89.

84. Tisdel to Frelinghuysen, November 23, 1884, *Miscellaneous Correspondence*, 349–50.

85. Senate Report no. 393, *Correspondence Concerning the Berlin Congo Conference*, 161.

86. Fry, *Henry S. Sanford*, 137–38; Plesur, *America's Outward Thrust*, 144–50.

87. "The Question of West Africa," *New York Times*, December 11, 1884, 4.

88. Rev. J. N. Murdock to Kasson, January 29, 1885, enclosed in Kasson to Frelinghuysen, February 16, 1885, *Correspondence Concerning the Berlin Congo Conference*, 178–79.

89. Mark Hopkins and J. N. Stearns to Kasson, January 26, 1885, enclosed in Kasson to Frelinghuysen, February 9, 1885, *Correspondence Concerning the Berlin Congo Conference*, 176.

90. Charles G. Leland, "Leland's Letter," *Chicago Daily Tribune*, December 6, 1884, in Jones, et al., "To Enter Africa from America," accessed July 26, 2016, http://greystoke.unl.edu/doc/llg.ber.007.01.html (emphasis added).

91. Francis to Frelinghuysen, May 15, 1883, *FRUS*, 1883, 741.

92. Protocol 9—Meeting of February 23, 1885, *Correspondence Concerning the Berlin Congo Conference*, 253; Kasson to Frelinghuysen (with enclosure), November 20, 1884, *Correspondence Concerning the Berlin Congo Conference*, 33–34.

93. Crowe, *Berlin West Africa Conference*, 177.

94. Kasson to Frelinghuysen, December 22, 1884, *Correspondence Concerning the Berlin Congo Conference*, 136.

95. See Kasson to Frelinghuysen, January 7, 1885; Kasson to Frelinghuysen, January 12, 1885, *Correspondence Concerning the Berlin Congo Conference*, 141–42. Although Leopold issued decrees against slavery and the slave trade, both in effect continued and were extended under his rule. For details, see Hochschild, *King Leopold's Ghost,* 117–35.

96. Kasson to Frelinghuysen, December 22, 1884, *Correspondence Concerning the Berlin Congo Conference*, 136.

97. Kasson to Frelinghuysen, January 26, no. 144, RG 59, M44, reel 55, NARA.

98. Younger, *John A. Kasson*, 333–34. Although Younger does concede that "Kasson could not conceal his inner urgings for imperialism."

99. "Statement Read by Mr. Kasson at the Sitting of the Commission, December 10, 1884," in Gavin and Betley, *Scramble for Africa*, 219–21.

100. Enclosure no. 2 to dispatch 95, *Correspondence Concerning the Berlin Congo Conference*, 63; Kasson to Frelinghuysen, no. 171, February 16, 1885, RG 59, M44, reel 55, NARA. See also Kasson to Frelinghuysen, January 12, 1885, *Correspondence Concerning the Berlin Congo Conference*, 142–43.

101. Tisdel to Bayard, June 29, 1885, *Miscellaneous Correspondence*, 367.

102. Tisdel to Bayard, April 25, 1885, *Miscellaneous Correspondence*, 359; Tisdel to Bayard, June 29, 1885, *Miscellaneous Correspondence*, 369. The exceptions were, he said, the Kabinda and Loango tribes. Tisdel had traveled with a group of Loangos from the coast up the Congo River through territory controlled by other groups, which were hostile but had allowed the Loangos to pass. Perhaps in part because the Loangos (like Tisdel) spoke Portuguese, he found them to be "brave, obedient, loyal men" who "rarely ever complained of the hardships they had to endure."

103. Tisdel to Bayard, June 29, 1885, *Miscellaneous Correspondence*, 364.

104. Tisdel to Bayard, April 25, 1885, *Miscellaneous Correspondence*, 359–60.

105. Tisdel to Bayard, June 29, 1885, *Miscellaneous Correspondence*, 369.

106. Frelinghuysen to Kasson, October 13, 1884, RG 59, M77, reel 68, NARA; Declarations between the United States of America and the International Association of the Congo, April 22, 1884, *Correspondence Concerning the Berlin Congo Conference*, 260; Pletcher, *Awkward Years*, 79–86.

107. Frelinghuysen to Baron von Alvensleben, October 17, 1884; Frelinghuysen to Kasson, October 17, 1884, *Correspondence Concerning the Berlin Congo Conference*, 12–13; Frelinghuysen to Kasson, February 17, 1885, RG 59, M77, reel 68, NARA.

108. Blaine to Arthur, July 3, 1882, reel 2, series 1, Chester A. Arthurs Papers, Manuscript Division, Library of Congress, Washington, DC; Russell H. Bastert, "Diplomatic Reversal: Frelinghuysen's Opposition to Blaine's Pan-American Policy in 1882," *Mississippi Valley Historical Review* 42, no. 4 (1956): 653–71.

109. "The Congo Conference: Mr Perry Belmont Explains His House Resolution," *New York Times*, January 16, 1885, 5; "New Treaties in Congress," *New York Times*, January 6, 1885, 1; "The Congo Diplomacy," *New York Times*, January 31, 1885, 1; Pletcher, *Awkward Years*, 342–43.

110. "The Congo Conference," *New York Herald*, November 17, 1884, 4; Pletcher, *Awkward Years*, 320–22. Pletcher suggests that the *New York Times* also turned against U.S. participation, but I have not found evidence of this. Instead, it broadly maintained its position that the United States had every right to take part because of its growing commercial and humanitarian interests in Africa, and because it had not become involved in "any polemic discussion whatever." See "West African Projects," *New York Times*, January 17, 1885, 2; "The Berlin Conference," *New York Times*, January 30, 1885, 3; "Free State of the Congo," *New York Times*, August 31, 1885, 2.

111. "Interests in the Congo," *New York Times*, January 8, 1885, 1; "British-American Alliance," *New York Times*, February 4, 1885, 1; "A Newspaper's Prophecy," *Los Angeles Times*, February 4, 1885, in Jones, et al., "To Enter Africa from America," accessed July 27, 2016, http://greystoke.unl.edu/doc/llg.ber.034.01.html.

112. De Leon, "The Conference at Berlin on the West African Question," 137–39. These legal precedents concerned the "discovery" and "constructive possession" of a piece of coastline or mouth of a river, which he claimed the State Department had employed during American exploration of the Louisiana territory, and had now abandoned.

113. Tisdel to Bayard, March 20, 1885, *Miscellaneous Correspondence*, 379–87.

114. Sanford to Frelinghuysen, January 14, 1885, *Correspondence Concerning the Berlin Congo Conference*, 159–61.

115. John A. Kasson, "The Congo Conference and the President's Message," *North American Review* 142 (February 1886): 119–33. See also Kasson to Frelinghuysen, February 16, 1885, *Correspondence Concerning the Berlin Congo Conference*, 177–78; Kasson to Bayard, April 13, 1885, *Correspondence Concerning the Berlin Congo Conference*, 194–95.

116. See, for example, Kasson to Frelinghuysen, December 15, 1884, no. n/k, RG 59, M44, reel 54, NARA.

117. Kasson to Bayard, March 16, 1885, *Correspondence Concerning the Berlin Congo Conference*, 190–91.

118. Kasson to Frelinghuysen, January 7, 1885, RG 59, M44, reel 55, NARA; Kasson to Bayard, January 7, 1885, *Correspondence Concerning the Berlin Congo Conference*, 139–40.

119. Kasson to Frelinghuysen, January 12, 1885, *Correspondence Concerning the Berlin Congo Conference*, 143; Kasson to Bayard, March 16, 1885, *Correspondence Concerning the Berlin Congo Conference*, 188.

120. Kasson to Frelinghuysen, January 7, 1885, RG 59, M44, reel 55, NARA; Kasson to Bayard, January 7, 1885, *Correspondence Concerning the Berlin Congo Conference*, 139–40.

121. Kasson to Frelinghuysen, February 3, 1885; Frelinghuysen to Kasson, February 17, 1885, *Correspondence Concerning the Berlin Congo Conference*, 173–75.

122. Bayard to von Alvensleben, April 16, 1885, *Miscellaneous Correspondence*, 321–22.

123. Bayard to von Alvensleben, April 6, 1885, *Miscellaneous Correspondence*, 325–26.

124. Bayard to Tree, September 11, 1885, *FRUS*, 1885–1886, 60–61.

125. Grover Cleveland, First Annual Message, December 8, 1885, in Richardson, *A Compilation of the Messages and Papers of the Presidents*, 11:4915.

126. Kasson to Frelinghuysen, March 2, 1885, *Correspondence Concerning the Berlin Congo Conference*, 184. The General Act of the Berlin Conference can be found in *Correspondence Concerning the Berlin Congo Conference*, 297–305.

127. "London's Saturday Night: Khartoum the Topic That Absorbs and Oppresses All," *New York Times*, February 8, 1885, 1.

128. George Washington Williams, "An Open Letter to His Serene Majesty Leopold II, King of the Belgians and Sovereign of the Independent State and the Congo (18 July 1890)," in *Apropos of Africa: Sentiments of Negro American Leaders from the 1800s to 1950s*, ed. Adeleide Cromwell Hill and Martin Kilson (London: Frank Cass, 1969), 98–107; 100; Shepperson, "Aspects of American Interest in the Berlin Conference," 288; Lisa Lowe, *The Intimacies of Four Continents* (Durham, NC: Duke University Press, 2015); W. E. B. Du Bois, "The African Roots of War," *Atlantic Monthly* 115 (May 1915): 707–14.

Conclusion

1. Albert G. Browne Jr., "Latin and Saxon America," *Atlantic Monthly* 64, no. 386 (December 1889): 834–41.

2. Thomas Bender, *A Nation Among Nations: America's Place in World History* (New York: Hill & Wang, 2006), 183.

3. Browne, "Latin and Saxon America," 837.

4. For a sense of the continuing heated debates about how to define the American empire, see a recent public discussion between Paul Kramer and Daniel Immerwahr. Daniel Immerwahr, "The Greater United States," *Diplomatic History* 40, no. 3 (2016): 373–91; Paul A. Kramer, "How Not to Write the History of U.S. Empire," *Diplomatic History* 42, no. 5 (2018): 911–31; Daniel

Immerwahr, "Writing the History of the Greater United States: A Reply to Paul Kramer," *Diplomatic History* 43, no. 2 (2019): 397–403. It should be noted that both of these authors agree that the United States is an empire; they disagree on how to define the term.

5. Frederick Cooper, *Colonialism in Question: Theory, Knowledge, History* (Berkeley: University of California Press, 2005), 153–58.

6. Walter LaFeber, *The New Empire: An Interpretation of American Expansion, 1860–1898* (Ithaca, NY: Cornell University Press, 1963), 29.

7. George C. Herring, *From Colony to Superpower: U.S. Foreign Relations Since 1776* (Oxford: Oxford University Press, 2008), 293.

8. David M. Pletcher, "1861–1898: Economic Growth and Diplomatic Adjustment," in *Economics and World Power: An Assessment of American Diplomacy Since 1789*, ed. William H. Becker and Samuel F. Wells Jr. (New York: Columbia University Press, 1984), 119–71, esp. 123–25.

9. Lawrence A. Clayton, "The Nicaragua Canal in the Nineteenth Century: Prelude to American Empire in the Caribbean," *Journal of Latin American Studies* 19, no. 2 (1987): 323–52.

10. Clayton, "Nicaragua Canal in the Nineteenth Century," 327.

11. Merze Tate, "Twisting the Lion's Tail Over Hawaii," *Pacific Historical Review* 36, no. 1 (1967): 27–46.

12. Clayton, "Nicaragua Canal in the Nineteenth Century," 349.

13. Henry Cabot Lodge, "England, Venezuela, and the Monroe Doctrine," *North American Review* 160, no. 463 (1895): 651–58.

14. Cui Zhihai, "The United States and the Sino-Japanese War of 1894–1895," *Social Sciences in China* 36, no. 4 (2015): 164–92.

15. Grover Cleveland, Special Message to Congress, December 17, 1895, in *A Compilation of the Messages and Papers of the Presidents*, ed. James D. Richardson (New York: Bureau of National Literature, 1902), 9:655–58.

16. Louis A. Pérez Jr., "The Meaning of the Maine: Causation and the Historiography of the Spanish-American War," *Pacific Historical Review* 58, no. 3 (1989): 293–322.

17. Herring, *From Colony to Superpower*, 325.

18. Daniel Immerwahr, *How to Hide an Empire: A Short History of the Greater United States* (London: Bodley Head, 2019).

19. Matthew Frye Jacobson, *Barbarian Virtues: The United States Encounters Foreign Peoples at Home and Abroad, 1876–1917* (New York: Hill & Wang, 2000), 221–59.

20. Patrick M. Kirkwood, " 'Lord Cromer's Shadow': Political Anglo-Saxonism and the Egyptian Protectorate as a Model in the American Philippines," *Journal of World History* 27, no. 1 (2016): 1–26; Thomas R. Metcalf, "From One

Empire to Another: The Influence of the British Raj on American Colonialism in the Philippines," *Ab Imperio* 3 (2012): 25–41.

21. On this point, see, for example, Paul A. Kramer, *The Blood of Government: Race, Empire, the United States, and the Philippines* (Chapel Hill: University of North Carolina Press, 2006).

22. Cooper, *Colonialism in Question*, 4.

23. Cooper, *Colonialism in Question*, 3.

24. Amy Kaplan, "'Left Alone with America': The Absence of Empire in the Study of American Culture," in *Cultures of United States Imperialism*, ed. Amy Kaplan and Donald Pease (Durham, NC: Duke University Press, 1993), 3–21.

25. Charles Bright and Michael Geyer, "Where in the World Is America? The History of the United States in the Global Age," in *Rethinking American History in a Global Age*, ed. Thomas Bender (Berkeley: University of California Press, 2002), 63–100; 73–74.

26. Afaf Lutfi al-Sayyid-Marsot, "The British Occupation of Egypt from 1882," in *The Oxford History of the British Empire*, vol. 3, *The Nineteenth Century*, ed. Andrew Porter (Oxford: Oxford University Press, 1999), 651–64; 655.

27. Bright and Geyer, "Where in the World Is America," 74.

Bibliography

Primary Sources

Boston, Massachusetts Historical Society
  Papers of Edward Atkinson
College Park, MD, National Archives and Records Administration
  Record Group 59, Records of the Department of State
    M31 Despatches from U.S. Ministers to Spain, 1792–1906
    M34 Despatches from U.S. Ministers to France, 1789–1906
    M44 Despatches from U.S. Ministers to the German States and Germany,
    1799–1906
    M77 Diplomatic Instructions of the Department of State, 1801–1906
    T41 Despatches from U.S. Consuls in Cairo, Egypt, 1864–1906
Rochester, NY, University of Rochester
  Papers of William H. Seward (microfilm)
Washington, DC, Manuscript Division, Library of Congress
  Chester A. Arthur Papers
  Hamilton Fish Papers
  Frederick Theodore Frelinghuysen Papers
  James A. Garfield Papers
  William Henry Seward Papers

Published Newspapers and Periodicals

American Whig Review
Atlantic Monthly
Century: A Popular Quarterly
Continental Monthly
Galaxy
Harper's New Monthly Magazine
New Englander and Yale Review
New York Daily Tribune
New York Herald
New York Times
North American Review
Overland Monthly
Scribner's Monthly
Southern Literary Messenger
Westminster Review

Internet Sources

Jones, Jeanette Eileen, et al. "To Enter Africa from America: U.S. Empire, Race, and the African Question, 1847–1919." Accessed July 27, 2016. http://greystoke .unl.edu/.

Government Publications

Byrd, Robert C. *The Senate, 1789–1989: Classic Speeches, 1830–1993.* Washington, DC: United States Government Printing Office, 1994.

Congressional Globe, 26th Congress, 2nd Session, February 12, 1840.

Congressional Globe, 37th Congress, 2nd Session, December 30, 1861.

Congressional Globe, 37th Congress, 3rd Session, February 3, 1863.

Congressional Globe, 38th Congress, 1st Session, April 4, 1864.

Congressional Globe, 39th Congress, 1st Session, December 11, 1865.

Congressional Globe, 40th Congress, 1st Session, April 19, 1867.

Congressional Globe, Appendix, 41st Congress, 1st Session, April 9, 1869.

Public Papers of the Presidents of the United States: Barack Obama, 2009, Book 1. Washington, DC: United States Government Printing Office, 2010.

Public Papers of the Presidents of the United States: Barack Obama, 2011, Book 1. Washington, DC: United States Government Printing Office, 2014.

Richardson, James D., ed. *A Compilation of the Messages and Papers of the Presidents.* 20 vols. New York: Bureau of National Literature, 1897–1916.

Senate Executive Document 196, 49th Congress, 1st Session. *A Report of the Secretary of State Relative to the Affairs of the Independent State of the Congo, Part I, Correspondence Concerning the Berlin Congo Conference Together with the Protocols and General Act.*

Senate Executive Document 196, 49th Congress, 1st Session. *A Report of the Secretary of State Relative to the Affairs of the Independent State of the Congo, Part II, Miscellaneous Correspondence Concerning the Independent State of the Congo.*

Senate Executive Journal, 37th Congress, 2nd Session, February 19, 1862.

Senate Report no. 393, 48th Congress, 1st Session. *Correspondence Concerning the Berlin Congo Conference.*

Sumner, Charles. "Our Claims on England." Appendix to the *Congressional Globe,* 41st Congress, Special Session, April 13, 1869, 21–26.

United States Department of State. *Foreign Relations of the United States.* Washington, DC: United States Government Printing Office, 1861–1886.

Published Primary Sources

Abbott, John S. C. *The History of Napoleon III, Emperor of the French.* Boston: B. B. Russell, 1869.

Adams, John Quincy. *Address Delivered at the Request of the Committee of the Citizens of Washington, July 4, 1821.* Washington, DC: Davis & Force, 1821.

——. *Writings of John Quincy Adams.* Ed. Worthington Chauncey Ford. 7 vols. New York: Macmillan, 1913–1917.

Baker, George E., ed. *The Life of William H. Seward with Selections from His Works.* New York: J. S. Redfield, 1855.

Chase, Salmon P. *The Salmon P. Chase Papers.* Ed. John Niven. 5 vols. Kent, OH: Kent State University Press, 1993–1998.

Child, Lydia Maria. *A Lydia Maria Child Reader.* Ed. Carolyn L. Karcher. Durham, NC: Duke University Press, 1997.

Delany, Martin R. *Martin R. Delany: A Documentary Reader.* Ed. Robert S. Levine. Chapel Hill: University of North Carolina Press, 2003.

——. *Official Report of the Niger Valley Exploring Party.* London: Thomas Hamilton, 1861.

De Leon, Daniel. "The Conference at Berlin on the West African Question." *Political Science Quarterly* 1, no. 1 (1886): 103–39.

Douglass, Frederick. *The Frederick Douglass Papers, Series One: Speeches, Debates, and Interviews.* Ed. John W. Blassingame and John R. McKivigan. 5 vols. New Haven, CT: Yale University Press, 1979–1992.

Foner, Philip S., ed. *The Life and Writings of Frederick Douglass.* 4 vols. New York: International Publishers, 1950–1955.

Franklin, Benjamin. *Observations Concerning the Increase of Mankind, Peopling of Countries, &c.* Boston: S. Kneeland, 1755.

Garrison, William Lloyd. *The Letters of William Lloyd Garrison.* Ed. Walter M. Merrill and Louis Ruchames. 6 vols. Cambridge, MA: Belknap Press of Harvard University Press, 1981.

Gavin, R. J., and J. A. Betley, eds. *The Scramble for Africa: Documents on the Berlin West African Conference and Related Subjects, 1884/1885.* Ibadan: Ibadan University Press, 1973.

Gladstone, W. E. *Bulgarian Horrors and the Question of the East.* New York: Lovell, Adam, Wesson, 1876.

Goldman, Lawrence, ed. *The Federalist Papers.* Oxford: Oxford University Press, 2008.

Grant, Ulysses S. "A Threatened Invasion of California: Letter to Major General McDowell by General U. S. Grant." *California Historical Society Quarterly* 13, no. 1 (1934): 38–42.

———. *The Papers of Ulysses S. Grant.* Ed. John Y. Simon. 31 vols. Carbondale: Southern Illinois University Press, 1967–2009.

Howe, Julia Ward. *A Trip to Cuba.* Boston: Ticknor and Fields, 1860.

Jefferson, Thomas. *Summary View of the Rights of British America.* Williamsburg, VA: Clementina Rind, 1774.

Johnson, Andrew. *The Papers of Andrew Johnson.* Ed. Paul H. Bergeron, LeRoy P. Graf, and Ralph W. Haskins. 16 vols. Knoxville: University of Tennessee Press, 1967–2000.

Kingsley, Vine Wright. *French Intervention in America.* New York: C. B. Richardson, 1863.

Leavitt, Joshua. *The Monroe Doctrine.* New York: Sinclair Tousey, 1863.

Lincoln, Abraham. *The Collected Works of Abraham Lincoln.* Ed. Roy P. Basler. 9 vols. New Brunswick, NJ: Rutgers University Press, 1953.

Lodge, Henry Cabot. "England, Venezuela, and the Monroe Doctrine." *North American Review* 160, no. 463 (1895): 651–58.

Schurz, Carl. *Speeches, Correspondence and Political Papers of Carl Schurz.* Ed. Frederic Bancroft. 6 vols. New York: Negro Universities Press, 1913.

Seeley, J. R. *The Expansion of England: Two Courses of Lectures.* London: Macmillan, 1914. First published 1883.

Seward, William H. *The Works of William H. Seward.* Ed. George E. Baker. 5 vols. New York: AMS, 1972.

Smith, Theodore Clarke, ed. *The Life and Letters of James Abram Garfield.* Vol. 1. New Haven, CT: Yale University Press, 1925.

Stanton, Elizabeth Cady. *Eighty Years and More: Reminiscences, 1815–1897.* Boston: Northeastern University Press, 1993.

Stevens, Thaddeus. *The Selected Papers of Thaddeus Stevens.* Ed. Beverly Wilson Palmer. 2 vols. Pittsburgh, PA: University of Pittsburgh Press, 1997.

Strong, Josiah. *Our Country: Its Possible Future and Its Present Crisis.* Revised ed. Cambridge, MA: Belknap Press of Harvard University Press, 1963. First published 1891 by Baker & Taylor.

Sumner, Charles. *Memoir and Letters of Charles Sumner.* Ed. Edward L. Pierce. 4 vols. Boston: Roberts Brothers, 1893.

——. *Naboth's Vineyard: Speech of Hon. Charles Sumner of Massachusetts on the Proposed Annexation of "The Island of Santo Domingo," Delivered in the Senate of the United States, December 21, 1870.* Washington, DC: F & J Reeves & Geo. A. Bailey, 1870.

——. *The Selected Letters of Charles Sumner.* Ed. Beverly Wilson Palmer. 2 vols. Boston: Northeastern University Press, 1990.

Sumner, William Graham. *Essays of William Graham Sumner.* Ed. Albert Galloway Keller and Maurice R. Davie. 2 vols. Hamden, CT: Archon, 1969.

Twain, Mark. *King Leopold's Soliloquy.* Boston: P. R. Warren, 1905.

Welles, Gideon. *The Diary of Gideon Welles.* Ed. Edgar T. Welles. 3 vols. Boston: Houghton Mifflin, 1911.

Williams, George Washington. "An Open Letter to His Serene Majesty Leopold II, King of the Belgians and Sovereign of the Independent State and the Congo (18 July 1890)." In *Apropos of Africa: Sentiments of Negro American Leaders from the 1800s to 1950s,* ed. Adeleide Cromwell Hill and Martin Kilson, 98–107. London: Frank Cass, 1969.

Woodull, Victoria. *Selected Writings of Victoria Woodhull: Suffrage, Free Love, and Eugenics.* Ed. Cari M. Carpenter. Lincoln: University of Nebraska Press, 2010.

Young, John Russell. *Around the World with General Grant.* Vol. 1. New York: Subscription Book Department, 1879.

Secondary Sources

Akpan, M. B. "Black Imperialism: Americo-Liberian Rule over the African Peoples of Liberia, 1841–1964." *Canadian Journal of African Studies* 7, no. 2 (1973): 217–36.

Aldrich, Robert. *Greater France: A History of French Overseas Expansion.* Basing-stoke, UK: Palgrave Macmillan, 1996.

Allen, H. C. *Great Britain and the United States: A History of Anglo-American Relations, 1783–1952.* New York: St. Martin's Press, 1955.

Bancroft, Frederic. "The French in Mexico and the Monroe Doctrine." *Political Science Quarterly* 11, no. 1 (1896): 30–43.

Bastert, Russell H. "Diplomatic Reversal: Frelinghuysen's Opposition to Blaine's Pan-American Policy in 1882." *Mississippi Valley Historical Review* 42, no. 4 (1956): 653–71.

Beisner, Robert L. *From the Old Diplomacy to the New, 1865–1900.* New York: Crowell, 1975.

Bemis, Samuel Flagg. *A Diplomatic History of the United States.* 5th ed. New York: Rhinehart & Winston, 1965.

——. *John Quincy Adams and the Foundations of American Foreign Policy.* New York: Alfred A. Knopf, 1949.

Bender, Thomas. *A Nation Among Nations: America's Place in World History.* New York: Hill & Wang, 2006.

Betts, Raymond F. "Immense Dimensions: The Impact of the American West on Late Nineteenth-Century European Thought About Expansion." *Western Historical Quarterly* 10, no. 2 (1979): 149–66.

Bhagat, Goberdhan. *Americans in India, 1784–1860.* New York: New York University Press, 1970.

Bickham, Troy. *The Weight of Vengeance: The United States, the British Empire, and the War of 1812.* Oxford: Oxford University Press, 2012.

Bixler, Raymond W. *The Foreign Policy of the United States in Liberia.* New York: Pageant, 1957.

Blumberg, Arnold. *The Diplomacy of the Mexican Empire, 1863–1867.* Philadelphia: American Philosophical Society, 1971.

Blumenthal, Henry. *France and the United States: Their Diplomatic Relations, 1789–1914.* Chapel Hill: University of North Carolina Press, 1970.

Botero, Rodrigo. *Ambivalent Embrace: America's Relations with Spain from the Revolutionary War to the Cold War.* Westport, CT: Greenwood, 2000.

Bourne, Kenneth. *Britain and the Balance of Power in North America, 1815–1908.* London: Longman, 1967.

Bowen, Wayne H. *Shades of Blue and Grey: Spain and the American Civil War.* Columbia: Missouri University Press, 2011.

Boyd, Julian P. "Thomas Jefferson's 'Empire of Liberty.'" *Virginia Quarterly Review* 24 (1948): 538–54.

Bradford, Richard H. *The Virginius Affair.* Boulder: Colorado Associated University Press, 1980.

Brauer, Kinley J. "The Slavery Problem in the Diplomacy of the American Civil War." *Pacific Historical Review* 46, no. 3 (1977): 439–69.

———. "The United States and British Imperial Expansion, 1815–1860." *Diplomatic History* 12, no. 1 (1988): 19–37.

Bright, Charles, and Michael Geyer. "Where in the World Is America? The History of the United States in the Global Age." In *Rethinking American History in a Global Age*, ed. Thomas Bender, 63–100. Berkeley: University of California Press, 2002.

Brown, Philip Marshall. "Frederick T. Frelinghuysen." In *American Secretaries of State and Their Diplomacy*, vol. 8, ed. Samuel Flagg Bemis, 3–46. New York: Cooper Square, 1963.

Buzzanco, Robert. "Anti-Imperialism." In *Encyclopedia of American Foreign Policy*, ed. Alexander DeConde, Richard Dean Burns, and Fredrik Logevall, 49–60. New York: Scribners, 2002.

Campbell, Charles S. *From Revolution to Rapprochement: The United States and Great Britain, 1783–1900.* New York: John Wiley & Sons, 1974.

———. *Transformation of American Foreign Relations, 1865–1900.* New York: Harper & Row, 1976.

Castel, Albert. *The Presidency of Andrew Johnson.* Lawrence: University Press of Kansas, 1979.

Chang, Gordon H. *Fateful Ties: A History of America's Preoccupation with China.* Cambridge, MA: Harvard University Press, 2015.

———. "Whose 'Barbarism'? Whose 'Treachery'? Race and Civilization in the Unknown United States-Korea War of 1871." *Journal of American History* 89, no. 4 (2003): 1331–65.

Chapin, James B. "Hamilton Fish and American Expansion." In *Makers of American Diplomacy: From Benjamin Franklin to Alfred Thayer Mahan*, ed. Frank J. Merli and Theodore A. Wilson, 223–51. New York: Scribner, 1974.

———. "Hamilton Fish and the Lessons of the Ten Years' War." In *Perspectives on American Diplomacy*, ed. Jules Davids, 131–63. New York: Arno, 1976.

Cobbs Hoffman, Elizabeth. *American Umpire.* Cambridge, MA: Harvard University Press, 2013.

Cogliano, Francis D. *Emperor of Liberty: Thomas Jefferson's Foreign Policy.* New Haven, CT: Yale University Press, 2014.

Conroy-Krutz, Emily. *Christian Imperialism: Converting the World in the Early American Republic.* Ithaca, NY: Cornell University Press, 2015.

Cooper, Frederick. *Colonialism in Question: Theory, Knowledge, History.* Berkeley: University of California Press, 2005.

Cortada, James W. "Diplomatic Rivalry Between Spain and the United States over Chile and Peru, 1864–1871." *Inter-American Economic Affairs* 27, no. 4 (1974): 47–57.

———. *Spain and the American Civil War: Relations at Mid-Century, 1855–1868*. Philadelphia: American Philosophical Society, 1980.

———. *Two Nations over Time: Spain and the United States, 1776–1977*. Westport, CT: Greenwood Press, 1978.

Crapol, Edward P. *America for Americans: Economic Nationalism and Anglophobia in the Late Nineteenth Century*. Westport, CT: Greenwood Press, 1973.

Crowe, S. E. *The Berlin West African Conference, 1884–1885*. Westport, CT: Negro Universities Press, 1970.

Cumings, Bruce. *Dominion from Sea to Sea: Pacific Ascendency and American Power*. New Haven, CT: Yale University Press, 2009.

Cunningham, Michele. *Mexico and the Foreign Policy of Napoleon III*. Basingstoke, UK: Palgrave Macmillan, 2001.

Darwin, John. "Imperialism and the Victorians: The Dynamics of Territorial Expansion." *English Historical Review* 112, no. 447 (1997): 614–42.

Davis, Mike. *Late Victorian Holocausts: El Niño Famines and the Making of the Third World*. London: Verso, 2001.

Davis, Sue. *The Political Thought of Elizabeth Cady Stanton: Women's Rights and the American Political Traditions*. New York: New York University Press, 2008.

DeGuzmán, María. *Spain's Long Shadow: The Black Legend, Off Whiteness, and Anglo-American Empire*. Minneapolis: Minnesota University Press, 2005.

Dennett, Tyler. "Seward's Far Eastern Policy." *American Historical Review* 28, no. 1 (1922): 45–62.

Doenecke, Justus D. *The Presidencies of James A. Garfield and Chester A. Arthur*. Lawrence: University Press of Kansas, 1981.

Donald, David Herbert. *Charles Sumner and the Rights of Man*. New York: Da Capo, 1996.

Doyle, Don H. *The Cause of All Nations: An International History of the American Civil War*. New York: Basic Books, 2015.

Duncan, Robert H. "Political Legitimation and Maximilian's Second Empire in Mexico, 1864–1867." *Mexican Studies* 12, no. 1 (1996): 27–66.

Egan, Clifford L. "The United States and the Spanish Intervention in Mexico, 1861–1862." *Revista de Historia de América* 63, no. 4 (1967): 1–12.

Egnal, Marc. *A Mighty Empire: The Origins of the American Revolution*. Ithaca, NY: Cornell University Press, 1988.

Federici, Michael P. *The Political Philosophy of Alexander Hamilton*. Baltimore, MD: Johns Hopkins University Press, 2012.

Ferguson, Niall. *Colossus: The Rise and Fall of the American Empire*. London: Penguin, 2004.

Ferrer, Ada. *Insurgent Cuba: Race, Nation, and Revolution, 1868–1898*. Chapel Hill: University of North Carolina Press, 1999.

Field, James A., Jr. *America and the Mediterranean World, 1776–1882.* Princeton, NJ: Princeton University Press, 1969.

Fleche, Andre M. *The Revolution of 1861: The American Civil War in the Age of Nationalist Conflict.* Chapel Hill: University of North Carolina Press, 2014.

Foner, Philip S. *A History of Cuba and Its Relations with the United States.* Vol. 2. New York: International Publishers, 1962.

Foreman, Amanda. *A World on Fire: An Epic History of Two Nations Divided.* London: Penguin, 2010.

Frazer, Robert W. "The Role of the Lima Congress, 1864–1865, in the Development of Pan-Americanism." *Hispanic American Historical Review* 29, no. 3 (1949): 319–48.

Fry, Joseph A. *Henry S. Sanford: Diplomacy and Business in Nineteenth-Century America.* Reno: University of Nevada Press, 1982.

——. "John Tyler Morgan's Southern Expansionism." *Diplomatic History* 9, no. 4 (1985): 329–46.

Fuller, Joseph V. "Hamilton Fish." In *American Secretaries of State and Their Diplomacy,* vol. 4, ed. Samuel Flagg Bemis, 125–214. New York: Cooper Square, 1963.

Gallagher, John, and Ronald Robinson. "The Imperialism of Free Trade." *Economic History Review* 6, no. 1 (1953): 1–15.

Gelfand, Lawrence E. "Hemispheric Regionalism to Global Universalism: The Changing Face of United States National Interests." *Mid-American Historical Review* 76, no. 3 (1994): 187–203.

Gibson, Charles. *The Colonial Period in Latin American History.* Washington, DC: Service Center for Teachers of History, 1958.

Gjersø, Jonas Fossli. "The Scramble for East Africa: British Motives Reconsidered, 1884–95." *Journal of Imperial and Commonwealth History* 43, no. 5 (2015): 831–60.

Gleason, David T., and Simon Lewis, eds. *The Civil War as Global Conflict: Transnational Meanings of the American Civil War.* Columbia: University of South Carolina Press, 2014.

Gleijeses, Piero. "Napoleon, Jefferson and the Louisiana Purchase." *International History Review* 39, no. 2 (2017): 237–55.

Go, Julian. *Patterns of Empire: The British and American Empires, 1688 to the Present.* New York: Cambridge University Press, 2011.

Goldwert, Marvin. "Matías Romero and Congressional Opposition to Seward's Policy Toward the French Intervention in Mexico." *The Americas* 22, no. 1 (1965): 22–40.

Gould, Eliga H. *Among the Powers of the Earth: The American Revolution and the Making of a New World Empire.* Cambridge, MA: Harvard University Press, 2012.

Gould, James W. "American Imperialism in Southeast Asia Before 1898." *Journal of Southeast Asian Studies* 3, no. 2 (1972): 306–14.

Graebner, Norman A. *Empire on the Pacific: A Study in Continental Expansion*. New York: Ronald Press, 1955.

——, ed. *Traditions and Values: American Diplomacy, 1865–1945*. Lanham, MD: Rowman & Littlefield, 1985.

Gray, Elizabeth Kelly. "American Attitudes Toward British Imperialism, 1815–1860." PhD diss., College of William and Mary, 2002.

Grenville, John A. S., and George Berkeley Young. *Politics, Strategy, and American Diplomacy: Studies in Foreign Policy, 1873–1917*. New Haven, CT: Yale University Press, 1966.

Guettel, Jens-Uwe. *German Expansionism, Imperial Liberalism, and the United States, 1777–1945*. New York: Cambridge University Press, 2012.

Guterl, Matthew Pratt. *American Mediterranean: Southern Slaveholders in the Age of Emancipation*. Cambridge, MA: Harvard University Press, 2008.

Guyatt, Nicholas. "America's Conservatory: Race, Reconstruction, and the Santo Domingo Debate." *Journal of American History* 97, no. 4 (2011): 974–1000.

Hahn, Steven. *A Nation Without Borders: The United States and Its World in an Age of Civil Wars, 1830–1910*. New York: Viking, 2016.

Hammond, Harold E. "American Interest in the Exploration of the Dark Continent." *The Historian* 18, no. 2 (1956): 202–29.

Handler, Edward. *America and Europe in the Political Thought of John Adams*. Cambridge, MA: Harvard University Press, 1964.

Hanna, Alfred Jackson, and Kathryn Abbey Hanna. *Napoleon III and Mexico: American Triumph over Monarchy*. Chapel Hill: University of North Carolina Press, 1971.

Hanna, Kathryn Abbey. "The Roles of the South in the French Intervention in Mexico." *Journal of Southern History* 20, no. 1 (1954): 3–21.

Hardy, William E. "South of the Border: Ulysses S. Grant and the French Intervention." *Civil War History* 54, no. 1 (2008): 63–86.

Harper, John Lamberton. *American Machiavelli: Alexander Hamilton and the Origins of U.S. Foreign Policy*. Cambridge: Cambridge University Press, 2004.

Hart, John Mason. *Empire and Revolution: The Americans in Mexico Since the Civil War*. Berkeley: University of California Press, 2002.

Haslip, Joan. *Imperial Adventurer: Emperor Maximilian of Mexico*. London: Weidenfeld & Nicolson, 1971.

Haynes, Sam W. "Anglophobia and the Annexation of Texas: The Quest for National Security." In *Manifest Destiny and Empire: American Antebellum Expansion*, ed. Sam W. Haynes and Christopher Morris, 115–45. College Station: Texas A&M University Press, 1997.

Heiss, Mary Ann. "The Evolution of the Imperial Idea and U.S. National Identity." *Diplomatic History* 26, no. 4 (2002): 511–40.

Hendrickson, David C. *Union, Nation, or Empire: The American Debate over International Relations, 1789–1941*. Lawrence: University of Kansas Press, 2009.

Herring, George C. *From Colony to Superpower: U.S. Foreign Relations Since 1776*. Oxford: Oxford University Press, 2008.

Hidalgo, Dennis. "Charles Sumner and the Annexation of the Dominican Republic." *Itinerario* 21, no. 2 (1997): 51–65.

Hietala, Thomas R. *Manifest Design: Anxious Aggrandizement in Late Jacksonian America*. Ithaca, NY: Cornell University Press, 1985.

Hochschild, Adam. *King Leopold's Ghost: A Story of Greed, Terror and Heroism in Colonial Africa*. London: Macmillan, 1999.

Hoganson, Kristin L. *Consumers' Imperium: The Global Production of American Domesticity, 1865–1920*. Chapel Hill: University of North Carolina Press, 2007.

Hoganson, Kristin L., and Jay Sexton, eds. *Crossing Empires: Taking U.S. History into Transimperial Terrain*. Durham, NC: Duke University Press, 2020.

Hopkins, A. G. *American Empire: A Global History*. Princeton, NJ: Princeton University Press, 2018.

——. "The Victorians and Africa: A Reconsideration of the Occupation of Egypt, 1882." *Journal of African History* 27, no. 2 (1986): 363–91.

Horsman, Reginald. "Dimensions of an 'Empire for Liberty': Expansion and Republicanism, 1775–1825." *Journal of the Early Republic* 9, no. 1 (1989): 1–20.

Hoskins, Halford L. "French Views of the Monroe Doctrine and the Mexican Expedition." *Hispanic American Historical Review* 4, no. 4 (1921): 677–89.

Hughes, David. "Unmaking an Exception: A Critical Genealogy of U.S. Exceptionalism." *Review of International Studies* 41, no. 3 (2015): 527–51.

Hunt, Michael H. *Ideology and U.S. Foreign Policy*. New Haven, CT: Yale University Press, 1987.

Hurtado, Albert L. "Empires, Frontiers, Filibusters, and Pioneers: The Transnational World of John Sutter." *Pacific Historical Review* 77, no. 1 (2008): 19–47.

Hyde, H. Montgomery. *Mexican Empire: The History of Maximilian and Carlota of Mexico*. London: Macmillan, 1946.

Immerman, Richard H. *Empire for Liberty: A History of American Imperialism from Benjamin Franklin to Paul Wolfowitz*. Princeton, NJ: Princeton University Press, 2010.

Immerwahr, Daniel. "The Greater United States." *Diplomatic History* 40, no. 3 (2016): 373–91.

——. *How to Hide an Empire: A Short History of the Greater United States*. London: Bodley Head, 2019.

——. "Writing the History of the Greater United States: A Reply to Paul Kramer." *Diplomatic History* 43, no. 2 (2019): 397–403.

Jacobs, Sylvia M. *The African Nexus: Black American Perspectives on the European Partitioning of Africa*. Westport, CT: Greenwood, 1981.

Jacobson, Matthew Frye. *Barbarian Virtues: The United States Encounters Foreign Peoples at Home and Abroad, 1876–1917*. New York: Hill & Wang, 2000.

Jampoler, Andrew C. A. *Congo: The Miserable Expeditions and Dreadful Death of Lt. Emory Taunt, USN*. Annapolis, MD: Naval Institute Press, 2013.

Johnson, Walter. *River of Dark Dreams: Slavery and Empire in the Cotton Kingdom*. Cambridge, MA: Belknap Press of Harvard University Press, 2013.

Jonas, Manfred. *The United States and Germany: A Diplomatic History*. Ithaca, NY: Cornell University Press, 1984.

Jones, Howard. *Blue and Gray Diplomacy: A History of Union and Confederate Foreign Relations*. Chapel Hill: University of North Carolina Press, 2010.

Kagan, Robert. *Dangerous Nation: America and the World, 1600–1898*. London: Atlantic Books, 2006.

Kaplan, Amy. "'Left Alone with America': The Absence of Empire in the Study of American Culture." In *Cultures of United States Imperialism*, ed. Amy Kaplan and Donald Pease, 3–21. Durham, NC: Duke University Press, 1993.

Kaplan, Lawrence S. *Thomas Jefferson: Westward the Course of Empire*. Wilmington, DE: Scholarly Resources, 1999.

Karp, Matthew. *This Vast Southern Empire: Slaveholders at the Helm of American Foreign Policy*. Cambridge, MA: Harvard University Press, 2016.

Kelly, Patrick J. "The North American Crisis of the 1860s." *Journal of the Civil War Era* 2, no. 3 (2012): 337–68.

Kennedy, Dane. "The Imperial History Wars." *Journal of British Studies* 54, no. 1 (2015): 5–22.

Kent, Marian, ed. *Great Powers and the End of the Ottoman Empire*. 2nd ed. London: Frank Cass, 1996.

Kirkwood, Patrick M. "'Lord Cromer's Shadow': Political Anglo-Saxonism and the Egyptian Protectorate as a Model in the American Philippines." *Journal of World History* 27, no. 1 (2016): 1–26.

Koebner, Richard. *Imperialism: The Story and Significance of a Political Word, 1840–1960*. Cambridge: Cambridge University Press, 1964.

Kramer, Paul A. *The Blood of Government: Race, Empire, the United States, and the Philippines*. Chapel Hill: University of North Carolina Press, 2006.

——. "Empires, Exceptions, and Anglo-Saxons: Race and Rule Between the British and United States Empires, 1880–1910." *Journal of American History* 88, no. 4 (2002): 1315–53.

——. "How Not to Write the History of U.S. Empire." *Diplomatic History* 42, no. 5 (2018): 911–31.

LaFeber, Walter. *Cambridge History of American Foreign Relations*. Vol. 2, *The American Search for Opportunity, 1865–1913*. Cambridge: Cambridge University Press, 1993.

———. *The New Empire: An Interpretation of American Expansion, 1860–1898*. Ithaca, NY: Cornell University Press, 1963.

Langley, Lester D. *The Cuban Policy of the United States: A Brief History*. New York: John Wiley, 1968.

Leary, John Patrick. "Cuba in the American Imaginary: Literature and National Culture in Cuba and the United States, 1848–1958." PhD diss., New York University, 2009.

Lee, Robert. "Accounting for Conquest: The Price of the Louisiana Purchase for Indian Country." *Journal of American History* 103, no. 4 (2017): 921–42.

Lewis, James E. *The American Union and the Problem of Neighborhood: The United States and the Collapse of the Spanish Empire, 1783–1829*. Chapel Hill: University of North Carolina Press, 1998.

Libby, Justin. "Hamilton Fish and the Origins of Anglo-American Solidarity." *Mid-America* 76, no. 3 (1994): 205–26.

Louis, William Roger. *Ends of British Imperialism: The Scramble for Africa, Suez and Decolonization*. London: I. B. Tauris, 2006.

Love, Eric T. L. *Race over Empire: Racism and U.S. Imperialism, 1865–1900*. Chapel Hill: University of North Carolina Press, 2004.

Lowe, Lisa. *The Intimacies of Four Continents*. Durham, NC: Duke University Press, 2015.

Maass, Richard W. "'Difficult to Relinquish Territory Which Has Been Conquered': Expansionism and the War of 1812." *Diplomatic History* 39, no. 1 (2015): 70–97.

Maier, Charles S. *Among Empires: American Ascendency and Its Predecessors*. Cambridge, MA: Harvard University Press, 2006.

Marsot, Afaf Lutfi Al-Sayyid. "The British Occupation of Egypt from 1882." In *The Oxford History of the British Empire*, vol. 3, *The Nineteenth Century*, ed. Andrew Porter, 651–64. Oxford: Oxford University Press, 1999.

Martínez-Fernández, Luis. "Political Change in the Spanish Caribbean During the United States Civil War and Its Aftermath." *Caribbean Studies* 27, nos. 1–2 (1994): 37–64.

May, Robert E. *Manifest Destiny's Underworld: Filibustering in Antebellum America*. Chapel Hill: University of North Carolina Press, 2002.

———. *The Southern Dream of a Caribbean Empire*. Baton Rouge: Louisiana State University Press, 1973.

Mayers, David. *Dissenting Voices in America's Rise to Power*. Cambridge: Cambridge University Press, 2007.

McCoy, Alfred W., and Francisco A. Scarano, eds. *Colonial Crucible: Empire in the Making of the Modern American State*. Madison: University of Wisconsin Press, 2009.

McCoy, Alfred W., Josep M. Fradera, and Stephen Jacobson, eds. *Endless Empire: Spain's Retreat, Europe's Eclipse, America's Decline.* Madison: University of Wisconsin Press, 2012.

McCoy, Drew R. "Republicanism and American Foreign Policy: James Madison and the Political Economy of Commercial Discrimination, 1789–1794." *William and Mary Quarterly* 31, no. 4 (1974): 633–46.

McGuinness, Aims. *Path of Empire: Panama and the California Gold Rush.* Ithaca, NY: Cornell University Press, 2008.

Merk, Frederick. *Manifest Destiny and Mission in American History*, with a new foreword by John Mack Faragher. Cambridge, MA: Harvard University Press, 1995.

Metcalf, Thomas R. "From One Empire to Another: The Influence of the British Raj on American Colonialism in the Philippines." *Ab Imperio* 3 (2012): 25–41.

Meyer, L. E. "Henry S. Sanford and the Congo: A Reassessment." *African Historical Studies* 4, no. 1 (1971): 19–39.

Miller, Robert Ryal. *Arms Across the Border: United States Aid to Juárez During the French Intervention in Mexico.* Philadelphia: American Philosophical Society, 1973.

——. "Matias Romero: Mexican Minister to the United States During the Juarez-Maximilian Era." *Hispanic American Historical Review* 45, no. 2 (1965): 228–45.

Milne, David, *Worldmaking: The Art and Science of American Diplomacy.* New York: Farrar, Straus & Giroux, 2015.

Mowat, R. C. "From Liberalism to Imperialism: The Case of Egypt 1875–1887." *Historical Journal* 16 (March 1973): 109–24.

Murphy, Martin F. *Dominican Sugar Plantations: Production and Foreign Labor Integration.* New York: Praeger, 1991.

Nakajima, Hiroo. "The Monroe Doctrine and Russia: American Views of Czar Alexander I and Their Influence upon Early Russian-American Relations." *Diplomatic History* 31, no. 3 (2007): 439–63.

Nevins, Allan. *Hamilton Fish: The Inner History of the Grant Administration.* New York: Dodd Mead, 1936.

Ninkovich, Frank. *Global Dawn: The Cultural Foundations of American Internationalism, 1865–1890.* Cambridge, MA: Harvard University Press, 2009.

Nugent, Walter. *Habits of Empire: A History of American Expansion.* New York: Alfred A. Knopf, 2008.

O'Connor, Richard. *The Cactus Throne: The Tragedy of Maximilian and Carlota.* London: George Allen & Unwin, 1971.

Ogelsby, J. C. M. "The Cuban Autonomist Movement's Perception of Canada, 1865–1898: Its Implications." *The Americas* 48, no. 4 (1992): 445–61.

Onuf, Peter S. "A Declaration of Independence for Diplomatic Historians." *Diplomatic History* 22, no. 1 (1998): 71–83.

——. *Jefferson's Empire: The Language of American Nationhood*. Charlottesville: University Press of Virginia, 2000.

Oren, Michael B. *Power, Faith, and Fantasy: America in the Middle East, 1776 to the Present*. New York: Norton, 2007.

Owen, Roger, and Bob Sutcliffe, eds. *Studies in the Theory of Imperialism*. London: Longman, 1972.

Palen, Marc-William. *The "Conspiracy" of Free Trade: The Anglo-American Struggle over Empire and Economic Globalisation, 1846–1896*. Cambridge: Cambridge University Press, 2016.

Paolino, Ernest N. *The Foundations of the American Empire: William Henry Seward and U.S. Foreign Policy*. Ithaca, NY: Cornell University Press, 1973.

Parton, James, ed. *Life of Andrew Jackson*. Vol. 3. New York: Mason Brothers, 1861.

Pérez, Louis A., Jr. *Cuba and the United States: Ties of Singular Intimacy*. 3rd ed. Athens: University of Georgia Press, 2003.

——. *Cuba: Between Reform and Revolution*. 4th ed. New York: Oxford University Press, 2011.

——. *Cuba in the American Imagination: Metaphor and the Imperial Ethos*. Chapel Hill: University of North Carolina Press, 2008.

——. "The Meaning of the Maine: Causation and the Historiography of the Spanish-American War." *Pacific Historical Review* 58, no. 3 (1989): 293–322.

Perkins, Bradford. *The Cambridge History of American Foreign Relations*. Vol. 1, *The Creation of a Republican Empire, 1775–1865*. Cambridge: Cambridge University Press, 1993.

——. *The First Rapprochement: England and the United States, 1795–1805*. Berkeley: University of California Press, 1967.

——. *The Great Rapprochement: England and the United States, 1895–1914*. London: Victor Gallanz, 1969.

Perkins, Dexter. *A History of the Monroe Doctrine*. Boston: Little, Brown, 1955.

Phelps, Nicole M. *U.S.-Hapsburg Relations from 1815 to the Paris Peace Conference: Sovereignty Transformed*. New York: Cambridge University Press, 2013.

Plesur, Milton. *America's Outward Thrust: Approaches to Foreign Affairs, 1865–1890*. DeKalb: Northern Illinois Press, 1971.

Pletcher, David M. *The Awkward Years: American Foreign Relations Under Garfield and Arthur*. Columbia: University of Missouri Press, 1962.

——. *The Diplomacy of Annexation: Texas, Oregon, and the Mexican War*. Columbia: University of Missouri Press, 1973.

——. *The Diplomacy of Trade and Investment: American Economic Expansion in the Hemisphere, 1865–1900*. Columbia: University of Missouri Press, 1998.

———. "1861–1898: Economic Growth and Diplomatic Adjustment." In *Economics and World Power: An Assessment of American Diplomacy Since 1789*, ed. William H. Becker and Samuel F. Wells Jr., 119–71. New York: Columbia University Press, 1984.

Plummer, Brenda Gayle. *Haiti and the United States: The Psychological Moment.* Athens: University of Georgia Press, 1992.

Polyné, Millery. *From Douglass to Duvalier: U.S. African Americans, Haiti, and Pan Americanism, 1870–1964.* Gainesville: University Press of Florida, 2010.

Porter, Bernard. *Empire and Superempire: Britain, America and the World.* New Haven, CT: Yale University Press, 2006.

Pratt, Julius W. *America's Colonial Experiment: How the United States Gained, Governed, and in Part Gave Away a Colonial Empire.* New York: Prentice Hall, 1951.

———. *Expansionists of 1812.* New York: P. Smith, 1957.

Press, Steven. *Rogue Empires: Contracts and Conmen in Europe's Scramble for Africa.* Cambridge, MA: Harvard University Press, 2017.

Priest, Andrew. "Imperial Exchange: American Views of the British Empire During the Civil War and Reconstruction." *Journal of Colonialism and Colonial History* 16, no. 1 (2015).

———. "Thinking About Empire: The Grant Administration, Spanish Colonialism, and the Ten Years' War in Cuba." *Journal of American Studies* 48, no. 2 (2014): 541–58.

Prochaska, Frank. *Eminent Victorians and the United States: The View from Albion.* Oxford: Oxford University Press, 2012.

Reeves-Ellington, Barbara. *Domestic Frontiers: Gender, Reform, and American Intervention in the Ottoman Balkans and the Near East.* Amherst: University of Massachusetts Press, 2013.

Reid, Donald Malcom. "The 'Urabi Revolution and the British Conquest, 1879–1882." In *The Cambridge History of Egypt*, vol. 2, *Modern Egypt from 1517 to the End of the Twentieth Century*, ed. M. W. Daly, 217–38. Cambridge: Cambridge University Press, 1998.

Reuter, Paul H., Jr. "United States-French Relations Regarding French Intervention in Mexico: From the Tripartite Treaty to Querétaro." *Southern Quarterly* 6, no. 4 (1968): 469–89.

Roberts, Tim. "Lajos Kossuth and the Permeable American Orient of the Mid-Nineteenth Century." *Diplomatic History* 39, no. 5 (2015): 793–818.

Roberts, Timothy Mason. *Distant Revolutions: 1848 and the Challenge to American Exceptionalism.* Charlottesville: University of Virginia Press, 2009.

Rosenberg, Emily S. "Economic Interest and United States Foreign Policy." In *American Foreign Relations Reconsidered*, ed. Gordon Martel, 37–51. London: Routledge, 2003.

———. "The Invisible Protectorate: The United States, Liberia and the Evolution of Neocolonialism, 1909–40." *Diplomatic History* 9, no. 3 (1985): 191–214.

Royle, Charles. *The Egyptian Campaigns, 1882 to 1885.* London: Hurst & Brackett, 1900.

Russell, Greg. *John Quincy Adams and the Public Virtues of Diplomacy.* Columbia: University of Missouri Press, 1995.

Sainlaude, Stève. *France and the American Civil War: A Diplomatic History,* trans. Jessica Edwards. Chapel Hill: University of North Carolina Press, 2019.

Sanderson, G. N. "The European Partition of Africa: Origins and Dynamics." In *The Cambridge History of Africa,* vol. 6, *From 1870 to 1905,* ed. Roland Oliver and G. N. Sanderson, 96–158. Cambridge: Cambridge University Press, 1985.

Schmidt-Nowara, Christopher. *Slavery, Freedom, and Abolition in Latin America and the Atlantic World.* Albuquerque: University of New Mexico Press, 2011.

Schmitt, Karl M. *Mexico and the United States, 1821–1873: Conflict and Coexistence.* New York: Wiley, 1974.

Schölch, Alexander. *Egypt for the Egyptians! The Socio-Political Crisis in Egypt, 1878–1882.* London: Ithaca Press, 1981.

———. "The 'Men on the Spot' and the English Occupation of Egypt in 1882." *Historical Journal* 19, no. 3 (1976): 773–85.

Schoonover, Thomas. *Dollars over Dominion: The Triumph of Liberalism in Mexican-United States Relations, 1861–1867.* Baton Rouge: Louisiana State University Press, 1978.

———. *The French in Central America: Culture and Commerce, 1820–1930.* Wilmington, DE: Scholarly Resources, 2000.

———. "John A. Kasson's Opposition to the Lincoln Administration's Mexican Policy." *Annals of Iowa* 40, no. 8 (1971): 585–93.

———. "Napoleon Is Coming! Maximilian Is Coming? The International History of the Civil War in the Caribbean Basin." In *The Union, the Confederacy, and the Atlantic Rim,* ed. Robert E. May, 101–30. West Lafayette, IN: Purdue University Press, 1995.

Schoultz, Lars. *Beneath the United States: A History of U.S. Policy Toward Latin America.* Cambridge, MA: Harvard University Press, 1998.

Schrecker, John. "'For the Equality of Men—For the Equality of Nations': Anson Burlingame and China's First Embassy to the United States, 1868." *Journal of American East-Asian Relations* 17, no. 1 (2010): 9–34.

Scott, Rebecca J. *Degrees of Freedom: Louisiana and Cuba After Slavery.* Cambridge, MA: Belknap Press of Harvard University Press, 2005.

———. *Slave Emancipation in Cuba: The Transition to Free Labor, 1860–1899.* Princeton, NJ: Princeton University Press, 1985.

Seager, Robert, II. "Ten Years Before Mahan: The Unofficial Case for the New Navy, 1880–1890." *Mississippi Valley Historical Review* 40, no. 3 (1953): 491–512.

Sexton, Jay. *The Monroe Doctrine: Empire and Nation in Nineteenth-Century America.* New York: Hill & Wang, 2011.

———. "Toward a Synthesis of Foreign Relations in the Civil War Era, 1848–77." *American Nineteenth Century History* 5, no. 3 (2004): 50–73.

———. "The United States in the British Empire." In *British North America in the Seventeenth and Eighteenth Centuries*, ed. Stephen Foster, 318–45. Oxford: Oxford University Press, 2013.

———. "The United States, the Cuban Rebellion, and the Multilateral Initiative of 1875." *Diplomatic History* 30, no. 3 (June 2006): 335–65.

———. "William H. Seward in the World." *Journal of the Civil War Era* 4, no. 3 (2014): 398–430.

Sha'ban, Fuad. *Islam and Arabs in Early American Thought: The Roots of Orientalism in America.* Durham, NC: Acorn Press, 1990.

Sharkey, Heather Jane. *American Evangelicals in Egypt: Missionary Encounters in an Age of Empire.* Princeton, NJ: Princeton University Press, 2008.

Sharrow, Walter G. "William H. Seward and the Basis for American Empire." *Pacific Historical Review* 36, no. 3 (1967): 325–42.

Shepperson, George. "Aspects of American Interest in the Berlin Conference." In *Bismarck, Europe, and Africa: The Berlin Africa Conference 1884–1885 and the Onset of Partition*, ed. Stig Förster, Wolfgang J. Mommsen, and Ronald Robinson, 281–93. Oxford: Oxford University Press, 1988.

———. "The Centennial of the West African Conference of Berlin, 1884–1885." *Phylon* 46, no. 1 (1985): 37–48.

Sim, David. *A Union Forever: The Irish Question and U.S. Foreign Relations in the Victorian Age.* Ithaca, NY: Cornell University Press, 2013.

Smith-Rosenberg, Carroll. *This Violent Empire: The Birth of American National Identity.* Chapel Hill: University of North Carolina Press, 2010.

Sneider, Allison L. *Suffragists in an Imperial Age: U.S. Expansion and the Woman Question, 1870–1929.* New York: Oxford University Press, 2008.

Stahr, Walter. *Seward: Lincoln's Indispensable Man.* New York: Simon & Schuster, 2011.

Stephanson, Anders. "An American Story? Second Thoughts on Manifest Destiny." In *Manifest Destinies and Indigenous Peoples*, ed. David Maybury-Lewis, Theodore Macdonald, and Biorn Maybury-Lewis, 21–49. Cambridge, MA: Harvard University Press, 2009.

Stokes, Eric. "Late Nineteenth-Century Colonial Expansion and the Attack on the Theory of Economic Imperialism: A Case of Mistaken Identity?" *Historical Journal* 12, no. 2 (1969): 285–301.

Stout, Joseph A., Jr. *Schemers and Dreamers: Filibustering in Mexico.* Fort Worth: Texas Christian University Press, 2002.

Strout, Cushing. *The American Image of the Old World.* New York: Harper & Row, 1963.

Stuart, Reginald C. *United States Expansionism and British North America, 1775–1871.* Chapel Hill: University of North Carolina Press, 1988.

Sturgis, James. "Britain and the New Imperialism." In *British Imperialism in the Nineteenth Century,* ed. C. C. Eldridge, 85–105. London: Macmillan, 1984.

Suri, Jeremi. *Liberty's Surest Guardian: American Nation-Building from the Founders to Obama.* New York: Free Press, 2011.

Tate, Merze. "Twisting the Lion's Tail over Hawaii." *Pacific Historical Review* 36, no. 1 (1967): 27–46.

Thompson, Julius E. "Hiram Rhodes Revels, 1827–1901: A Reappraisal." *Journal of Negro History* 79, no. 3 (1994): 297–303.

Tollefson, Harold H., Jr. "The 1894 British Takeover of the Egyptian Ministry of Interior." *Middle Eastern Studies* 26, no. 4 (October 1990): 547–60.

Troutt Powell, Eve M. *A Different Shade of Colonialism: Egypt, Great Britain, and the Mastery of the Sudan.* Berkeley: University of California Press, 2003.

Tucker, Robert W., and David C. Hendrickson. *Empire of Liberty: The Statecraft of Thomas Jefferson.* New York: Oxford University Press, 1990.

Tuffnell, Stephen. "'Uncle Sam Is to Be Sacrificed': Anglophobia in Late Nineteenth Century Politics and Culture." *American Nineteenth Century History* 12, no. 1 (2011): 77–99.

Tulloch, H. A. "Changing British Attitudes Towards the United States in the 1880s." *Historical Journal* 20, no. 4 (1977): 825–40.

Tyrrell, Ian. "American Exceptionalism in an Age of International History." *American Historical Review* 96, no. 4 (1991): 1031–55.

Tyrell, Ian, and Jay Sexton, eds. *Empire's Twin: U.S. Anti-imperialism from the Founding Fathers to the Age of Terrorism.* Ithaca, NY: Cornell University Press, 2015.

Valone, Stephen J. "Weakness Offers Temptation: William Seward and the Reassertion of the Monroe Doctrine." *Diplomatic History* 19, no. 4 (1995): 583–99.

Van Alstyne, R. W. *The Rising American Empire.* Chicago: Quadrangle, 1960.

Vevier, Charles. "American Continentalism: An Idea of Expansion, 1845–1910." *American Historical Review* 65, no. 2 (1960): 323–35.

Vivian, Cassandra. *Americans in Egypt, 1770–1915: Explorers, Consuls, Travelers, Soldiers, Missionaries, Writers and Scientists.* Jefferson, NC: McFarland, 2012.

Vlahos, Michael. *America: Images of Empire.* Washington, DC: Johns Hopkins Foreign Policy Institute, 1982.

Walker, Charles S. "Causes of the Confederate Invasion of New Mexico." *New Mexico Historical Review* 8, no. 2 (1933): 76–97.

Walther, Karine V. *Sacred Interests: The United States and Islamic World, 1821–1921.* Chapel Hill: University of North Carolina Press, 2015.

Warren, Gordon H. "Imperial Dreamer: William Henry Seward and American Destiny." In *Makers of American Diplomacy: From Benjamin Franklin to Alfred Thayer Mahan,* ed. Frank J. Merli and Theodore A. Wilson, 195–221. New York: Scribner, 1974.

Weeks, William Earl. *Building the Continental Empire: American Expansion from the Revolution to the Civil War.* Chicago: Ivan R. Dee, 1996.

——. *John Quincy Adams and American Global Empire.* Lexington: University of Kentucky Press, 1992.

White, Richard. *The Middle Ground: Indians, Empires, and Republics in the Great Lakes Region, 1650–1815.* Cambridge: Cambridge University Press, 1991.

——. *The Republic for Which It Stands: The United States During Reconstruction and the Gilded Age, 1865–1896.* New York: Oxford University Press, 2017.

Williams, William Appleman. *The Tragedy of American Diplomacy.* New York: Norton, 1991.

Yokota, Kariann Akemi. *Unbecoming British: How Revolutionary America Became a Postcolonial Nation.* Oxford: Oxford University Press, 2011.

York, Neil L. *Turning the World Upside Down: The War of American Independence and the Problem of Empire.* Westport, CT: Praeger, 2003.

Younger, Edward. *John A. Kasson: Politics and Diplomacy from Lincoln to McKinley.* Iowa City: State Historical Society of Iowa, 1955.

Zhihai, Cui. "The United States and the Sino-Japanese War of 1894–1895." *Social Sciences in China* 36, no. 4 (2015): 164–92.

Index

Page references to figures are in *italics*.

Abbott, John S. C., 55, 60, 69
Abdulmejid I, Sultan, 32
Adams, Henry, 134
Adams, John, 24, 27
Adams, John Quincy, 209n26; and
    acquisition of Florida, 37, 39;
    disdain for revolutionaries in
    Spanish colonies, 26–27; and Greek
    rebellion against Ottoman Empire,
    46; and nonintervention policies,
    44–45; objections to British
    imperialism, 25; and territorial
    expansion, 37, 39, 40; views on First
    Opium War, 42–43
Africa: American travelers to, 154–55,
    158, 164, 173–74, 240n1, 246n102;
    and Belgian imperialism (*see* Congo
    Free State; International Association
    of the Congo; Leopold II, king of
    Belgium); Berlin West Africa
    Conference (*see* Berlin West Africa

Conference); and British
    imperialism, 161 (*see also* British
    occupation of Egypt); and
    "civilization" discourse, 12, 158, 167,
    171, 175–82; European interests in,
    120, 156–57, 159–60, 171–72; and
    French imperialism, 17, 55–56, 135,
    160–61; and German imperialism,
    161–62 (*see also* Berlin West Africa
    Conference); and Islam, 31;
    missionaries, 131, 145, 158, 176,
    178–79; and Monroe Doctrine,
    182–86; racialized views of Africans,
    12, 19, 177–82; scramble for Africa,
    12, 120, 156–57, 159–60; U.S.
    interests in, 12, 155, 157–64, 169–75;
    and warfare, 173–74, 180–81, 184,
    189. *See also* British occupation of
    Egypt; Congo; Congo Free State;
    International Association of the
    Congo; *specific countries*

Belmont, Perry, 182

Bemis, Samuel Flagg, 39

Bender, Thomas, 192

Benjamin, Judah P., 59

Berlin West Africa Conference, 154–89; Arthur and, 12, 152, 164, 166, 167, 182, 184, 187; Bismarck and, 155, 160, 187; and "civilization" discourse, 152, 175, 175–82; Cleveland's repudiation of, 157, 165, 186, 187, 197; critics and defenders of U.S. participation, 182–86, 188, 194; Frelinghuysen and, 164, 169–71, 182, 186, 187; lack of African representatives, 155; Leopold II and, 155, 160, 169, 183; and Liberia, 241n11; and Monroe Doctrine, 182–86, 188; signing of, 187; topics of discussion at, 155; and U.S. interests in Africa, 171–72; U.S. participation, 12, 152, 155, 157, 162, 164–69, 182–87, 194, 241n11 (see also Kasson, John; Sanford, Henry S.; Stanley, Henry Morton; Tisdel, Willard Parker)

Bigelow, John, 67

Bismarck, Otto von, 97, 155, 160, 162–64, 184, 187

Blaine, James G., 122, 123, 165, 182, 188, 190

Boker, George H., 135–36

Booth, John Wilkes, 71–72

Bradford, Richard, 114

Brauer, Kinley, 63

Brazil, 53, 96

Bright, Charles, 203

Bright, John, 172

British East India Company, 18, 90, 128, 129

British Empire, 21, 122–31; and Africa, 161 (see also British occupation of Egypt); American views on, 17, 24, 121–22, 126–31, 193, 202, 232n27; and Asia, 130–31; Clay's objections to, 24; and colonialism viewed as beneficial to colonized peoples, 126, 127; compared to French imperialism, 57; cruelty of, 128–31, 147; Disraeli and, 124; and Egypt, 12 (see also British occupation of Egypt); expansionism as "natural" process, 125; formally and informally controlled colonies, 13, 23, 120, 150; mishandling of disease epidemics, 138–39; and missionaries, 234n55; Seward's views on, 68; U.S. mimicry of British approach to imperial dominance, 13, 19, 121–22, 199; and Venezuela, 196, 197; white settler colonies, 125, 193. See also British occupation of Egypt; India

British Guyana, 196–97

British occupation of Egypt, 12, 118–22, 139–46, 171, 199, 202, 231n6; Alexandria riots of 1882 and British response, 118–19, 143–45; American sympathy for anti-foreign movement, 142; American views influenced by race theories, 148–49; and anti-foreign movement, 141–42; British control of Egyptian affairs in spite of lack of official rule, 120, 150; British misrule, 147–48; and "civilization" discourse, 151; drunkenness among British troops, 146–48; Egyptian population's resentment of, 141–42; half measures/hybrid system of control, 150; as model for U.S. after 1898, 121–22; and race issues, 146–50; Urabi's rebellion, 119–20, 142–45; U.S. responses to, 121, 143–45, 151

Brooks, Charles Wolcott, 131

Browne, Albert G., Jr., 190–91, 192, 193

Bryant, William Cullen, 113, 134
Bryce, James, 1
Bulgaria, 136
Burma, 130–31
Burriel, Don Juan N., 86
Butler, Benjamin, 110

Calhoun, John C., 38–39
California, 37, 128
Campbell, Lewis D., 72, 75
Canada, 6, 34, 193; and Great Britain,
    77, 195; and U.S. territorial
    expansion, 36, 105, 191
Canning, Stratford, 25
Cardwell, John, 146, 147, 148, 152
Caribbean: and British imperialism, 23;
    and French imperialism, 34; obstacles
    to republics in, 95; and race issues, 88,
    115; and Spanish imperialism, 17; and
    U.S. Civil War, 83; U.S. economic
    interests in, 36, 91–92, 109, 198; and
    U.S. territorial expansion, 1, 46, 83,
    84, 96–100, 105, 116, 166, 170, 173.
    See also Cuba; Cuban rebellion;
    Haiti; Santo Domingo
Carlota, empress of Mexico, 50–51,
    164–65
Catholicism, 32–33, 191
Chamberlain, J. E., 127–28
Chandler, William E., 152
Chang, Gordon, 42, 130
Chase, Salmon P., 74
Child, Lydia Maria, 97–98, 128–29
Chile, 103
China, 195; Opium Wars, 42, 130, 131,
    238n125; Sino-Japanese War
    (1894–1895), 197; treaty port system,
    130; and U.S. foreign policy, 42–43
cholera, 138–39
"civilization," advancement of, 3, 202;
    and Africa, 12, 158, 167, 171, 175–82;

and assimilation of Native
    Americans, 8, 42; and British
    occupation of Egypt, 12, 151; and
    colonialism viewed as beneficial to
    colonized peoples, 19, 42, 126, 127;
    and commerce and trade, 175–82,
    188; and French imperialism, 55; and
    lack of enthusiasm for incorporating
    people of color into the U.S., 9
    (see also under race and racism); and
    missionaries in Africa, 158, 178–79;
    and potential annexation of Santo
    Domingo, 99; and republicanism, 81;
    and sense of Anglo-Saxon
    superiority, 9, 126; and U.S.
    discourse on sub-Saharan Africa, 12;
    and U.S. leadership in the Americas,
    81; and U.S. participation in Berlin
    West Africa Conference, 152; and
    U.S. territorial expansion, 42, 199;
    and white settler colonies, 126
Civil War, U.S., 82, 83; and anti-
    imperialist views, 48; connection
    between slavery and empire, 60–65;
    and cotton industry in Egypt, 131;
    and French intervention in Mexico,
    52, 71; and Haitian independence,
    26; Napoleon III as Confederate ally,
    57; possible recognition of the
    Confederacy by European powers,
    54, 58, 59, 63–65; possible
    recognition of the Confederacy by
    Mexico under Maximilian, 71;
    and Prussia, 161; and U.S. foreign
    policy, 16, 48–49. See also
    Reconstruction
Clarendon, Lord, 79
Clay, Henry, 24, 45, 209n26
Clayton-Bulwer Treaty (1850), 123, 196
Cleopatra's Needle (Egyptian obelisk),
    133

Cleveland, Grover, 185; as anti-imperialist, 197; and Monroe Doctrine, 197; repudiation of Berlin West African Conference, 157, 165, 186, 187, 197; and Sino-Japanese War, 197

Clive, Robert, 90

Cobden, Richard, 172

colonialism: American objections to, 17–18, 24, 25, 57 (see also anti-imperialist views, American); British colonialism (see British Empire; British occupation of Egypt; India); French colonialism in Africa and Asia, 55–57, 130; Kasson and, 173; and Liberia, 159; and Monroe Doctrine, 8, 20; Spanish colonialism viewed as exceptionally aggressive and violent, 27, 87, 89–90; U.S. "imperial anticolonialism" (Williams's concept), 5; viewed as beneficial to colonized peoples, 13, 19, 42, 55, 126, 127; viewed as outdated system, 10, 25. See also Africa; "civilization," advancement of; imperialism, European; specific countries

Comanos, N. D., 142–45, 148, 237n94

commerce: and alcohol, 179, 181; British free trade policies, 7, 21, 23–25, 58, 123–24; and "civilization" discourse, 175–82, 188; cotton industry, 23, 58, 59, 63, 131, 170, 173; and European informal imperialism, 120; European trade practices, 18, 172; fur trade, 36; Open Door policy, 157, 169, 173; Spanish protectionist policies and U.S. response, 92; sugar trade, 26, 91–92, 198; and U.S. acceptance of British models of empire, 10; and U.S. interests in Africa, 12, 159,

169–75; and U.S. interests in Madagascar, 160–61; U.S. search for new markets, 43, 159, 170, 171, 175; and U.S. territorial expansion, 5, 36, 83, 84. See also economics

Confederacy. See Civil War, U.S.

Congo, 9; humanitarian crisis in, 155–56, 169, 188–89, 245n80, 246n95; Tisdel's mission to, 154–55, 164, 173–74, 246n102; U.S. interests in, 169–71. See also Berlin West Africa Conference; International Association of the Congo

Congo Free State, 155–56, 187

Cooper, Frederick, 200

Cortada, James, 28

Corwin, Thomas, 65

Costa Rica, 78

cotton, 23, 58, 59, 63, 131, 170, 173

Crapol, Edward, 13

Creoles, 27

Crowe, Sybil, 169, 179

Cuba, 1, 6, 9; American attitudes toward, 47, 87–90; and diplomacy, 92–93; Frelinghuysen and, 195; potential U.S. annexation of, 40, 47, 79, 88, 89, 95; racialized views of Cubans, 19, 87–89, 95, 99–100, 110, 114, 116; rebellions against Spanish rule (see following headings); and slavery, 12, 47, 53, 87, 88, 90–91, 96; Spain's diminished influence over, 195; and Spanish-American War (1898), 197–98; and Spanish imperialism, 17, 89–92; and sugar trade, 92, 198; symbolic power for Americans, 89; U.S. control of, 198–99; and U.S. economic interests, 92, 109, 198

Cuban rebellion (Cuban War of Independence; 1895–1898), 197–98

Cuban rebellion (Ten Years' War;
1868–1878), 11–12, 85–117, 194;
American beliefs about Cubans' lack
of capacity for self-rule, 11–12, 90,
93, 198; American misgivings over
"uncivilized" warfare, 108–15; and
Americans living in Cuba, 103–4,
109; American support for Cuban
independence, 94–95, 100–104, 116;
desire of some Cubans to join the
U.S., 93; Douglass and, 102–3; end of
war, 115; "filibustering" expeditions
to Cuba, 47, 90–91; Fish and, 93–95,
99–100, 104, 107–16; Garfield and,
105, 124; Grant and, 86–87, 94,
100–102, 105, 107–12, 116, 227n72;
Hayes and, 115; and limits of U.S.
anti-colonial sentiment, 11; and
Monroe Doctrine, 87, 107, 116;
origins of, 92–95; pressure for U.S.
intervention, 100–104, 116; pressure
from groups within Spain to
attenuate rule in Cuba, 109; and
racial dimensions of American
imperial thought, 11–12, 87–88,
99–100, 110, 114; Rawlins and, 100;
Sickles and, 100, 108; and slavery,
92–93, 108, 110–11; Sumner and, 105,
110; and U.S. nonintervention
policies, 104–8, 115; U.S. relations
with Spain prioritized over support
for Cuban rebels, 11, 87, 90, 94,
107–8, 112, 116; U.S. responses to,
87–89, 90–92, 94–95, 104–8, 115–17;
Virginius affair, 86–87, *101*, 113–14
Cunningham, Michelle, 60
Cushing, Caleb, 43, 75, 111, 114, 115
Cyprus, 135

Dalton, Francis, 125
Darwin, Charles, 125

David, Jacques-Louis, 54
Davis, Henry Winter, 166
Davis, J. C. Bancroft, 182
Davis, Jefferson, 71
Dayton, William L., 73, 76
de Brazza, Pierre Savorgnan, 161
de Céspedes, Pedro, 85, 92
Declaration of Independence, 21, 48
deGuzmán, María, 27–28
Delany, Martin, 39–40
de La Reintre, Henry R., 100
De Leon, Daniel, 162, 184
De Leon, Edwin, 31
de Lhuys, Édouard Drouyn, 78
democracy. *See* republicanism
Democrats, 8, 31, 38
demography, 169
Dennison, William, 74
disease, 138–39
Disraeli, Benjamin (Lord Beaconsfield),
124, 136, 139, 232n27
Dominican Republic. *See* Santo
Domingo
Douglass, Frederick, 3, 61, 70, 98–99,
101–3, 127
Doyle, Don, 52
Draper, John W., 57–58
Du Bois, W. E. B., 189
Dwinelle, John W., 58

economics: American objections to
European economic practices, 7, 18,
21, 23–24; and American Revolution,
18–19; British economic power and
free trade policies, 13, 21, 23–25, 58,
123–24; and Cuba, 92, 109; European
interests in Africa, 120, 156–57,
159–60, 171–73; and German
imperialism, 163; and post–Civil War
commercial growth, 167; and slavery,
53 (*see also* slavery); and transoceanic

canal in the Americas, 195–96; U.S. companies' growing influence in Latin America, 47; U.S. interests in Africa, 12, 131, 159, 169–75; U.S. interests in the Caribbean, 26, 36, 91–92, 109, 198; U.S. search for new markets, 43, 159, 170, 171. *See also* commerce; cotton; sugar trade

Egypt, 9, *140*; Alexandria riots of 1882, 118–19, 143–45; Americans in Egyptian government service, 141; American travelers to, 134; American views of European influence in the Ottoman Empire and Egypt, 135–39; anti-foreign movement, 141–42; British occupation (*see* British occupation of Egypt); cotton production, 131; debts, 120, 133, 137, 140, 141, 150; famine and disease, 138–39; as khedivate of the Ottoman Empire, 120; legal system, 134; missionaries, 131, 145; problems with alcohol, 146–48; racialized views of Egyptians, 19, 148–50; and slavery, 134–35; and the Suez Canal, 120; territorial expansion by, 133–34; U.S. influence in, 131–35

Eliot, William Greenleaf, 101

Emerson, Ralph Waldo, 134

empire. *See* anti-imperialist views, American; colonialism; ideology; imperialism, American; imperialism, European

eugenics, 125

Europe: American affinity for European powers, in spite of anti-imperial sentiment, 9, 26, 153; and American anti-imperialist sentiment (*see* anti-imperialist views, American); American objections to European economic practices, 7, 18, 21, 23–24; American views of European influence in the Ottoman Empire and Egypt, 135–39; contrast to the U.S., 5, 10, 20, 193, 202; early American views on European empires, 21–28, 48; economic depression in the late nineteenth century, 171; economic interests in Africa, 120, 156–57, 159–60, 171–73; economic practices, 7 (*see also* economics; *specific countries*); and French intervention in Mexico, 66; and Monroe Doctrine, 45 (*see also* Monroe Doctrine); possible recognition of the Confederacy by European powers, 54, 58–59, 63–65; potential for warfare, 173–74, 180; relations with Native Americans, 42. *See also* imperialism, European; *specific countries*

Evarts, William M., 122, 159, 165

Everett, Edward, 45

expansion. *See* territorial expansion, U.S.

Expansion of England, The (Seeley), 125

Farman, Elbert E., 137–42, 237nn 105, 116

Federalist Papers, The, 22, 30, 36, 211n58

Ferrer, Ada, 99

"filibustering" (interference in foreign countries by private individuals), 47, 90–91, 111

Fish, Hamilton, *93, 101*; Beardsley and, 139; and Cuban rebellion, 93–95, 99–100, 103–4, 107–16; Grant and, 225n31, 227n72; and Great Britain, 124; and Hawaii, 195; and Liberia, 159; naval expedition to Korea (1971), 117; racial attitudes, 88, 95, 99, 114, 116; and territorial expansion, 122

Florida, 34, 36–37, 39, 40

Foner, Philip, 111, 113

foreign policy, U.S.: and Africa, 156–64, 182–86 (*see also* Berlin West Africa Conference); African Americans and, 3; and American exceptionalism, 5, 12, 20, 157, 201–2; American ignorance about much of the world, 30, 32, 33; and Asia, 42–43; and Berlin West Africa Conference (*see* Berlin West Africa Conference); and British imperialism in Africa, 161; and Civil War era, 16, 48–49, 52, 59–60 (*see also* French intervention in Mexico); and Cuba, 11–12, 47, 86–89, 94–95, 104–8 (*see also* Cuban rebellion); and differences between U.S. and European powers, 10; and diplomatic and consular services, 3, 121, 134–35; and early American views on European empires, 21–28; and Egypt, 12, 131–35, 143, 150–51; elitist nature of approach to foreign affairs, 3–4, 9, 11, 16, 121, 137, 157, 160, 162, 195, 200; expansionist thought in the U.S., 2, 5, 18, 192, 199; and French imperialism in Africa, 160–61; and French intervention in Mexico, 11, 51–53, 66–74; and Germany, 161–62; and global influence, 94; and Greece, 31, 45–46; and Haiti, 26, 98, 159; Hamilton and, 22–23; and ideology, 6 (*see also* race; religion); increasing U.S. assertiveness, 116–17, 156, 166, 187–88, 192, 195–96; and interference viewed as beneficial to other nations, 202; and International Association of the Congo, 155, 164, 169, 170, 182; and internationalism, 8–9, 15, 123, 129, 182, 187; and Korea, 117, 159;

lack of material support for independence movements abroad, 20, 26, 46; and Liberia, 158–59; maintaining good relations with France, 59, 74; Monroe Doctrine (*see* Monroe Doctrine); and navy, 152; necessity of interactions with other imperial powers, 14, 17–20, 48, 122; and Northern vs. Southern visions of the U.S., 16; Open Door policy, 157, 169, 173; and the Ottoman Empire, 31–32, 120–21, 151; and Pan-American conference, 190–91; Pickens and, 25; rapprochement with Great Britain, 25–26, 122, 123, 151–52, 184, 196; and regional interests (*see* regional interests in U.S. foreign policy); relations with Spain prioritized over support for Cuban rebels, 11, 87, 90, 94, 107–8, 112, 116; and Republican elites, 8; rhetorical support for independence movements, 24, 26, 31, 45–46, 94–95; and Russia, 68–69; strained relations with Mexico, 47; strained relations with Spain, 86–87, 89; and transoceanic canal in the Americas, 195–96; U.S. self-awareness as international power, 117, 151–52; and weakness of U.S. in the Civil War and post–Civil War eras, 48, 87; women and, 3. *See also* interventionism, U.S.; isolationism, U.S.; neutrality, U.S.; nonintervention policies, U.S.; territorial expansion, U.S.; *specific countries, presidents, and secretaries of state*

France: American affinity for, 9; and American Revolution, 18–19; American views of French

Grant, Ulysses S., *101*; attempt to purchase Santo Domingo, 96–100; and British bombardment of Alexandria, 144; and Cuban rebellion, 11, 86–87, 94, 100–102, 104, 107–12, 116, 227n72; Fish and, 225n31, 227n72; Frelinghuysen and, 123; and French intervention in Mexico, 71–72; and Liberia, 159; visit to Egypt, 134

Granville, Lord, 147, 150

Gray, Elizabeth Kelly, 122

Great Britain: abolition of slavery, 23; Adams (John Quincy) and, 25; American affinity for, 9, 161; and American Revolution, 18; American views of British imperialism, 10, 19, 161, 232n27; and Canada, 77, 195; Caribbean colonies, 23; Clay and, 24; economic drivers of imperialism, 173; economic power and free trade policies, 13, 21, 23–25, 58, 123–24; and French intervention in Mexico, 79; Hamilton and, 22–23; Jefferson and, 22; Monroe and, 25; and Monroe Doctrine, 45; and nonintervention in Mexico, 65; occupation of Egypt (*see* British occupation of Egypt); Opium Wars, 42, 130, 131, 238n125; and Oregon territory, 37; and Ottoman Empire, 135; Pickens and, 25; and possible recognition of the Confederacy, 58; and Quadruple Alliance, 45; rapprochement with U.S., 25–26, 122, 123, 151–52, 184, 196; relations with Spain, 36; and scramble for Africa, 160; and Suez Canal, 120, 141, 237n94; and U.S. Civil War, 58; U.S. mimicry of British approach to imperial dominance, 13, 19, 121–22,

199; Washington and, 22. *See also* British Empire

Greece, 19, 31, 45–46

Guam, 1, 198

Guernsey, Alfred H., 129–30, 137

Haight, Sarah, 134

Haiti, 19, 26, 78, 91–92, 95, 98, 114, 159

Hall, James, 103

Hamilton, Alexander, 22, 29, 30, 34, 36–37, 211n58

Hapsburg Empire, 17, 30, 32–33

Harrison, Benjamin, 190, 195

Hartshorn, Newton T., 232n27

Hawaii, 6, 83, 167, 196; annexation of, 1, 195, 198; British interests, 77; and U.S. search for new markets, 43

Hayes, Rutherford B., 115, 122

Heard, Augustine, 130

Heinzen, Karl, 33

Heiss, Mary Ann, 60

Hendrickson, David, 15

Herbert, Hilary A., 182–83

Herring, George, 198

Hietala, Thomas, 38

Honduras, 77

Howe, Julia Ward, 3, 89

Hungary, 19, 32

Hunt, Michael, 6

ideology, 6, 7; and American republicanism, 78–82; and Civil War, 48; and Cuban rebellion, 87, 89; and debates about economic growth, 7; and foreign policy, 6 (*see also* "civilization," advancement of; regional interests in U.S. foreign policy; religion; territorial expansion, U.S.); and French intervention in Mexico, 11, 52; ideological objections to colonialism,

17–18, 24, 39; and Manifest Destiny, 38, 40; and race issues, 7–8 (*see also* African Americans; Native Americans; race and racism); and use of term "empire" in early U.S., 33–34; and U.S. nonintervention policies, 44–45. *See also* "civilization," advancement of; race and racism; religion

Immerman, Richard, 33–34

immigrants, 8, 32–33, 197, 199, 200

imperialism, American, 198–99, 202, 232n27; acceptance of/appreciation for British models of empire, 10, 19, 121–22, 126–28, 161, 232n27; ambiguity of U.S. position, 157, 193, 203; and American exceptionalism, 5, 12, 20, 157, 201–2; British occupation of Egypt as model for, 121–22, 199; and colonialism viewed as beneficial to colonized peoples, 13, 19, 42, 202; and commerce and trade, 5, 10 (*see also* commerce); connection between slavery and empire, 60–65; contemporary global role of the U.S., 13–14; contrast to European imperialism, 5, 10, 20, 193, 202; and Cuba, 198–99; "democratic imperialism" (Sharrow's concept), 67; expansionist thought in the U.S., 2, 5, 18, 19, 192, 199 (*see also* territorial expansion, U.S.); first known use of term "imperialism" in the U.S., 29–30; and French intervention in Mexico, 52; historiography of, 6, 14; "imperial anticolonialism" (Williams's concept), 5; "imperial dominance" (White's concept), 42; and interdependence with European powers, 200; Kasson and, 166–67;

and Northern vs. Southern visions of the U.S., 16; public and academic debates over, 192–93, 198–99; and race issues (*see* race and racism); sense that interventions could be a necessary evil, 10; Seward and, 67; transimperialism, 14; U.S. as an imperial power, 13, 193–97, 201–2; U.S. as successor to British Empire, 19, 127–28; U.S. mimicry of British approach to imperial dominance, 13, 19, 121–22, 199; and U.S. national identity, 200–201; and Wisconsin school, 5. *See also* anti-imperialist views, American; ideology; territorial expansion, U.S.

imperialism, European, 2, 27–28; and American views of autonomous British settler colonies vs. less autonomous colonies, 193; American views of European influence in the Ottoman Empire and Egypt, 135–39; contrast to U.S. imperialism, 5, 10, 20, 193, 202; decline of Europe influence in the Americas, 196; Douglass and, 99; early American views on, 21–33, 48; economic drivers of, 173 (*see also* economics); and ideas about racial hierarchy, 38 (*see also* race and racism); "new" or "high" imperialism, 48, 117, 120; and scramble for Africa, 12, 120, 156–57, 159–60; Seward and, 68; and slavery, 63 (*see also* slavery). *See also* British Empire; France; Germany; Great Britain; Hapsburg Empire; Russia; Spain

imperialism, Ottoman. *See* Ottoman Empire

India, 23, 63, 90, 128–30, 199, 202

Indochina, 55, 128, 130

International Association of the Congo: Cleveland and, 186; and free trade, 172; and nonintervention policies, 182; supposed mission of, 176–77; U.S. recognition of, 155, 164, 169, 170, 182

internationalism, U.S., 8–9, 15, 123, 129, 182, 187

interventionism, U.S., 94, 209n26

Islam, 30–31, 210n38

Ismail Pasha, khedive of Egypt, 133, 134, 137–38, 140

isolationism, U.S., 14, 17, 94

Italy, 32

Jackson, Andrew, 39

Jacobs, Sylvia M., 176

Jamaica, 103

Japan, 43, 195, 197

Jefferson, Thomas, 21–22, 28–29, 34–36, 35

Jervis, Alfred, 71

Jesup, Thomas S., 46

Johnson, Andrew: and French intervention in Mexico, 52, 72, 75–78; and Haiti, 78; and Madagascar, 160–61; and Reconstruction, 79; and republicanism in Mexico, 81; and republics in the West Indies, 95; Seward and, 59; and territorial expansion, 83–84

Juárez, Benito, 51, 52, 54, 70, 72

Kaplan, Amy, 200

Kapp, Friedrich, 33

Kasson, John, 165, 166; and Berlin West Africa Conference, 155, 162, 164, 166–69, 169, 187; Bismarck and, 162–63; and "civilization" discourse, 179–80; defense of U.S. participation in Berlin Conference, 185–86; and free trade, 172–73; Frelinghuysen

and, 166, 167, 170, 185; and French ambitions in Africa, 160; and Monroe Doctrine, 166, 185; and potential for European warfare, 173–74, 180; racial attitudes, 180; and slave trade, 178, 179; and territorial expansion, 170

Kennedy, Dane, 14

King Leopold's Soliloquy (Twain), 156

Kingsley, Vine Wright (pseudonym), 56, 79–80, 222n126

Kipling, Rudyard, 199

Knox, Thomas W., 130, 136

Koebner, Richard, 29

Korea, 117, 159

LaFeber, Walter, 195

Latin America: American preference for European powers over colonized peoples of the Americas, 9; British intervention in, 196–97; calls for U.S. expansion in, 46; lack of enthusiasm for U.S. territorial expansion in, 191 (*see also under* race and racism); and Pan-American conference, 190–91; and republicanism, 80–82; Spanish intervention in, 65; transoceanic canal, 166, 167, 195–96; and U.S. companies' growing influence, 47; and U.S. policy of nonintervention, 43, 66. *See also* Cuban rebellion; French intervention in Mexico; Monroe Doctrine; race and racism; Western Hemisphere; *specific countries*

Leavitt, Joshua, 56–57, 70, 74

Lee, Robert, 35

Leland, Charles G., 178

Leopold II, king of Belgium: and Berlin West Africa Conference, 155, 160, 169, 183; and "civilization" discourse,

Moret Law of 1870 (Cuba), 111
Morgan, John Tyler, 164, 167, 177
Morocco, 31
Morrill, Justin S., 96, 124
Morton, Levi P., 160, 161

Napoleonic Wars, 29
Napoleon III, 54; and Algeria, 55;
    American views on, 29, 55–57;
    duplicity toward allies, 57; and
    Egypt, 137; failure of intervention in
    Mexico, 11, 53; interest in restoring
    France's colonial empire, 55–56; and
    intervention in Mexico, 10, 51, 57,
    66, 74, 76 (see also French
    intervention in Mexico); loss of
    power, 97; and possible recognition
    of the Confederacy, 59; Seward and,
    76; and slavery and tensions in
    Mexico, 64; and U.S. Civil War, 58,
    59, 60, 64–65; and U.S. foreign
    policy, 60
Nast, Thomas, 101, 106, 140, 183
National Temperance Society, 178
Native Americans, 194; and alcohol,
    179; Americans' views on, 7–8, 19,
    180; and assimilation, 8, 42; cruelty
    of tribal warfare compared to cruelty
    of European imperialism, 128–29;
    and European diplomacy, 42; and
    European powers, 60–61; and Florida,
    39; and Spanish settlers, 36; Stanton
    and, 234n47; U.S. coercion of/
    violence toward, 42; and U.S.-Mexico
    border, 60–61; and U.S. territorial
    expansion, 10, 18, 19, 33, 35–37, 41, 67,
    192. See also race and racism
navy, British, 118–19
navy, German, 162, 163
navy, U.S., 94, 117, 152, 163–64, 170,
    238n121

neutrality, U.S., 21–22, 104–5,
    116. See also nonintervention
    policies, U.S.
New Mexico, 37
Ninkovich, Frank, 2–3, 122, 126
nonintervention policies, U.S., 20,
    43–47; Adams (John Quincy) and,
    44–45; and Africa, 182–86; and
    Cuban rebellion, 104–8; and Egypt,
    150–51; and "filibustering"
    (interference by private individuals),
    47; Frelinghuysen and, 170; and
    French intervention in Mexico, 11,
    52, 72–78, 82, 83; Garfield and, 105;
    justifications for, 44; and Latin
    America, 43, 66, 103; Lincoln and,
    75; and Monroe Doctrine, 10, 20,
    45–46, 72–74 (see also Monroe
    Doctrine); objections to policy,
    46–47; and Pan-American
    conference, 190–91; Seward and,
    75–77, 83; U.S. rejection of British
    proposal for joint declaration against
    Russian and French control in the
    Americas, 45–46; Washington and,
    10, 44, 75, 77
North, the. See regional interests in U.S.
    foreign policy

Obama, Barack, 1, 4, 14, 201, 207n22
Observations Concerning the Increase of
    Mankind (Franklin), 33
On the Origin of Species (Darwin), 125
Open Door policy, 157, 169, 173
Opium Wars, 42, 130, 131, 238n125
Ostend Manifesto, 47
O'Sullivan, John, 38
Ottoman Empire, 17, 30–32; American
    views of European influence in the
    Ottoman Empire and Egypt, 135–39;
    American views on, 30–32, 136–39;

railroads, 43, 135, 178

Rawlins, John A., 100

Reconstruction, 6, 11, 79, 87, 107, 167, 169

regional interests in U.S. foreign policy, 6; and Berlin West Africa Conference, 167; and Caribbean and South America as potential outlets for slavery, 90; and Civil War, 48–49; and connection between slavery and empire, 60–65; and cotton industry, 23; and Cuba, 47, 90–91; and French intervention in Mexico, 52–53, 57, 69–70; and Hapsburg Empire, 32–33; and Napoleon III, 57; Northern vs. Southern views on territorial expansion, 38–39; Northern vs. Southern visions of the U.S., 16; and slavery, 90 (*see also* slavery); Southern and Western objections to European imperialism based on economic factors, 24–25; Southern objections to British economic practices in India and the West Indies, 23

religion, 6; and American views of Mexican people, 69; and American views of the Ottoman Empire, 30–31; Catholicism, 32–33, 56, 98, 191; and "civilization" discourse, 176, 178–79; and French imperialism, 56; and Hapsburg Empire, 32–33; Islam, 30–31, 210n38; missionaries, 30–31, 55, 77, 131, 145, 158, 176, 178–79, 234n55, 238n125; and objections to annexation of Santo Domingo, 98; Protestantism, 30, 131

republicanism: American republicanism, 78–82; Europe viewed as not suited to, 32; and French intervention in Mexico, 66, 78; and Great Britain, 123; hopes for pan-republicanism in the Americas, 24; and Mexico, 76, 80–81, 83; and Spain, 114; and territorial expansion, 35; and U.S. dominance in the Americas, 53, 81–82; and U.S. policy of nonintervention, 76–77

Republicans, 8, 9, 59, 124, 182

Revels, Hiram, 99

Revolutionary War, U.S., 4, 17–19

Riotte, Charles N., 78

Robinson, Ronald, 23

Roosevelt, Theodore, 202

Rush, Benjamin, 79

Rush, Richard, 40

Rush-Bagot Pact of 1817, 26

Russell, Greg, 37

Russell, Lord, 77

Russia: acquisition of Alaska from, 67, 83; and American Northwest, 45; American views on, 136; emancipation of the serfs, 91; Jefferson and, 28–29; and Ottoman Empire, 136–37, 140; and Quadruple Alliance, 45; Russian imperialism, 17, 28–29, 46; Seward's views on, 68–69; and U.S. Civil War, 136; and Young America movement, 31

Ryan, George Washington, 85–86

Saint Thomas, 79

Samoa, 162

Sandwich Islands, 77

Sanford, Henry S., 164–65; beliefs about U.S. interests in Africa, 169–70, 178; and Berlin West Africa Conference, 155, 164–67, 169, 187; and "civilization" discourse, 179; as representative of Leopold II, 156, 165–66; Tisdel's criticisms of, 184

194; and Santo Domingo, 79,
96–100; and sense that new lands
were "untrodden," 41; sense that
U.S. expansion differed from
European imperialism, 10, 20, 34,
35, 38, 40–41; Seward and, 67–68;
and slavery, 4, 36, 38–40, 47, 48; and
Spanish-American War (1989), 198;
and Texas, 37, 38, 40–41; and the
War of 1812, 36; and Young
America movement, 31
Tewfik Pasha, Mohammed, khedive of
Egypt, 120, 133, 137–38, 143
Texas, 37, 38, 40–41, 128
Tisdel, Willard Parker: cautions on U.S.
involvement in Africa, 173–74, 184,
188; mission to West Africa, 154–55,
164, 173–74, 246n102; views on
Africans, 177, 180–82
Transcontinental Treaty (1819), 39
Treaty of London (1861), 55, 65
Treaty of Washington (1871), 227n69
Trent crisis, 55
Trist, Nicholas, 39
Tuffnell, Stephen, 123
Tunisia, 135
Twain, Mark, 134, 156

Uganda, 134
United States: American exceptionalism,
5, 12, 20, 157, 201–2; Civil War (see
Civil War, U.S.); contemporary
global role of, 13–14; contrast to
European powers, 5, 10, 20, 193, 202;
demography, 125–26, 169; and
leadership in the Americas, 59,
80–83; Mexican-American War
(1846–1848), 37–38, 73, 74, 144;
Monroe Doctrine (see Monroe
Doctrine); national identity, 199; as
postcolonial nation, 4; race issues (see

race and racism); Reconstruction, 6,
11, 79, 87, 107, 167, 169;
Revolutionary War, 4, 17–19;
self-awareness as international power,
117, 151–52; and social Darwinism,
126–27; Spanish-American War
(1898), 6, 197–98; and Suez Canal,
121; and transimperialism, 14; War of
1812, 25, 36. See also anti-imperialist
views, American; economics; foreign
policy, U.S.; imperialism, American;
navy, U.S.; press, U.S.; territorial
expansion, U.S.; specific presidents and
secretaries of state
Urabi, Ahmed, 119–20, 142–43, 145,
146, 230n4, 238n116
USS Maine, 198

Van Alstyne, Richard, 34
Venezuela, 196, 197, 202
Virginius affair, 86–87, 101, 113–14
Vlhahos, Michael, 34
Von Gerolt, Friedrich, 95

Wallace, Lew, 143
Walther, Karine, 30, 31
Warner, Charles Dudley, 126
War of 1812, 25, 36
Washington, George, 10, 22, 44, 75, 77
Webster, Daniel, 45
Weeks, William Earl, 37
Welles, Gideon, 51, 69, 72, 74, 83
Wells, William V., 58
Western Hemisphere: and British
imperialism, 23; decline of
European influence in, 196; and
French imperialism, 17 (see also
French intervention in Mexico); and
Monroe Doctrine, 20 (see also Monroe
Doctrine); Pan-American conference,
182, 188, 190; pan-republicanism, 24;